SCIENCE FICTION THEATRE

A HISTORY OF THE TELEVISION PROGRAM
1955–57

BY MARTIN GRAMS, JR.

Science Fiction Theatre
A History of the Television Program, 1955-57
©2011 Martin Grams, Jr.

All rights reserved.

No part of this book may be reproduced or distributed, in print, recorded, live or digital form, without express written permission of the copyright holder. However, excerpts of up to 500 words may be reproduced online if they include the following information, "This is an excerpt from *Science Fiction Theatre: A History of the Television Program*, by Martin Grams, Jr."

Published in the USA by:

BearManor Media
P.O. Box 71426
Albany, Georgia 31708
www.BearManorMedia.com

ISBN-10: 1-59393-657-5 (alk. paper)

ISBN-13: 978-1-59393-657-0 (alk. paper)

Design and Layout: Valerie Thompson

TABLE OF CONTENTS

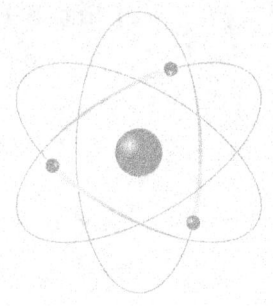

INTRODUCTION . . . 1

CHAPTER ONE: FREDERIC ZIV, FATHER OF SYNDICATION
BY PATRICK LUCANIO . . . 5

CHAPTER TWO: TRUMAN BRADLEY, FROM FORENSICS TO
SCIENCE FICTION—REVUES, AUDIO & CELLULOID BETWEEN
BY JIM COX . . . 21

CHAPTER THREE: BIOGRAPHY OF IVAN TORS . . . 36

CHAPTER FOUR: THE HISTORY OF THE SERIES . . . 42

EPISODE GUIDE: SEASON ONE . . . 128

EPISODE GUIDE: SEASON TWO . . . 301

APPENDIX A:
AN ESSAY ABOUT SCIENCE FICTION
BY IVAN TORS . . . 474

Appendix B:
Truman Bradley's Lab Demonstrations ... *478*

Appendix C:
"Y**O**R**D**" A Teleplay Treatment
by Ivan Tors & George Van Marter ... *487*

Selected Bibliography ... *494*

Index ... *497*

About the Author ... *523*

Introduction

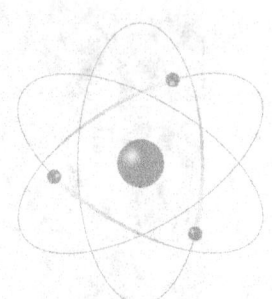

Historically, though this tends to be forgotten, the invention of cinematography came about not because of a search after some new kind of entertainment, but because of the desire of scientists and technicians to evolve from photography, an instrument for recording and reproducing visible motion. Popular science documentaries of a worthwhile nature never found steady fiscal backing from private industry. It took producer Ivan Tors, a lover of both science and nature, to convince Frederic W. Ziv, a pioneer in the development of now-standard broadcasting, to produce and syndicate an anthology series based on scientific fact.

If anyone in the 1950's doubted the public's interest in science and technology, they needed only to go so far as to recall the 40 million people who attended the 1939 New York World's Fair with its theme, "the World of Tomorrow." This was where the fluorescent light was introduced, the new automatic dishwasher, and Elecktro, a seven-foot tall walking, talking robot. Elecktro was later joined by Sparko, a robot dog that could bark, sit and beg. RCA introduced television to the American public at the same event, even publishing a brochure for their factory authorized dealers to explain just what television is. The opening ceremonies were even televised, but it's been estimated that only a few hundred receiving television sets had been manufactured by that time—and more than half of those were on display at the Fair!

The concept of bringing a semi-documentary anthology series to American living rooms was never conceived in 1939 but, less than twenty years later, ZIV-TV syndicated a program that would allow

the medium of television to inform, educate and fascinate Americans. The world of tomorrow did not require a trip to the World's Fair—only a trip to the living room.

By avoiding the growing popularity of juvenile clichés commonly found in science fiction films of the fifties, *Science Fiction Theatre* was able to entertain television audiences without the use of giant insects on the loose, killer robots or Martian invaders. A young couple woke to find themselves in a secret laboratory on a moon of Jupiter, then return to Earth with a scientific calculation that would save mankind. An average American couple suspects their secretive new neighbors, who possess fantastic scientific advancements, might be time travelers from the future. A scientist replicates the atmospheric conditions of the planet Venus, only to create a threatening new life form.

While a bit on the fantastic side, the stories were based (partially) on scientific fact and placed an emphasis on science before fiction. Unlike *The Twilight Zone* and *The Outer Limits*, every episode focused on the technology, not the society that was based upon it. What little conflict between social interaction appeared on the screen was limited to the exhaustive attempts to find a solution to a problem which only science could solve.

Introduction

When I was first exposed to *Science Fiction Theatre*, I found myself entertained not by the dramatic stories, but the lab experiments performed by host Truman Bradley. Dressed in a dark suit and striped tie, he introduced a scientific fact and would then demonstrate the principals for which that fact originated. Thousands of short story anthologies and magazines have explored all the conceivable (and inconceivable) possibilities of the future, so bug-eyed aliens or giant insects would not impress me in the least. Imagine how pleased I was to discover the dramatic plots were based more on science than fiction.

After deciding to do this book, I felt a fact-based approach would be required to not only document a piece of broadcasting history, but satisfy those fans who today, thanks to new technology, can re-watch the episodes at their convenience without consulting the current television listings. This approach includes biographies on the men responsible for the formation of the program, Frederic W. Ziv, Ivan Tors, and the program host, Truman Bradley. I also took advantage of the opportunity to work with two good friends, Jim Cox and Patrick Lucanio, who each contributed a chapter. These friends underscore and support such endeavors. Such loyalty can only be counted in halos.

I'd also like to take a moment and explain the photographs in this book. While I had the luxury of accessing over 2,000 photographs related to *Science Fiction Theatre*, I was not permitted to scan them directly into my computer scanner. As a result, I applied a primitive technique that allowed me to acquire copies of photos, but certainly not at the level of quality a first-generation scan would permit. While some book reviewers are never satisfied until they find a "glaring flaw" to make mention in their book review, I would like to explain that I chose this option for one positive reason: something is better than nothing. For most *Theatre* fans, behind-the-scenes photographs are treasured, regardless of their condition. My advance apologies if someone feels the quality is not up to par with today's standard print jobs. For all others, enjoy the photographs!

A book like this cannot be possible without the endeavors of close friends who took the time to review the manuscript, and offer suggestions and encouragement. In no particular order: Ben Ohmart, Paul Adomites, Beverly Garland, Terry Salomonson, Roy Bright,

Alex Daoundakis, Bridget Grams, Randy A. Riddle, Bob Cockrum, Warren Stevens, Don Ramlow, Steven Thompson, Mike Martini, Mark Phillips, Tom Weaver, Derek Tague and my loving wife who doesn't care much for the series (but put up with my love for the program long enough to see this book through).

On a closing note about giving credit and acknowledgment, it has become a growing trend for people to lift material from published books like this one and post it on the internet without giving due credit for their source. While some feel not applying their name as author and researcher is the same as not stealing credit, misleading others into believing they are responsible for the information is the same as stealing. Thousands of dollars went into researching the material contained in this book. It is my hope that enough copies will sell to reimburse all my expenses before someone steals the material and posts it on the Internet, without any consideration for the author's time and expense. If you have a friend who loves *Science Fiction Theatre* as much as you and I, please tell them about the book and encourage them to buy a copy. And now I'll get off my soapbox so you can enjoy all the imaginative adventures.

MARTIN GRAMS
AUGUST 2010

Chapter One
FREDERIC ZIV, FATHER OF SYNDICATION
BY PATRICK LUCANIO

There are certain names that have come to possess unmistakable influence in the history of broadcasting. William S. Paley and David Sarnoff, for example, remain forever linked to the concept of network broadcasting. Paley's Columbia Broadcasting System and Sarnoff's National Broadcasting Company remain active titans in both radio and television, despite the advancement of cable television channels. But in the pantheon of broadcasting innovators there remains one name that serves as the antithesis to Paley and Sarnoff. Frederic W. Ziv, a one-time advertising executive and author of an influential book on composition called *The Business of Writing*, and nearly single-handedly developed the concept of program syndication which, unlike network programming, is programming that eschews network authority for direct and independent control of the programming by local broadcasters.

Frederic W. Ziv was born August 17, 1905, in Cincinnati, Ohio, the son of a salesman for a buttonhole machine and a research assistant to the president of Hebrew Union College in Cincinnati. Ever since high school Ziv considered himself a writer. While attending the University of Michigan as an English major, Ziv wrote for *The Gargoyle*, a campus humor magazine. The magazine not only allowed Ziv to develop his writing style, but it allowed him to become acquainted with magazine advertising as well as the practical applications of design, layout and printing. He eventually became editor-in-chief, and among his staff were Gurney Williams, who would become humor editor of *Cosmopolitan* and *Look*, and Lichty née George M. Lichtenstein, who drew the syndicated cartoon strip "Grin and Bear It."

Frederic Ziv circa 1970.
(Photo courtesy of Mike Martini/Media Heritage.)

Ziv was also selling short stories to several magazines during his last years in college, including *Saturday Review of Literature* and *Redbook*. In 1928, Ziv graduated from the University of Michigan Law School and abandoned his writing for, as he would say bitterly, "something more practical." He passed the Ohio bar but never practiced law. And it was while waiting to take the bar exam that he was approached by the publishers of *Writer's Digest* and asked to write a book that eventually became *The Business of Writing*. He soon found a position with the Julian Behr Advertising Agency in Cincinnati, for which he wrote copy for $10 per week. Knowing royalties for book sales were going to be extremely small, he ventured into advertising.

In 1930, at the request of one of his clients, he formed the Frederic W. Ziv Advertising Agency where he soon discovered a lucrative market in the fledgling radio business. "I realized there were dozens of agency men who knew ten times what I did about magazine and newspaper advertising," he once said. "But nobody knew anything about radio in those days. It was the one field where a young man could be an expert."

Ziv, in an article in the June 4, 1956, *Broadcasting/Telecasting* journal, noted that, "we approached radio with the view that the local baker, for example, was able to compete as far as buying trucks were concerned. He paid the same price. He would hire salesmen. He could hire bakers. But when it came to radio, he had no opportunity to compete. He had to be a poor second-rater, yet his product wasn't second rate, and his position in the market would need not be second rate. So we felt that we were rendering a very genuine service in producing shows for the local and regional sponsor."

In the mid-1930s, Ziv developed a print campaign for the Rubel Baking Company that featured a young boy saying that the bakery's product was "The Freshest Thing in Town." The campaign proved successful, and Ziv reasoned that the same slogan with the boy would prove likewise for radio. With the bakery's blessing, Ziv devised a 15-minute program combining comedy, American wholesomeness, and sentimentality that was broadcast five times per week in Cincinnati. The show was titled *The Freshest Thing in Town* and was one of the first series in south western Ohio designed specifically for radio. *The Freshest Thing in Town* proved to be the beginning of the Ziv broadcasting empire.

News of the local success of *The Freshest Thing in Town* spread, and Ziv found himself receiving requests from other markets for the program. He realized that the program was already packaged and ready for broadcast, and so it was a simple matter of shipping the transcription discs to any station or sponsor interested in buying the episodes. Ziv embarked on a sales campaign, traveling throughout the South and Midwest, eliciting interest in the program. Interest was keen, and Ziv realized that there was a future in syndicating original programming.

Syndication, originating in the newspaper business, was a simple enterprise. Ziv understood that talent, be it a comic strip writer/artist or a radio program producer, could be compensated by direct payment from a single source or the talent could be compensated by many sources that split the payments. Many broadcast historians cite Robert L. Ripley, himself a newspaper syndicator, as being the first to syndicate radio programs.

Ziv realized that the radio program itself was nothing more than a product, and in order to get a product sold, the organization needed a sales force. In 1938, Ziv hired his first sales officer, Bud Rifkin, thereby establishing the foundation upon which the Ziv organization dominated radio and television syndication until 1960 when the organization was purchased by United Artists Television. Also in 1938, Ziv changed the corporate name from the Frederic W. Ziv Company to the Frederic W. Ziv Company-Radio Productions to better denote the organization's primary purpose, which by this time was moving away from an advertising agency to producer of programming to secure clients. As such, Ziv was dedicating more time to hiring and training a sales force that would write sales presentations and research new clients and markets. Salesmen were paid a ten percent commission on top of their salary, encouraging the sale. The actual production responsibilities fell to John Sinn, who would stay in that capacity through the television years.

Ziv's earliest programs were produced at Cincinnati's WLW and WKRC, but in 1938 he moved production to Chicago because the quality of recording programs was superior. The Windy City, at that time, was the central base of many soap operas. His first soap opera for Chicago was *Dearest Mother*. Ziv's sales force described the program as "a thrilling day-by-day drama of heart-stirring romance and pulse-quickening action. It is the story of a young girl alone in a strange city and her gallant struggle for happiness. Warm and true to life, each days' episode opens and closes with the young girl writing a letter to her mother."

Ziv followed *Dearest Mother* with *Forbidden Diary* in the same year, and also introduced a second staple of his library, the sports program. *Fans in the Stands* featured Dick Bray, roving among "fans in the stands" of various sporting events, to get the spectators' view of the events transpiring on the fields. Famed sportscaster Sam Balter narrated anecdotes about famous sport personalities in *One for the Books.* WKRC in Cincinnati accepted Oklahoma Bob Albright and his "mountain music."

By 1940, however, Ziv Company-Radio Productions was expanding into all genres of radio programming. In 1940, Ziv released yet a new soap opera, *The Career of Alice Blair* with Martha Scott, followed in 1941 with *The Korn Kobblers*, a comedy and music variety series with Alan Courtney, and *The Old Corral*, a country and western variety series featuring Pappy Cheshire, Merle Travis and Sally Foster. But the early 1940s in radio were dominated by action-adventure series, and as the March 9 edition of *Radio Guide* indicated, programs such as *Gang Busters, The Lone Ranger, Mr. District Attorney* and *The Adventures of Ellery Queen* were proven successes. To Ziv that meant proven formulas for successful marketing. To this end, Ziv produced *Manhunt*, described by the Ziv organization as a "dynamic, fast-moving mystery that sustains interest to the last minute." The 15-minute program was made available to markets in 1943, and *Variety* concluded that the series "looms up as a good buy for sponsors looking for low-priced shows."

"If you read the trade papers, you will find that I'm usually referred to as the 'father of syndication.' That's the tag that followed me and is still being used," Ziv told author Irv Broughton (*Producers on Producing*, McFarland, 1986). "I developed the technique; I didn't originate it. I'm not sure if anyone preceded me. I did expand on it and brought it to what was probably its highest level."

But Ziv's next production proved to be the organization's most valuable property. In January 1944, Ziv was granted a six month option to sell *Boston Blackie*, a successful literary series, as well as film series for Columbia Pictures. Like the Columbia Pictures interpretation of writer Jack Boyle's amoral self-appointed detective, radio's Blackie was a champion of justice and an advocate for the "little guy." Ziv employed the star of the Columbia series, Chester Morris, in the title role, paying Morris $1,000 per week for the first 13 weeks with increases of $200 per year if the show continued.

Boston Blackie premiered on NBC on June 23, 1944, and the "enemy to those who make him enemy, friend to those who have no friends" proved so successful that by February 1945, Ziv was able to syndicate the series by negotiating a purchase by the Rubsam and Horman Brewing Company for a "live" production of the series on

Transcription label from the Frederic W. ZIV Company.
(Photo courtesy of Randy A. Riddle).

WOR in New York. The brewery received exclusive rights to the series within 100 miles of New York City. The deal also included distribution outside the New York area of the recorded broadcast. Since the syndicated series was originating in New York, Chester Morris was replaced by Richard Kollmar, and a total of 220 episodes of *Boston Blackie* were ultimately recorded and syndicated.

Ziv also purchased the rights to a second famous detective whose exploits appeared in several best-sellers by S.S. Van Dine and in successful motion pictures for such diverse studios as Paramount, Warner Brothers, and MGM. *Philo Vance* had already been a radio series for NBC in the summer of 1945, when Ziv was granted exclusive radio rights to the character in 1946, for the initial production of 52 half-hour "electronic transcriptions." Jackson Beck portrayed Vance for a total of 104 episodes through 1952.

Ziv's business acumen was also evident in his reissuing of previously produced programming. In 1945, Ziv signed Goodman Ace and Jane Ace to re-record and re-edit their series of 1,400 15-minute shows called *Easy Aces*. Between 1945 and 1949, 763 quarter-hour episodes of the program were syndicated with great success.

Musical series were also a staple of the Ziv library. During the 1940s, Ziv produced and syndicated *Sincerely, Kenny Baker* with Baker; *Pleasure Parade* hosted by Vincent Lopez; *The Barry Wood Show* with Wood and Margaret Whiting; *The Wayne King Show* which was described by *Variety* as "just sweet music, with a fine baritone solo by Larry Douglas;" and *The Guy Lombardo Show*, which was the first Ziv production to be recorded on audio tape.

In 1943, Ziv made overtures to purchase the radio rights to *The Cisco Kid*, a successful film series based on a character in O. Henry's story titled "The Caballero's Way," published in 1907. At the same time, Philip N. Krasne, an acquaintance of Ziv's, was interested in acquiring the television rights to the character so Ziv advanced Krasne the money to secure the television rights. Ziv and the company's vice-president John Sinn, with Krasne, formed Cisco Kid Productions, and by 1948 the rights to *The Cisco Kid* were now controlled by Ziv.

In 1946, The Cisco Kid began radio production with O. Henry's "Robin Hood of the Old West" toned down considerably from the original. Just as Boston Blackie had become a champion of justice in the modern age, so did Cisco and his sidekick, Pancho, become defenders of truth and justice in the Old West. The series was recorded live for Don Lee Broadcasting, originating at station KHJ in Los Angeles, and carried along the 50-station Don Lee Network. Each episode was recorded, and the recordings were syndicated throughout the country beginning in February 1946.

In securing a sponsor for the series, Ziv found himself in familiar company. Interstate Bakeries, makers of Weber Bread, bought the series, and Cisco and Pancho proved so successful at selling bread that after three years, Interstate agreed to sponsor not only the radio series but also the television series through 1954. Moreover, Interstate expanded its sponsorship into the Midwest, selling another of its products, Butter-Nut Bread, through association with Cisco and Pancho.

ZIV-TV's *The Cisco Kid*

In the late 1940s and into the early 1950s, *The Cisco Kid* proved successful with audiences in radio, television and film. Between 1946 and 1955, 833 radio episodes were produced, and in 1946 the trade journal, *Radio Showmanship,* reported that *The Cisco Kid* "had gained a larger audience than either *The Lone Ranger* or *Red Ryder!*"

In 1947, Ziv's company was labeled by the trade papers as the "largest of the open-end transcription producers in the country." His company grossed a whopping $10 million that year, a thirty percent growth from the year previous.

In 1948, the Ziv organization announced that vice-president John Sinn would become president of the newly formed Ziv Television Programs, Inc. With little fanfare, Ziv had broadened the broadcasting horizon to include television, and he saw *film* as the vehicle by which television programs could be syndicated to regional markets. At the time, television was primarily "live" from New York, and Ziv reasoned correctly that just as the transcription disc or the audio tape could be distributed to hundreds of regional and local radio stations, motion picture film could do the same for regional and local television stations.

Chapter One: Frederic Ziv, Father of Syndication

With radio ratings high and the image omnipresent in motion pictures, Ziv's decision to convert *The Cisco Kid* to television was only reasonable. But *The Cisco Kid* was not Ziv's first effort at TV syndication. Following the purchase of the World Broadcasting System from Decca Records in 1948, the world's oldest and largest transcription library, Ziv then purchased the General Film Library which consistsed of newsreel footage that dated back to the turn of the century. Using this priceless newsreel footage, Ziv produced two 15-minute fillers titled *Sports Album* and *Yesterday's Newsreel*. With the success of these programs and the phenomenal success of the *Hopalong Cassidy* programs edited from the feature films, Ziv believed the time was right to enter the television market with dramatic programming. Thus in October of 1949, he produced a pilot episode of *The Cisco Kid* with the two actors who had been playing the roles in a series of feature films produced by Krasne. Duncan Renaldo and Leo Carrillo made the transition to television as Cisco and Pancho, respectively, much to the delight of the kids who had followed their adventures at Saturday matinees. Upon seeing the pilot episode, courtesy of Ziv's sales division, Interstate Bakeries immediately agreed to a 10-year contract, and in January 1950, *The Cisco Kid* went into production as a weekly series in 16 major markets on the West Coast.

Production on *The Cisco Kid* ended in 1955, following a total of 156 episodes. Filming was halted not because the series fell out of favor with audiences, but for financial reasons. With 156 episodes in the can, reruns simply yielded higher profits than producing new episodes. Looking back at his career with Nick Clooney in a video interview in November of 1990, Ziv recalled that television was in the lab during World War II. No one predicted broadcasting in color but Ziv felt the added expense for *The Cisco Kid* would, at the very least, sell sponsorship if not program loyalty. "Everyone said I was wrong," Ziv recalled, making the effort to film *The Cisco Kid* in color.

In addition, by the late 1950s, color television was becoming more prevalent and Ziv had wisely shot the episodes on color film stock in anticipation of TV's transition into color. This decision led to even more profit as *The Cisco Kid* was rediscovered, as it were, for color broadcasting. Additionally, as more and more syndicators joined

The popular ZIV-TV brand name.

the crowded market in the early 1960s, color programming was essential. As such, Ziv netted a considerable yield when he sold the entire *Cisco Kid* series in 1964 to Walter Schwimmer Inc., the television syndication subsidiary of Bing Crosby Productions Inc. *The Cisco Kid* remained popular in its new color form through the mid-seventies, some 25 years after its television debut.

Recognizing the emerging importance of television, in 1950 Ziv signed a five-year $100,000 lease with California Studios in Hollywood to produce television programming. By 1952, Ziv Television Programs Inc. had nine series available for syndication including *Sports Album* and *Yesterday's Newsreel*, as well *The Cisco Kid, Boston Blackie, The Unexpected, The Living Book* and *Story Theatre*. Ziv also offered a package of feature films reportedly leased from distributor Budd Rogers, and a cartoon package leased from Walter Lantz.

Realizing that the company was truly in the television production business, Ziv purchased American National Studios (formerly Eagle-Lion Pathé Studio) on Santa Monica Boulevard in late December 1954, for a reported $1.7 million. Ziv Television Programs, Inc. bought 92 percent of the A.N.S. from the two groups which had majority control. The Fred Levy syndicate, which owned 60 percent, was paid $1,400,000 for its interest. The Bernard Prockter group was given about $750,000 for its share of the property. Initially announced to trade papers as being "used to house administrative offices," the newly christened Ziv Television Studios took immediate possession of the facilities, which included completely equipped sound stages covering more than six acres. The new facilitiy offered twice as much space as Ziv occupied at the former Studios. Only two episodes (including Bradley's lab demonstrations) were filmed at the old studio, "Beyond" and "Y··O··R··D··." The remaining episodes of the series were filmed at the new studio.*

According to the January 1, 1955 issue of *Billboard*, "Ziv badly needed the additional space for some of its new ventures, which will double its production rate in 1955. First show skedded is a science fiction series developed by Ivan Tors." To compensate for the cost factor, the new studio facilities were rented out to a number of tenants filming television and motion pictures, including a number of feature films produced by the fledgling and independent American International Pictures.**

But despite Ziv's entry into television production, his radio unit continued to prosper, producing some of the finest radio programs of the 1950s. Among them were Morton Fine and David Friedkin's *Bold Venture* with Humphrey Bogart and Lauren Bacall; Robert E.

---

* The only ZIV program affected by the move was *I Led Three Lives*. The purchase happened halfway through filming of the second season so the script writers incorporated a major change. The characters of Eva and Herbert Philbrick were asked by the Communist Party to move into a new house, which only added to the risk of exposure for the characters, and a subplot for a number of second-season episodes. Behind the scenes, it allowed the crew to create sets of the new Philbrick house and not have to recreate the same sets featured in prior episodes.

** The purchase of American National did not go unnoticed by Ziv's competition, MCA and UTP, which publicly stated in the last week of December 1954, that the reason for the purchase of the latter organization by MCA was that neither distribution firm could achieve saturation selling by itself. It was hoped that with its 50-odd salesmen and 22 programs, it would now be able to match ZIV-TV's thoroughness in coverage of markets.

Advertisement for Ziv's radio program, *Bold Venture*.

Lee and Jerome Lawrence's *I Was a Communist for the FBI* with Dana Andrews; and a remake of *Mr. District Attorney* with David Brian, who also appeared simultaneously in a television version.

The years 1953 through 1960 are considered the television years for Ziv as radio gradually faded, leaving Ziv Television Programs Inc. as the sole business entity. In 1953, Ziv produced its most successful series up to that time, a series that was touted for its realism and patriotism. Based on a 1951 book of the same title by Herbert Philbrick, an FBI counterspy, *I Led Three Lives* broke records within four weeks of its release. By September 1953, the series had been sold in ninety-four markets besting CBS's top-rated program, *I Love Lucy*, by fifteen.

"The public is getting more and more selective in its choice of TV fare as well as in cars and other goods," wrote Frederic Ziv in an essay for the January 1956 issue of *Television Magazine*. "From the program point of view, TV film is but in the pioneering stage. It will prove equal to the challenge, I believe, and move beyond any conventional lines anyone might try to draw today." Ziv's track record went unsurpassed as he expanded his television operations.

In succession, twenty-five series followed: *Mr. District Attorney, Meet Corliss Archer, The Eddie Cantor Comedy Theatre, Science Fiction*

Theatre, Highway Patrol, The Man Called X, Dr. Christian, West Point, Men of Annapolis, The New Adventures of Martin Kane, Harbor Master (later retitled *Adventure at Scott Island*), *Harbor Command, Tombstone Territory, Sea Hunt, Target, Dial 999, Bat Masterson, The Rough Riders, MacKenzie's Raiders, Bold Venture, Lock Up, The Man and the Challenge,* and *This Man Dawson.* These were in addition to Ziv's earlier TV series such as *Sports Album, Yesterday's Newsreel, The Cisco Kid, The Living Book, Story Theatre, Boston Blackie, The Unexpected* (later retitled *Times Square Playhouse*) and *Favorite Story* making a total of 33 successful television series.

Among the strengths used to sell his television programs to stations and sponsors was the ratings. But ratings services were difficult for the programs Ziv produced, because they aired in various time slots and days of the week. So Ziv arranged for individual ratings in various cities, used for promoting and sales pitches, revealing how well they did in Peoria, New York, Seattle, etc.

Of all the Ziv programs, three remain not only the most recognized of syndicated success but also the most favored by audiences in the popularity polls: *Science Fiction Theatre*, an anthology series hosted by Truman Bradley; *Highway Patrol* with Broderick Crawford as the chief of a state law enforcement agency that was not necessarily California despite the similar milieu; and *Sea Hunt* with Lloyd Bridges as an "underwater troubleshooter." (*Bat Masterson* was a close fourth.)

"Most of our shows were not offered to the network," Ziv recalled to interviewer Irv Broughton. "A program like *Sea Hunt*, for example, was turned down by the network. We showed it to each of the networks, showed them the pilot. They liked the pilot, but they figured—and each one seemed to be of the same opinion—'Well, what do you do the second week and what do you do the third week—you've done it all the first week.' Well, of course, they were wrong; we produced it year after year."

Ziv dominated the field. Of the six distributor categories in *Billboard*'s fourth annual TV film service awards, ZIV-TV won first place in four and was second in one. As far as the poll was concerned, ZIV-TV in 1955 maintained its leadership in TV film syndication. The company's status in the *Billboard* polls remained constant through most of the 1950s in the same manner.

Advertisement for ZIV-TV's *Dr. Christian* series.

Eventually, radio was consumed by television, and the networks began to dominate the television airwaves. In early 1960, Ziv sold his company to United Artists Television for $20 million. The corporate name became Ziv-United Artists, but in 1962, Ziv was dropped and the corporate name returned to United Artists Television. Fred Ziv remained at UA-TV for five years, serving as a consultant for three series that definitely had the Ziv mien: *King of Diamonds* (a second series for Broderick Crawford), *Everglades* and *Ripcord*.

In 1968, Ziv moved into the next phase of his career as professor at the University of Cincinnati. In addition to sharing his vast knowledge, he agreed to participate in interviews with authors and historians and donate much of his collection of material to the University archives.

Despite the Hollywood connection, Ziv's corporate headquarters remained in Cincinnati. Ziv himself once stated that he was basically a shy man, and staying in Cincinnati allowed him to remain in the background. In his later years, he once remarked that "there's more violence and very little intellectual material" in current television fare, adding that "the sad thing about television is that it had such gigantic possibilities."

ZIV RADIO SERIES

The Freshest Thing in Town	1936
Dearest Mother	1938
Forbidden Diary	1938
One for the Books	1939
Career of Alice Blair	1940
Korn Kobblers	1941
Old Corral	1941
Eye Witness News	1942
War Correspondent	1943
Songs of Good Cheer	1943
Manhunt	1943
Boston Blackie	1944
Calling All Cars	1944
Parents' Magazine of the Air	1945
Lightning Jim	1945
Easy Aces	1945
Sincerely, Kenny Baker	1945
Pleasure Parade	1945
The Barry Wood Show	1946
The Wayne King Show	1946
Philo Vance	1946
The Cisco Kid	1946
It's Showtime From Hollywood	1947
The Guy Lombardo Show	1947
Favorite Story	1947
Bright Star	1949
Meet the Menjous	1950
Bold Venture	1951
Movietown Radio Theatre	1951
I Was a Communist for the FBI	1952
Freedom USA	1952
Hour of Stars	1953
The Red Skelton Show	1954
The Eddie Cantor Show	1954
Mr. District Attorney	1954
Dorothy and Dick	1955
The Fred Waring Show	1956

ZIV TELEVISION SHOWS

Sports Album	1948
Yesterday's Newsreel	1948
The Cisco Kid	1950
The Living Book	1951
Story Theatre	1951
Boston Blackie	1951
The Unexpected	1952
Favorite Story	1952
I Led Three Lives	1953
Mr. District Attorney	1954
Meet Corliss Archer	1954
Eddie Cantor Comedy Theatre	1955
Science Fiction Theatre	1955
Highway Patrol	1955
The Man Called X	1956
Dr. Christian	1956
West Point Story	1956
Men of Annapolis	1956
Martin Kane	1957
Harbor Master	1957
Harbor Command	1957
Tombstone Territory	1957
Sea Hunt	1958
Target	1958
Dial 999	1958
Bat Masterson	1958
Rough Riders	1958
McKenzie's Raiders	1958
Bold Venture	1959
Lock Up	1959
The Man and the Challenge	1959
This Man Dawson	1959
Men Into Space	1959
The World of Giants	1959

Chapter Two
Truman Bradley
From Forensics to Science Fiction—Revues, Audio & Celluloid Between
By Jim Cox

"Know what you're talking about, and enjoy talking about it," explained Truman Bradley, when asked what he felt was the secret of his success.

The future host-narrator of *Science Fiction Theatre* was born in Sheldon, Missouri, on February 8, 1905. As a youth there he captured first place in a Show-Me State high school debating competition, an early sign of his ultimate occupational direction. Bradley enrolled at Missouri State Teacher's College on a scholarship, attended three years, and transferred to the Kansas City School of Law where he concentrated on forensics.

With his formal education done, including studying law, in the early 1920s Bradley exhibited marketing proficiency by peddling Westinghouse electric appliances. As a vendor, he was eventually compensated at $500 weekly—profoundly stimulating wages by 1920s standards. In spite of the lucrative sums, as time went on he grew restless. Based in Kansas City and seeing little chance to apply the skills for which he had specifically trained, at 22 he took the advice of a pal. Goodman Aiskowitz, drama critic for *The Kansas City Post-Journal*—six years Bradley's senior—persuaded the youthful salesman to cut his Westinghouse ties and chase his heart's desire on the stage.

Aiskowitz undoubtedly continued to inspire Bradley long afterward as the journalist altered his handle to Goodman Ace and simultaneously reviewed films for KMBC Radio from 1927-31. In 1930 with his wife, Jane Sherwood Ace, he developed a couple of self-characterizations that—in a little while—gave them instant recognition in American households as the venerable *Easy Aces*,

Truman Bradley demonstrates medical apparatus.

"radio's distinctive laugh novelty." Media historians claimed she "never met a malaprop she didn't like," sometimes applying such foolishness to ludicrous extent. The Aces' humorous exchanges, written by Goodman and eventually aired nationally from Chicago, continued into the late 1940s. He also authored a *Saturday Review* column while penning gags for the likes of entertainers Tallulah Bankhead, Milton Berle, Perry Como, Danny Kaye and Bob Newhart.

Truman Bradley poses for the camera for a publicity photo.

In the meantime, Truman Bradley was enchanted from his early moments in front of the footlights. Entering vaudeville as his personal conduit to entertainment, in a short while he signed with the Henry Duffy Players, one of the nation's most respected performing touring outfits circulating from the West Coast to the Midwest. He played six weeks with Edmund Breese.

Possibly to alleviate a family crisis, in 1928 Bradley interrupted his own career quest to assume management of his sister's Hollywood publishing enterprise. Within a year, however, he was also on the air just like his chum Goodman Ace back in Kansas City: Bradley signed as an announcer at KFI and his first show was with the Boswell Sisters. He would also be heard in 1929 on Tinseltown's KMTR, and was the announcer for Olsen and Johnson's variety program, *The Swift Revue*, originating from KHJ in Los Angeles.

Within a short while a new mentor appeared on the Hollywood horizon to tempt him. When Harry Von Zell, 24—Bradley's junior by a year and an ethereal colleague—left the Coast in 1930 for New York's more developed airwaves' challenges, Von Zell induced the young word-slinger to join Columbia's staff in New York and Bradley agreed. The latter tarried only a brief two years. When it became abundantly clear that Chicago at that moment in time was the center of America's broadcasting universe, in 1932 he auditioned at the Windy City's CBS affiliate, WBBM, and was hired. He was soon announcing and acting in myriad nationwide broadcasts, interspersed with local assignments as a newscaster and sportscaster. His voice training had at last found a venue of diverse proportions!

Bradley's most impressive audio duty was his appointment in 1932 as announcer of the glitzy network series, *The Ford Sunday Evening Hour*, airing live every week from Detroit. CBS publicists ultimately observed that he racked up 39,000 air miles on round-trip jaunts each week via propeller-driven craft between Chicago and Detroit, for broadcasts that persisted from 1932-38. During that era, all of his other radio work originated in the Windy City.

While that was going on, he was also penning, announcing, producing and acting in multiple shows locally and nationally. Among the better known were *The Story of Mary Marlin, Then and Now, Og, Son of Fire* and *Jack Armstrong, the All-American Boy*. One of his most fulfilling features from the Loop included appearances with Goodman and Jane Ace on *Easy Aces*—they had arrived in Chicago in 1931, just ahead of him. Theirs was a gratifying reunion. On their comedy serial, he was cast in the debuting role of Brad, a departure from his normal announcing assignments. Two decades later, when Bradley took on the hosting chores for *Science Fiction*

Truman Bradley before the radio microphone.

Theatre, television critics would be quick to point out Bradley's prior association with the *Ford* program, a testament to his skills as a radio announcer.

Delivering the news for American Family Soap and American Family Flakes (Procter & Gamble) over WBBM in Chicago, Bradley found himself under scrutiny when *Variety* commented: "News-reviewer has pleasing voice and the art of injecting color into what he talks about." Bradley was not limited to just news, but also commentary. For the broadcast of February 24, 1938, for instance, he told about the latest Black Legion killing and then went into the history of the other hooded organization, the Ku Klux Klan, telling how it originated, how it functioned, and how it died.

In early 1938 Bradley once more migrated to the West Coast, that time for permanent residence. Considered MGM's new great white hope, Bradley found himself under studio contract, making several flickers. Norma Shearer saw his picture in a Chicago paper in 1936 and sent a cutout of the photo to a studio biggie with the suggestion that Bradley looked like screen material. Nothing happened. In early 1938, she saw another picture and sent it to another producer.

Bradley was tested, signed and made his screen debut in *Vacation from Love* (1938). Always playing minor and supporting roles in his earliest films, Bradley planted roots at the radio microphone to supplement his income.

The sunshine state offered airtime opportunities that had significantly flourished in California in the half-dozen years he had been living in the Midwest. In 1940, he won news casting and announcing posts at CBS-owned KNX, Los Angeles, and picked up several chain-fed chores. He opened series for some of the biggest names in the business including Don Ameche, George Burns and Gracie Allen, Tony Martin, Dinah Shore, Tommy Dorsey, Frank Sinatra, Red Skelton, Shirley Temple, and Rudy Vallee. Shortly before each of Frank Sinatra's radio programs, Bradley was on stage before the juvenile audience to remind them to refrain from showing their enthusiasm while Sinatra was in the middle of a number.

During his initial season as announcer for *The Hinds Honey and Almond Cream Program,* starring George Burns and Gracie Allen, *Variety* remarked: "Truman Bradley fills the announcing portfolio expertly."

As announcer for the *Lady Esther Screen Guild Theatre*, Bradley made it a habit of introducing the studio audience before the broadcast with his "warm up" patter. To make them feel at ease, he repeatedly told them, "We have a number of celebrities with us tonight, in fact, there in the third row from the back I see Gary Cooper." Then Bradley would point and everyone would crane their necks. Whereupon Bradley would add, "No, I guess I was mistaken. It's not Gary, it's Asta." A big laugh followed. After doing this for a number of weeks, word reached Cooper. On the sixth week, Bradley repeated the gag, pointed, and there was Cooper—with Asta, the famous film pooch from the *Thin Man* movies. The joke was on Bradley.

Bradley accepted the announcing chores for *Screen Guild Theatre* for little or no pay. A charity show, he (along with all of the Hollywood guest stars) donated all of his fees to the Motion Picture Relief Fund.

In February 1942, Bradley interrupted a network run as comic Red Skelton's interlocutor to fulfill an obligation in Uncle Sam's Army. But by October of that year, he was back in his accustomed spot on

Truman Bradley received fifth billing in *Treat 'Em Rough* (1942).

Truman Bradley posing for the camera on the first day of filming, September 11, 1954.

the Skelton show. When Ozzie and Harriet made arrangements to star in their own weekly program, they invited Bradley to jump on board but prior contracts with other agencies prevented their friend from making the transition.

Subsequently, from 1943-47, while presenting episodes of "radio's theater of thrills," *Suspense*, Bradley became the unofficial audio commercial spokesman of the Roma Wine Company. Roma underwrote that mystery narrative.

By September 1947, Bradley was still in Hollywood but confessed publicly that he had to give up a number of his air shows (including Red Skelton) because of picture commitments.

Bradley's motion-picture work certified him as a bit player for a handful of memorable celluloid works among them: *Northwest Passage* (1940), *The Horn Blows at Midnight* (1945), *I Wonder Who's Kissing Her Now* (1947) and *Call Northside 777* (1948). He played the role

Truman Bradley on the newly-constructed laboratory.
(Photo taken on September 11, 1954.)

of Dr. William Collins, a young physician who is sent up for drunk driving in *Millionaires in Prison* (1940). Actor Paul Guilfoyle played the plausible role of Ox in the same movie. Ironically, Guilfoyle would later direct numerous episodes of *Science Fiction Theatre,* including a number of segments with Truman Bradley as the host. Throughout the forties and early fifties, Bradley's on-camera roles in the movies would turn to off-screen narrations and the radio announcer voices—often un-credited—and a brief cameo for Columbia Pictures' *Behind the Mike* in 1947.

When *The Night Before the Divorce* (1942) was released in theaters, critics noted that the picture itself was somewhat short of the best that Hollywood could do. To have written otherwise would have been to compromise honesty, but the critics would have been equally remiss in their duty not to have cited the performance of Truman Bradley, whom columnist Vic Boesen of the *Albuquerque Journal* remarked was, "the one virtue of the offering," and praised him in the deserved measure.

Truman Bradley poses for the camera in between takes.

During his tenure in the limelight, Bradley displayed an entrepreneurial streak. In August 1937, he purchased all the stock in Mme. Huntingford, Inc., a 42-year-old cosmetics manufacturing company. After reviewing the necessities of the reputed Chicago toiletries-cosmetics firm, which produced 30 cosmetics including face creams, he turned the day-to-day management of the operation over to his sister Elene, who had extensive experience in the field. He owned the business venture for a good while, too, viewing it as supplementary to his entertainment livelihood.

Hollywood Columnist Frederick Othman interviewed Bradley when he made his screen entrance in late 1938. "If movie actor I am," laughed Bradley, "I hope it works out, but if it doesn't, I guess I still can go back to radio announcing. If that doesn't pan out either, then I still have my cosmetics business."

Bradley's final contribution to celluloid was *Confidence Girl* in 1952, supplying the voice of the off-screen narrator. With the exception of his role as announcer for ZIV's radio program *I Was A Communist for the F.B.I.* (78 episodes starring Dana Andrews as counterspy Matt Cvetic), Bradley's career and personal life remain a mystery until late 1954 when he agreed to play host for Ivan Tors' *Science Fiction Theatre*. Many speculate that he attempted the shoe manufacturing business venture which he started in November of 1949. One thing can be agreed upon: his job as announcer for the ZIV radio program was most likely the reason why he was approached with the offer to do *Theatre*. Perhaps his prior interest in forensics peaked his interest?

Having begun his entertainment career on stage, then adding radio and film to an expanding portfolio, Bradley completed his professional cycle in television by hosting-narrating 78 episodes of *Science Fiction Theatre* from 1955-57, the true capstone of his career. The pilot was filmed in July of 1954, but Bradley's on-screen duties were not filmed until September 11, which also included off-screen narration for the pilot and the second episode produced, "Y..O..R..D..," which never went into production until December. When the remainder of the series began production in late February of 1955, Bradley began routine visits to the studio for his hosting chores, often filmed in batches of two, three and four episodes at one time. On February 28, for example, Herbert Strock directed Bradley for all the pickups and off-screen narrations for episodes 3, 4 and 5. He would return two weeks later for pickups and off-screen narrations for episodes 6 and 7, and so on.

After *Science Fiction Theatre*, Bradley found it difficult to appear before television cameras, having been associated and possibly typecast as the host of a series syndicated on local stations across the country throughout the late '50s and early '60s. His final performance was in 1960 as narrator for one episode of the *Perry Mason* TV series, titled "The Case of the Madcap Modiste."

Truman Bradley holds binoculars for one of his lab demonstration.

Then, noted one source, "he was the man who got to utter one of television's most deathless phrases, if that's a possible superlative. After conning the audience into sitting through the last commercial by telling them he'd be right back, he'd look straight into the camera and say: 'This is Truman Bradley saying...see you next week!'"

When *Science Fiction Theatre* premiered on television, Bradley's hometown heralded his comeback. The November 16, 1955 issue of the *Joplin Globe* reported:

> "Truman Bradley, longtime top-rated newscaster and network announcer comes back to his home area via television at 9:30 o'clock Monday night on KOAM, channel 7. This entirely new kind of TV series is sponsored by Standard Oil Company."

Bradley's personal life never seemed to fare as well as his professional pursuits. He wed three times and divorced three times. His first wedding was in Chicago about 1935 when his bride was Evelyn Jane Esenther. That union ended prior to 1939 when she remarried.

On January 12, 1940, Bradley—then almost 35—took actress Myrla Ethel Bratton, 24, as his wife—"the girl with the most beautiful figure in the United States," an MGM dance director assessed. Married in Las Vegas, within weeks the couple were living apart. They separated numerous times, in fact, reconciling at his recurring promise "to reform"; she sued for divorce in the summer of 1940 but they got together again before permanently going in opposite directions in March of 1941. The newspapers were quick to dig into the juicy details, even pointing out that she sued her husband—twice—in less than two weeks during the month of March. At formal divorce proceedings on April 15, 1941, she accused him of acting like a prima donna, argued that he had a "violent temper" and brought uncontested charges of cruelty. "It made a nervous wreck out of me," she told reporters.

On June 27, 1942, Bradley wed film actress-amateur golfer Phyllis Ruth in Hollywood. *The Los Angeles Times* reported on August 29, 1945, that their marriage was headed for divorce, too, although the duo stuck it out a while longer. Having heard them out in the courtroom, a judge ruled that they attempt to live in the same house together for a period of time, though separate. The couple soon reconciled and had a baby together.

In November 1947, the marriage hit a rocky road as Ruth filed divorce after having testified that he once referred to her as a "stupid little blond without a brain in her head." Attorneys announced to the press that the couple had reached a property settlement and that Mrs. Bradley was to have custody of their one-year-old daughter. Fortunately for him, he had much better luck in the entertainment arena.

Bradley suffered a stroke in later years and spent most of his decline at the Motion Picture Country Home along with scores of movie notables and less famous people from behind the scenes of the industry. Ironically, the *Screen Guild Theatre* radio program he served as announcer, partially funded the very same home he spent his remaining years. He died of a heart attack at the age of 69 at the Home on July 28, 1974, in Woodland Hills, Calif.

Chapter Three
Biography of Ivan Tors

With a sense of mission impervious to the commercial pressures of motion picture and television production, Ivan Tors produced a series of films that brought science and wildlife conservation into American homes. He was often compared with Walt Disney in numerous trade columns, not so much because of his style and content of his work, but because of the economic success he achieved in the limited market of family fare. The Ivan Tors Films, Inc., reportedly grossed about $26 million in 1967. Through his far-flung enterprises in California, Florida, the Bahamas, and East Africa, he set an unmatched record of spinning off numerous television programs including *Man and the Challenge, Sea Hunt, Daktari, Gentle Ben, Cowboy in Africa* and of course, *Science Fiction Theatre*. Tors rejected violence and sadism for its own sake in favor of exciting exploits in science, natural science and adventurous exploration. While the name of ZIV television graced the screen in large type with each episode, Ivan Tors' name was limited to the small print in the closing credits—but viewers of *Science Fiction Theatre* know who was truly responsible.

Ivan Lawrence Tors was born on June 12, 1916, in Budapest, Hungary, to Anthony Tors, a dairy chemist, and Margaret (Bohm) Tors. He grew up in Budapest with a sister, Eva, and a brother, Erwin, who later became treasurer of Ivan Tors Studios. In boyhood, Ivan Tors acquired an interest in science that developed into a lifelong hobby. When he was seven he became fascinated with astronomy, and later, at Saint Stephens secondary school, he showed an unusual talent in mathematics. After his graduation in 1934,

Ivan Tors relaxing on the set of *Science Fiction Theatre*.

he entered the University of Budapest, where as a premedical student he gained some knowledge of zoology.

While at the university, Tors was discovered by a leading European literary agent as a promising playwright. In 1935 his first play, *Mimi*, was produced. His later productions included *Keep Your Distance* and *Wind Without Rain*. He also worked as a newspaperman in Hungary. As the Nazi menace began to spread throughout Europe, Tors left Budapest in 1939 for New York, where he studied English for several months at Fordham University.

Producer Ivan Tors gives instructions on the set of "Postcard From Barcelona."

Like many other talented Hungarian expatriates, Tors was attracted to Hollywood. In 1941, he joined Columbia Pictures' staff of screenwriters, and he just established himself in the film capital when he was called for military duty in World War II. Entering the Army Air Forces in 1942, he served in the technical training command branch as a radio writer with the Glenn Miller band, stationed at Yale University. Later, at his own request, he was transferred to the Office of Strategic Services. During training, he was injured in a premature explosion and in 1945 he received a medical discharge.

An Air Force veteran involved in a gambling racket served as the hero of the 1946 Monogram release, *Below the Deadline*, for which Tors wrote the original story. On his return to Hollywood in 1945, he became a writer for MGM. He collaborated on the screenplays for *Song of Love* (1947), *In the Good Old Summertime* (1949), *That Forsythe Woman* (1949) and *Watch the Birdie* (1951). He also collaborated on the screenplays of some of the motion pictures of which he had been producer or co-producer. The first of those, *Storm Over Tibet*, a 1952 Columbia release, explored the unknown regions of the Himalayas and keynoted the theme of much of his later work—man's exploration of the little-known. Using stock footage from a German-Austrian film titled *Demon of the Himalayas* from 1936, *Storm Over Tibet* was produced under a modest budget and this inspired Tors to use stock footage from a German film to produce *The Magnetic Monster*.

His lifelong interest in wildlife, science and education was reflected in the pictures he produced. His interest in space exploration was responsible for *The Magnetic Monster* (1953), *Riders to the Stars* (1954) and *Gog* (1954). These inventive science fiction adventures for United Artists are today considered "serious-minded" fiction, compared to the growing trend of the times. Ivan Tors, Curt Siodmak, Andrew 'Bundy' Marton and Lazlo Benedek were the Hungarian clan in Hollywood—there was a sign over their writing department at MGM, "Being Hungarian Is Not Enough." His first of these productions, *The Magnetic Monster*, also established his working relationship with a cast and crew that would be responsible for the creative process on television's *Science Fiction Theatre*; among them director Herbert L. Strock who started out as a film editor.

After two or three days into the picture, Ivan was very unhappy with the dailies," recalled Herbert Strock to author Tom Weaver. "He called me and said, 'Come on down to the sound stage.' I said, 'I can't. If I come down, you won't have your dailies on time.' He said, 'To hell with the dailies. Come down to the stage.' So I jumped on a bicycle and went down to the stage. Here was the star Richard Carlson, Ivan Tors, the camerman and Harry Redmond, the special effects man—standing around, doing nothing! The script supervisor, a charming lady by the name of Mary Whitlock Gibson, very prim and proper, like a Gibson girl, said, 'They want

(LEFT TO RIGHT) **Herbert L. Strock, Truman Bradley and Ivan Tors.**

you to take over the picture!' I said, 'What? I'm not a director, I'm a film editor!' And she said, 'This picture has so much stock from the German film we have, and you know exactly how everything must go together.' And Curt couldn't understand it. Ivan came over and said, 'Don't worry, I've call the Director's Guild, you're in the guild, take over.'"

Strock stuck with Tors as the producer made the move to television. Not only did Strock direct a number of *Science Fiction Theatre* episodes, but he directed most of the first season opening and closing segments featuring Truman Bradley and his lab demonstrations, and was responsible for establishing the pan and scan of Bradley's laboratory for the title segment of each episode.

"Ivan Tors came to Ziv through Richard Carlson [*Riders to the Stars*]," Strock recalled to interviewer Tom Weaver. "He ended up on *Science Fiction Theatre*, and I worked with Ivan on many of those. I enjoyed working on that show with actors like Victor Jory, Gene Barry, Gene Lockhart and others that the studio would hire because it was a prestige series. But eventually Ivan came to resent the fact that I would want to rewrite certain things in order to make them work better. There was really no argument between us, but he resented a little bit and I was moved off *Science Fiction Theatre* onto other series—as well as doing one of those every once in a while."*

After production of *Science Fiction Theatre* was completed, Tors' interest in underwater exploration led him in 1957 to the MGM feature, *Underwater Warrior* and afterwards, 155 episodes of *Sea Hunt*, which he produced for four television seasons. He then completed 32 hour-long shows for the CBS series, *The Aquanauts*.

Turning to animals as a source of entertainment, Tors filmed the highly successful *Flipper*, first as a motion picture and then as a television series. Next came the African adventure feature, *Rhino!*

Tors took pride in the fact that his company specialized in making films others deemed impossible. His camera crews pioneered filmmaking in skydiving, underwater and scientific photography. And Tors wanted all of his films designed for the entire family. When Tors later co-owned with Ralph Helfer of a private zoo, "Africa, U.S.A.," located fifty miles from Hollywood in Soledad Canyon, this was where his *Daktari* television series was filmed. The compound sheltered more than 400 animals, seen regularly in the series. Tors also owned a studio in Miami, Florida, where the *Flipper* series was produced.

---

* Strock went on to direct numerous episodes at ZIV-TV including *I Led Three Lives, Favorite Story, Sea Hunt, Meet Corliss Archer, Highway Patrol, Men of Annapolis, Harbor Command,* and *Dr. Christian*. In 1959, Strock made the switch to Warner Brothers where he directed a number of television productions including *The Alaskans, 77 Sunset Strip, Colt .45, Bronco, Cheyenne* and *Maverick*.

Chapter Four
THE HISTORY OF THE SERIES

In October 1955, retired General Douglas MacArthur told the *New York Times*, "The nations of the world will have to unite, for the next war will be an interplanetary war." While we are still waiting on our back porch on summer evenings, looking up at the stars, for the initial signs of a galactic war between the human race and aliens from outer space, writers have conjured up their own visions in the form of short stories, television scripts and motion-pictures, giving us a taste of the hazards and fallout resulting from such combat. While dismissive folks reading this chuckle at the thought, keep in mind that Pierre Pachet, Professor of Psychology at Toulouse remarked in 1872, "Louis Pastueur's theory of germs is ridiculous fiction." And Dr. Lee De Forest, inventor of the vacuum tube and labeled "father of invention," remarked in 1957, "Man will never reach the moon regardless of all future scientific advances." Science fiction author Arthur C. Clarke once commented that no first-rate scientist made fun of science fiction, and he pointed out a number of scientists who did write for the field. After all, scientists took the next step in technological evolution thanks to some form of imagination.

Perhaps anthologist Groff Conklin described the journey of science fiction best when he wrote, "It is difficult to pinpoint when science fiction originated because it is a form of writing that encompasses a wide range of ideas and incorporates many styles of literature." From Lucian of Samosata's Greek travel tale *True History* or *True Story* (written in the second century) to Jonathan Swift's *Gulliver's Travels* (1726), imaginary voyages and monsters were scientific ideas even before the days of H.G. Wells and Jules Verne. Groff

William Hudson and Lisa Gaye in between takes of "Gravity Zero."

also wrote, "Let us admit it: fantasies based upon extrapolation of scientific or quasi-scientific ideas are definitely upon us, at least for as long as our society is based upon a complex technology." During the 1930s, science fiction became a staple of newspaper comics, pulp magazines and Saturday matinees. Buck Rogers, Flash Gordon and Captain Future took us through interplanetary adventures and were subject to attacks of ignorant and downright malicious critics, citing the genre as childish. It wasn't until the 1950s that science fiction stories reached a pinnacle with an outgrowth of books, magazines, comics, motion pictures and television programs. It wasn't until the 1940s that Isaac Asimov, Ray Bradbury and Theodore Sturgeon (among others) took the genre into a playing field of serious literature. And it wasn't until 1947 that Kenneth Arnold saw in the sky what he termed a "flying saucer" and from that day forward, numerous citizens, pilots and scientists were quick to jump in on the phenomenon by using the "flying saucer" as an excuse for anything flying through the air for which they could not decipher detail with the human eye.

First jet planes, then the atomic bomb, color television, the electronic computer and a host of other technological innovations, were all foretold in one manner or another by science fiction writers. Inventions, dangerous and otherwise, interplanetary and dimensional travel, contact with alien beings and mechanical monsters were certainly colorful themes of the times. But there were two factors that fought Ivan Tors, the producer of *Science Fiction Theatre*, and they were attributed to technology of the times. Tors had to create a series that would meet the approval of station managers who generally felt that science fiction was still a limited market, gaining only the attention of juveniles who read comic books and viewed *Captain Video* and *Tom Corbett, Space Cadet*. Second was that the stories had to contain a happy ending or promising resolution, unlike the stories that appeared in top-grade science fiction magazines that bore little (if any) censorship.

Thirteen years before the premiere of *Theatre*, the mature-appeal science fiction story had only one outlet—Street and Smith's *Astounding Science Fiction*. By 1952, the magazine had severe competition from three sources: *The Magazine of Fantasy and Science Fiction*, *Fantastic* and *Galaxy Science Fiction*. Television's *Tales of Tomorrow* (1951-1953) garnished attention from the faithful readers of those magazines, but sadly it was short-lived. By the time *Theatre* premiered on television, the motion-picture industry was picking up on the growing popularity of the genre. This would spawn a number of low-budget science fiction flicks, each attempting to out-do the other while justifying the lack of quality and intelligence that could have given them a longer life span. Hollywood started out trying to make the science fiction genre a bit more respected on the big screen with films such as *Destination: Moon* (1950), *Rocketship X-M* (1950), *The Day The Earth Stood Still* (1951) and *Project Moon Base* (1953).

Regardless of the competition, what Ivan Tors had going for him was the stories which proved successful when well plotted, with character analysis, depth of observation, and the imaginary element often referred to as "the Idea" (not to overlook the successful distribution process of the Ziv Television facilities). Tors preferred to cut closer to the bone and make evil invaders would look exactly like those who lived next door. *Donovan's Brain* (1953), promoted in the theatrical trailer as a thriller containing "satanic vibrations of evil," revealed the dangers of science without use of make-up or clever lighting tricks. *Flight to Mars* (1951) borrowed the same space suits created for *Destination Moon* (1950), and the story of man's conquest of space was equally fascinating and suspenseful. Inspired by these documentary-style approaches, Tors began a moderately successful movie career producing science fiction films of his own that would receive critical acclaim. Tors eventually became frustrated because studio executives were crying for science fiction of the giant insect nature, women who dominated the population of an entire planet and rubber monsters from outer space. His A-Men Production company (named for a TV pilot written by Siodmak) had produced two successful films of the cerebral and a third best described as a speculative brand of science fiction. And still theatergoers were not satisfied.

THE MOVIES

Ivan Tors' first motion-picture was *The Magnetic Monster*, which was a bit misleading to theater goers who saw the promotional posters or the movie trailer. There was no monster, per se, like the two-legged creatures the audience expected to see, but more of a mystery story that gets resolved through police and detective work. While much of the film was produced on location throughout Los Angeles and the Hal Roach studio, to keep the budget to a minimum, Ivan Tors purchased the rights to use footage from *Gold*, a 1934 German film from UFA with sets so breathtaking that supposedly during WWII, Americans confiscated a copy of the movie to find out just how advanced the Germans were in using radioactivity.

Tors utilized the best scenes from the movie including the high-voltage generator in an underground shaft beneath the sea, and the final explosion which blew up the mine, engulfing everything in water. Curt Siodmak, the author of *Donovan's Brain*, was also the director and cleverly filmed a number of scenes and shots to match the footage from the movie. Unless the viewer is aware of this, the difference between stock footage and new footage is remarkably undetected. The script was written just so—the giant

Chapter Four: The History of the Series | 47

cyclotron (a particle accelerator) became the fictional deltatron. The story climaxes 7,800 feet below the surface in an old mine shaft in Canada under the ocean floor, which helps add credibility to the stock footage during the climax. Actor Richard Carlson switches into a total of three different suits during the movie's final 20 minutes so the audience would assume the obscured actor in stock footage was the same actor. Carlson even dubbed his voice for the stock footage scenes, so the audience would never suspect a German film was being utilized.

Movie poster promoting *Gold* (1934).

Stock footage from *Gold* and special effects shots (courtesy of Maxwell Smith and Leonard Baurmash) that appear in *The Magnetic Monster,* also appear in a number of *Science Fiction Theatre* episodes (as noted under those specific episode entries in the episode guide). Initially intended as a television pilot with Richard Carlson in the lead, there was the stipulation that if the pilot was unable to be sold, the footage could be used as a major motion picture. For an idea of the intended television pilot, viewers today need only watch the first thirty minutes and observe how the story comes to an abrupt conclusion after the arrest on the airplane.

Michael Fox brushes up on his sociology in "The Flicker."

"The first science fiction film I did for [Ivan Tors] was *The Magnetic Monster*, and that was shot for $96,000 cash and $20,000 deferred," actor Michael Fox recalled for author/interviewer Tom Weaver. "You couldn't make a trailer for that today [*laughs*]! Curt Siodmak wrote it and we put that together—I was the casting director, the dialogue director, and I also acted in it."

> **THE FEBRUARY 11, 1953 ISSUE OF *VARIETY* REVIEWED *THE MAGNETIC MONSTER*:**
>
> "With public interest in science fiction material steadily growing, *The Magnetic Monster* has favorable b.o. prospects on the lower half of twin-bills if properly exploited. Aside from its exploration possibilities, the film generally shapes up as a routine programmer. Basic appeal of the script, with producer Tors co-authored with director Curt Siodmak, is keyed toward juvenile filmgoers. Moreover, although the small cast tries hard to make the proceedings credible, the plot places a distinct strain upon the imagination . . . Director Siodmak builds the suspense nicely and skillfully handles the climax, in which the menacing element is tamed. Numerous stock shots were employed in the footage. These were blended in well and help give a touch of realism that's badly needed. Budget is an obviously modest one on this release. However, overall result shows that Tors expertly held the production reins. Charles Van Enger's camerawork is good, as is the Blaine Sanford musical score."

Richard Carlson, who is accorded top billing, is a young, married scientist who is suddenly confronted with the problem of controlling a newly discovered element that threatens to devour the world. Exerting a powerful magnetic attraction, this substance has the capacity of doubling its size every 11 hours by seizing energy in its vicinity. Fiendish characteristics of the element give Carlson and his co-workers an uneasy time before it is decided to bombard the dangerous, radioactive material with high voltage at a Canadian experimental station. The attempt is, of course, successful.

For Ivan Tors' second venture, stock footage was discarded for a fairly basic plot: outstanding young men of science are arbitrarily gathered from the four quarters of the United States to serve as pilots of rocket ships destined to pluck meteors from outer space. Hush-hush research in an isolated deserted area where jets and

Chapter Four: The History of the Series

rockets constantly sizzle across the sky, requires to know how iron meteors withstand cosmic rays, when Earth's processed iron crystallizes and crumbles under their effect. In *Riders to the Stars*, men obeyed scientific dictators, being given their choice in such a way that refusal looked unpatriotic. The climax, designed to be realistic (not every man survives the ordeal) gave viewers the illusion of reality and one is left with the impression that return trips from outer space were within the realm of possibility.

The film also capitalizes on the then present day space race which would herald front page headlines in the advancing years. The government scientists built the rocket ship in a race to conquer space before some other country, unnamed, beats us to it. Scientific fact was clearly lifted from numerous issues of *Scientific American*, including the March, June and September 1953 issues. The magazine was a favorite of Tors.

When Government technicians recover fragments of a rocket which hurled into the sky at 18,000 mph, pieces of the most refined steel crumble because of crystallization. They realize they must devise some sort of shield to protect space travel against bombardments of cosmic rays. The plan is to capture meteors flying 150 miles above the Earth, using specifically constructed rockets that fly a few miles faster than the meteors, and scoop them into nose cone compartments. The meteors would then be returned to Earth for study before they are burned away by air-friction. William Lundigan plays a young flyer/scientist chosen to handle one of the ships, with Richard

> **VARIETY REVIEWED *RIDERS TO THE STARS* IN JANUARY OF 1954:**
>
> "Exploitation aspects of this science fiction entry are high, its imaginative subject being given expert treatment right down the line. Followers of this type of flint will find it intelligently handled and it stands a good chance to rack up better-than-average returns in both the exploitation and general program field. Film would benefit, however, by tighter editing, to eliminate conversational drags and snap up the action. Major premise of the Curt Siodmak original, revolving around a rocket ship flying into space and capturing a meteor in flight, is carefully developed into a legitimate story, which Richard Carlson, also co-starred, direct in know-how style for slick entertainment. Effect is considerably heightened by Color Corporation of America's above average tints, vitalizing the action visually as well as emotionally . . . Ivan Tors provides slick production mounting. On the technical end, Stanley Cortez' color photography is impressive, Jerome Pycha, Jr.'s art direction atmospheric and Harry Sukman's musical score suitable."

Carlson and Robert Karns flying the other two. The majority of the narrative shows them being trained for the job and finally their takeoff to pursue the approaching meteors. Lundigan is successful in a thrilling climax, but the other two are lost—Carlson when his ship goes off course and shoots out into space, Karns when his ship disintegrates.

Both William Lundigan and character actor Michael Fox would also appear in the pilot episode of *Science Fiction Theatre*, with Tors reusing some of the same props and sets created for *Riders to the Stars*. United Artists Corporation issued a press release on January 18, 1954, referring to the science fiction melodrama as "a comic strip story with lots of thrills and excitement." Box office receipts, however, revealed otherwise.

The Curt Siodmak screenplay was adapted into a full-length novel in 1953 by Robert Smith. The book was designed to help promote the motion picture, with photos from the movie on the back cover, and for Ballantine to promote their Science Fiction Preview Club, which convinced readers to buy 12 additional science fiction novels and short story collections in one purchase, for full cover price.

Today, *Riders to the Stars* is considered a period piece and a product of the times. The film documents in dramatic fashion, the selection and training of three men who establish their pioneering efforts to pilot a craft outside of the Earth's atmosphere. This would become outdated less than a decade after the movie was released in theaters. Fans of

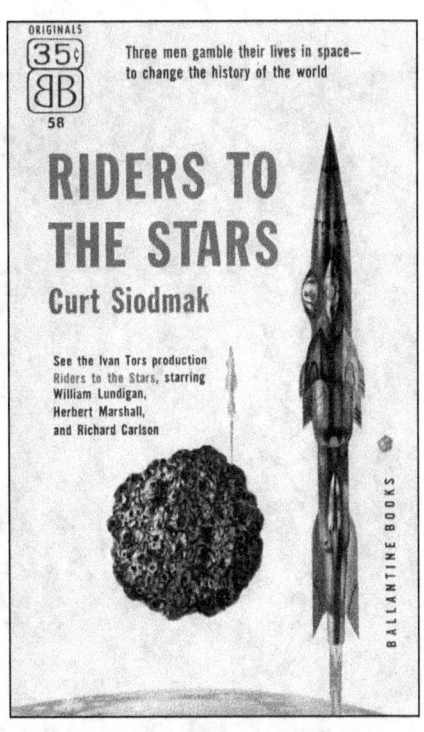

Book Cover of *Riders to the Stars*.

Science Fiction Theatre will recognize stock footage of the U.S. military V-2 rocket tests that appeared in more than one episode of the television series. The exterior shot of the science hall where Richard Carlson is recruited, appears in a number of *Theatre* episodes. Footage of the white mice in the pressurized space capsule, appeared in at least two television episodes. Props that appear in this movie also make appearances on *Theatre* including microphones, speakers, fake computers and the charts hanging on the wall in Herbert Marshall's office. The red visual ports on the wall and the walls of glass squares were also featured in his next motion picture, *Gog* (1954), Tors' third big-screen production and the film that established his romantic connection with actress Constance Dowling, whom he would marry months after the film's production.

Gog was a slow-moving science fiction story that could have succeeded if it was edited down to a faster-pace. Richard Egan plays Investigator David Sheppard of the OSI, sent to an underground installation in the middle of the desert, to check on the status of the scientific tests to construct the first space station, where scientists

are spending their time trying to iron out the complex bugs involved with putting man into space. Soon after his arrival, someone or something is controlling the various scientific equipment, killing human beings and scientists. As the body count rises, the acts of sabotage suggest an enemy agent, until it is learned that the special computer called NOVAC (Nuclear Operated Variable Automatic Computer), which operates most of the equipment in the complex, is being maneuvered by an enemy plane located high above the complex, using radio equipment to sabotage America's plans for winning the space race. Sheppard battles the complex devices, including two robots named Gog and Magog, until the enemy plane (using high frequency electronics to control the computer) is destroyed.

For fans of *Science Fiction Theatre*, the movie offers a checklist of varied props, stock footage and scientific equipment that would be reused in numerous television episodes. The scientific and electronic equipment in *Gog* was furnished by the Bendix Aviation Corporation and Minneapolis Honeywell Regulator Company. The Bendix Aviation Corporation also supplied the computer equipment seen in the *Theatre* episode, "Survival in Box Canyon."

Gog contains a suspenseful scene involving an attempted murder by means of a solar mirror, which is mounted in the desert and channels the collected heat down to a focusing device that proves an effective and powerful heat ray. The mirror system used to shoot deadly rays at one intended victim was reused during Truman Bradley's lab demonstrations (courtesy of stock footage from *Gog*) in two episodes of *Theatre*.

Shortly after Gog and Magog are demonstrated, the character of Dr. Zeitman explains how the robots detect the location of human beings in the room through infrared lenses, which he learned from rattlesnakes. Zeitman explains that when you blindfold a rattlesnake, it can still find its prey. This same scientific principal was applied in two episodes of *Theatre*, including "Friend of a Raven," and Truman Bradley's lab demonstrations with a blindfolded rattlesnake, striking at a balloon filled with hot water. Obviously, the same stock footage was applied, but through the magic of movie making, none of the television viewers suspected otherwise.

Garco the robot and actress Sally Mansfield (presently playing the role of Vena Ray on television's *Rocky Jones, Space Ranger*) for a publicity photo for *Gog* (1954).

When Dr. Van Ness introduces David Sheppard to the model of the space station, hanging on strings, he refers to the model as "Man's first attempt to conquer space." This same space station prop can be seen in three *Theatre* episodes: "Postcard From Barcelona," "The Missing Waveband" and "The Strange People at Pecos," though dressed up in the latter episode with red paint to avoid the possibility of being recognized by observant viewers.

Publicity photo taken on September 11, 1954, with Truman Bradley. Notice the framed art work on the wall that appears in numerous television episodes and doubled for the background art during the opening credits of *Gog* (1954).

The two rods touching and creating sparks was used as stock footage for a second season episode of *Science Fiction Theatre*. The monitor chamber visual screen appears in "The Long Day." The art work featured in the opening credits was later framed and can be found hanging on the walls in numerous episodes. Posters hanging on the walls and whole sections of the wall—including the glass square pattern—can be found among other episodes of the television series to mask the background décor.

The shooting schedule was fifteen days on two sets at Hal Roach Studios, with exteriors at the George Air Force Base in Victorville, Ca. Actor Richard Carlson, who had starred and co-starred in Tors'

(LEFT TO RIGHT) **Ivan Tors, Richard Carlson, Osa Massen, Madge Kennedy (known as Aunt Martha Bronson on television's *Leave it to Beaver*) and Kent Smith on the set of "The Unexplored."**

two former productions, had by this time ventured into the realm of television production in a joint venture with Frederic W. Ziv, in which he would receive a share of the profits. Carlson was introduced to Ziv, courtesy of Tors. Carlson agreed to star in his own television series, at minimum scale, in exchange for ten percent of the profits. This business arrangement suited Ziv, but originated from Ivan Tors who couldn't pay Herbert Marshall or Richard Carlson's normal salary for his movies, and instead offered a piece of the profits.

Filming two pilots in April and June of 1953 for *I Led Three Lives*, based on the best-selling novel of the same name by Herbert A. Philbrick, Carlson was unavailable for *Gog*, making way for actor Richard Egan to play the lead character of David Sheppard. Ivan Tor's fourth motion-picture, a tale concerning the invention of an artificial space satellite, was rejected by numerous film producers in Hollywood, even after he convinced Carlson to appear in the movie after filming was completed on the first season of *Lives*. The anti-Communist propaganda series was an instant success in the fall of

1953. Tors, meanwhile, took his unused satellite story, combined it with several other "unmarketable" science fiction story proposals, and sold the entire package as a weekly series to ZIV. The satellite story, however, was never used on *Theatre*.

SCIENCE FICTION THEATRE

"What makes this telefilm series outstanding is that its stories, however fantastic, are based on scientific fact," reviewed a critic for *TV Guide*. "Moreover, the show doesn't permit phony romance to interfere with more intellectual excitement. True, some researcher might have a beautiful girl assistant, but she concentrates on her work without disturbing the plot." Point taken. As the producer, Ivan Tors insisted that a love interest would distract the viewer from the scientific aspect of the plots. While this rule was broken in *Gog* and *Riders to the Stars*, any romantic interests featured on *Science Fiction Theatre* remained a mere hug at the conclusion and usually with tidings of relief from the resolution of their escapade.

Tors' first effort was to launch a series about a fictional government agency called the Office of Scientific Investigation, or OSI, as featured in his motion pictures, *The Magnetic Monster* and *Riders to the Stars*. His first filmed effort was incorporated into *The Magnetic Monster* (discussed earlier) and when the pilot failed to attract attention, additional footage was filmed and footage from *Gold* (1934) was incorporated to complete a full-length motion picture. *

After producing two major motion-pictures, and presently filming his third, Tors tried to raise $100,000—a mere pittance as movie budgets went at the time—to film a motion-picture about a scientific development that had not yet happened. The screenplay was titled "Operation Satellite," a docudrama about the launching of an artificial Earth satellite. Tors was unable to convince enough backers that the film would earn a profit and supposedly one backer suggested to shelve the screenplay until science caught up with it—which it did in 1957. Tors decided to find a new venue—television.

---

* A number of episodes, including "Miracle of Doctor Dove," featured a similar organization known as the Office of Scientific Security.

Bill Williams as Dr. Alan Cathcart in "Mind Machine."

In February 1954, Tors sought to produce a science fiction anthology when Joe Harris failed to take over United Artists Television. Through April and May, Tors discussed his proposal with Flamingo Films but the deal never went through. (Flamingo instead chose to produce Marion Parsonnet's 15-minute science adventure, *Top Secret*.) In early June 1954, Ivan Tors began negotiating with Ziv and promised that the science fiction anthology would avoid the type of stories seen on *Tales of Tomorrow* and *Captain Video*. The third time was the charm. Before the end of the month, a contract was signed between Tors and Ziv and a color pilot was produced in July. If sales for a first-run syndication were sufficient enough to warrant production of 38 additional episodes, Ziv would agree to syndicate the series. In the first week of November 1954, the announcement of the new science fiction series went public. Ziv would syndicate—and Tors would produce—a scientific series totalling 39 segments to be filmed in Eastman color. The contract originally stated the series would be filmed at California Studios. That would change with the purchase of American National Studios, two months later. In November, Maurice (Babe) Unger, vice-president in charge of TV production, explained to the press that color filming resulted in increased production cost which could not be recouped on a first run. Ziv-TV expected that in the long run the series would be more profitable than if it was shot in black and white.

Normally a treatment was created for every television series so that the writers would retain continuity, ensuring that the characters would remain the same for every episode. Ziv himself wrote the continuity and the first script so that writers would read it and know how to write future plot outlines. For *Science Fiction Theatre*, Ziv did not write the treatment. That task was up to Ivan Tors, who, as acting producer, supervised every episode and wrote about half of the plot outlines. (Many of these story proposals and treatments were very brief and can be found reprinted under their respective episode entries.)*

Tors' deal with ZIV called for gross participation in the show on a graduated scale. The more successful the series, the more money Tors would receive. This proved to be a very profitable and mutual agreement. Tors contended that without the ZIV know-how in getting a wider appeal for such shows, he might have produced a series of projects which would appeal only to scientists. *Science Fiction Theatre* proved so successful that he formed Ivan Tors Films and under a new deal, ZIV had first refusal on all of the company's pilots. This led to *Sea Hunt, The Man and the Challenge* and *The Aquanauts*. This was followed by *Ripcord* and *Flipper*—six pilots

---

* Numerous press releases and magazine articles claimed Tors was granted permission to spend a budget of $1.5 million, including provisions, for location shooting at Air Force bases, universities and private laboratories. This, of course, was pure fiction. If the series could not be filmed on stage in the studio, or on location within an hour's drive from the studio, stock footage would be required.

and six successful television series—a rare batting average considering most produce six or seven pilots before one sold.

THE PILOT, "BEYOND"

The pilot episode was produced in July 1954, with William Lundigan in the lead as Fred Gunderman and Ellen Drew as his wife. It comes as no surprise that Lundigan, having played the lead in Tors' *Riders to the Stars* less than a year previous, would star in the pilot. Tors had struck up a friendship with the actor and his agency, Famous Artists, who secured the arrangements for casting. Tors then assembled a staff composed of many who worked on his three motion pictures. Scientific advisor Maxwell Smith agreed to assist with the pilot and the entire series. George Van Marter, who was the art director for *The Magnetic Monster*, was hired on a free-lance basis to temporarily serve as a writer for the first two episodes. "Beyond" concerned a test pilot who may have encountered an unidentified flying object, with baffled scientists unable to find definite proof that his story was anything but a hallucination. "Y..O..R..D.." concerned a group of scientists stationed in the Arctic who receive telepathic communication from visitors from outer space, seeking a means of escape from the Earth's gravitational pull.

"Beyond" and "Y..O..R..D.." were both produced at American National. While Tors had the Hal Roach Studios at his disposal (the same studio responsible for producing *You Are There* and *My Little Margie*), it was Ziv who insisted that production be kept at American National to limit the expenses. Made at the same time as producer Art Arthur's *Battle Taxi*,* Ivan Tors borrowed some of Arthur's

---

* Art Arthur was responsible for *Battle Taxi*, released theatrically in January of 1955, which had a working title of "Operation Air Rescue," during production in the summer of 1954. The movie (assigned Prod. No. 9941) took place during the Korean war, and told the story of the commander of an Air Rescue helicopter team who must show a hot-shot former jet pilot how important helicopter rescue work is, and turn him into a team player. The pilot, "Beyond," had Prod. No. 9072, revealing that production numbers at ZIV were not assigned in sequence.

William Lundigan as Col. Edward McCauley in "Beyond."

production staff to assist with the pilot. A clause in the contract protected ZIV-TV with an option to reject the proposal should ZIV deem the pilot insufficient.

Herbert L. Strock, who directed *Battle Taxi*, also directed the pilot. "I felt that Ivan had a fetish for doing scientific things that an audience didn't understand," Strock recalled in the March/April 1996 issue of *Filmfax*. "He would lose the human element—emotions that were going on—and get into technicalities. I had to constantly bandy him to try to change something that had meaning. He wasn't very good at dialogue; his physical dialogue had that European convolution of expressing oneself."

Herbert L. Strock on the set of *Science Fiction Theatre*.

Strock served as an associate producer for a number of television programs and movies before script clerk Mary Whitlock Gibson recommended him for the job of both editor and director, filling in for director Curt Siodmak, who was disappointing Tors. As a film editor, Strock knew how to best incorporate stock footage into newly filmed footage. For Tors' second film, *Riders to the Stars*, also scripted by Curt Siodmak, Strock became an associate producer and soon found himself taking over as director when Richard Carlson overextended himself by directing, acting and rewriting the film. It started when Carlson asked Strock to direct the scenes he acted in, and Strock quickly took over the task for the remainder of the film. Strock remains un-credited for both movies as director. *

---

* Herbert L. Strock would continue to go silent as a ghost director for *Science Fiction Theatre*, directing a large handful of the first season opening and closing segments featuring Truman Bradley, which were filmed separately from the dramatic stories.

"Curt and Ivan disagreed constantly, there's no question about that," recalled actor Michael Fox. "And Curt's knowledge of directing was, in my opinion, not particularly great. Curt's brother Robert was an extremely successful director, and I think Curt—who certainly ranks very highly among screen-writers—always was somewhat envious of Robert."

Also joining the *Theatre* troupe was Harry Redmond Jr. as a special effects technician. Redmond's father had worked during the years of silent cinema and quickly rose in the ranks to special effects supervisor for RKO Studios. He taught his son the craft while working together for *The Princess and the Pirate* (1944) and *The Secret Life of Walter Mitty* (1947), the latter of which was the senior's final contribution to Hollywood, passing on the torch to his son.

Redmond quickly jumped into television with *Dangerous Assignment* before moving on to Ziv Television at the request of Ivan Tors. It was Redmond who succeeded in bringing *Donovan's Brain* to life in 1953, and the skilled elements that made up Ivan Tors' three former science fiction motion-pictures. Many of Redmond's personal props that appear in *Donovan's Brain* (1953), such as test tubes, water tanks, lab equipment, Oscillograph and scientific charts hanging on the wall, make appearances in numerous *Theatre* productions. After production of *Science Fiction Theatre* concluded, Redmond would stay with the studio to help assist with *Sea Hunt, The Man and the Challenge, The Aquanauts* and then concluded at the peak of his career with the first season of *The Outer Limits* from 1963 to 1964.*

"Beyond" was conceived by Ivan Tors and scripted by Robert Smith and Van Marter. On April 13, 1954, Maurice Unger at ZIV consulted Tors regarding the story premise, temporarily titled "Saucer," offering insight into story structure since television production required careful plotting and pace. The exposition,

---

* It was Redmond's balanced magnetic field that holds the ball bearing in mid-air as demonstrated by Truman Bradley in "Beyond." The same prop can be seen on Bradley's desk at the close of "Beyond," and "Y··O··R··D··," and the lab demonstration for the U.S. military in one key scene of *Earth vs. the Flying Saucers* (1956).

Truman Bradley's laboratory before his desk was placed in the center of the room.

rising action, climax, falling action and concluding with dénouement, catastrophe or resolution.

"Generally speaking, the first thirteen pages seems to be about right, but we have decided that in some manner we must get the story started from Fred's point-of-view," Unger wrote. "One suggestion in this connection is to have a short scene in or around the control room where Fred is receiving a last-minute briefing and also is getting into his latest model, highly technical gear. We establish who he is and the purpose of his flight. If we handle it in this matter, it would be well to give Fred the bulk of the dialogue because, at this point, it is Fred in whom we are interested."

Another suggestion was to do a complete switch in point-of-view and play the second half of the story to an ending completely from the point-of-view of the General and the scientist. Also suggested was the questioning. "When the matter is being discussed we must knock out the possibility of everything that is suggested such as another one of our planes, an enemy plane, a guided missile, atmospheric reflections, etc. We also have to set up some reason why, if the General knew that Fred saw something in the sky, he felt it necessary to convince Fred that he didn't." Another suggestion was to retain the computers but remove all company logos that might be misinterpreted as product placement, including IBM.

On May 28, 1954, after reviewing the revised script, Unger offered a number of other suggestions for improvement. Among these was suggesting the television audience catch more glimpses of Fred Gunderman before take-off, particularly seeing his face before he put on his flying helmet, "otherwise we'll never recognize his face when we see it in the hospital." Another suggestion was to not mix dialogue and narration. Fading out the dialogue as the narrator overtakes the soundtrack was considered a no-no. "Once the narration stops, leave it out of the scene until all the dialogue has been completed." This explains why Truman Bradley's off-screen narrations overlaps only visual scenes—but not verbal—throughout the series.

On June 19, 1954, just a couple weeks before the pilot went before the cameras, Maurice Unger of Ziv Television Programs, Inc. submitted Ivan Tors with a list of nine names for the lead role in "Beyond." Gary Merrill, Frank Lovejoy, Robert Preston, Steve McNally, John Lund, Howard Duff, Lloyd Bridges (who was not

Truman Bradley poses with the Oscillograph.

Truman Bradley being filmed with the Oscillograph.

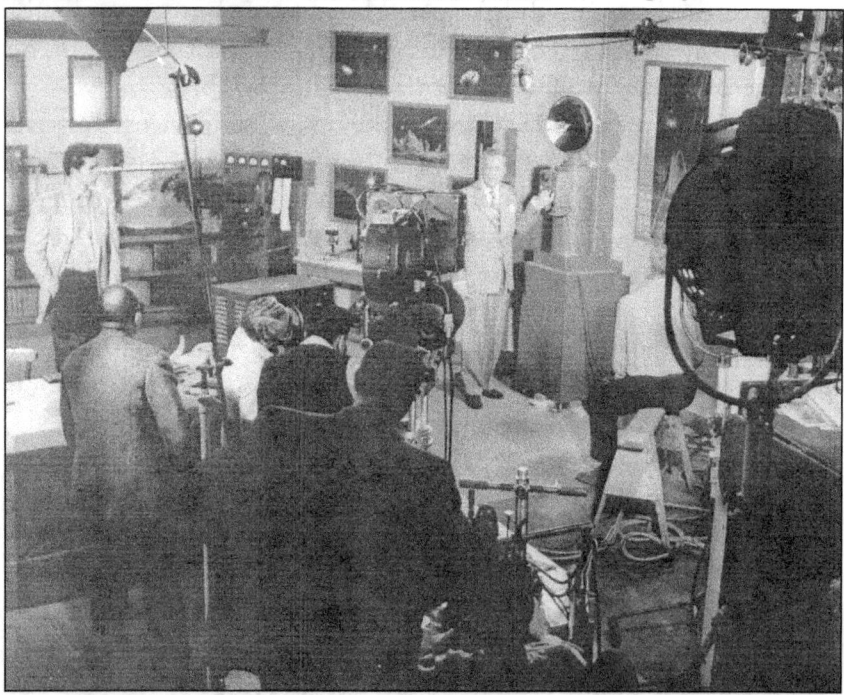

yet starring in *Sea Hunt*), William Lundigan and John Ireland. Dane Clark and Scott Brady were also up for consideration but were quickly ruled out. Tors replied back to Unger with three names, Frank Lovejoy, John Lund and William Lundigan, with Lovejoy being his top preference and John Lund second. "Of course, my suggestions might not be in line with what the sponsors want," Tors explained. "My yardstick is acting ability in these selections."

On June 23, 1954, Ralph Winters submitted a list of cast suggestions for the pilot.

WIFE
Lynn Bari
Helena Carter
Janis Carter
Marguerite Chapman
Nancy Davis
Ellen Drew
Colleen Gray
Barbara Hale
Ruth Hussey
Andrea King
Angela Lansbury
Anita Louise
Maria McDonald
Alexis Smith
Phyllis Thaxter
Arleen Whelan

SCIENTIST
John Loder
John Emery
Shepperd Strudwick
John Carradine
Eduard Franz
Clark Howat
John Wengraf
John Qualen
Donald Randolph
George Dolenz
Steven Geray
Antony Eustrel
Hans Conried
Robert Cornthwaite
John Hoyt

GENERAL
Gene Evans
Henry Wilcoxan
Donald Woods
Victor Jory
Barry Kelly
Paul Guilfoyle
William Conrad

DOCTOR
Louis Jean Heydt
Regis Toomey
Tristram Coffin
Robert Emmett Keane
Ray Collins
Roy Roberts

PROFESSOR
Gene Lockhart
Basil Ruysdale
Everett Glass
Lloyd Corrigan
Edward Earle
Raymond Greenleaf
Taylor Holmes
Selmer Jackson

ADDITIONAL LEADS
Wendell Corey
John Hodiak
Arthur Kennedy
Wayne Morris
Edmund O'Brien
Robert Ryan
Forest Tucker

The production crew creates a laboratory for a first season episode. Notice one of the crew smoking on the set and the charts hanging on the wall that re-appear on the walls in numerous episodes.

PROFESSOR
Edward Keane
Walter Kingsford
Francis Pierlot
Ralph Morgan
Charles Winninger

For the role of the wife, Ivan Tors requested three women, numbered one through three in the order of preference: Ruth Hussey, Ellen Drew and Barbara Hale. For the role of the General, William Conrad was his only choice. For the role of the professor, Ralph Morgan, followed by Basil Ruysdale and Gene Lockhart.

Perhaps the most significant casting was actor and dialogue director Michael Fox. Known today as a character actor in more than 200 television and motion pictures and the reason why actor Michael J. Fox (*Back to the Future*) inserted a middle initial in his name. Having played the role of doctors in *The Magnetic Monster* (1953), *The Lost*

Chapter Four: The History of the Series

> Science Fiction Theatre was Frederic Ziv's eighth television series having followed seven other programs including The Cisco Kid and I Led 3 Lives. Ironically, playwright Rod Serling wrote to Herbert Gordon, executive producer at ZIV, in late January 1951 proposing a science fiction television series, pre-dating ZIV's efforts to produce Science Fiction Theatre. "Although you do not go into much detail regarding your show, I can see where it could be quite interesting," wrote Gordon on February 3. "However, due to our present commitments, which will carry us well through 1951, we cannot consider taking on any new projects at this time."

Planet (1953), *Beast With 20,000 Fathoms* (1953), *Riders to the Stars* (1954) and *Gog* (1954), he built a friendship with Ivan Tors. "While I was doing *Home of the Brave* [an acting-directing stint in a Players Ring production], Ivan Tors also had come to see the play," Fox recalled for author/interviewer Tom Weaver. "Ivan and I became very good friends. Ivan was then wooing Constance Dowling, later they married, and Constance and [her actress-sister] Doris and I all became extremely good friends." As a result, Fox secured acting jobs for seven episodes of *Science Fiction Theatre*, six of which he played the role of a doctor. (His only non-doctor role was that of a radar man in the "Beyond" pilot.)

Y**O**R**D**

"Y..O..R..D.." was conceived by Ivan Tors on Halloween 1954, and typed into a short story format on November 1. It was produced because ZIV felt the series had potential, but only if there were two pilots available for screening for potential sponsors. Tors handed the story to Van Marter, who then expanded the conception into a nine-page teleplay treatment. Dr. H.J. Lawton of the Department of Parapsychology, was consulted for the second entry, to ensure accuracy in the science depicted in the script. On December 8,

Maurice Unger offered his criticism. Among his concerns was the opening. "There is no impact," he explained. "I think that to open up with the magnetic typewriter is okay, but this should be only a first step to something more dramatic and with more impact as a second experiment, followed by a third which perhaps can be not only dramatic, but can also point strongly toward the direction in which our story is to go."

"You will undoubtedly remember, Ivan, that we had these same discussions about the opening in the first picture," Unger continued, "and none of us were quite happy until we came up with the group of three experiments now in the picture and consequently we now have what we feel is a good opening in Picture #1." It was here that Tors affirmed the decision to include more than one lab demonstration before every filmed science-fiction story.

Ivan Tors was interested in science to a point where many consider his early motion pictures too talky. Often overusing language, Tors felt that it was much cheaper to describe something than it was to present something. Thanks to Unger's supervision of the scripts, the final drafts of each teleplay were polished evenly and the educational dialogue was limited to Truman Bradley's opening introductions.

With assistance from Leon Benson, who had directed episodes of *Mr. District Attorney* and *Meet Corliss Archer* for ZIV, Van Marter co-wrote the revised teleplay to fit the demands of the television director and grasp a feel of what could and could not be accomplished with the limitations and budget of television production. Whether Van Marter found the task of composing the stories and script revisions too demanding, or his love as an art director beckoned strongly, he left after the second production and never returned to the series.

More important was the foundation of "Y..O..R..D.." for *Science Fiction Theatre*. Not only did it kick off production of the remaining 37 episodes but establish the format the rest of the series would be molded during production, including the hosting chores of Truman Bradley which varied from the pilot and the rest of the episodes, but Bradley's comments describe the program to a tee—something not found in "Beyond."

Tales of fiction, from the borderlands of science. Science fiction today, but how about tomorrow?

—Truman Bradley

Maurice Unger expressed his disappointment with the script for "Y..O..R..D.." in December of 1954. Minor complaints included removing a joke about Eddie Cantor, the removal of stock footage of a dog sled team because it "might seem to come completely out of left field," replacing phraseology uncommon to the average television audience with substituted words that the audience would understand, and when Edna is being tested for comparative purposes, he questioned whether she was off target on the Bible question. The word used repeatedly by Unger was "hokey," which he expressed to Ivan Tors towards the end of his memo. "By this time, Ivan, you must feel that I've used the word 'hokey' a great number of times in this memo, and this is not accidental. It is probably the greatest single fault in the script at the present writings. Some of the corrections in this will have to be fairly radical; others are a simple re-write of language."

Ziv had a financial interest in the productions because he was responsible for the distribution of the series and it was his studio and staff that would produce the films. Ivan Tors was responsible for hiring a few individuals from his motion-picture days including cinematographer Charles Van Enger, who helped photograph *The Magnetic Monster*. While others were credited with photography during the closing credits of the first season, Van Enger served as supervisor to ensure a professional touch would be applied on the sound stage and on location.

SCIENTIFIC STUDIES

Maxwell Smith's relationship with Tors for *The Magnetic Monster, Riders to the Stars* and *Gog* assured that he was credible when it came to television production. Smith was billed in all publicity as "a leading scientist in the field of design and development, electronics, nuclear work, optics and physical science."

Maxwell Smith poses for the camera.

Smith has been credited with pioneering the development of the radar equipment then being used by the U.S. Armed Forces, and received on-screen credit as a "scientific advisor" for electronics and radiation. Working closely with Harry Redmond Jr., Smith ensured that all of the science demonstrated was accurate and up-to-date. Redmond often brought props from his own house to the studio sound stages for use on the series. After *Theatre*, Smith would reuse many of the props for Ziv's *Men Into Space* series. How much Smith was paid to supervise the technical babble that would be written into the scripts remains unknown, but the April 18, 1955 issue of *Broadcasting-Telecasting* reported: "A budget of approximately $75,000 for scientific research has been allocated by Ziv Television programs, Inc. in connection with its film series, *Science Fiction*

(LEFT TO RIGHT) **Producer Ivan Tors, actor Dick Foran and scientific advisor Maxwell Smith on the set of "The Missing Waveband."**

Theatre. A spokesman for the company said the funds will be used to obtain the mechanical devices used by Truman Bradley, host-narrator, in his pre-program demonstrations; in checking scientific theories on which the series is based and in following up newly announced scientific development as possible story lines." Had this factoid not been a work of fiction for the sake of publicity, the total amount of money spent would have been $2,925,000, which was beyond the exaggeration of $1.5 million pointed out in a previous footnote. $75,000 for the entire season, possibly.

While Unger reviewed every script that crossed his desk, attempting to prevent the dialogue from going over the viewers' heads, Tors attempted to make every word of dialogue reasonably credible from the numerous out-of-this-world problems, forcing him to call on scientists throughout the U.S. for advice on subjects as varied as mental telepathy to the crystallizing of sound waves. Naturally, they were paid for their efforts and Tors once told a newspaper columnist that he estimated his research budget ran to $2,500 a week. This is perhaps the most realistic figure to come from the trade columns.

Six American universities cooperated with Ivan Tors to ensure the scientific authenticity of the series. These were: University of California at Los Angeles; University of Southern California; California Institute of Technology; University of Pennsylvania; Massachusetts Institute of Technology; and the Johns Hopkins University of Baltimore. In addition, a number of scientific institutions, research laboratories and industrial organizations including the Smithsonian Institution, the U.S. Department of Defense, the Garrett Corporation, the Los Angeles County Museum, and the Douglas, Lockheed and North American aircraft companies also worked closely with Ziv on the scientific aspect of the program.

Dr. Kenneth E. Stager, for instance, received an S.O.S. when scriptwriter Donn Mullally came up with a batty script, "Out of Nowhere." Dr. Stager, professor of zoology at the University of Southern California and curator of birds and mammals at the Los Angeles County Museum, filled an order for "a dozen live bats by day after tomorrow," even though they were out of season. After traveling 140 miles to a high plateau along the Colorado River, on the California-Arizona border, and descending 500 feet into an abandoned mine shaft, Dr. Stager was able to cast every one of the 12 parts.

Dr. Konrad Buettner, German V-2 rocket developer and an authority on space medicine, contributed script assistance when Ivan Tors and scriptwriter Sloan Nibley wanted to ensure accuracy for the episode, "Brain Unlimited." Buettner acted as a consultant for Ivan Tors' production of *Riders to the Stars*, for which he was billed in the opening credits for space-medicine research. Buettner has been credited for assisting Dr. Hubertus Strughold, Heinz Haber

Stock footage of the V-2 rocket which appears in numerous episodes of *Science Fiction Theatre*.

and Fritz Haber authoring a seminal paper in the *Journal of Aviation Medicine*, titled "Where Does Space Begin?: Functional Concepts of the Boundaries between the Atmosphere and Space," a thesis concerning the human potential for space exploration.

Dr. Robert S. Richardson, of Palomar Observatory, advised scriptwriter Lou Huston on the hazards of that trip to Mars, but ensured the facts involving space travel to the red planet were accurate in the episode "Project 44." Richardson himself even appeared on the broadcast with Truman Bradley, discussing the possibility of finding water and plant life on Mars.

Sometimes the fanciful ideas of the show's writing staff taxed even the ingenuity of its research and special effects staffs. Since no "sonic broom" for cleaning a house by remote control existed, *Science Fiction* technicians invented one for the episode, "Time Is Just A Place." The broom was supposed to run about the floor by itself, tidying up electronically owned by a couple from the

The crew prepare to install tusks on the baby elephant so it will resemble a baby mammoth for "Dead Storage."

distant future. Thanks to the invisible wires and trick lighting, the broom, designed by radar expert Maxwell Smith, performed so convincingly that several people wrote in asking where they could buy one. (Perhaps this was where Hanna-Barbera got their ideas for *The Jetsons*?)

Freezing an elephant for the episode, "Dead Storage," was impossible—but easy. It didn't involve any recipe beginning with, "take one plump, tender elephant . . ." Instead, for a story in which scientists revive a baby mammoth frozen in Arctic ice since prehistoric

Truman Bradley poses for the camera.

times, a four-year-old elephant was rented and equipped with tusks. No elephant would lie still long enough to simulate a frozen beast, so Tors and crew photographed him lying down, then repeated the same single frame from the negative over several yards of film. Result: a frozen elephant.

Animals and insects figured as prominently in *Science Fiction* scripts as they do in most research laboratories . . . and for the same reason. "In science," Tors remarked, "we learn always from the same source—nature." This led to some tricky doings on the set. One script required a "blindfolded rattlesnake," to demonstrate that a mysterious "heat pit" between rattlesnake' eyes, and not vision, guides them to their prey.

According to a press release (if it can be believed): In order to find the queen among 3,000 bees provided by California's Claremont

College, Tors let several dozen escape on the ZIV lot, one at a time, until the lady herself appeared, the escapees presumably taking up residence in Hollywood. No original bee footage was featured in that episode, however, and stock footage was clearly evident.

Another escapee—but not by design—was a chimpanzee who fled the *Science Fiction* set and wandered into the production office of *The Cisco Kid*. When the staff got back to lunch, the monkey was sitting in the producer's chair, waving a ballpoint pen. Did the staff summon the fire department or the dogcatcher? Not in Hollywood. According to that press release, they rushed to a phone to call the studio press agent. In one trade column, Government experts who had experience in these things provided several dozen mice that continually ran in circles. This, of course, was a little white lie as the same footage appeared prior in *Riders to the Stars*. Another stretch of truth was that of a Malayan giant lizard, one of the last remnants of the dinosaur age, that had to be imported for another episode. Maxwell Smith was quoted of saying that the most difficult task was the creation of a typewriter that could be manipulated by a chimpanzee. This, too, was a stretch of the truth to help with publicity.

THE EPISODES

"The stories retain an appealing human touch," reviewed a critic for *TV Guide*. "For example, when a ship from outer space, trying to visit the Earth, is destroyed just short of its goal, is our Army elated at thus escaping a potential menace? Not at all. The authorities regret losing an opportunity to learn from an obviously superior species of life. This particular story dealt with extra-sensory perception. Others have told of a search for a new artificial foodstuff, a visit by residents of a future world, mankind's first flight into outer space. The films, featuring well-known Hollywood actors, are well acted, directed and produced."

The genre of science fiction is divided into a number of themes including the advancement of human evolution, space exploration, the creation of new life forms, alternate worlds, the disruption of social systems and apocalyptic scenarios. Time travel has always been

Vincent Price and Jean Byron prepare to film an important scene in "One Thousand Eyes."

among the more intriguing plot devices for science fiction stories, mastered by greats such as Robert Heinlein and Fritz Leiber. Wanting to deal with the impact of imagined innovations in science or technology, producer Ivan Tors preferred to keep mankind planted firmly on the ground. *Science Fiction Theatre* never strayed too far from reality; half of the stories involving flying saucers and visitors from other worlds were left to mere speculation. Exceptions to the time travel theory were explored in "Time Is Just A Place," in which strange neighbors living next door are suspected of being time travelers from the future. In "Operation Flypaper," Vincent Price and his colleagues discover time is misplaced with minutes—and even hours—missing from their day. But this was as far off the beaten track as Tors would allow.

If fantasy is considered fiction that could never happen, science fiction is considered fiction that could happen. "Time Is Just A Place," for example, was more than an intriguing first season episode. For Tors, it also served as a pilot for another television series. According to the June 11, 1955, issue of *Billboard*, "Ivan Tors is already at work on a new series to be developed from 'Time Is Just A Place,' which was one of the *Science Fiction Theatre* segments. Show would be patterned along scientific detection lines." This obviously was an attempt to revive his Office of Scientific Investigation premise but Tors could never grab the interest of a sponsor or a network.

Sometimes *Theatre* episodes helped establish science as a necessity in the field of investigation. "Ivan Tors wanted to make the point that science can obtain facts that dispel harmful or useless superstition," recalled Lou Huston to Mark Phillips. "In this story, several people, on different occasions, are found dead under a tree. Conclusion: the tree must have killed them. A scientist couple investigates and learns that carbon dioxide is seeping up from the ground. Anyone sleeping by the tree will fill their lungs with the gas and suffocate. The source is coming from volcanic action unusually near the surface. A year or two after the episode aired, some animals and, it is believed, several people died near the shores of an African lake. Cause: deep waters in the lake 'burped' pockets of gas."

"Story conferences at the Frederic Ziv lot in Hollywood are among the most fantastic in the film capitol," quoted Bill Ladd, television critic for the *Courier-Journal*. "One of the traps into which such a series may fall is complete dependence on science for interest. This is avoided at the story conference by excluding the scientist at the start and depending on the writers and the producer to come up with a story with human interest, suspense and other components of any half-hour drama."

One early episode of *Science Fiction Theatre* originated from the very style of science fiction Ivan Tors attempted to avoid. Writer Robert M. Fresco recalled to interviewer Tom Weaver: "Jack Arnold had produced and directed a documentary [*With These Hands*, 1950] on the Triangle Shirtwaist fire of 1911, and it went up for an Academy Award. He was very proud of that, as he should have been. But in 1955 when I met him, he was making a living directing wonderful garbage, *Creature from the Black Lagoon* and blah, blah, blah. He was directing this 'No Food For Thought' that I had come up with for *Science Fiction Theatre* and it had a marvelous cast ... Jack said to me, 'Hey, stay on the set,' so I did—he had me on the set all three days. And we liked each other. He liked the script and liked

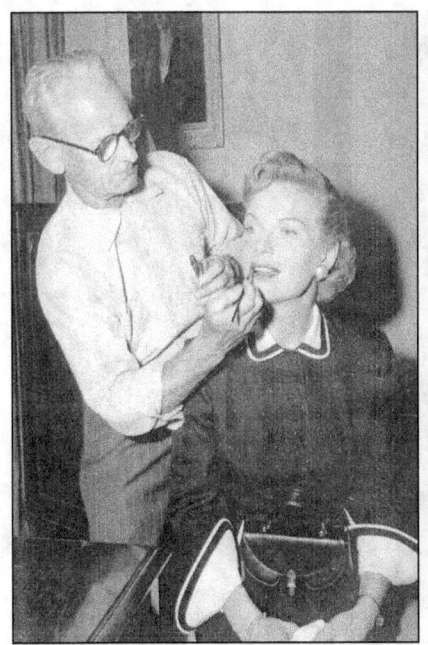 

Make-up artist George Gray touches up actress Kristine Miller for multiple episodes of *Science Fiction Theatre*.

the quality of the dialogue, and one day he said, 'You know, there may be a movie in this.' I said, 'Okay with me.' Then he added, 'But you gotta put a monster in it.' There was no monster in 'No Food For Thought,' believe me, it was about a bunch of scientists developing an artificial nutrient. And the lab animal in the show was not a tarantula, it was a mouse named Moses [*laughs*]."

"Yes, he suggested that we do something," Fresco continued. "I brought him up to my office after the episode was done and we had lunch a couple of times and talked and I came up with the idea of the spider instead of the mouse. He went away and I developed the story, seven pages. According to the screen credits of *Tarantula*, it's a story by . . . I believe the order is Jack Arnold and Robert M. Fresco, although maybe it's Robert M. Fresco and Jack Arnold."

A number of *Science Fiction Theatre* episodes demonstrate scientific concepts in their relative infancy; the stepping stones for a not too distant future. In the episode, "The Brain of John Emerson," Truman Bradley demonstrated a thinking machine using a robotic mouse in a maze, an application that is theorized to have had a large impact on the development of humanity, since the advancement of

Truman Bradley and the robotic mouse.

computers in the past fifty years. Applying the theory that machines might replace the brains of man, this episode revealed an advancement of neuroscience. John Emerson, a police sergeant, wakes from a coma after having a bullet removed from his brain, only to discover he possesses memories of another man's life. The solution comes in the form of the operating surgeon, a dying man, who before his death had successfully transferred his own memory units electronically to John Emerson's brain cells. Emerson, realizing first-hand the importance of this discovery, resigns to spend the remainder of his life devoted to the advancement of this science.

The same theory was applied in other episodes. In the episode "Mind Machine," a special electronic computer stores groups of electrical impulses deciphered as language. The episode "Doctor Robot" explored the possibility of computers being able to analyze facts and figures and then provide the answers for which a decision based on the outcome of a human life is dictated by a thinking machine.

Thinking machines, also referred to as super computers, however, were certainly not original and were not always considered a blessing. In John W. Campbell's "The Machine," originally published in the February 1935 issue of *Astounding Science Fiction*, a futuristic society became so dependent on machines doing all the work that when the electronic gadgets discovered that mankind was going to revert to a savage breed, they broke down. In fear of not knowing where to stay warm or how to find food, mankind starts to fall apart like a den of frightened rabbits.

Fredric Brown dreamt of the worse case scenario in his 1954 short story, "Answer," in which the monster computing machines of all the populated planets in the universe—96 billion planets—are tapped into the super circuit that would connect them all into a cybernetics machine that would combine all the knowledge of all the galaxies. Once powered, the first question submitted to the thinking machine was one which no cybernetics machine was able to answer. "Is there a God?" The mighty voice answered without hesitation, without the clicking of a single relay. "Yes, *now* there is a God."

"Sometimes the science took out the drama," recalled director Herbert Strock to author Mark Phillips. "I tried to show things rather than explain them. I demanded intelligent, coherent scripts with speakable dialogue. I didn't want any story holes. Ivan was a nut for getting stock footage and using it to explain scientific principles. The science approach worked well, but sometimes Ivan had a bad habit of explaining things with specific details and the story would stop. I had to find ways to make those stories work dramatically."

In another interview with interviewer Tom Weaver, Strock recalled: "Ivan did come to resent the fact that I would want to re-write certain things in order to make them work better. There was really no argument between us but he resented a little bit and I was moved off *Science Fiction Theatre* onto other series."

One such example was "The Last Barrier," set in the near future, which concerned the unmanned flight of XR-1, a new type of space ship sent out into space to photograph shots of the moon. Loaded with stock footage and containing very little interaction with the fictional characters, the only conflict in the episode arises from

Keefe Brasselle and Christine Larson in "Postcard From Barcelona."

confusion when two unidentified objects are noticed on the radar screen accompanying the XR-1. Four more flying objects follow. Various explanations are put forth but the fact remains that the objects cannot be thrown off by maneuvers of the XR-1. The experimental craft is flown back to Earth where it finally crashes and analysis of the components show that the disabled parts of the ship were burned out by some high powered ray, unknown to scientists. No explanation or resolution to the story is given.

"The Last Barrier," originally produced under the title "Breakthrough," underwent a considerable amount of research by scripter Rik Vollaerts, his fourth and final contribution to the series, but with assistance of Ivan Tors, who provided the script writer with numerous magazine articles regarding the past endeavors of the U.S. Air Force and the development of two-stage rockets.

This episode may be dated when compared to present NASA programs, space shuttles and man-made satellites circling around the globe. Since the film was produced in the summer of 1956 and dramatizes in documentary fashion the first rocket to break through the Earth's atmospheric envelope and beyond, courtesy of a new ion booster, this episode can only be enjoyed when the viewer accepts the context of historical timelines.

The first American-built rocket to leave the Earth's atmosphere (the WAC) was launched on March 22, 1946. It was launched from White Sands, and attained 50 miles of altitude. It wasn't until October 4, 1957, months after this television episode aired on American television, that the Soviet Union stunned the world by placing the first satellite, Sputnik, into space. From that day forward, satellites were the scientific marvels of the twentieth century.

Science Fiction Theatre also approached science as a social field of forces, struggles and relationships of power among the protagonists. Often a recurring theme throughout the program, scientists kept their secrets closely guarded until a third party threatened exposure, hence the only conflict in the 22-minute drama. Only in a fictitious world do human guinea pigs agree to be subjected to a scientist's serum, an unethical practice that the real world would find vulnerable to charges of illegal experimentation. In "Three Minute Mile," a biology professor finds a way to speed up bodily processes electronically with the result that his best student can now lift a 1,000 pound weight and run a mile in three minutes. In "The Human Experiment," a humanitarian biochemist believes that through an insect serum that pre-determines the development of the egg in the insect society, the same adjustment to her surroundings can be given to the psychological misfit, the mentally ill, unable to cope with life around them. Instead, the doctor finds herself being held captive, a veritable slave by the very misfits she helped to cure—replicating the pattern of an insect society. Rarely a reference was made during

Beverly Garland in "The Other Side of the Moon."

the episodes suggesting that the doctors would lose their license or face criminal charges. In two cases, law enforcement offered to assist them after learning of their motives and the untapped potential of their new discovery.

In "When A Camera Fails," Dr. Richard Hewitt (played by Edmund Gwenn), geo-physics professor at a Mid-Western University, finds a way of amplifying light within the range of his ultra microscope. Looking at a piece of green glass under his microscope, he is amazed to see an exact image of the atom bomb blast that fused the rock itself. Believing that the evolution of the Earth can be found within other rocks, he sees images of dinosaurs, the glacial age and ancient Egypt. No one else can see them, however, and the doctor is suspected of suffering delusions. Only by accident does someone discover that Hewitt had a special prescription calling for polarized lenses. It is deduced that the images are actually present, but invisible unless seen through polarization.

This episode parallels the classic story of the micro-world in Fitz James O'Brien's "The Diamond Lens" (1858), written when the author was still in his twenties, with only four years of life ahead of him before his brilliant career would be cut short by the Civil War. "The Diamond Lens" is the tragedy of a scientist who falls in love with a woman too small to be visible to the naked eye, and who lives in the world of a water drop. No one else can see her, of course, and the story has a tragic ending. It would not be until sixty years later that the nuclear nature of the atom was discovered and the potential of microscopic discoveries reached a new playing field.

Another recurring theme was man adapting to new surroundings. In "Beyond Return," a biochemist at a big hospital, asks permission from the head of the hospital to experiment on one of its patients with a new hormone he has isolated from the highly adaptive fruit fly. Dan believes that curing a disease is causing the patient to adapt to it and has already been successful with experimental animals. With consent, the injections are given to Kyra Zelas, a pathetic, unattractive waif in the last stages of tuberculosis. Kyra has a miraculous recovery but the doctors find themselves faced with a frightening situation when it is discovered that Kyra, now an ultimate adaptive, can change her physical characteristics under pressure; in revolt against her former drab existence, becoming a beautiful blonde, dangerous and immortal. Risking borderline asphyxiation, the doctors trick Kyra into unconsciousness so they can cure her back to normal, which she is grateful at the conclusion.

This was one of two episodes adapted from a previously published short story, "The Adaptive Ultimate," by Stanley G. Weinbaum, originally published in the November 1935 issue of *Astounding Science Fiction*, under the pen name of John Jessel. The same story was also the basis for a low-budget motion picture titled *She Devil*, released theatrically in April of 1957. Jack Kelly played the role of

Dr. Dan Scott and Albert Dekker played the role of Dr. Richard Bach. Mari Blanchard played the role of Kyra Zelas in the big screen version, a woman who faces a horrible demise unlike the version dressed up for *Science Fiction Theatre*.

Prior, "The Adaptive Ultimate" had been dramatized twice. The first on radio's *Escape* on March 26, 1949 under the original title. The second on television's *Studio One* on September 12, 1949, titled "Kyra Zelas" (the same name of the title character).

Astounding Science Fiction magazine, November 1935

There are cases where people are tricked into false results by a lack of understanding about what human beings can do to themselves in the way of being led astray by subjective effects, wishful thinking or threshold interactions. These are examples of pathological science, as evidenced in the frightening chiller, "End of Tomorrow." In this episode, Dr. Keith Brandon, a government bacteriologist, is introduced to a newly arrived scientist named Professor Reimers. The latter claims to have discovered a universal antibiotic which is capable of eradicating all known virus and diseases. Keith's job is to validate the said anti-biotic. According to experiments which Keith witnesses, the serum appears to be valid. However, Keith's laboratory assistant and wife, Jane, accidentally discovers that the drug has a decomposing effect on the genes of the injected animals. This effect manifests itself in the sole regeneration of the female species, which will cause the human race to die out within 100 years. Since Congress has already passed a bill approving general inoculation, it becomes Keith's and Jane's responsibility to bring their findings to the attention of the government, over the many hurdles placed by Reimers and the enemies of reason. After they succeed in breaking red tape and proving the side effect of the antibiotic, Reimers mysteriously disappears without a trace . . . after almost succeeding to sabotage the survival of the human race.

One message that comes through after viewing multiple episodes of *Science Fiction Theatre* is that man will never conquer space.

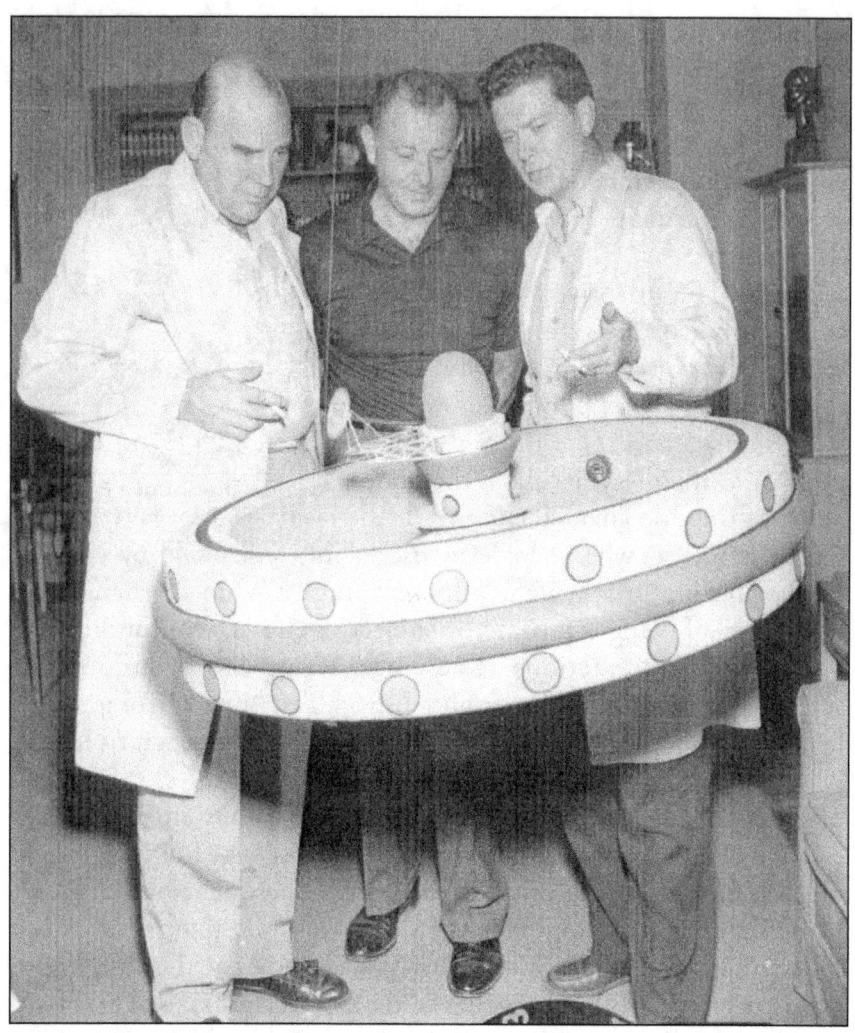

James Westerfield, Ivan Tors and Arthur Franz look over a scale model of a proposed space station.

Explore, yes. As Robert Heinlein once wrote, "The vast area of space stretches into infinity and therefore, the only means of exploring beyond the tools we build are visitations from visitors from outer space." Could man receive visits from residents of other worlds? That subject was explored more than once in "Are We Invaded?" and "Hour of Nightmare." Scientists have speculated whether or not we would receive such visits from extra-terrestrials, and this certainly makes good fiction. But on *Theatre*, such visitors were in human form and only speculation.

Solar expert Robert S. Richardson studying sun's spectrum on 40-ft. long strip of photographs. Photo taken in Los Angeles, sans glasses.
(PHOTO COURTESY OF *LIFE MAGAZINE*)

It's a known fact that many scientists of the twentieth century enjoyed reading science fiction. A number of them were, themselves, respected writers of the field. In the episode "Project 44," Truman Bradley had the honor of interviewing Dr. Robert S. Richardson, an American astronomer of Mt. Wilson and Palomar Observatories, who appeared in the beginning of the episode discussing the realistic possibility of finding water and plant life on the planet Mars, even with its thin atmosphere, and man's attempt to land on the planet's surface. Dr. Robert S. Richardson also wrote science fiction under the name of Philip Latham. Under his real name, Richardson wrote *Five Against Venus* (1952) and *Missing Men of Saturn* (1953). He had served as technical advisor for the movies *The War of the Worlds* (1953) and *Conquest of Space* (1955), and wrote numerous scripts for television's *Captain Video*.

THE STAFF

Jon Epstein was the production chief at ZIV-Television, billed unofficially as a "story editor," who oversaw final approval of the scripts and ensured production never went over budget or beyond two days filming per episode (without good reason). Epstein was born and raised in New York City, where as a youth he came under the spell of radio broadcasting. Upon graduation from Lehigh University in 1947 at the age of 18, he got a job at the Ziv Corporation, which was by then heavily involved in the syndication and production of radio programs. He spent several years as an office boy and mimeograph operator, but soon found himself directing a number of the radio programs. After serving in Korea and Japan from 1950 to 1952, Epstein returned to resume his career in radio. In 1953, he moved to Hollywood with the Ziv Corporation and entered the world of syndicated television and series production. He oversaw *Meet Corliss Archer* and *I Led Three Lives*, to name a few.

"Well, that company was the hottest company in the business in the syndication field, and we made everything cheaper than anyone else," Epstein recalled to interviewer Irv Broughton (*Producers on Producing*, McFarland, 1986). "I gotta tell you, plenty of people went by the wayside, but other people used that as a learning experience. When you're given no money, you can't buy the best writers in town or the best directors in town, and you have to hang in there on your ingenuity and your own abilities—you know, when they're not giving you all the tools and they're giving you less tools than the next guy, you're either going to collapse under the effort or you're going to acquire more abilities because you're forced to. I would like to think in my case that's what happened. I really learned from the ground up with not a lot of help. I mean, they said, 'Here it is. This is all we've got. Now go make it.'"

Tors originally intended for George Van Marter to write all 39 teleplays but after Van Marter's departure after the second teleplay, Stuart Jerome was hired to take his place.

Jerome was one of the first radio writers to gain prominence in the new medium of television. The son of the late Warner Bros. songwriter M.K. Jerome, he began his career in radio writing for several hundreds of shows, the first of which was "Winter Holiday" with Barbara Stanwyck for the prestigious *Lux Radio Theatre*. He scripted numerous episodes for ZIV-TV including *Mr. District Attorney, Tombstone Territory, The Unexpected, Favorite Story, The Cisco Kid* and the pilot for *Highway Patrol*. Jerome also accepted the task of scripting for the new *I Led Three Lives* series as *Science Fiction Theatre* began production, keeping him busy behind the typewriter. Jerome was so reliable he became one of the only writers to work under contract with ZIV.

Doris Gilbert was a frequent freelance contributor, who also got her start writing radio scripts for such programs as the Kate Smith show and *Junior Miss*. Her television credits included *The Adventures of Superman, Mr. and Mrs. North* and ZIV's *The Unexpected*.

Lou Huston, who scripted eight episodes of *Science Fiction Theatre*, didn't have a strong background in science. His formal education in science consisted of one year in Freshman Biology at USC in 1931. He contributed radio scripts for the blood and thunder program, *The Hermit's Cave*, and television scripts for *Dr. Christian* and *Space Patrol* (which he would also adapt from his radio scripts), all based on fiction instead of science. Huston's eye caught an announcement in a trade paper about Ivan Tors and Frederic Ziv's joint venture for a science fiction program. Huston introduced himself to the studio as a writer of science fiction plays and quickly found himself working on the series. Ironically, of the handful of scripts he wrote for the series, the only one that had anything to do with biology was "Killer Tree," and someone else wrote the short story for which he wrote the teleplay.

Two episodes were based on published short stories and a few from original plot proposals. More than half, however, originated from Ivan Tors who either acquired stock footage and wrote a premise around the use of that footage, or got a germ of an idea adapted from a magazine article. An avid reader of *Scientific American* magazine, Tors borrowed more ideas from that magazine than any other.

"TV in those days was exhilarating and demanding," recalled director Henry Kesler. "We had only several days time to shoot an entire half-hour episode and a lot of directors just couldn't stack up.

Candid photo of producer Ivan Tors circa 1966.

As a result, in addition to producing and directing my own material, I was often called on to 'trouble shoot.'"

Screen actor Paul Guilfoyle who received great acclaim for his role as Garth Esdras, the haunted and hunted accessory to murder in *Winterset* (1936), served both as actor and director for a number of *Science Fiction Theatre*. Memorable as the weasel convict who tries to kill James Cagney at Steve Cochran's behest, but gets his just desserts in the trunk of a car in *White Heat* (1949), Guilfoyle learned the craft of film making by working closely with the technicians. He specialized in becoming victims of drowning, strangulation, being thrown from a skyscraper, buried in landslides and run over by automobiles.

Production supervisor Barry Cohon consults director Paul Guilfoyle on the set of "The Long Sleep."

After two decades as a film actor, he made a small foray into film directing for such television programs as *Racket Squad* and *Public Defender*. He played supporting roles for three episodes of *Science Fiction Theatre* and supplied an off-screen voice (un-credited) for at least two episodes on top of directing 15 episodes of the series. He was paid for his acting talent on top of his directing chores.

Lew Ayres attempts to phone for help from *Donovan's Brain* (1953).

While producing *Donovan's Brain* (1953), Tom Gries (rhymes with rise) worked with a number of individuals who later worked on *Science Fiction Theatre*. A tight-knit group, Gries was invited to jump on board by Ivan Tors at the request of Harry Redmond and Herbert Strock. Gries ultimately wrote and directed a number of episodes of *Science Fiction Theatre*. Having worked as a writer for newspapers in Chicago, Gries went to Hollywood in 1950 as a talent agent and later became a successful screenwriter. It was during his period with Ziv that he learned the complexities of the craft.

"At that point in time, television was far ahead of motion pictures in techniques, far ahead in the ability and willingness to make relevant statements. During that period, television hurt movies not just because it was free, but because there was so much said, so much to be seen, so many things that audiences rarely could see in local theaters. Television had better writing and directing, far better acting and more trenchant subject matter than feature films."

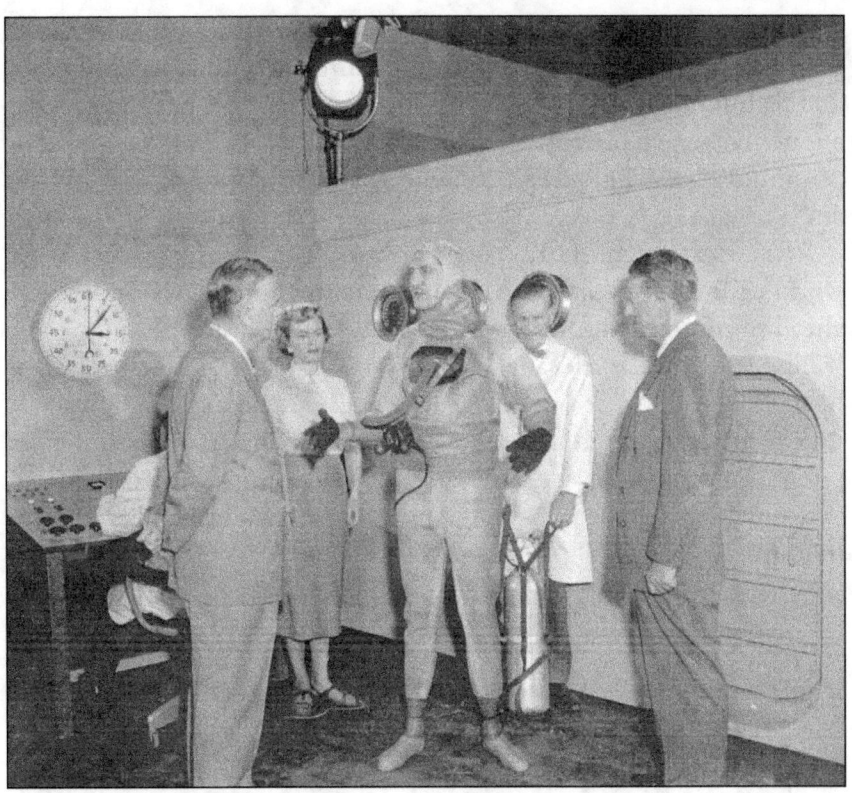

Vincent Price demonstrates the "Second Skin," an experimental diving suit for underwater exploration in "Operation Flypaper."

While most major film studios operated five days a week, ZIV Television worked six days a week excluding Sundays—unusual for television production during the fifties. "Filmmaking was fun, but it was also hard to be a Latter-day Saint and work in the picture business during Hollywood's heyday," recalled Kesler. "The system itself worked to make it difficult to observe church teachings."

"The folks at ZIV were more concerned with budget than our creative talents," recalled director Leon Benson for a trade column in the early seventies. "I often felt the pressures when something went wrong. They passed around an internal memo one afternoon reminding those of us underpaid that each television production was to be completed within two shooting days. The next day a power outage put us a full hour behind schedule one morning and I was sweating every minute we waited for the power to return to the set."

"Television was very good to me," recalled Tom Gries. "It was a school and a laboratory where a young director could learn the tools and techniques of film at small risk to himself or his producer. After all, no matter what we did, *any* of us, the show would be better than 26 minutes of blank screen. Come what may, it would go on the air."

"There was the satisfaction of good work, sometimes even significant work," continued Gries. "At that point in time television was far ahead of motion pictures in techniques, far ahead in the ability and willingness to make relevant statements. During that period, television hurt movies not just because it was free, but because there was so much to be said, so much to be seen, so many things that audiences rarely could see in their local theaters. Television had better writing and direction, far better acting and more trenchant subject matter than feature films."

THE MUSIC

Since the program was not affiliated with ASCAP or BMI, the composer of the theme music was never credited on the screen during any of the 78 productions. It is suspected that Ray Bloch was the composer since he was given conducting credit on "Science Fiction Theatre Signature" when the piece appeared in the World Broadcasting System production music library. Some sources cite Ray Llewelyn as the composer, but this has since been proven to be a pseudonym of several musicians who composed the theme songs for ZIV-TV productions, usually because they worked under a specific buyout contract. Other names tossed about were David Rose, John Seely or William Loose, with Seely the least likely for numerous reasons.

With the exception of the theme, the music was clearly stock, pulled from a stock library and used with permission for a flat fee paid by ZIV-TV. The same music bridges can be heard on other fifties television productions including Republic's *Commando Cody* series, which is credited to Stanley Wilson.

For most of the second season, Milton Lustig served as the music editor. Choosing which pieces to incorporate into the film to bridge scenes and elevate important shock scenes, Lustig worked solo

Gene Barry as Bat Masterson, another ZIV-TV production.

without the assistance of other musicians. Beginning with production #1060, titled "One Thousand Eyes," Lustig's name appeared on screen during the closing credits, lasting till the end of the series. There is no documentation to verify whether or not he was the music editor for the first season. Lustig never composed any music but he helped edit stock music into other ZIV-TV finished films including *Harbor Command, Men Into Space* and *Bat Masterson*.

SYNDICATION

By March of 1955, science began to hog space in newspapers and magazines. The mounting public excitement over high-altitude rockets, guided missiles, anti-polio vaccine, artificial diamonds and other signs of progress impelled Ziv to the conclusion, according to an inter-office memo, that the sooner they could get *Science Fiction*

Theatre on the air, the better. Ziv's sales promotion staff in Cincinnati was alerted to start work on presentations and merchandising tie-ins for the new show. While top sales execs began screening the pilot for major ad agencies who had not yet signed, attempts to have merchandise produced for the program failed due to the hurried schedule. The sales department was ultimately given less than two months for its sales drive. A release date was already set for April 1.

At the time *Science Fiction Theatre* premiered on television in April of 1955, only ten programs were in the can and 19 still in pre-production. Ironically, accusations were being leveled by Frederic W. Ziv that same month against the television industry for failing to "maintain a continuously high level of quality, ingenuity and inventiveness in its programs."

Ziv, in a prepared statement, warned that deficiency could result only "in a loss of audiences, a loss of impact, and, finally, a greater cost per thousand to the advertiser who is paying the bills." The statement was released in conjunction with the first quarter report, which revealed a stepping up of the company's activities. An increase of thirty-two percent in the first quarter of 1955 revenue, over the same period a year before, verified Ziv's growth.

"Television is growing out of its infant stages and all of us who are engaged in this great industry must face up realistically to maturity in our thinking and planning and our execution," Ziv asserted. "We must dedicate ourselves to find and develop, encourage and nourish great new writers . . . men and women who can approach this vast new medium of communication and entertainment in a spirit of courageous explorers, without being shackled by the formulas, formats and inhibitions associated with the earlier forms of stagecraft." This same dedication was certainly evident in *Science Fiction Theatre*.

The same month gave Ziv financial stability when his *Mr. District Attorney* was renewed by 94 percent of present clients. The statistics of retention was remarkable.

"No one else created the kind of sales and promotional helps that we did," Ziv recalled to author Jeff Kisseloff (*The Box: An Oral History of Television, 1920-1961*, Viking/Penguin Group, 1995). "Let's say a bakery in Indianapolis bought one of our programs. He would receive posters, window displays, newspaper ads, and newspaper stories to feed to the editors. We also sent a man to conduct a meeting of his sales organization."

Ziv had a sales organization that was very shrewd when it came to business. After securing an offer from a television station, the salesman would cross the street to another television station and encourage them to beat their competition by offering more money. The sponsor was easier. The salesman would carry a 16-millimeter projector and film of the shows with them on the sales trips. Whether it was set up at a bakery or in the back of a hardware store, the owner of the business would personally see the product.

"Advertisers will demand a greater quality of film product and a constantly improving quality," Ziv wrote in late 1955. "Our own 1956 plans call for growth in both directions. We now have 12 series in production, four of them released during the past year."

One year after the premiere of *Science Fiction Theatre*, the April 16, 1956, issue of *Broadcasting-Telecasting* reported Ziv with heavy renewals. An estimated $1,225,000 in business contracts were signed during March by ZIV television programs with advertisers or their agencies on four different television film series, as reported by M.J. Rifkin, vice president in charge of sales. Renewals were responsible for 80 percent of the dollar volume. Renewals for the month included 17 for *Science Fiction Theatre*, 26 for *I Led Three Lives* and 27 for *Mr. District Attorney*. *The Man Called X*, a new program finishing production, had just been sold for 11 spot TV advertisers and five TV stations.

One of the success factors may have been ZIV-TV's offer to have the star or host of each program do the commercials. In the seven largest West Coast markets, *Science Fiction Theatre* was sponsored alternately by The Olympia Brewing Company* and PictSweet Frozen Foods, and Truman Bradley was paid to stand before the camera and make a sales pitch for the beer and food commercials. In addition, Progress Brewing Company sponsored the series in

---

* During the 1950s, Breweries were the major single product type among regional sponsors. Ziv's sales force was aware of this and often targeted their programs to companies selling beer. Olympia's distribution covered the three West Coast States plus Idaho, Montana, Nevada and Arizona.

Oklahoma City; Arizona Public Service sponsored the series in Phoenix and Yuma; and Tobin Packing Company in Rochester, New York. The Emerson Drug Company sponsored *Theatre* when it premiered in 1955 on WRCA, New York. Olympia had sponsored Ziv's *Favorite Story* for two seasons and was looking for a different program to attract a different audience. The contract between Olympia and Ziv was signed on February 12, 1955.

Sales ranking for *Science Fiction Theatre* compared to the competition is evident from the listing below.

JULY 1955

CHICAGO, SATURDAY AT 10:30 P.M.
WNBQ	*Science Fiction Theatre*	14.8
WGN	Wrestling	10.9
WBBM	Pee Wee King	11.4

CINCINNATI, SATURDAY AT 10 P.M.
WLW	*Science Fiction Theatre*	18.5
WCPO	*Million Dollar Movie*	14.9
WKRC	News; *Best in Hollywood*	12.4

COLUMBUS, SATURDAY AT 10 P.M.
WLW	*Science Fiction Theatre*	19.7
WBNS	*Meet Corliss Archer*	18.0 *
WTVN	*Saturday Playhouse*	15.5

DAYTON, SATURDAY AT 10 P.M.
WLW	*Science Fiction Theatre*	24.3
WHIO	*Famous Playhouse*	20.8

MINNEAPOLIS, ST. PAUL, FRIDAY AT 9 P.M.
WCCO	*Science Fiction Theatre*	18.9
KEYD	Baseball	19.4
WTCN	*Adventure Theatre*	15.9

---

* *Meet Corliss Archer* was also a ZIV-TV production.

JANUARY 1956

CHICAGO, SATURDAY AT 10:30 P.M.
WNBQ	*Science Fiction Theatre*	18.8
WGN	Wrestling	11.4
WBBM	Pee Wee King	8.7

NEW YORK, FRIDAY AT 7 P.M.
WRCA	*Science Fiction Theatre*	10.8
WCBS	*Rain or Shine;* CBS News	7.8
WOR	*Million Dollar Movie*	4.9

OKLAHOMA CITY, FRIDAY AT 9:30 P.M.
WKY	*Science Fiction Theatre*	24.2
KWTV	*Our Miss Brooks*	23.7

SEATTLE-TACOMA, THURSDAY AT 9:30 P.M.
KING	*Science Fiction Theatre*	16.2
KOMO	*Lux Video Theatre*	19.5
KTVW	Baseball	13.7

WASHINGTON, SUNDAY AT 6 P.M.
WMAL	*Science Fiction Theatre*	10.3
WRC	*Meet the Press*	6.3
WTOP	*Telephone Time*	9.3

For the local television affiliates, a kit detailing a special public service promotion campaign was practically standard equipment on each of ZIV-TV's releases. It was designed to cash in on the documentary slant on most of Ziv's shows. Three separate promotional kits were given to sponsors after the purchase. The regular kit contained the basic publicity, photos, mats and announcement copy. The "enthusiasm" kit was designed to help the sponsor stir up interest in the show within his own organization. Beginning with *Science Fiction Theatre*, the public service campaign kit was produced and offered for all of Ziv's programs. In the promotional kit for *Theatre*, Ziv suggested that the local sponsor stage a science exposition to get local industries, hospitals and universities to cooperate. Such staged events were obvious

Actor Peter Hanson comforts Joyce Holden in "Signals from the Heart."

promotional gimmicks to encourage free publicity from local newspapers.

Ziv even attempted to interest an international appeal. The first season was dubbed in Spanish and lip-synched for the Latin-American market. The science fiction show was the eighth Ziv property to go on the Latin-American market, and the second to go into Spanish dubbing in 1955. Latin-American sponsors were renewing programs like *The Cisco Kid* for a second year and sought new programs. In Puerto Rico, four of Ziv's programs were among the 15 highest-rated programs and were the only film shows on the list. In May of 1955, Ziv announced success with its largest single foreign deal, selling six of its programs to Goar Mestre's CMBF-TV in Havana. The purchase included *The Unexpected, Boston Blackie, The Cisco Kid, I Led Three Lives, Mr. District Attorney* and *Science Fiction Theatre*. *

---

* *Science Fiction Theatre* was also dubbed in French, German and Italian.

SEASON ONE SPONSORS

The following is a list of sponsors for the first season of *Science Fiction Theatre*, beginning with the season premiere in April of 1955.

Olympia Beer	22 West Coast markets
Pictsweet	13 markets
Bromo-Seltzer	17 markets
White King Soap	5 markets
Geritol	5 markets
Genesee Beer	3 markets

BANKS

First National of Miami, First National of Atlanta
First National of Tulsa, American National Bank & Trust Co. of Chattanooga
Security Federal Savings & Loan of Columbia, South Carolina

UTILITIES

Arizona Public Service in Phoenix, Arizona
New England Gas & Electric in Boston, Massachusetts
Central Maine Power Co. in Portland, Oregon
Natural Gas Companies in Pittsburgh
Providence Gas Co. & Blackstone Valley Gas & Electric in Providence, Rhode Island
Manufacturers Light & Heat Company in Wheeling, West Virginia

FOODS

Tobin Packing Co. in Utica, Rochester and Buffalo, New York
Marmat Packing in Charlotte, North Carolina
Acme Supermarkets in Syracuse, New York
Pevely Dairy in St. Louis, Missouri

Make-up artist George Gray (FAR LEFT) **and director Herbert L. Strock** (FAR RIGHT) **decide on which wig the actor will wear on** *Science Fiction Theatre.*

Associated Grocers in Billings, Montana
Strietmann Biscuit in Huntington, West Virginia
Kotarides Baking in Norfolk, Virginia
Hathway Bakeries in Providence, Rhode Island
Woodhaven Dairy in Mobile, Alabama
Texas Coffee Co. in Beaumont, Texas

GASOLINE

Wisconsin Oil Co. in Milwaukee
Continental Oil Co. in Dallas, Texas
Bell Oil Co. in Ada, Oklahoma
Phillips Petroleum in Greensboro, North Carolina

AUTOS

Ford Motors	5 Western markets
Plymouth Motors	2 big city markets
Pontiac	1 market

SEASON TWO

"We have maintained a policy from the outset right straight through to today of shooting a great deal of our product in color," Ziv explained in an interview for *Broadcasting-Telecasting*. "*The Cisco Kid*, for example, has been produced in color for six consecutive years . . . We avoid violence in our shows, just as we avoid sex and horror and some of the other things that theatrical producers state sell tickets at the box office."

In January of 1954, Ziv learned from a trade paper that he was not the only producer considering color. MPT (Motion Pictures for Television) and Guild Films had made the decision to think outside the box. In late 1954, MCA-TV had begun shooting occasional color segments in some of its shows on an experimental basis.

Ziv's first television series was *The Cisco Kid*, initially shot on 16mm color. The network-owned-and-operated stations seemed to prefer 35mm, so Ziv quickly switched production to 35. For *Science Fiction Theatre*, the first season (39 episodes) was filmed on 35mm Eastman Kodak color stock. For the second season, it was decided to film the series on 35mm black and white. According to an inter-office memo, first-year sponsors were "not clamoring for renewal." This could be substantiated by the March 31, 1956, issue of *Billboard* which reported: "About half the first-year sponsors of *Science Fiction Theatre* have now signed for the second year of the show." Ziv had a discussion with Ivan Tors and it was agreed a second season would be produced, but only in black and white to retain a profit. "We were not competitive to the stations, and in many cases I would say, most cases, the stations welcomes us because we not only furnished programming, but we furnished substantial sponsors, sometimes local, sometimes regional, and sometimes national," Ziv explained.

Collectors today seek out 16mm reels of television episodes, and the general belief is that the series was originally shot on 16mm. Some even claim the series was kinescoped. Neither of these are true. The 16mm market was created for home viewing and are second-generation dupes from the original 35mm masters. Over time, Eastman color holds true on 35mm masters, provided they are stored in the proper atmospheric conditions. But Eastman color, compared

Marshall Thompson examines the periodic table of elements in "Bullet Proof."

to Technicolor of the times and digital feeds of today, was primitive and cheap and a number of viewers question whether it would be better to view the first season episodes in black and white since faded color can sometimes be a distraction.

This was not the only time Ziv produced specific seasons in color instead of the entire series. The first and third seasons of *I Led Three Lives* were shot in black and white while the second season was shot in color. Black and white prints do exist for second season episodes (and first season *Science Fiction*) but those exist in 16mm format when it was considered too costly by the purchaser to pay for color prints.

In January of 1956, Ziv issued a press release for the trade columns, including *Variety* and *Broadcasting*. He issued a warning to syndicated film sponsors to beware of the "one-season wonders."

"Advertisers should be cautious of buying a syndicated film series, no matter how good it is, when the production of the series is likely to be limited to only a season's output," he declared. This statement may have been directed against his competition, but to prove his worth, Ziv signed contracts on January 14 to renew *Science Fiction Theatre*. The major influence was the Emerson Drug Company (pitching Bromo-Seltzer), who renewed the series for 17 markets spot-booked throughout the United States. According to the contract, filming on 26 new half-hour dramas would get under way in February. Emerson also renewed another ZIV show on the same day, *I Led Three Lives*, which was extremely popular at the time. Ziv was offering subsequent year production when various sponsors signed in 1955, but the deciding factor was whether other sponsors would make a request for a renewal. Emerson did not want to pick up the entire tab. Alternating sponsors or sharing commercial time was granted as long as they were not sharing with competing companies. During the first week of February, *Science Fiction Theatre* was re-ordered by Olympia Brewing for 21 West Coast markets, and by the Arizona Public Service Company for a number of stations in that state. After the purchase of eight single-station renewals, Ziv agreed to add 13 additional productions to an amended contract, allowing for an additional total of 39 episodes to be produced for the second season.

For the second season of *Science Fiction Theatre*, Arrid Deodorant sponsored the series over WFIL in Philadelphia. Bromo-Selzter over WBAL in Baltimore, and WNBQ in Chicago. Super Anahist Products and Bromo-Seltzer shared sponsorship time over WXYZ in Detroit. Morton Frozen Foods and Bromo-Seltzer shared sponsorship duties over WMAL in Washington. Peter Paul Candy Bars, Bromo-Seltzer and Polident Denture Cleaner shared sponsorship duties over WPIX. Robert Burns Cigars and Olympia Beer alternated sponsorship over KRON in San Francisco. Robert Curley Products and Sustain 2-12 Tablets were both promoted over KMGM in Minneapolis-St. Paul. National Bohemian sponsored the series on 23 stations along the West Coast. Alka-Seltzer picked up the series on

Dr. Hugh Bentley (Bruce Bennett) hypnotizes one of his students in "Who Is This Man?"

20 stations nationwide. Conoco Oil and Gas sponsors six stations in the Southwest. Continental Oil sponsored the program in Fort Worth. King Soap took *Science Fiction Theatre* for four California markets and one in Reno, Nevada. Also for the second season, Olympia Brewing added Alaska to its West Coast spread. Glass Wax signed for a Chicago market, Wisconsin Oil in Milwaukee, Tobin Packing in Buffalo, and Auto-Lite along the East Coast in New York and Philadelphia.

Convincing existing sponsors to renew during mid-season, or picking up new sponsors, especially during the month of March, was difficult. Businesses were not focused on sponsoring a program that would begin syndication in mid-season—in this case, the month of April. While the second season productions of *Theatre* were being produced, Ziv's sales force got aggressive and Bud Rifkin, sales vice-president of ZIV-TV, reported in late April that the volume was "noticeably higher" than that of a year ago and that 80 percent of the profits was renewal business, mostly on *Science Fiction Theatre*.

TRUMAN BRADLEY

When compared to other science fiction television programs, *Science Fiction Theatre* lacked a number of outer space visitors which were more prominent on juvenile series such as *Rocky Jones, Space Ranger* and *Space Patrol*. On *Theatre*, extra-terrestrials were not bug-eyed. They did not contain lizard-like skin. They looked just like human beings and their identities were always verified after their disappearance—a tease to witnesses of flying saucers and the television viewers. "That which we do not understand, sometimes causes apprehension," explains Truman Bradley in the first-season episode, "Are We Invaded?"

Bradley was quick to point out that there had been over 2,000 flying saucer sightings and no one person was ever reported being injured by one. "And yet, has there been any phenomenon in our time that has stimulated so much speculation? Or are they like Haley's Comet—just one more harmless phenomenon of the skies?" Ironically, the only aspect of the series talked about and referenced more than the stories themselves was Truman Bradley, the host. Synonymous with the program, Bradley entered people's living rooms and invited them to witness a scientific marvel, captivating the television audience for a glimpse of the world of tomorrow.

The first two episodes produced, "Beyond" and "Y..O..R..D..," were learning experiences for both Bradley and the crew. Inter-office memos reveal debates whether or not he was allowed to wear his ring on the pinky finger of his right hand, because a number of insert shots might require a stand-in to use his hand and therefore, the need of a ring to be worn to match. It appears the decision to remove the ring was discarded since he wore the ring throughout the first season.

Bradley's wardrobe, however, became an issue that was quickly resolved when Maurice Unger viewed the rough cut for "Y..O..R..D..," and discovered that Bradley's tie was a solid red before the drama but the closing scene with Bradley at his desk, inviting the viewers to return again next week, was polka dotted. When Bradley had been filmed for "Beyond," he wore a polka dot tie and his closing invite was purposely filmed with no commentary, so the closing minute (which contained the cast and crew credits) would be reused

A rare photo of Truman Bradley wearing the tan colored suit from one of the very first productions.

Another photo of Bradley wearing the tan colored suit.

for all of the episodes—a cost saving device that was used for the closing of "Y..O..R..D.." and Unger's disappointment.

On December 10, Unger sent both Ivan Tors a memo requesting the closing shot be re-filmed with a striped tie, and beginning with the third episode put before the cameras, Bradley would officially wear a striped tie. On the morning of February 28, 1955, Bradley reported to Stage 6 at American National to film the lab demonstrations (known as pickups) for episodes 3, 4 and 5, and wore the striped tie as requested. But he wore a textured suit, tan in color, which went overlooked until after the rushes were viewed. Fearing the cost to re-film, these are the only episodes to feature Bradley wearing the tan colored suit. (Only the first five productions were filmed at American National.)

On the afternoon of March 14, Bradley reported to the set at Ziv Television Studios wearing a dark blue suit, for productions 6 and 7. By this time a script had been written: "I hope you enjoyed our story. We'll be back with you a week from today with another exciting adventure from the world of fiction and science. Until then, this is your host, Truman Bradley, saying . . . see you next week." The closing scene was filmed on this date and again Unger viewed the rushes and requested Bradley wear the dark suit from now on. Observant television viewers will note that with the exceptions noted above, Bradley always wore the striped red and white tie and the dark blue suit.

Truman Bradley's opening and closing scenes were filmed in batches of two, three and four episodes at a time. For much of the first season, Bradley reported to the set to film the episodes as a separate production, usually filmed on different days than the episodes filmed. For most of the second season, Bradley reported to the set on the same day the episodes were produced, filming his scenes either during lunch breaks or during the afternoon and evening after the cast was dismissed and the crew remained.

Truman Bradley's lab demonstrations were not just for educational value. They set the stage for the drama the audience was about to view by presenting a deeper understanding behind the scientific principal that was used by the fictional characters. Bradley's narratives also provided commentary for the viewer to think about. In "Y..O..R..D..," for example, Bradley demonstrated how his voice was picked up by

Truman Bradley plays around between takes.

a small broadcast receiver attached to an electronic typewriter which then deciphered his words into text. Bradley then applied this same concept with tiny nerve cells in the human brain that receive signals and demonstrated how the human body is a battery that stimulates the cells. Bradley then pondered whether the electrical activity of our brains is confined within our own nervous system. Could it be broadcast to other minds? Could we, perhaps one day, master the secret to broadcast from one mind to another?

In "Stranger in the Desert," Bradley reveals the history of the atomic age and the discovery of radium. In "Sound of Murder," Bradley uses an Oscilloscope, a device which reduces sound into electrical energy, revealing how his voice appears on a graph (and was the same prop seen in *Riders to the Stars*). Bradley also started a fire with the sound from a tuning fork. With these gimmicks, he demonstrated different kinds of sound, each giving a different physical reaction.

The advancement of high-speed brain activity was explored in "Brain Unlimited," in which Truman Bradley explains how the human brain operates with chemical and electrical fuel, and theorized whether the brain could be supercharged like an automobile motor.

This served as the premise for that episode, also explored in numerous science fiction programs including *The Outer Limits*, which often featured stories of human beings pushing themselves beyond their present-day capabilities by using scientific means of advancing their body chemistry.

In "The Human Circuit," Bradley closed the episode commenting that unexplainable events happen every day and in the years to come, scientists are hopeful of understanding mind over matter and such unexplained phenomena as telepathy, clairvoyance and hypnotism as ordinary functions of the human brain.

Very little has been documented regarding Truman Bradley's lab demonstrations. Those scenes were filmed as separate productions and the few lab assistants that appear on screen went mostly un-credited. What little is known can be found under their retrospective episode entries, and Appendix B.

IN CLOSING

Science Fiction Theatre was syndicated, principally over NBC stations, between April 1955 and April 1957. In May of 1957, just one month after *Theatre* ended its first run of second season episodes, Ziv turned the series over to Economee TV, a rerun affiliate of Ziv, and the series began making the rounds of smaller, local affiliates. By 1958, as the last of *Science Fiction Theatre* was making the initial rounds on the television circuit, Tors' second project came to fruition: *Sea Hunt*. He had received a number of letters from other television and motion picture producers, accusing him of distorting the purpose of such films to the extent that "science fiction has become an ugly word." One such letter also accused him of wasting the genre and said that he "made it vulgar." They emphasized that horror to such a degree that "the scientific aspects have become secondary."

"I believe a picture with a scientific background stimulates the minds of young people," Tors wrote in defense. "The pictures made now are in bad taste and have a bad effect on juveniles because they are so sensational and vulgar. I dropped my [theatrical] projects because I can't compete with this low-budget sensational type of

Marilyn Erskine poses for the camera in "Sun Gold."

product. Today, the average theater owner will only pay about a $30 rental for such pictures; they're not paying for better ones."

In February of 1957, before the second season of *Science Fiction Theatre* finished it's initial run, Ivan Tors convinced Ziv to take up a new science series, this time taking Ziv for an underwater swim with a property known as *Sea Hunt*. The lead was originally intended for two freelance skin divers, but would ultimately be narrowed down to one with Lloyd Bridges. Tors would also attempt other projects and eventually form New Venture Productions with Andrew Marton. Plans for a sequel to *Gog* fell through, and his attepts at an "Office of Scientific Investigation" series ceased (though a suspiciously similar "Office of Scientific Security" turned up in several *Science Fiction Theatre* episodes).

The conquest of space, one of the repeated themes in science fiction television programs, became a natural exploitation programmer, with both syndicators and stations dusting off reruns for a fresh round. Official Films, on the basis of a simple mailing, corralled eight stations within a few days for its *Rocky Jones, Space Ranger* series of 39 episodes.

Laika, the first animal ever sent to space, rode to orbit in Sputnik II on November 3, 1957. The dog's trip into outer space warranted newspapers headlines for weeks. The editors of *TV Guide* remarked shortly thereafter: "Producers of *Science Fiction Theatre* wonder what all the shouting is about. One of their shows last year spotlighted animals as the first space travelers." In 1958, with interest in space, Muttnik and Sputnik high, Ziv began tallying up many station sales on multiple-run deals on *Science Fiction Theatre*. Among stations inking were WGR-TV, Buffalo; WDSU-TV, New Orleans; WTVJ-TV, Miami; KMGM-TV, Minneapolis; WBRE-TV, Wilkes-Barre, Pa.; and WTVN-TV, Columbus. All told, 57 stations made deals on the reruns of the skein during the first quarter of the year.

Walt Disney displays a model on one of his *Tomorrowland* television specials.

In New York, WOR-TV was giving its space telefilms a big play, telecasting *Science Fiction Theatre* Sunday and Monday evenings, and for the moppets in the afternoons, *Rocky Jones Space Ranger* and *Flash Gordon*. The station was also pruning through the RKO library for a science fiction feature for telecasting on "Million Dollar Movie."

Months after *Science Fiction Theatre* concluded its initial run on network television, Walt Disney successfully attempted to piggyback by producing dramatic and illuminating scientific films. Discussion stages concerned sightings of flying saucers; astronomy; mysterious, unsolved scientific phenomena through the ages; and the world of electronics. But the animator's brush moved slower than news events and a great deal of story and artwork about the projected launching of a U.S. satellite was scrapped after the Russian disclosure of their successful launching. Disney learned from this failure one important rule to avoid a recurrence of this sort: deal with scientific subjects in general, non-news matter.

"I'm not trying to teach anything to anybody," remarked Disney. "I want to entertain the public. And response to past shows proves that people are entertained when they see new subjects, new facts, new areas of life treated in an interesting way." In the hour-long film, "Mars and Beyond," the television audience was treated to a sweeping survey of the known universe and an imaginative glance into the unknown. It was rushed into production as a result of the Russian Sputnik triggered a new fever-interest in the realm of outer space. Doctors Wernher von Braun and Ernst Stuhlinger, well-known experts on rockets and where they may go, discussed the possibility of outer-space travel. The high point was the realistically animated sequence dealing with a future flight to Mars in an atomic-powered space ship.

From 1957 to 1958, CBS-TV offered a short-run series titled *Conquest*, with each of the three entries offering different scientific stories. The highlight of the show was the report on the development of the blunt-nosed missile. Featuring excellent shots of wind-tunnel experiments, a series of schematic drawings and explanatory comments by the designers themselves, the reasons why missiles were converted from needlepoint to blunt-nose shapes were turned into a dramatic lesson on the methods of the laboratory scientists.

Another fine sequence was devoted to Dr. Gerard Kuiper, head of the Yerkes Observatory in a fascinating account of an astronomer at work. The focus of that segment was on Dr. Kuiper's work in charting a detailed map of the moon. Along with CBS reporter George Herman, television viewers were given a peek of the moon through the observatory telescope and it was as good as any science fiction creation. The topography of the moon was further detailed via an extensive series of photos and Dr. Kuiper's comments.

In February of 1958, ABC-TV presented a special hour-long documentary titled *The Unchained Goddess*, a science documentary produced by Frank Capra. With the help of animated characters and actor Richard Carlson, Dr. Research (Dr. Frank Baxter) talked about the weather and described what scientists were doing about it. They illustrate the origins of such weather elements as winds, clouds, rain, snow, hail and lightning; show how these elements combine to produce weather; and depict scientific attempts to predict and control weather.

From 1959 to 1960, ZIV-TV offered *The Man and the Challenge*, another program utilizing factual science into a dramatic form of entertainment. What some might consider a spin-off from a number of *Science Fiction Theatre* episodes, the theme of *Challenge*—the scientific search to ascertain the limits of man's ability to endure physical and mental pain—lent itself to a variety of story ideas. The series borrowed science fiction clichés such as women scientists and lab assistants, military and Air Force personnel working on top-secret projects, and human beings subjected to unorthodox experiments that would normally receive harsh criticism in the scientific community, rather than praise from close associates at the conclusion of the story.

One such example was "The Sphere of No Return," which centered on man's reactions in a balloon ascent to 100,000 feet. The tendency toward hallucinations at that height and a sequence with a thunderstorm were a few of the challenges. There was also a near-collision with power lines on the way up, a malfunction of the carbon-dioxide regenerating system, exhaustion of the oxygen supply, an impossible descent because of 70-mile winds below, a "weather inversion" that prevented them from dropping when the coast is clear, and plummeting descent that's stopped when the emergency parachute opened. "It's impossible to tell the legitimate from the hokum," remarked a columnist for *Variety*. And of course, stock footage of an Air Force balloon was used so much that Tors was obviously borrowing material from the *Riders to the Stars* and *Science Fiction Theatre*, which helped provide scientific angles that otherwise would have been too costly to reproduce.

Another episode of *Challenge* included the subjecting of two volunteers to an extended period in which astronauts awaited retrieval after returning from space. In another, volunteers were subjected to the psychological torture and stress of brainwashing. Positive results were not always guaranteed—especially when an emergency occurred.

When preparing an episode of *The Man and the Challenge*, Tors learned of some Army experiments in hypnosis. Flying to Washington, he got an appointment with a psychiatrist in the Surgeon General's office, where he learned that GIs under hypnosis could lift 40 percent more weight than they could under normal circumstances and that even Sad Sacks were memorizing difficult texts. Back in Hollywood, Tors turned this unclassified material over to a scriptwriter as a vehicle for the series, but he soon ran into trouble. When the script did not read convincingly, the producer and his writer discovered they didn't really understand hypnosis. Tors phoned a

Lucky Strike advertisement for *Men Into Space*.

hypnotist recommended by the Los Angeles Medical Association and arranged for a series of trances with himself as the suspect. He described the script's flaw: "It isn't the hypnotist who hypnotizes you. You hypnotize yourself. The hypnotist is just the medium." When Tors combined hypnosis and psychic phenomena for an episode of *Science Fiction Theatre* a few years previous, the scriptwriter had understood the subject matter and the problem was averted.

The same television season premiered another of ZIV's science fiction offerings, *Men Into Space*. Unlike *Challenge*, Ivan Tors was not the producer, but the program certainly had the Ivan Tors feel.

Told through a documentary approach, the program was made to depict an accurate account of man's likely experiences and problems venturing away from the Earth to help colonize the moon. *Men Into Space* hopped off the CBS launching pad giving the television viewers a closer look at the technical difficulties, challenges and ordeals of the "space race."

Starring in the lead was William Lundigan as Col. Edward McCauley, who appeared in the pilot episode of *Science Fiction Theatre*. Produced with the cooperation and assistance of the Army, Navy, Air Force and numerous scientific organizations, the series was something of a novelty even if sooner or later, all the dial-twitching, knob-pushing, radar screen scanning and pip popping was going to become second nature to the television viewer. *Variety* laughed at the program, remarking: "At times the picture resembled a snip out of an old George Pal flicker. The results, while not entirely unsatisfactory, proved that even the most painstaking authenticity may manufacture something of a dud."

Early episodes depicted attempts to refuel spacecraft by tankers in orbit, construction of a space telescope, an experiment to dispose of high level atomic waste by launching it into the sun, the search for life-sustaining frozen water on the moon, exploration and destruction of an asteroid whose orbit threatened Earth and exo-fossil evidence of extraterrestrial life. Not content on the exploration of the moon—not having learned the true dangers of space exploration as a result of the early episodes—towards the end of the series' run McCauley and the gang set their sights toward the red planet, and made plans for colonization of Mars.

The series was advertised as being for its era an extremely accurate preview of manned spaceflight, based on scientific studies and buttressed by technical assistance from the USAF's ballistic missile and space medicine offices. However, the spacecraft designs veered incoherently between early 1950s Wernher Von Braun concepts, and later, totally scaled-down proposals. Visual backdrops and conceptual designs of spacecraft, space stations and a moon base depended somewhat on contributions from notable astronautics artist Chesley Bonestell (*Conquest of Space*). The series also availed itself of extensive documentary footage of early missile launches. Footage, costumes and props created specifically for

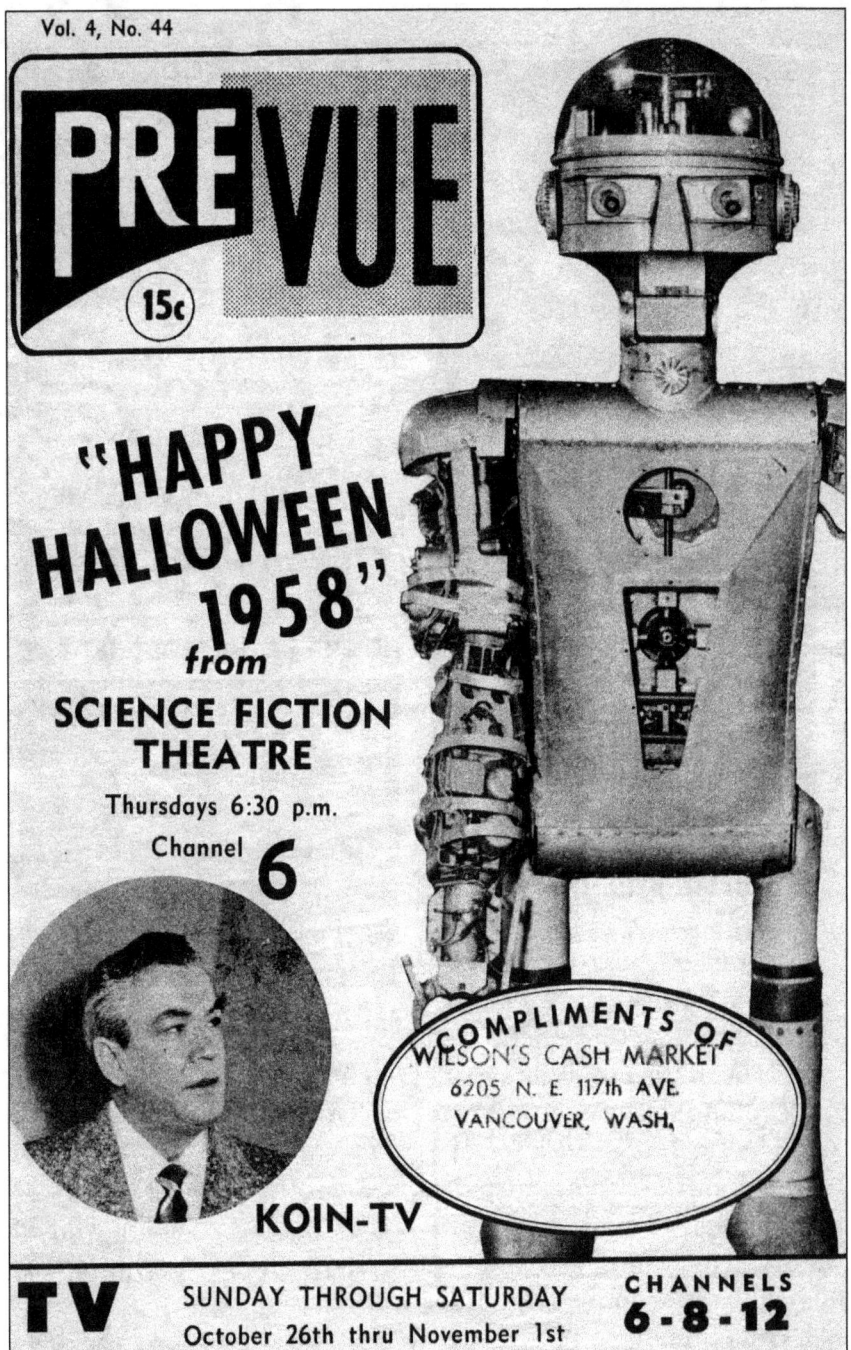

Cover of the October 26 – November 1, 1955 issue of *PreVue*.
PHOTO COURTESY OF PATRICK LUCANIO.

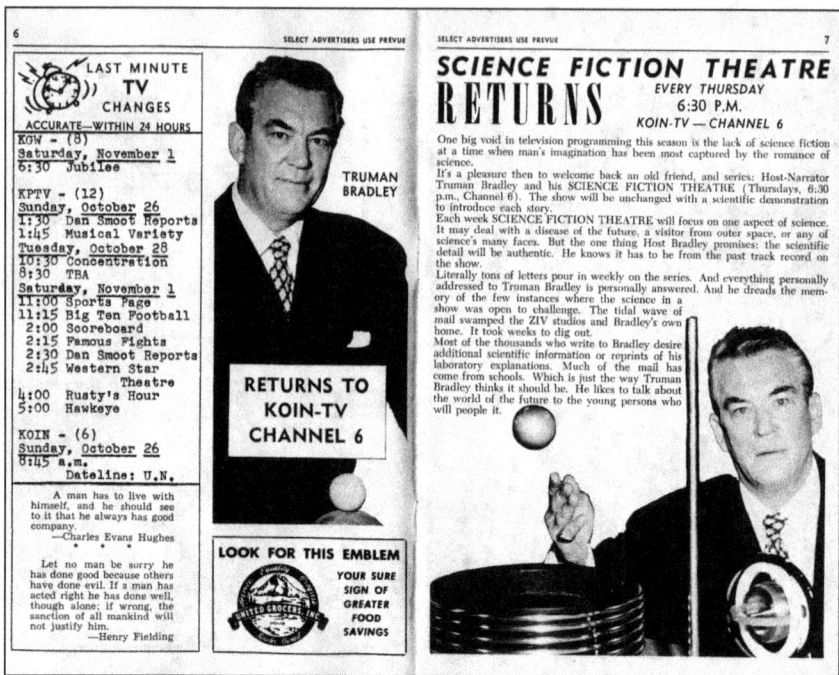

Article as it appeared in *PreVue*, promoting the return of *Science Fiction Theatre*. Photo courtesy of Patrick Lucanio.

Men Into Space were later reused for a number of *Outer Limits* episodes.

Even without the vocal talents of Truman Bradley, the narrator successfully explained to the audience why the astronauts needed magnetic boots to walk in or upon their free-falling spacecraft, how a jet-thruster backpack could propel an astronaut through the vacuum of space, and why a wrong angle of attack could doom a spacecraft upon atmospheric re-entry.

In 1960, during its twelfth year of business in television production, ZIV's company was bought out by United Artists, becoming ZIV-UA. *Science Fiction Theatre* was syndicated again but this time under a different title, *Beyond The Limits*. In 1981, MGM attempted to rebuild its production capacity by purchasing United Artists, which presently retains copyright and ownership of the television series and is responsible for television reruns.

ZIV commented in an interview in the May 9, 1955, issue of *Broadcasting-Telecasting*, thought that he had "achieved a truly adult series in a field that could have been completely juvenile. This

achievement has not been easy; it's entailed a laborious load of meticulous research. But it has paid off." This author could not disagree with that statement.

The Episode Guide
Season One

The episode titles were superimposed on the screen at the beginning of every episode. The accurate spelling of each episode's title is featured appropriately. If the on-screen title varied from the script title, it is noted accordingly. Example: the on-screen title for production 57b was "Miracle of Doctor Dove." The word "the" is not in the title and "Doctor" is spelled out, not abbreviated. For the next episode, the title is not "1000 Eyes." The number was spelled out on-screen so the correct title is "One Thousand Eyes."

All known production crew, credited or un-credited, have been listed alongside their respective productions. Only half of the production crew received on-screen credit. Unless mentioned otherwise, production crew listed were credited on-screen.

A complete cast is offered for each episode, along with their talent fees, according to salary contracts found among legal files and corporate records.

EPISODE #1 "BEYOND"

Production #1001 / 1B
Dates of Production: July of 1954
Directed by Herbert L. Strock

SCRIPT & STORY
Teleplay by Robert Smith and George Van Marter, from a story by Ivan Tors

PRODUCTION CREDITS
1st Asst. Cameraman: Dick Rawlings (*un-credited*)
1st Co. Grip: Mel Bledsoe (*un-credited*)
2nd Asst. Cameraman: Jack Kenny (*un-credited*)
2nd Asst. Director: George Loper (*un-credited*)
2nd Cameraman: Monroe "Monk" Askins (*un-credited*)
2nd Co. Grip: Walter Culp (*un-credited*)
Art Director: William Ferrari
Assistant Director: Joe Wonder (*credited*) and Donald Verk (*un-credited*)
Asst. Film Editor: George Reid (*un-credited*)
Asst. Prop man: Sam Heiligman (*un-credited*)
Best Boy: Lotus Davidson (*un-credited*)
Boom Man: Elmer Haglund (*un-credited*)
Cableman: J.R. McDonald (*un-credited*)
Camera Operator: Lee Davis (*un-credited*)
Casting: Patricia Harris (*un-credited*)
Construction Chief: Archie Hall (*un-credited*)
Director of Photography: L.B. Worth
Executive Production Secretary: Bea Lisse (*un-credited*)
Film Coordinator: Donald Tait
Film Editor: Charles Craft, A.C.E.
Gaffer: Joseph Wharton (*un-credited*)
Make-up Artists: George Gray (*un-credited*) and Harry Thomas (*credited*)
Property Master: Charles Henley (*credited*) and Lyle Reifsnider (*un-credited*)
Publicity: Frank Perrett (*un-credited*)

Recorder: Bob Post (*un-credited*)
Script Supervisor: Jack Herzberg
Secretary: Constance Morris (*un-credited*)
Set Dresser: Lou Hafley (*un-credited*)
Set Labor: Felex Caelecia (*un-credited*)
Sound Mixer: Jack Goodrich (*credited*) and Garry Harris (*un-credited*)
Special Effects Director: Harry Redmond, Jr. (*un-credited*)
Still Man: Bill Thomas (*un-credited*)
Wardrobe: Paul McCardle

Cast: Bruce Bennett (General Troy, $750); Robert Carson (Captain Ferguson, the security officer, $70); Tom Drake (Dr. James Everett, $500); Ellen Drew (Helen Gunderman, $750); Michael Fox (the radar man, $70); Douglas Kennedy (Colonel R.J. Barton, $300); Mark Lowell (the switch board operator, $70); William Lundigan (Major Fred Gunderman, $1,500); and Basil Ruysdael (Prof. Samuel Carson, $300)

Plot: A test pilot flying with twice the speed of sound meets a torpedo-shaped flying object 30,000 feet high in the sky. Afraid of collision, the pilot bails out. Medical experts suspect that his sighting was nothing but a visual hallucination and he is subjected to a lie detector test, hypnosis and various mental and physical examinations. In the meantime, retracing the curve of the test flight, some prominent scientists arrive at the conclusion that the angle and the speed of the ascent equalized the Earth's gravitational pull with the result that the pilot's brain was floating inside his skull. They conclude that the effect of this unusual condition was the misinterpretation of a floating fountain pen inside the cockpit. The pilot insists he was not hallucinating, but his insistence is met with opposition. When pieces of the wrecked airplane are recovered in the desert, the metal is highly magnetized, indicating that the plane brushed against something traveling through the atmosphere powered with magnetic force. Was it a spaceship, a flying saucer or a monitoring instrument from outer space? Only science and tomorrow will reveal that answer.

William Lundigan comforts Ellen Drew for a publicity photo.

NOTES

- The closing credits of every episode acknowledged Ivan Tors being "in charge of production." This is the only episode of the series that acknowledges his middle initial, "Ivan L. Tors."
- Because this episode was constructed as a pilot and not produced along with the remaining episodes of the season, Truman Bradley's laboratory set was different from that seen in the remaining first-season episodes, including different props along the wall during the initial pan and scan. This was also the only episode to feature the official ZIV Television logo in color.

- The square glass wall surrounding the doorway in the professor's room was the same one featured prominently in the 1954 movie *Gog*.
- Truman Bradley's introduction for this episode, as verified by the script, was originally intended to open with Bradley in a dark room. The cameraman was then instructed to change the lenses by placing a tube in front of the camera showing Bradley standing in the center of the screen, revealing an instrument developed by the Defense Department to find targets in the night. Instead, the opener features the camera pointed directly to Bradley's chair and Bradley speaks off-camera before finally walking into the frame. The remaining scenes were filmed as instructed, revealing a number of demonstrations of how the human eye could not see what was clearly there.
- Eddie Davis directed Truman Bradley for the opening and closing lab demonstrations on September 11, 1954, as well as the introductory pan and scan of the lab that was intended for the opening and closing on-screen credits. This pan and scan, however, was discarded for a revised pan and scan when Bradley's lab was reconstructed (with revisions) six months later for the production of the remaining episodes.
- Props featured in this drama would be reused repeatedly throughout numerous episodes of *Science Fiction Theatre* including the speaker in the Operation Center and the textured painting of the solar system hanging on the wall in the professor's office.
- The Eastman Kodak company provided the stock footage of the slow motion effect of the bullet hitting the glass. Every episode of the first season was filmed on 35 mm Eastman Kodak color film.
- A poster mapping out the layers of Earth's atmosphere hangs on the wall in two separate rooms, in two separate scenes, in this same episode! This is the same poster that would appear on the wall in numerous episodes such as "Project 44," "Postcard From Barcelona" and "Hour of Nightmare," and the wall of Truman Bradley's laboratory during the initial opener of every episode, located behind the oscillator cone.

The magnetic ball bearing device demonstrated by Truman Bradley in "Beyond" is the same prop featured in *Earth vs. the Flying Saucers* (1956). In that movie, Hugh Marlowe demonstrates an anti-gravity device using the same prop to reverse the effects.

- After the initial filming for this pilot was completed, Bruce Bennett insisted on having the same identical billing that William Lundigan received—equal size and position on the screen. ZIV-TV obliged to please both actors, but when Basil Ruysdael insisted on first feature billing, this posed a problem. Ruysdael only had a brief scene in the entire episode. ZIV's solution was to give him top billing on the list of supporting cast (not the lead stars). Ruysdael was not satisfied when he learned about the arrangement, threatening in a letter never to endorse *Science Fiction Theatre*. This may explain why he never appears in any other episode of the series.
- The footage of the white mice in the weightlessness of space would be reused for another episode, "Marked Danger."

- The scene of the missile launching into the Earth's atmosphere in this episode utilizes the same stock footage that appears in "The Strange People at Pecos," and the same footage that closed the movie *Gog* (1954).

The April 13, 1955 issue of *Variety* reviewed this episode:

"There's too much science and too little fiction in the opener of ZIV's new series. It was a smart move on ZIV's part to start an offbeat series in a market glutted with imitations, but the show will have to be much better than the tee-off stanza to hold an audience.

"Semi-documentary approach is used, or mis-used, to put it more accurately. Narrator Truman Bradley gives little lectures on science both before and after the picture, thus leaving only about 20 minutes for the telling of the yarn. This leaves little time for proper building up of characterizations or situations.

"William Lundigan is seen as pilot of an experimental jet who zips into the stratosphere, and bails out when he sees an object he calls a flying saucer coming right at him. Key sequence, wherein the pilot sees the alleged saucer, is omitted from the vidpic, a big mistake since at the same time it eliminated suspense and tension. Viewer is told what is happening and while this might be fine for radio, on TV it is a dud. Scientists figure out pilot actually saw his fountain pen suspended in weightlessness, but later on there's proof he probably did see an unidentified object which might have been a platter.

"Ivan Tors, the pix producer, is making this series for Ziv as his TV debut. His first shot is a disappointing one, particularly in view of the unlimited horizons for a different kind of series such as scientifiction.

"William Lundigan as the pilot, Bruce Bennett, Tom Drake, Ellen Drew, Basil Ruysdael and Douglas Kennedy perform their chores well. Herbert L. Strock's direction is handicapped by the script limitations."

EPISODE #2 "TIME IS JUST A PLACE"

PRODUCTION #1002 / 4B
DATES OF PRODUCTION: FEBRUARY 8 AND 9, 1955
DIRECTED BY JACK ARNOLD

SCRIPT & STORY

FIRST DRAFT BY LEE BERG, JANUARY 21, 1955
SECOND DRAFT BY LEE BERG, JANUARY 26, 1955
FINAL DRAFT (REVISED MIMEO) BY LEE BERG, JANUARY 26, 1955
TELEPLAY BY LEE BERG, BASED ON THE SHORT STORY "SUCH INTERESTING NEIGHBORS" BY JACK FINNEY

PRODUCTION CREDITS

1ST ASST. CAMERAMAN: DICK JOHNSON (*UN-CREDITED*)
1ST CAMERAMAN: ROBERT HOFFMAN (*UN-CREDITED*)
1ST CO. GRIP: MEL BLEDSOE (*UN-CREDITED*)
2ND ASST. DIRECTOR: HARRY JONES (*UN-CREDITED*)
2ND CAMERAMAN: BUD MAUTINO (*UN-CREDITED*)
ASSISTANT DIRECTOR: ED STEIN
BOOM MAN : BILL FLANNERY (*UN-CREDITED*)
CONSTRUCTION CHIEF: ARCHIE HALL (*UN-CREDITED*)
DIRECTOR OF PHOTOGRAPHY: ROBERT HOFFMAN
FILM COORDINATOR: DONALD TAIT
FILM EDITOR: JOHN B. WOELZ
GAFFER: J.C. BARTON (*UN-CREDITED*)
MAKE-UP ARTIST: GEORGE GRAY
PROPERTY MASTER: MAX PITTMAN
RECORDER: BILL DENBY (*UN-CREDITED*)
SCRIPT SUPERVISOR: HELEN GAILEY
SCIENTIFIC ADVISOR ON ELECTRONICS AND RADAR OPERATION: MAXWELL SMITH
SET DECORATOR: LOU HAFLEY
SOUND MIXER: JAY ASHWORTH
SOUND SUPERVISOR: SIDNEY SUTHERLAND
SPECIAL EFFECTS: HARRY REDMOND, JR.
WARDROBE: ALFRED BERKE

Truman Bradley poses with Garco.

CAST: Don DeFore (Al Brown, $2,000); Peggy O'Connor (Ann Heller, $100); Warren Stevens (Ted Heller, $500); and Marie Windsor (Nell Brown, $500)

PLOT: Flight engineer Al Brown and his wife Nell become suspicious of the peculiar behavior of their new neighbors, Ted and Ann Heller. Their suspicion becomes compounded by confusion and a tinge of fear when Al, an amateur inventor and an authority on science fiction, discovers that Ted is the possessor of an automatic vacuum cleaner referred to as a "sonic broom," an X-ray flashlight and other unusual gadgets. In a discussion of the world of tomorrow, Ted paints a picture of time traveling and offers the theory that time is just a place, that in the future man will be able to travel backward into any year or month or day for recreation. Al has his suspicions but fails to find proof because the story ends with the mysterious disappearance of Ted and Ann, giving the impression that they were visitors from tomorrow.

Notes

- The small robot toy picked up by actor Warren Stevens and referred to by Don DeFore as "The Man of Tomorrow," was really Ideal's Robert the Robot, which was being sold on toy store shelves at the time this episode was produced. Had the actors turned the small crank feature on the back, the toy robot would have spoke, "I am Robert the Robot, mechanical man . . ."
- The stock footage of the model airplane melting in this episode as a result of air friction was reused for Truman Bradley's lab demonstration in the second season episode, "The Last Barrier."
- Don DeFore was one of the few actors to earn residuals for reruns of *Science Fiction Theatre.* His initial talent contract agreed on a salary of $2,000 for up to three days filming (even though production was completed in two) with $200 per showing, starting with the third repeat broadcast, on any station that choose to air the episodes more than twice.
- This is one of only two episodes of *Science Fiction Theatre* to be based on a published short story. Jack Finney's "Such Interesting Neighbors" was originally published in the January 6, 1951 issue of *Collier's*. It told the story of Al and Nell Lewis, a suspicious couple living in San Rafael, California, a

The January 6, 1951 issue of *Collier's*.

neighborhood of small houses, and their preoccupation with Ted and Ann Hellenbek. The Hellenbeks are unaware of United States currency and are the proud possessors of remarkable gadgets. Ted explains he and his wife are from South America and have come to the States to acquire patents on his inventions. In reality, the Hellenbeks are among the world's population who accepted the convenience and luxury of time traveling, to places that best suit their own temperament. Within weeks, the twenty-first century is deserted like a sinking ship as the population dwindles away to a tiny minority.

- The same short story was later adapted for an episode of TV's *Amazing Stories*. Retaining the story's original title, "Such Interesting Neighbors," it was initially telecast on March 20, 1987.
- There is a reference in this episode about a man of the future who escapes to the present. The secret police of the future come for him and take him back. This was a direct reference to Ray Bradbury's "The Fox and the Forest," which was also alluded to in Finney's time travel story from which this episode was adapted. Rather than make reference to a nightmarish

> "THEY KEPT MAKING ODD LITTLE MISTAKES—AND ALMOST UNCANNY PREDICTIONS. I GUESS WE'LL NEVER AGAIN HAVE SUCH INTERESTING NEIGHBORS . . ."
> — TEASER IN THE JANUARY 6, 1951 ISSUE OF *COLLIER'S*

future as Finney's story concluded, it makes reference to the Bradbury story instead.

- The title listed on the first draft of the script was "Such Interesting Neighbors," the same title of the Jack Finney story. By the time the final draft of the script was composed, the title had been changed to "Time is Just a Place."

A HISTORY OF GARCO

Before the drama, Truman Bradley introduces Garco, an "automated man," designed and built in 1953 by Harvey Chapman Jr., an engineer for the Garrett Supply Company of Los Angeles.

Garco was a well-oiled machine consisting of Convair gear trains, Constellation electrical actuators, and DC-6 cabin pressure regulators, plus electronic circuits and enough sheet metal to make him decent. Through the aim of a vacuum applied through his rubber-tipped fingers, he could pick up light objects with delicacy. His brain was electronic, an accumulation of six aircraft servo systems. His nervous system consisted of 1,200 feet of wire cable. A two-way radio transmitter enabled him to make pertinent remarks.

When Truman Bradley fiddled with a box of controls on the screen, this was clearly staged because Garco was really operated through a control arm and push buttons. While the television audience wasn't aware of that, what they may have known was that producer Ivan Tors had worked previously with Garco prior to *Science Fiction Theatre*. In June of 1954, Garco was called into service as "Hollywood's first mechanical press agent" for the recently released science fiction film, *Gog*. According to a press release, "Garco, who represents a million dollars in electronic research, plans a personal appearance tour of the country in behalf of the movie." Starlet Sally Mansfield, from the *Rocky Jones, Space Ranger* television series, posed with the robot for a publicity photo that was widely circulated.

Truman Bradley poses with Garco.

Truman Bradley operates Garco from a control box.

Garco hard at work.

Chapman, interviewed for the December 1953 issue of *Popular Mechanics*, felt his robot should have been taken more seriously. Thanks to Tors, Truman Bradley demonstrated the possibilities for the robot, substituting hazardous tasks men would normally be exposed to. (Bradley's pre-*Jetsons* prediction of an automatic man baby-sitting the children may have been shunned by Chapman, but the audience at the time the episode premiered probably dismissed this laugh for the advanced technology demonstrated on-screen.)

Others, however, took to using the robot for a variety of promotional gimmicks from stacking boxes at a warehouse to acting as a baseball umpire with uniform. Chapman insisted that robots like Garco could braze titanium in a vacuum, work under any degree of atmospheric pressure, handle radioactive materials—even pilot the first rocket to the moon.

Soon afterwards, Walt Disney took advantage of Garco's potential for the December 4, 1957 broadcast of *Disneyland*, "Mars and Beyond," demonstrating the robot's potential.

The April 28, 1955 issue of *Variety* reviewed this episode:

"Ziv's new scientifiction series, off to a fumbling start last week, more than compensated for that on its second offering, a spine-tingler in the best flesh-creeping tradition. 'Time' holds the viewer all the way. A well-executed expedition into the unknown is simulated by Lee Berg's teleplay, from an original by Jack Finney. Tale manages a good deal of suspense in its half hour.

"A couple visitors from the future, who have crossed the time barrier into the present, are the prime 'Place' protagonists. It seems the future is a rigidly mechanical age with joy of living, and inhabitants of that distant time are scramming into the past. The overlords of the future, worried at the escape of so many into the past, go back into time and kidnap the fugitives, returning them to the future, and that happens to the fugitive couple who topline 'Time.' Through it all there's a taut air of tension and well-manipulated fear of that unknown world of tomorrow.

"Don DeFore, seen as an inventor-neighbor of the couple from the future, plays his role very well. Marie Windsor is satisfactory, as his wife, while fine performances are given by Warren Stevens and Peggy O'Connor, the twosome from tomorrow. Jack Arnold's direction is still another plus for the stanza which ranks as a good credit for producer Ivan Tors."

EPISODE #3 "NO FOOD FOR THOUGHT"

PRODUCTION #1003 / 5B
DATES OF PRODUCTION: FEBRUARY 22 AND 23, 1955
DIRECTED BY JACK ARNOLD

SCRIPT & STORY

FIRST DRAFT BY ROBERT M. FRESCO, CIRCA FEBRUARY 16, 1955
FINAL DRAFT BY ROBERT M. FRESCO, FEBRUARY 16, 1955
TELEPLAY BY ROBERT M. FRESCO

PRODUCTION CREDITS

1ST ASST. CAMERAMAN: DICK RAWLINGS (*UN-CREDITED*)
1ST CAMERAMAN: CURT FETTERS (*UN-CREDITED*)
1ST CO. GRIP: CARL MIKSCH (*UN-CREDITED*)
2ND ASST. DIRECTOR: HARRY JONES (*UN-CREDITED*)
2ND CAMERAMAN: MONROE "MONK" ASKINS (*UN-CREDITED*)
2ND CO. GRIP: COLEY KESSINGER (*UN-CREDITED*)
ASSISTANT DIRECTOR: JOE WONDER
ASST. PROP MAN: CECIL SMITH (*UN-CREDITED*)
BOOM MAN: ELMER HAGLUND (*UN-CREDITED*)
CAMERA OPERATOR: MONROE "MONK" ASKINS
CONSTRUCTION CHIEF: ARCHIE HALL (*UN-CREDITED*)
DIRECTOR OF PHOTOGRAPHY: CURT FETTERS
FILM COORDINATOR: DONALD TAIT
FILM EDITOR: JOHN B. WOELZ
GAFFER: JIM VAIANA (*UN-CREDITED*)
MAKE-UP ARTIST: GEORGE GRAY
PROPERTY MASTER: MAX PITTMAN
RECORDER: BOB POST (*UN-CREDITED*)
SCRIPT SUPERVISOR: GLORIA MORGAN
SCIENTIFIC ADVISOR ON ELECTRONICS AND RADAR OPERATION: MAXWELL SMITH
SET DECORATOR: LYLE REIFSNIDER
SET LABOR: SOL INVERSO (*UN-CREDITED*)
SOUND MIXER: GARRY HARRIS
SOUND SUPERVISOR: SIDNEY SUTHERLAND
SPECIAL EFFECTS: HARRY REDMOND, JR.

Truman Bradley in "No Food for Thought."

WARDROBE: ALFRED BERKE

CAST: Stanley Andrews (Sheriff Simpson, $100); Hal K. Dawson (Silas Baker, $100); John Howard (Dr. Paul Novak, $500); Otto Kruger (Prof. Emanuel M. Hall, $1,250); Clarence Lung (Dr. Lee Su-Yin, $75); Vera Miles (Dr. Jan Corey, $500); and Hank Patterson (Joe Green, $75)

PLOT: An unexplained corpse named John Corey upsets the peace and quiet of the little desert town of Santa Rosa. Investigating, the young County Health Officer discovers that a Nobel Prize-winning biologist is living in seclusion on the desert doing research into nutrients and artificial food. Because of the growing population, Professor Hall and his associates have been trying to create a synthetic nutrient that will give human beings the needed vitamins and minerals they require. Instead, the Professor has created a mixed blessing because the nutrient dramatically decreases the immune system and creates a new virus. Following a number of clues, the officer accuses the scientist of testing this synthetic nutrient on himself and his co-workers. Professor Hall admits this and discloses that after taking the nutrient, they cannot return to eating food normally. John Corey died from the virus and they fear they will become victims of the same. Rather than fight a losing battle, the Health Officer assists the scientists in finding a safer nutrient to combat the virus and—thanks to a series of blood transfusions and anti-bodies—saves their lives, thus opening the road for a successful artificial nutrient for mankind.

Notes

- Actor Charles Wagenheim was originally slated for the role of Joe Green. Wagenheim took ill the day before filming so actor Hank Patterson took his place.
- This episode was produced under the title, "The Hot House People," the same title featured on the front page of the shooting script.
- This plot may have been inspired by an article in the November 1954 issue of *Scientific American* entitled "How Antibodies Are Made," by Sir Macfarlane Burnet.

The May 5, 1955 issue of *Variety* reviewed this episode:

"'Food,' meaty scientifiction, maintains a fast and suspenseful pace. Jack Arnold's direction is a big plus; as is Robert M. Fresco's teleplay, well constructed and original in its conception. Yarn deals with a few scientists who isolate themselves in a desert, seeking to evolve a substitute for food which can be taken like pills. They believe, with the world's population continually increasing, there won't be enough food eventually for mankind. Their experiments backfire and one man dies.

"Otto Kruger is very good as the dedicated scientist; Vera Miles and Clarence Lung are fine as the aides, and John Howard gives a well-polished picture of the local doctor who stumbles onto the hush-hush project and saves the scientists. The quality of the production is the only jarring factor. Screen was blurry and camera work not good."

EPISODE #4 "OUT OF NOWHERE"

Production #1004 / 3B
Dates of Production: February 3 and 4, 1955
Directed by Herbert L. Strock

SCRIPT & STORY

First Draft by Donn Mullally, December 3, 1954
Second Draft by Donn Mullally, January 19, 1955
Third Draft by Donn Mullally, January 26, 1955
Final Draft by Donn Mullally, January 31, 1955
Teleplay by Donn Mullally

PRODUCTION CREDITS

1st Asst. Cameraman: Dick Johnson (*un-credited*)
1ts Co. Grip: Mel Bledsoe (*un-credited*)
2nd Asst. Director: Harry Jones (*un-credited*)
2nd Cameraman: Bud Mautino (*un-credited*)
3rd Grip: Delmar Hollaway (*un-credited*)
Assistant Director: Joe Wonder
Asst. Prop Man: Cecil Smith (*un-credited*)
Boom Man: Bill Flannery (*un-credited*)
Construction Chief: Archie Hall (*un-credited*)
Director of Photography: Robert Hoffman
Film Coordinator: Donald Tait
Film Editor: John B. Woelz
Gaffer: J.C. Barton (*un-credited*)
Property Master: Max Pittman
Recorder: Bill Denby (*un-credited*)
Script Supervisor: Helen Gailey
Scientific Advisor on Electronics and Radar Operation: Maxwell Smith
Set Decorator: Lou Hafley
Set Labor: Phil Casazza (*un-credited*)
Sound Mixer: Jay Ashworth
Sound Supervisor: Sidney Sutherland
Special Effects: Harry Redmond, Jr.
Wardrobe: Alfred Berke

Truman Bradley in a tan suit with a model plane in "Out of Nowhere."

CAST: Richard Arlen (Dr. Osbourne, $750); Elsie Baker (the scrub lady, $70); Jess Barker (Dr. Jeffries, $150); Dallas Boyd (Henry, the elevator operator, $70); Grant Davis (the man at lunch stand #1, $70); Craig Duncan (Robb, $70); Hal Forrest (Fleming, $70); Jonathan Hale (Dr. Hugo Milton, $125); Frank Hunt (the man at lunch stand #2, $70); Gus Hyland (the maintenance man, $70); Joe La Cava (the F.B.I. man, $70); Carlyle Mitchell (General Kenyon, $125); Irving Mitchell (the superintendent, $70); Bob Peterson (uniformed policeman, $70); Ben Pollock (Dr. Kennedy, $70); Gail Robinson (the milkman, $70); and Robert Templeton (the general's aide, $70)

Plot: There is tragedy at the price of progress when a flight of migratory birds crashes into the King Tower Building on a dark, foggy night. When several red bats are found amongst those birds . . . it becomes another matter altogether. It's a suspension of natural law . . . a bat being equipped with a kind of natural sonar which should prevent such accidents. Ornithologist Dr. Osborne, an expert on bird migration, is called in to investigate and suspects a synthetic vibration. With the cooperation of the U.S. Air Force, they discover a secret microwave signal that is being transmitted toward the building from an unknown stationary point. The mystery beam is traced and they soon expose a Communist attempt to cripple the U.S. radar network protecting the United States from foreign attack.

Notes

- This is the only episode in which Truman Bradley receives on-screen credit as the host of the series. This was acknowledged during the closing credits.
- The plot for this episode was tipped off when a colony of bats suddenly crashed into a tall building. Scientists were called in to solve this mystery and discovered that the bats' sense of direction could be upset. By projecting their findings they got a location for the machine that was fouling up the radar. Thus a great disaster was averted. The scientific fact was that a flock of birds did crash into a New York building.
- Actor Leo Needham was originally slated for the role of Dr. Kennedy, but actor Ben Pollock got the job when Needham was unavailable for filming.
- The opening stock shot of the antenna was also used in "Time Is Just A Place."
- The entire episode was filmed on Stages 1 and 2 at the American National Studio.
- The first draft of this script was entitled "Bat Story." The second draft was entitled "Beam from Nowhere." Beginning with the third draft, the title was "Out of Nowhere."
- Donn Mullally wrote this teleplay based on Donald R. Griffin's article in the March 1954 issue of *Scientific American*, titled "Bird Sonar."

The May 12, 1955 issue of *Variety* reviewed this episode:

"Even the most avid scientifiction fan is apt to be bored with the type of stuff presented in the latest in ZIV's new series, 'Nowhere.' Apparently with an eye on low budgets, action is kept at a minimum and talkiness at a maximum. Result: static that holds little interest.

"Teleplaywright Donn Mullally's yarn revolves about a mysterious sound beam which fouls up the U.S. protective radar system. First it's suspected the source is a space station from another planet, but denouement reveals beam is directed by enemy agents out to sabotage out radar setup. Premise is interesting, but not its presentation. Long, scientific discussions on radar and its ramifications don't make for pop-consumption TV entertainment.

"Richard Arlen, Jess Barker, Carlyle Mitchell, Irving Mitchell and Jonathan Hale do the best they can under adverse circumstances. Herbert L. Strock's direction lacks imagination."

EPISODE #5 "Y··O··R··D··"

PRODUCTION #1005 / 2B
DATES OF PRODUCTION: DECEMBER 22 AND 23, 1954
DIRECTED BY LEON BENSON

SCRIPT & STORY

FIRST DRAFT BY LEON BENSON, NOVEMBER 24, 1954
SECOND DRAFT BY LEON BENSON AND GEORGE VAN MARTER, DECEMBER 2, 1954
THIRD DRAFT BY LEON BENSON AND GEORGE VAN MARTER, DECEMBER 13, 1954
REVISED PAGES DATED DECEMBER 17, 1954
TELEPLAY BY LEON BENSON AND GEORGE VAN MARTER FROM AN ORIGINAL STORY BY IVAN TORS AND GEORGE VAN MARTER

PRODUCTION CREDITS

1ST ASST. CAMERAMAN: DICK RAWLINGS (*UN-CREDITED*)
1ST CO. GRIP: MEL BLEDSOE (*UN-CREDITED*)
2ND ASST. DIRECTOR: BOBBY RAY (*UN-CREDITED*)
ASSISTANT DIRECTOR: ED STEIN

Boom Man: Elmer Haglund (*un-credited*)
Camera Operator: Monroe "Monk" Askins
Construction Chief: Archie Hall (*un-credited*)
Director of Photography: Robert Hoffman
Film Coordinator: Donald Tait
Film Editor: Charles Craft, A.C.E.
Gaffer: Joseph Wharton (*un-credited*)
Make-up Artist: George Gray
Property Master: Max Pittman
Recorder: Bob Post (*un-credited*)
Script Supervisor: Larry Lund
Scientific Advisor on Electronics and Radar Operation: Maxwell Smith
Set Decorator: Lou Hafley
Set Labor: Sal Inverso (*un-credited*)
Sound Mixer: Garry Harris
Sound Supervisor: Sidney Sutherland
Special Effects: Harry Redmond, Jr.
Wardrobe: Alfred Berke

Cast: Judith Ames (Edna Miner, $75); John Bryant (Millican, $70); Louis Jean Heydt (Colonel Van Dyke, $150); Clark Howat (Captain Boyce, $70); DeForest Kelley (Captain Hall, $70); Walter Kingsford (Dr. H.J. Lawton, $150); and Kenneth Tobey (Lt. Dunne, $300)

Plot: An Arctic weather station near the Magnetic Pole reports that scientists stationed there have displayed unusual mental powers including having the psychic ability of reading each other's minds. A parapsychologist in Washington D.C. is sent out to investigate this strange phenomenon. Recording the brainwaves of the scientists, he finds that their brain cells are extremely active, and that the electric charges in the neurons are much stronger than those in other latitudes. A definite pattern is indicated. The impulses are decoded and it is established that the men are receiving telepathic messages from a space ship that has lost its way and has fallen into the gravitational pull of the Earth. The passengers of the ship are desperate and are sending out telepathic signals for help while the Earth's pull keeps

DeForest Kelley, Judith Ames and Walter Kingsford in "Y‥O‥R‥D‥."

attracting them toward our atmosphere. They know that when the ship reaches the Earth's atmosphere it will be destroyed by heat from the resulting friction . . . but the inevitable happens. We, on Earth, witness a gigantic fireball as the people from another planet are destroyed. The telepathic stimulation ceases but our scientists are sure that sooner or later people from another planet will make contact . . . and they will be peaceful.

Notes

- The title listed for this episode entry is the exact spelling featured on the opening title screen. On production sheets, it is specifically noted in pencil from 1955 to keep the title spelled "Yord" with upper and lowercase letters.
- Michael Fox supplied the un-credited voice coming over the speaker.
- Actress Judith Ames, a frequent co-star on *Science Fiction Theatre*, would later be known as Rachel Ames when she appeared regularly as Nurse Audrey on the soap *General*

Hospital for more than forty years.
- The opening stock footage of the Science Hall (side and front view) is the same footage later reused in five other first season episodes: "Death at 2 A.M.," "A Visit From Dr. Pliny," "The Unexplored," "Project 44" and "Operation Flypaper."
- The photo of the rocket blasting through the Earth's atmosphere that hangs on the wall during the beginning of the second act is the same original artwork that appears on screen during the opening credits of *Gog*.
- The original plot proposal by Ivan Tors and George Van Marter (reprinted in this book) offers a deeper glimpse into the character of Edna Miller, who, after arriving at the wintery base, remains in a constant state of unconsciousness. Of all the plot proposals, the one for this episode was the longest in length.

The May 19, 1955 issue of *Variety* reviewed this episode:

"Scientifiction addicts will enjoy 'Y..O..R..D..,' a well-done yarn about spaceships from another planet, magnetic waves, etc. One of the better stanzas in this series, it sustains interest all the way.

"Presence of a spaceship somewhere above the North Pole is detected when weather personnel stationed there receive strange messages which give them strong mental telepathic powers. Investigation determines the presence of the spaceship which is in trouble and sending out an SOS—spelled Y..O..R..D.. in the other planet's lingo. Attempts to save it via mental telepathic messages fail and it burns to a crisp in its plunge toward Earth. It's questionable U.S. intelligence could decipher an SOS sent in an unknown language from an unknown planet, but overall quality of the vidpic compensates for that point.

"There are good performances by Walter Kingsford, Judith Ames, Louis Jean Heydt, DeForest Kelley and Ken Tobey, and fine direction by Leon Benson."

EPISODE #6 "STRANGER IN THE DESERT"

Production #1006 / 7B
Dates of Production: March 5 and 7, 1955
Directed by Henry S. Kesler

SCRIPT & STORY

First Draft (annotated) by Curtis Kenyon and Robert M. Fresco, no date
Revised Draft by Curtis Kenyon and Robert M. Fresco, March 10, 1955
Teleplay by Curtis Kenyon and Robert M. Fresco, based on an original short story by Ivan Tors

PRODUCTION CREDITS

1st Asst. Cameraman: Jim Bell (*un-credited*)
1st Co. Grip: Mel Bledsoe (*un-credited*)
2nd Asst. Director: Harry Jones (*un-credited*)
2nd Cameraman: Bill Mautino (*un-credited*)
2nd Co. Grip: Ted Mathew (*un-credited*)
Assistant Director: Joe Wonder
Boom Man: Jim Flannery (*un-credited*)
Chief Set Electrician: Joseph Wharton
Construction Chief: Archie Hall (*un-credited*)
Director of Photography: Robert Hoffman
Electrician: Joseph Wharton (*un-credited*)
Film Coordinator: Donald Tait
Film Editor: John B. Woelz
Gaffer: J.C. Barton (*un-credited*)
Make-up Artist: George Gray
Property Master: Max Pittman
Recorder: Larry Golding (*un-credited*)
Script Supervisor: Helen Gailey
Scientific Advisor on Electronics and Radar Operation: Maxwell Smith
Set Decorator: Lyle Reifsnider
Set Labor: Sol Inverso (*un-credited*)
Sound Mixer: Jay Ashworth

SOUND SUPERVISOR: SIDNEY SUTHERLAND
SPECIAL EFFECTS: HARRY REDMOND, JR.
WARDROBE: ALFRED BERKE

CAST: Ray Bennett (Deputy Hayes, $75); Gene Evans (Bud Porter, $1,000); Lowell Gilmore (Mr. Ballard, $300); John Mitchum (Sheriff Grayson, $75); and Marshall Thompson (Gil Collins, $500)

PLOT: Gil Collins and Bud Porter, two prospectors searching for uranium in the Utah desert, defy warnings from the local authorities. After a hot find on their Geiger counter, they discover the area is occupied by Mr. Ballard, a hermit-style dweller who claims his only interest is the local plant life. Suspicious, Bud suspects the old man is lying and sets out for town to verify whether Ballard truly filed a claim. If he hasn't, Bud plans to file one for themselves and return to force the old man off the land . . . and kill him if necessary. Gil remains behind to keep tabs on Ballard, who claims his home land is unable to support life and he seeks plants that might help replenish the oxygen levels. Gil, suspicious, follows the old man into the desert and finding an abandoned mine, forces Ballard inside, hoping to find uranium deposits. Ballard saves Gil's life when the cave-in pins Gil to the ground. Before Ballard leaves, he tells Gil to avoid hunting for riches. Real value is what you make of life, just like the plants he digs up. Bud returns to find Ballard has disappeared and no signs of the uranium. Evidence on the ground outside the mine suggests Ballard departed by means of a spaceship, the source of the radioactivity that was initially registered on the Geiger counter.

NOTES
- This is the first of only two episodes of the series that credits Joseph Wharton, who was the chief set electrician during the entire first season.
- The first day of production consisted of location shots at Bronson canyon. Rather than rent a bus, a green Plymouth station wagon, Ivan Tors' personal station wagon and a jeep were used. The cast and crew returned on the morning of the

This map of the solar system in this episode is also featured in two second season episodes, "Sun Gold" and "The Miracle Hour."

Make-up artist George Gray revealing his trophy autograph collection.

second day to finish location shots, before returning to the studio to film interior shots. This was one of the few episodes produced on a Saturday.
- The first draft script for this episode was titled "Eagle in the Sky," but changed to "Stranger in the Desert" by the final draft.
- The green police car in this episode is really the green Plymouth station wagon disguised as a police car. The cameraman made sure the back half of the station wagon was not featured on the screen so the audience did not realize it was a station wagon.
- A number of the scenes featuring the jeep riding along the rough terrain do not have Marshall Thompson and Gene Evans inside. Stand-ins Grant Davis and Bob Lawson are the men driving and riding in the jeep, but with the jeep far enough in the distance, the TV audience would never have known the difference.

The May 26, 1955, issue of *Variety* reviewed this episode:

"Producer Ivan Tors has fallen into the habit of letting his audience decide what the end of his scientifiction plots is, and while this may intrigue once or twice, on a week-to-week basis it becomes downright exasperating, much like reading a book with the final chapter missing. This same weakness is inherent in 'Stranger,' yarn about uranium hunters in the desert. They come across a weird stranger who explains he's plant-hunting, and eventually disappears, apparently returning to his planet. So much more is unsaid than said it becomes a guessing game, and a monotonous one at that.

"Marshall Thompson, Gene Evans and Lowell Gilmore topline, and do the best they can under adverse circumstances. Ditto for director Henry S. Kesler. Only thing wrong with the teleplay by Curtis Kenyon and Robert M. Fresco, from an original yarn by Tors, is they didn't finish it."

EPISODE #7 "SOUND OF MURDER"

PRODUCTION #1007 / 8B
DATES OF PRODUCTION: MARCH 15 AND 16, 1955
DIRECTED BY JACK ARNOLD

SCRIPT & STORY
FIRST DRAFT BY STUART JEROME, MARCH 7, 1955
REVISED PAGES DATED MARCH 8 AND 9, 1955
FINAL DRAFT BY STUART JEROME, MARCH 9, 1955
TELEPLAY BY STUART JEROME, FROM AN ORIGINAL STORY BY IVAN TORS

PRODUCTION CREDITS
1ST ASST. CAMERAMAN: JIM BELL (*UN-CREDITED*)
1ST CO. GRIP: MEL BLEDSOE (*UN-CREDITED*)
2ND ASST. DIRECTOR: HARRY JONES (*UN-CREDITED*)
2ND CAMERAMAN: BUD MAUTINO (*UN-CREDITED*)
2ND CO. GRIP: TOM MATHEWS (*UN-CREDITED*)
ASSISTANT DIRECTOR: EDDIE BERNOUDY
ASST. PROP MAN: STAN WALTERS (*UN-CREDITED*)
BOOM MAN: BILL FLANNERY (*UN-CREDITED*)
CONSTRUCTION CHIEF: ARCHIE HALL (*UN-CREDITED*)
DIRECTOR OF PHOTOGRAPHY: ROBERT HOFFMAN
FILM COORDINATOR: DONALD TAIT
FILM EDITOR: THOMAS SCOTT (*CREDITED*) AND JOHN B. WOELZ (*UN-CREDITED*)
GAFFER: J.C. BARTON (*UN-CREDITED*)
MAKE-UP ARTIST: GEORGE GRAY
PROPERTY MASTER: MAX PITTMAN
RECORDER: BILL DENBY (*UN-CREDITED*)
SCRIPT SUPERVISOR: HELEN GAILEY
SCIENTIFIC ADVISOR ON ELECTRONICS AND RADAR OPERATION: MAXWELL SMITH
SET DECORATOR: LYLE REIFSNIDER
SOUND MIXER: JAY ASHWORTH
SOUND SUPERVISOR: SIDNEY SUTHERLAND
SPECIAL EFFECTS: HARRY REDMOND, JR.
WARDROBE: ALFRED BERKE

CAST: Whit Bissell (Mr. Grayson, $200); Wheaton Chambers (Prof. Van Kamp, $150); Russ Conway (Charles S. Lyons, $300); Rod De Medici (the man); Howard Duff (Dr. Tim Mathews, $2,000); Edward Earle (Dr. Joe Kerwin, $100); Ann Howard (the woman); Julie Jordan (the secretary, $70); Christine Larson (Wilma Mathews, $250); Charlotte Lawrence (the telephone operator, $70); Charles Maxwell (Security Agent Randall, $100); Ruth Perrott (Mary Kerwin, $150); Paul Peters (guard #1, $70); and Olan Soule (Mr. Wilkins, $75)

PLOT: During a top-secret conclave of scientists in Washington, one of the group, Dr. Kerwin, receives a phone message from his superior, Dr. Tom Mathews, to meet him in a certain hotel room. Kerwin is later discovered murdered, and key papers concerning a top-secret project are missing. Mathews is arrested both because of the phone call and more importantly because he had disappeared for six hours that evening, deliberately losing an FBI agent assigned to guard him. Tom's only explanation is that he went for a walk. But the ensuing Justice Department investigation turns up a number of phone calls which Mathews allegedly made to the other scientists on the same project, in each case requesting secret information. Mathews is indicted, regardless of how much he claims innocence. His case seems hopeless, until Mathews and a scientist friend mathematically figures out how the phone calls were made, and how not only his voice was duplicated, but also his knowledge of the workings of the project, through the use of an intricate instrument called a "Sound Synthesizer," used to replicate another man's voice and calculates an answer to a question by the recipient. By this means they trap the real murderer and traitor.

NOTES
- This episode was produced under the title "Murder by Sound."
- The insert shot with the hand pointing out the details of the sound synthesizer was stand-in Paul Cristo's hand.
- The Washington D.C. stock footage was used in a other ZIV-TV productions including numerous episodes of *The Man Called X*.

- The map of a small island hanging on the wall in this episode can be found hanging on the wall in other episodes of *Science Fiction Theatre*.

The June 2, 1955 issue of *Variety* reviewed this episode:

"'Murder,' a whodunit with scientific ramifications, is one of producer Ivan Tors' better entries, telling at rapid pace a good yarn via generally fine thesping. More in the science genre than scientifiction, Stuart Jerome's teleplay is suspenseful.

"Howard Duff, a scientist, engages in top-secret work, is accused of giving away some top U.S. secrets to the enemy. Tossed in the clink, Duff, by scientific deduction, learns how he was framed and who did the framing—a colleague. Episode, well developed, builds to an exciting climax.

"Emoting is good all along the line; top honors go to Duff's effective, restrained performance. He's given fine assistance by Wheaton Chambers, Christine Larson, Whit Bissell, Edward Earle, Charles Maxwell, Olan Soule. Jack Arnold's direction is a strong asset."

EPISODE #8 "THE BRAIN OF JOHN EMERSON"

PRODUCTION #1008 / 6B
DATES OF PRODUCTION: MARCH 1 AND 2, 1955
DIRECTED BY LESLIE GOODWINS

SCRIPT & STORY

FIRST DRAFT BY RIK VOLLAERTS, FEBRUARY 21, 1955
REVISED PAGES DATED FEBRUARY 25 AND MARCH 8, 1955
FINAL DRAFT BY RIK VOLLAERTS, MARCH 8, 1955
TELEPLAY BY RIK VOLLAERTS

PRODUCTION CREDITS

1ST ASST. CAMERAMAN: JIM BELL (*UN-CREDITED*)
1ST CO. GRIP: MEL BLEDSOE (*UN-CREDITED*)
2ND ASST. DIRECTOR: HARRY JONES (*UN-CREDITED*)
2ND CAMERAMAN: BILL MAUTINO (*UN-CREDITED*)
2ND CO. GRIP: TED MATHEW (*UN-CREDITED*)

ASSISTANT DIRECTOR: MARTY MOSS
ASST. PROP MAN: STAN WALTERS (*UN-CREDITED*)
BOOM MAN: JIM FLANNERY (*UN-CREDITED*)
CONSTRUCTION CHIEF: ARCHIE HALL (*UN-CREDITED*)
DIRECTOR OF PHOTOGRAPHY: ROBERT HOFFMAN
FILM COORDINATOR: DONALD TAIT
FILM EDITOR: JOHN B. WOELZ
GAFFER: J.C. BARTON (*UN-CREDITED*)
MAKE-UP ARTIST: GEORGE GRAY
PROPERTY MASTER: MAX PITTMAN
RECORDER: BILL DENBY (*UN-CREDITED*)
SCRIPT SUPERVISOR: HELEN GAILEY
SCIENTIFIC ADVISOR ON ELECTRONICS AND RADAR OPERATION: MAXWELL SMITH
SET DECORATOR: LOU HAFLEY (*UN-CREDITED*) AND LYLE REIFSNIDER (*CREDITED*)
SOUND MIXER: JAY ASHWORTH
SOUND SUPERVISOR: SIDNEY SUTHERLAND
SPECIAL EFFECTS: HARRY REDMOND, JR.
WARDROBE: ALFRED BERKE

CAST: Jackie Blanchard (the nurse, $70); Ellen Drew (Mrs. Turner, $750); Michael Fox (Dr. Franklin, $250); Joyce Holden (Joan, $200); John Howard (John Emerson, $500); Charles Maxwell (Dr. Norman Turner, *voice only*, $75); and Robert F. Simon (Capt. Damon, $150)

PLOT: John Emerson, a police sergeant, suffers multiple gunshot wounds to the head. A bullet is removed from his brain by a miraculous operation. It takes three months before Emerson regains consciousness. Discharged from the hospital, he finds his mental powers changed, his intelligence increased and he has a compulsion for medical research. His I.Q. was 119 before the injury, but after the surgery it is 173. He knows the names of the lab animals and equipment in Dr. Turner's office, but never knew them beforehand. This scares Emerson because he never met Dr. Turner. He was in a coma when the doctor treated him. After searching the laboratory of Dr. Turner, Emerson discovers the truth. The operating surgeon, a dying man, had successfully transferred his own memory units electronically to John Emerson's brain cells. John's pattern of behavior now explained, he agrees to pick up where Dr. Turner left off in his research.

Notes

- Actor Michael Fox, who appeared in a large number of television programs produced by the ZIV studios, recalled to interviewer Tom Weaver: "I did six or eight *Science Fiction Theatres*, including one called 'The Brain of John Emerson.' It was about a brain transplant operation—really, it was sort of a takeoff on *Donovan's Brain*. I did that with an actor I liked immensely, John Howard, and that was one of my all-time favorite roles. I liked working with Howard, and the script I loved. I played the psychiatrist in it."
- Produced under the title of "The Brain Transfusion."
- Jackie Blanchard, who plays the un-credited role of the nurse in the beginning of this episode, played supporting roles in dozens of television programs including *Peter Gunn* and *Gunsmoke*. This episode of *Science Fiction Theatre* marked her television debut.

The June 9, 1955 issue of *Variety* reviewed this episode:

"Science, says narrator Truman Bradley, is more amazing than fiction, and this figment of fantasy sets out to prove it. This it does and interestingly if the looker doesn't begin to ask himself questions and cast a doubt on the whole thing.

"Only five percent of the entire brain area is utilized, says a scalpel wielder, who proceeds to explore the unused gray matter when a police sergeant is brought to surgery with a bullet in his brain. The patient recovers, but the medic dies of a heart attack, leaving behind a heritage of his experiments with a memory machine. What has been stored up in the doctor's mind is transferred to the striper from headquarters and his IQ rises from 119 to 173, all of which baffles science and confounds fiction. At times it becomes confusing, this sudden change in his behavior pattern, but followers of this series must be conditioned to these miracles.

"John Howard, Ellen Drew, Joyce Holden, Robert Simon and Michael Fox play it straight for full dramatic impact without noteworthy acquittal, and the direction of Leslie Goodwins from Rik

Vollaert's script is estimable. Truman Bradley is a voice double of KRCA's Jack Latham and gives the narration authoritative clarity." *

EPISODE #9 "SPIDER, INC."

PRODUCTION #1009 / 9B
DATES OF PRODUCTION: MARCH 24 AND 25, 1955
DIRECTED BY JACK ARNOLD

SCRIPT & STORY

FIRST DRAFT BY JERRY SACKHEIM, MARCH 11, 1955
REVISED PAGES DATED MARCH 21 AND 24, 1955
FINAL DRAFT BY JERRY SACKHEIM, MARCH 24, 1955
TELEPLAY BY JERRY SACKHEIM

PRODUCTION CREDITS

1ST ASST. CAMERAMAN: BOB HAUSER (*UN-CREDITED*)
1ST CO. GRIP: MEL BLEDSOE (*UN-CREDITED*)
2ND ASST. DIRECTOR: BOBBY RAY (*UN-CREDITED*)
2ND CAMERAMAN: BUD MAUTINO (*UN-CREDITED*)
2ND CO. GRIP: TOM MATHEWS (*UN-CREDITED*)
ASSISTANT DIRECTOR: ERNIE BERNOUDY
ASST. PROP MAN: CECIL SMITH (*UN-CREDITED*)
BOOM MAN: BILL FLANNERY (MARCH 24 ONLY) AND ELMER HAGLUND (MARCH 25 ONLY) (*BOTH UN-CREDITED*)
CONSTRUCTION CHIEF: ARCHIE HALL (*UN-CREDITED*)
DIRECTOR OF PHOTOGRAPHY: MONROE "MONK" ASKINS
FILM COORDINATOR: DONALD TAIT
FILM EDITOR: JOHN B. WOELZ
GAFFER: JUDD LEROY (*UN-CREDITED*)
MAKE-UP ARTIST: GEORGE GRAY
PROPERTY MASTER: MAX PITTMAN
RECORDER: BILL DENBY (MARCH 24 ONLY) AND BOB POST (MARCH 25 ONLY) (*BOTH UN-CREDITED*)

---

* *Variety* incorrectly referred to the title of this episode as "The Brain of John Amerson."

Script Supervisor: Dick Chaffee
Scientific Advisor on Electronics and Radar Operation: Maxwell Smith
Set Decorator: Lou Hafley
Sound Mixers: Jay Ashworth (March 24 only) and Garry Harris (March 25 only)
Sound Supervisor: Sidney Sutherland
Special Effects: Harry Redmond, Jr.
Wardrobe: Alfred Berke

Cast: Phil Arnold (Schmidt, $75); Gene Barry (Joe Ferguson, $1,000); Robert Clarke (Frank, $75); Frank Hanley (Dr. Hemingway, $75); George Meader (Mr. Malloy, $75); Herbert Rudley (McAdoo, $150); Ludwig Stossel (Mr. Rodgers, $300); and Audrey Totter (Ellie Ferguson, $1,500)

Plot: Joe Ferguson, an assistant geologist working for a big oil company, finds in a second-hand store a piece of transparent rock (fossilized amber) with a giant spider imbedded in it. He has a wild hunch, but no money to fund the research. His expectant wife, Ellie, is concerned for their baby, but eventually reminds herself babies need love—not money. He takes on creditors who stake him in buying the rare specimen and thanks to his wife, forms Spider, Inc. Through lab testing, Joe proves that the stone and the spider are fifty million years old and the bubble inside the rock is a sample composition of the Earth's atmosphere from that time and age. Analyzing the oily mass inside, through the spider and the stone, he learns something about how oil was formed from vegetable and animal matter; This turns out to be an important discovery in the future creation of synthetic oil and a new age dawns.

Notes
- During production, the original title of this episode was "Spider, Incorporated." Before filming was completed, production notes from Ivan Tors specifically ensured the second word in the title be abbreviated.
- Stand-ins Rod De Medici and Ann Howard supply the insert shot consisting of Gene Barry's chipping of the rock, and

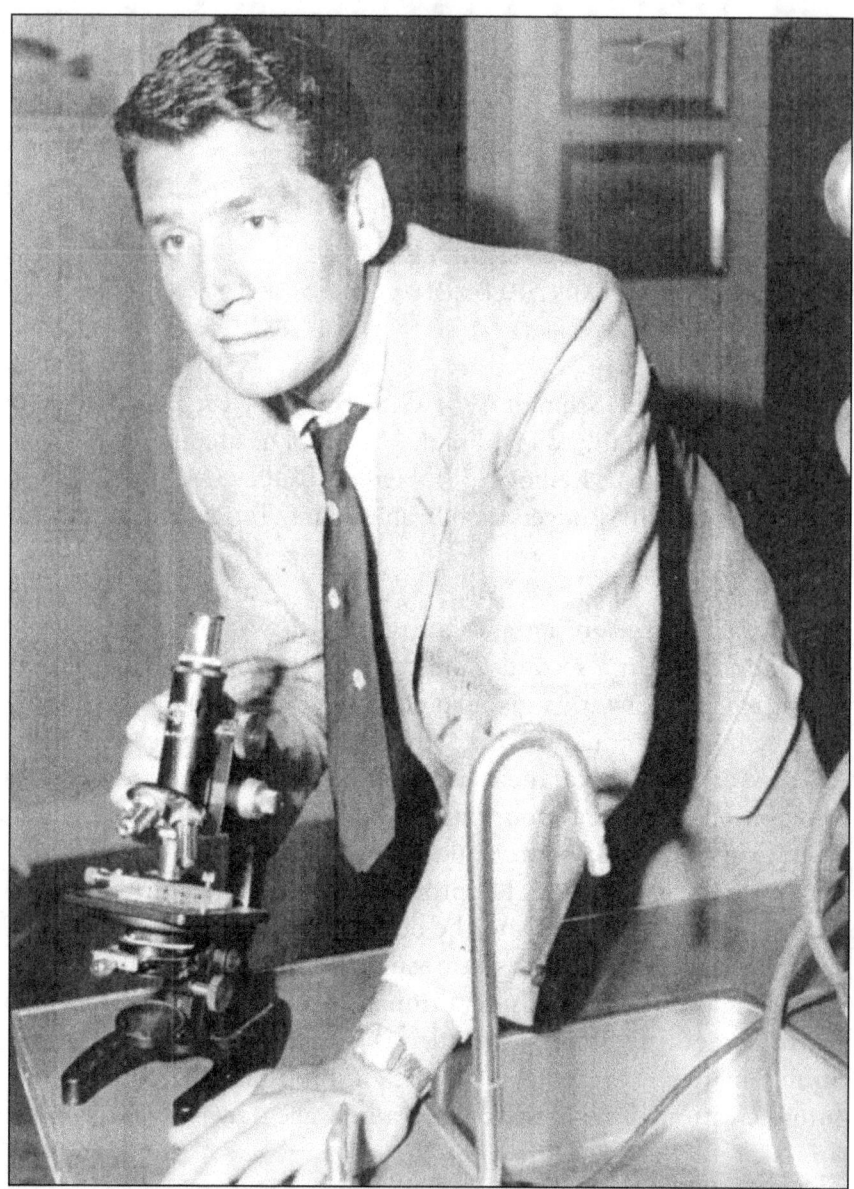

Gene Barry poses for this publicity shot in "Spider, Inc."

De Medici's hands supplied the insert shot of Barry's hands holding the rock between his fingers.
- Truman Bradley reported to the set at 5:30 p.m. on the second day, for filming the lab demonstrations for production 8b, which would ultimately be scrapped and re-shot later.

- Robert Clarke, who plays the role of Frank, was only paid $75 for his role, possibly one of the two lowest paid actors to appear on the series with a significant speaking role. (The other is Judith Ames in "Y··O··R··D··.")
- The electrical equipment on Truman Bradley's demonstration table—described as the carbon dating machine—and the green speaker, were really fake props that were reused in a number of *Science Fiction Theatre* dramas. The green speaker was the same one in the pilot, "Beyond," from which the Air Force pilot's voice supposedly originated.
- Jerry Sackheim's first draft of the script was titled "Wolf Spider."
- Jerry Sackheim wrote this teleplay based on Loren C. Eiseley's article "Fossil Man," in the December 1953 issue of *Scientific American*.

The June 22, 1955 issue of *Variety* reviewed this episode:
"Format of this series is given enough motivation in this latest segment to get by with followers of the program. Its by-plot structure is pretty flimsy, but the idea itself keeps the ball rolling.

"Yarn deals with a young geologist looking into the past of 50,000,000 years ago for modern advancement. When he discovers a piece of fossilized amber with a large spider encased, he's convinced it contains the secret of nature's process for making petroleum and makes use of latest scientific devices toward reaching his goals. One of these is a carbon dating process, explained in detail by narrator Truman Bradley in a lab demonstration of the story behind the spider specimen, an interesting recital.

"Gene Barry handles himself well as the scientist and Audrey Totter is his wife, in a part, however, dragged in by the heels. Ludwig Stossel provides a warm note in a character role, and Jack Arnold's direction of Jerry Sackheim's teleplay progresses at a good pace."

EPISODE #10 "DEATH AT 2 A.M."

Production #1010 / 10B
Dates of Production: April 1 and 2, 1955
Directed by Henry S. Kesler

SCRIPT & STORY
Final Draft by Ellis Marcus, March 30, 1955
Teleplay by Ellis Marcus, based on an original story by Ellis Marcus and Ivan Tors

PRODUCTION CREDITS
1st Asst. Cameraman: Jim Bell (*un-credited*)
1st Co. Grip: Carl Miksch (*un-credited*)
2nd Asst. Director: Bobby Ray (*un-credited*)
2nd Co. Grip: Coley Kessinger (*un-credited*)
Assistant Director: Ed Stein
Boom Man: Elmer Haglund (*un-credited*)
Camera Operator: Dick Rawlings
Construction Chief: Archie Hall (*un-credited*)
Director of Photography: Curt Fetters
Film Coordinator: Donald Tait
Film Editor: John B. Woelz
Gaffer: Joseph Wharton (*un-credited*)
Make-up Artist: George Gray
Property Master: Max Pittman
Recorder: John Allen (*un-credited*)
Script Supervisor: Larry Lund
Scientific Advisor on Electronics and Radar Operation: Maxwell Smith
Set Decorator: Lyle Reifsnider
Sound Mixer: Garry Harris
Sound Supervisor: Sidney Sutherland
Special Effects: Harry Redmond, Jr.
Wardrobe: Alfred Berke

CAST: Ted de Corsia (Sgt. Cox, $150); Douglas Henderson (Murray Lewis, $75); Skip Homeier (Bill Reynolds, $1,000); Virginia Hunter

(Paula Kennedy, $75); and John Qualen (Professor Samuel Avery, $500)

Plot: The violent death of ex-convict Eric Munson brings police to the University laboratory of Professor Samuel Avery and his assistant, Bill Reynolds. Evidence shows that Munson was attempting to blackmail Reynolds, who is considered the prime suspect in the crime. Reynolds, however, proves he was at the University at the time of the murder. Police Sergeant Cox remains suspicious of him. The true culprit is Professor Avery who somehow managed to kill Munson to protect his young assistant. The question is, how did a small man like Avery manage to strangle a large brute like Munson? The answer, Reynolds soon discovers, lies in Avery's secret experiments into the chemistry of muscle contraction. Avery has discovered a compound which gives tremendous strength to human muscles. An injection of this substance enabled him to overcome Munson, when his nervous system was unable to cope with the muscle reaction. With Reynolds' blessing, Avery decides to conceal the guilt so he can continue to work on the amazing new compound. A monkey that escaped from the lab, injected with the same compound, dies as a result and Avery, injected with the same compound eight hours after the monkey, realizes he is going to face the same fate.

Notes
- The character of Sergeant Cox was originally named Sergeant Gallagher in the rough drafts of the script. The original title was "The Brute of Man," but was changed before the final draft was composed.
- Produced under the title of "The Death of Man."
- Truman Bradley arrived on the set on the second day at 5 p.m. for filming the lab demonstrations for production 8b, since the previous filming for the same episode was apparently scrapped.
- The two posters hanging on the wall in this episode, displaying the human anatomy including blood vessels and muscles, appear in two other episodes: "The Unexplored" and "Three Minute Mile." Truman Bradley points out one of these posters in his lab demonstration in "100 Years Young."

The June 23, 1955 issue of *Variety* reviewed this episode:

"More of a whodunit than a science-fictioner, 'Death' is a so-so entry with more gab than action. The too-talky yarn about a young scientist accused of murder is static and never gets off the ground.

"Producer Ivan Tors, who also wrote the original, spends much footage in painstaking explanations of how a small-sized scientist is able to kill a king-sized murderer. Seems he discovers a magic compound which give him muscles, only flaw being at the end the stuff makes him more or less of a petrified man and he gets very dead. The lack of action and excess of verbiage makes it all rather slow, not too interesting fare.

"Skip Homeier, John Qualen, Ted de Corsia and Virginia Hunter acquit themselves well in the principal roles. Henry S. Kesler's meggish is sluggish, due to the script of the same description by Ellis Marcus."

EPISODE #11 "CONVERSATION WITH AN APE"

PRODUCTION #1011 / 13B
DATES OF PRODUCTION: APRIL 19 AND 20, 1955
DIRECTED BY HERBERT L. STROCK

SCRIPT & STORY

FIRST DRAFT BY RIK VOLLAERTS, APRIL 12, 1955
FINAL DRAFT BY RIK VOLLAERTS, APRIL 16, 1955
TELEPLAY BY RIK VOLLAERTS

PRODUCTION CREDITS

1ST ASST. CAMERAMAN: JIM BELL (*UN-CREDITED*)
1ST CO. GRIP: MEL BLEDSOE (*UN-CREDITED*)
2ND ASST. DIRECTOR: HARRY JONES (*UN-CREDITED*)
2ND CO. GRIP: TED MATHEW (*UN-CREDITED*)
ASSISTANT DIRECTOR: RALPH SLOSSER
BOOM MAN: ELMER HAGLUND (*UN-CREDITED*)
CAMERA OPERATOR: DICK RAWLINGS
CONSTRUCTION CHIEF: ARCHIE HALL (*UN-CREDITED*)
DIRECTOR OF PHOTOGRAPHY: ROBERT HOFFMAN

Film Coordinator: Donald Tait
Film Editor: Thomas Scott (CREDITED) AND John B. Woelz (UN-CREDITED)
Gaffer: S.H. Barton (UN-CREDITED)
Make-up Artist: George Gray
Property Master: Max Pittman
Recorder: Bob Post (UN-CREDITED)
Script Supervisor: Larry Lund (CREDITED) AND Billy Vernon (UN-CREDITED)
Scientific Advisor on Electronics and Radar Operation: Maxwell Smith
Set Decorator: Vincent Taylor
Sound Mixer: Garry Harris
Sound Supervisor: Gus Galvin
Special Effects: Harry Redmond, Jr.
Wardrobe: Alfred Berke

CAST: Hugh Beaumont (Dr. Guy Stanton, $500); Paul Birch (Pete Lane, $100); Barbara Hale (Nancy Stanton, $1,750); and Terry the Chimp (the chimp)

PLOT: Dr. Guy Stanton, head of the Anson Research Laboratory, brings home his bride and finds she is progressively more and more disturbed by what her husband didn't tell her about the circumstances of his life. It turns out his lab is located deep in a Florida swamp. There is also a penitentiary nearby. Worst of all, his research is such that large numbers of lab animals are required. She has a powerful and unreasoning fear of all living creatures. This combination of circumstances makes her so afraid that she decides she cannot live at the lab with her husband, threatening to ruin their marital relationship. Dr. Stanton pleads for time to discover the "X" factor in non-humans, capabilities humans don't have. Particularly, he is working with a chimp to give it sufficient understanding and vocabulary to communicate. The chimp has acquired word understanding and recognition both auditory and visual, and through the means of a combination word and pictorial 'typewriter' can communicate desires through words. Dr. Stanton wishes to prove that the ape, among other living creatures, has extra-sensory perception

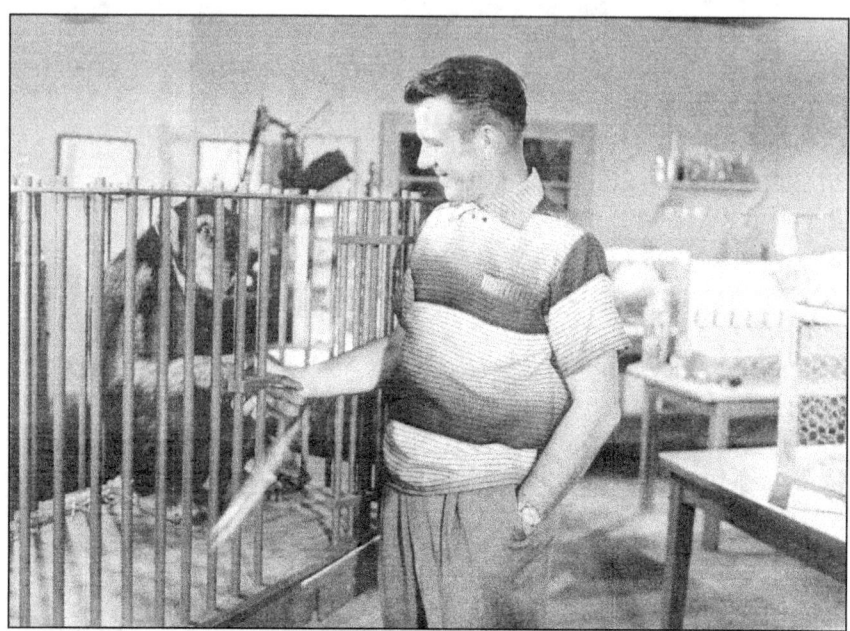

Hugh Beaumont and Terry the Chimp shake hands.

Terry the Chimp relaxes in between takes.

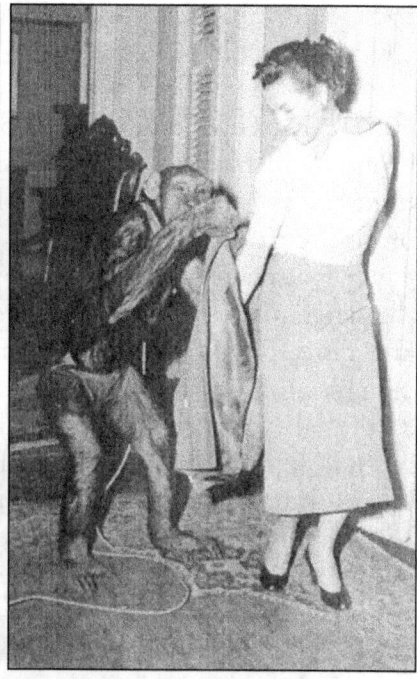

Terry the Chimp makes Barbara Hale on the set.

Terry the Chimp and Barbara Hale monkeys around between takes.

Hugh Beaumont and Barbara Hale introduce themselves to the laboratory animals in "Conversation With An Ape."

and can read minds. When an escaped convict holds them prisoner in their own house, Dr. Stanton mentally directs the chimp to bring him a gun and he does so. This permits Dr. Stanton and his wife to save their own lives. The "X" factor is proved to exist and the telepathic communication between man and animal is proved.

Notes

- The title ape's trainers were Henry Tyndall and a man named Kendal. Tyndall was a wrangler behind the scenes for *Around the World in Eighty Days* (1956).
- The entire episode was filmed on Stage 6.
- Stand-in Grant Davis was on hand for the insert shot of Guy Stanton reaching for the knife, but director Strock felt actor Beaumont could reach for the knife in a continuous shot so while Davis was on the set, he was never used and does not feature into the film.
- The footage of the car driving up to the Stanton house in the opening scene was originally filmed for "The Strange Doctor Lorenz," with actors Donald Curtis and Helen Tuttle. That is not Hugh Beaumont and Barbara Hale in the car.
- Rik Vollaerts wrote this teleplay based on scientific material contained within Robert A. Butler's article, "Curiosity in Monkeys," originally published in the February 1954 issue of *Scientific American*.

The June 30, 1955 issue of *Variety* reviewed this episode:
"Non-scientific audiences may feel that this story is far-fetched in reaching its climax, but the subject's premise that animals have extra-sensory perception is scientific reasoning and the unfoldment here is interesting. Segment fits handily into the *Science Fiction Theatre* format.

"Hugh Beaumont plays an animal psychologist who has had amazing success with his experiments, particularly on a pet chimp, and Barbara Hale has role of his bride, whom he has brought to his Florida Everglades station. When couple are held at bay in their home by an escaped convict, the scientist puts into practice his theory of the high degree of sensory perception in animals and sends the chimp upstairs to get a gun, with which he captures the con.

"Idea has been developed soundly in the Rik Vollaerts teleplay and given persuasive by Herbert L. Strock under Ivan Tors' production supervision. Beaumont registers impressively as the scientist, but about all Miss Hale is called upon to do is be frightened of animals. Paul Birch scored briefly as the con."

EPISODE #12 "MARKED DANGER"

PRODUCTION #1012 / 11B
DATES OF PRODUCTION: APRIL 8 AND 9, 1955
DIRECTED BY LEIGH JASON

SCRIPT & STORY

FIRST DRAFT BY STUART JEROME, JANUARY 31, 1955
SECOND DRAFT BY JERRY SACKHEIM AND STUART JEROME, APRIL 4, 1955
FINAL DRAFT BY JERRY SACKHEIM AND STUART JEROME, APRIL 4, 1955
TELEPLAY BY JERRY SACKHEIM AND STUART JEROME, BASED ON AN ORIGINAL STORY BY JOHN BENNETT

PRODUCTION CREDITS

1ST CO. GRIP: CARL MIKSCH (*UN-CREDITED*)
1ST ASST. CAMERAMAN: JIM BELL (*UN-CREDITED*)
2ND ASST. DIRECTOR: HARRY JONES (*UN-CREDITED*)
2ND CO. GRIP: COLEY KESSINGER (*UN-CREDITED*)
ASSISTANT DIRECTOR: RALPH SLOSSER
BOOM MAN: JIM FLANNERY (*UN-CREDITED*)
CAMERA OPERATOR: DICK RAWLINGS
CONSTRUCTION CHIEF: ARCHIE HALL (*UN-CREDITED*)
DIRECTOR OF PHOTOGRAPHY: MONROE "MONK" ASKINS
FILM COORDINATOR: DONALD TAIT
FILM EDITOR: JOHN B. WOELZ
GAFFER: J.C. BARTON (*UN-CREDITED*)
MAKE-UP ARTIST: GEORGE GRAY
PROPERTY MASTER: MAX PITTMAN
RECORDER: LARRY GOLDING (*UN-CREDITED*)

Scientific Advisor on Electronics and Radar Operation:
  Maxwell Smith
Script Supervisor: Billy Vernon
Set Decorator: Lou Hafley
Set Designer: Jack Collis
Sound Mixer: Jay Ashworth
Sound Supervisor: Gus Galvin
Special Effects: Harry Redmond, Jr.
Wardrobe: Alfred Berke

Cast: John Alvin (Dr. Lee Thomas, $75); Phyllis Cole (the nurse, $70); Arthur Franz (Fred Strand, $750); Nancy Gates (Lois Strand, $500); Otto Kruger (Dr. Werner Engstrom, $1,250); Steve Pendleton (Dr. Briggs, $100); and John Pickard (Sheriff Carson, $75)

Plot: Outside a government testing ground in the desert, mining engineer Fred Strand discovers a downed capsule. Learning that the Air Force base will pay for the return of their property, he phones the facility. Two white mice inside a sealed container, however, appear to be infected with a strange, completely unknown disease that is turning them green in color. Then the animals decompose, leaving only traces of green plant life cells. Fred's wife, Lois, becomes a victim of the disease. Her cells are turning to chloroplast and she begins craving sunlight. The doctors explain to Fred that the space capsule penetrated an ionic cloud containing cosmic particles, which pierced the capsule, to form an unknown, highly dangerous disease. The doctors promise to do the best they can to save Lois and seek help from Dr. Werner Engstrom, one of the great scientists of the world. He studies Lois' case and estimates she has only 15 days to live at most. Calling on Dr. Kraus in Geneva, they try an experimental procedure introducing glucose to the bloodstream, putting her into a coma, and praying she will get better—which she does.

Notes
- The role of Sheriff Carson was originally slated for actor John Mitchum.

- The entire second day of filming was shot on location at Bronson Canyon.
- The entire episode was produced under the title "Green-Out," which was also the title of the script. The title was later changed to "Danger" after filming was completed, and later changed to "Marked Danger" before the film was completely edited. *Variety*, using a press release from ZIV-TV, reviewed the episode in their paper, incorrectly referring to the title as "Danger" and not "Marked Danger."
- The original script was much darker than the revised one that was ultimately produced. On a lonely government base in the desert, experiments were being conducted by Dr. Alan Peters and his assistant, Dr. Elaine Forrest, trying to determine through experimental animals the physical changes occurring in humans who are sent two hundred miles into the stratosphere in rockets. After one such test, the doctors find that the animals have become infected with a strange, completely unknown disease that is turning them green. Then the animals decompose, leaving only traces of green plant life cells. And with that, the two scientists discover that they, too, have become victims of the green disease. Their cells are turning to chloroplast. They turn to Dr. Kraus, one of the great scientists of the world, for help. They estimate they have 30 days to live. Dr. Kraus calls on the scientists of the world for aid. They only come up with a theory; Man is in danger of extinction, like the dinosaurs. This is nature's reprisal against the growing threat of mankind's destruction of the world. Then, taking a desperate chance, Kraus puts them into a coma. Their lives are saved, but this is no permanent cure. Dr. Kraus questions what of the other inevitable cases to come?
- Besides the difference in lead characters, Dr. Briggs was originally Colonel Briggs in the initial draft.
- The footage of the white mice in weightlessness of space was also used for the episode "Beyond."

The July 7, 1955 issue of *Variety* reviewed this episode:
"One of producer Ivan Tors' better efforts, 'Danger' is packed solidly with suspense in the pure scientifiction genre. Finding an s-and-f

yarn which will have broad appeal, not limited to the science-fictioners, isn't an easy job, but 'Danger' fills the bill on all counts.

"Uranium hunter Arthur Franz finds a pair of white mice dropped by parachute in a sealed receptacle, after they've been sent to the ionosphere by rocket researchers. He leaves it with his wife while he goes off to notify the army, but she's too curious and presses a petcock on the receptacle. It releases an unknown gas which injects a form of plant life into her veins. Eventually she's saved from death by a w.k. scientist, played by Otto Kruger, who looks more like a scientist than a real-life one.

"Kruger, Franz and Nancy Gates give good portrayals, and Leigh Jason's direction holds to a consistent, taut tempo. The Jerry Sackheim-Stuart Jerome teleplay was well written."

EPISODE #13 "HOUR OF NIGHTMARE"

PRODUCTION #1013 / 14B
DATES OF PRODUCTION: APRIL 25 AND 26, 1955
DIRECTED BY HENRY S. KESLER

SCRIPT & STORY

FIRST DRAFT BY LOU HOUSTON, APRIL 20, 1955
FINAL DRAFT BY LOU HOUSTON, APRIL 22, 1955
TELEPLAY BY LOU HUSTON

PRODUCTION CREDITS

1ST ASST. CAMERAMAN: ED NUGENT (*UN-CREDITED*)
1ST CO. GRIP: MEL BLEDSOE (*UN-CREDITED*)
2ND ASST. DIRECTOR: HARRY JONES (*UN-CREDITED*)
2ND CAMERAMAN: BUD MANTINO (*UN-CREDITED*)
2ND CO. GRIP: TED MATHEW (*UN-CREDITED*)
ASSISTANT DIRECTOR: RALPH SLOSSER
BOOM MAN: BILL FLANNERY (*UN-CREDITED*)
CONSTRUCTION CHIEF: ARCHIE HALL (*UN-CREDITED*)
DIRECTOR OF PHOTOGRAPHY: ROBERT HOFFMAN
FILM COORDINATOR: DONALD TAIT
FILM EDITOR: JOHN B. WOELZ

William Bishop and Lynn Bari relax between takes with director Henry Kesler.

MAKE-UP ARTIST: GEORGE GRAY
PROPERTY MASTER: MAX PITTMAN
RECORDER: LARRY GOLDING (*UN-CREDITED*)
SCRIPT SUPERVISOR: BILLY VERNON
SCIENTIFIC ADVISOR ON ELECTRONICS AND RADAR OPERATION:
  MAXWELL SMITH
SET DECORATOR: VINCENT TAYLOR
SOUND MIXER: JAY ASHWORTH
SOUND SUPERVISOR: GUS GALVIN
SPECIAL EFFECTS: HARRY REDMOND, JR.
WARDROBE: ALFRED BERKE

On the set of "Hour of Nightmare" before filming.

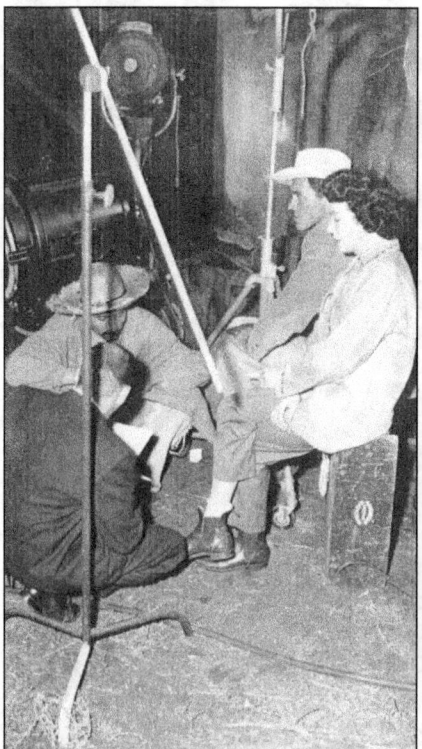

Christopher Dark, William Bishop and Lynn Bari relax between takes.

Candid camera shot of William Bishop and Lynn Bari on the set of "Hour of Nightmare." Note the stage lights caught on camera.

CAST: Lynn Bari (Verda Wingate, $750); Tony Barrett (Police Commandante, $150); William Bishop (Mel Wingate, $1,000); Christopher Dark (Ramon Sanchez, $150); and Charles Evans (Ed Tratner, $100)

PLOT: Mel and Verda Wingate, two top free-lance photographers, are sent into Mexico by an American picture magazine to investigate rumors of mysterious flying objects reported over a small Mexican village. They photograph an object with lights, but feel that what they saw was due to optical illusions in the hemisphere. In the dim light of dawn, Mel fires at a movement in the brush. Later they find a dead body of a creature so strangely formed that it could not be of this planet. They head back to the village with their amazing scientific discovery. That night the lights again appear in the sky. It is plain that the space ships are looking for their comrade and they are partially hostile. Their guide suddenly vanishes in a fantastic glare, along with the body of the visitor, confirming their suspicions. Back in the village the photographers find that all their films are fogged. They have no evidence of any kind to support their incredible story. Bowing to the inevitable, they permit the local police officer to reach the logical, 'reasonable' conclusion that the guide fell into a ravine during a storm. They phone the magazine editor to report there is 'no proof' of the existence of flying saucers.

NOTES

- The first day of production was filmed on location in Bronson Canyon for the scenes of Verda and Mel driving across the mountains and their meeting with Ramon Sanchez, and the scenes with the pack horses. Then the cast and crew reported back to the studio for filming on Stage 1. The second day of production was filmed on Stage 1 and Stage 6.
- All of the evening camp scenes were filmed in the studio, making it easier for the crew to shine the lights from the flying saucers on Ramon.
- A poster mapping out the layers of Earth's atmosphere hangs on the wall in this episode, which also appears in "Beyond," "Project 44," and on the wall of Truman Bradley's laboratory

during the initial opening of every episode, located behind the oscillator cone.
- The same footage of the flying saucer and the sound effect in the background track when the footage was on the screen was also used for the episode "Are We Invaded?"

The July 14, 1955 issue of *Variety* reviewed this episode:

"Inevitably for a series such as this, there had to be a flying saucer story. In 'Nightmare,' producer Ivan Tors turned out a suspenseful, engrossing yarn about the dishes from upstairs. Lou Huston's teleplay is well-written, and he packs excitement into every minute of his story.

"The yarn is pegged on those rumors that a saucer had actually landed in Mexico, with little men strolling around the countryside scaring the peons to death. Bill Bishop and Lynn Bari are U.S. mag photogs and went to the scene to see if there's anything to it, and grab pix to prove it. A native guides them to the mountain spot where the space ship reportedly landed, and they actually see the saucer flying above 'em. Bishop spots the body of a space man, decides to take it back with him as proof, but the saucer catches up with them, sends down a sheet of flame which destroys both the body and the guide. When they return to the village, they find they have no pix—the film's all been destroyed by radiation. It's all very bizarre and fanciful, as any saucer story must be, but it makes for interesting viewing.

"Bishop and Miss Bari turn in topnotch performances, and Christopher Dark is excellent as the guide, giving a realistic and sharply etched delineation. The direction by Henry S. Kesler had a fast tempo and was a decided asset to the overall production. Special effects men rate kudos for their handling of the weird lights denoting a space ship and the flame enveloping the guide."

EPISODE #14 "THE STRANGE DOCTOR LORENZ"

Production #1014 / 12B
Dates of Production: April 14 and 15, 1955
Directed by Leigh Jason

SCRIPT & STORY

Final Draft by Norman Jolley, April 11, 1955
Revised pages dated April 13, 1955
Teleplay by Norman Jolley, based on the short story "The Bee Story" by Ivan Tors

PRODUCTION CREDITS

1st Co. Grip: Mel Bledsoe (*un-credited*)
1st Asst. Cameraman: Dick Johnson (*un-credited*)
2nd Asst. Director: Dane Marks (*un-credited*)
2nd Cameraman: Fred Bentley (*un-credited*)
2nd Co. Grip: Ted Mathew (*un-credited*)
Assistant Director: Bert Chervin
Boom Man: Jim Gibbs (*un-credited*)
Chief Set Electrician: Joseph Wharton
Construction Chief: Archie Hall (*un-credited*)
Director of Photography: Robert Hoffman
Film Coordinator: Donald Tait
Film Editor: John B. Woelz
Gaffer: Joseph Wharton (*un-credited*)
Make-up Artist: George Gray
Property Master: Max Pittman
Recorder: William Hanks (*un-credited*)
Script Supervisor: Billy Vernon
Scientific Advisor on Electronics and Radar Operation: Maxwell Smith
Set Decorator: Vincent Taylor
Set Designer: Jack Collis
Sound Mixer: Phil Mitchell
Sound Supervisor: Gus Galvin
Special Effects: Harry Redmond, Jr.
Wardrobe: Alfred Berke

Dr. Lorenz (Edmund Gwenn) is pleased to demonstrate his scientific breakthrough to newcomers Helen Tuttle (Kristine Miller) and Dr. Fred Garner (Donald Curtis).

CAST: Madge Cleveland (Mrs. Le Blanc, $70); Donald Curtis (Dr. Fred Garner, $150); Edmund Gwenn (Dr. Lorenz, $2,250); Kristine Miller (Helen Tuttle, $300); Hank Patterson (George, $75); and Charles Wagenheim (Everett, $75)

PLOT: Dr. Fred Garner, a physician who is suffering from x-ray burns that will ultimately render his hands useless, is called out to a village in the swamplands to save the life of a little boy who has suffered third degree burns. When he gets to the village, he finds that the little boy was already treated by an old man who delivers honey to sick people. The wounds of the child heal miraculously so the doctor visits the keeper of the bees. He learns that the old man, Dr. Lorenz, has a hothouse where flowers grow in soil, radiated by isotopes. The radioactive pollens are carried by his bees into their beehives. Through their digestive systems, a new wonder drug is being manufactured as a substitute for honey. Fred has a taste of the honey and his hands are healed from the x-ray burns. When a local named Everett with a crippled leg breaks into the house to steal the honey, he falls victim to his own greed and Dr. Garner learns that

THE EPISODE GUIDE: SEASON ONE   183

Edmund Gwenn plays the role of a brilliant doctor in "The Strange Doctor Lorenz."

The cast consults the script for "The Strange Doctor Lorenz."

the honey is only a temporary cure—not a permanent one. Dr. Lorenz explains that he is going to die soon of old age and offers Dr. Garner the opportunity to carry on with his research until a permanent cure is discovered.

Notes

- Produced under the title of "Telling the Bees."
- The red viewers on the wall in Dr. Lorenz's lab are the same props featured on the wall in *Gog*.
- The periodic table of elements hanging on the wall in Lorenz's lab can also be seen hanging on the wall in a number of other episodes including "100 Years Young," "Operation Flypaper" and "Are We Invaded?"
- Ivan Tors based his plot proposal for this episode on Hans Kalmus' article that appeared in the July 1953 issue of *Scientific American*, titled "More on the Language of the Bees."

The July 21, 1955 issue of *Variety* reviewed this episode:

"Audiences will find it tough to wait out this laborious B picture. Scripter Norman Jolley keeps it singularly free from appeal, and tops this by giving Edmund Gwenn lengthy, pedantic speeches which might be interesting in some college biology class, but are deadening on TV.

"Producer Ivan Tors' penchant for having his scientists far afield from the civilization they're trying to aid holds true in this dull entry. Gwenn, a chemist researcher, is way off in some swamp country researching lots and lots of bees. He seems to get a buzz out of them, also a jelly which miraculously cures—or seems to cure—burns. A young doc with bad x-ray burns comes to him for healing, is helped, and then it develops the 'cure' is just temporary. Mucho research remains to be done and young doc and his g.f. agree to take over the work of the elderly chemist.

"Gwenn handles his role well, and so do Donald Curtis and Kristine Miller as the medico romancers. But they had little to work with in Jolley's static script. Leigh Jason's direction was similarly handicapped."

"THE BEE STORY"
BY IVAN TORS

A scientist finds a way to enlist the aid of bees as factory workers. He constructs a hothouse where flowers are planted in radioactive soil. The radioactive pollen is picked up by the bees and the digestive system of the bees, instead of making honey, makes a new product, a new wonder-drug. The drug turns out to be a miracle drug that saves many otherwise hopeless medical cases.

EPISODE #15 "100 YEARS YOUNG"

PRODUCTION #1015 / 15B
DATES OF PRODUCTION: MAY 9 AND 10, 1955
DIRECTED BY HERBERT L. STROCK

SCRIPT & STORY

FIRST DRAFT BY JERRY SACKHEIM AND ARTHUR FITZ-RICHARD, MAY 3, 1955
FINAL DRAFT BY JERRY SACKHEIM, MAY 6, 1955
TELEPLAY BY JERRY SACKHEIM, FROM AN ORIGINAL STORY IDEA BY ARTHUR FITZ-RICHARD

PRODUCTION CREDITS

1ST ASST. CAMERAMAN: ED NUGENT (*UN-CREDITED*)
1ST CO. GRIP: MEL BLEDSOE (*UN-CREDITED*)
2ND ASST. DIRECTOR: HARRY JONES (*UN-CREDITED*)
2ND CAMERAMAN: BUD MAUTINO (*UN-CREDITED*)
2ND CO. GRIP: TOM MATHEWS (*UN-CREDITED*)
ASSISTANT DIRECTOR: BERT CHERVIN
ASST. PROP MAN: GENE STONE (*UN-CREDITED*)
BOOM MAN: BILL FLANNERY (*UN-CREDITED*)
CONSTRUCTION CHIEF: ARCHIE HALL (*UN-CREDITED*)
DIRECTOR OF PHOTOGRAPHY: ROBERT HOFFMAN
FILM COORDINATOR: DONALD TAIT
FILM EDITOR: JOHN B. WOELZ
GAFFER: JOHN MILLMAN (*UN-CREDITED*)
MAKE-UP ARTIST: GEORGE GRAY

The chemist (Dick Ganz) discusses the mystery with Lt. Mike Redding (John Archer) in "100 Years Young."

PRODUCTION COORDINATOR: JOE WONDER
SCIENTIFIC ADVISOR ON ELECTRONICS AND RADAR OPERATION: MAXWELL SMITH
PROPERTY MASTER: MAX PITTMAN
RECORDER: LARRY GOLDING (*UN-CREDITED*)
SCRIPT SUPERVISOR: BILLY VERNON
SET DECORATOR: VINCENT TAYLOR
SET LABOR: TED McGASKEY (*UN-CREDITED*)
SOUND MIXER: JAY ASHWORTH
SOUND SUPERVISOR: GUS GALVIN
SPECIAL EFFECTS: HARRY REDMOND, JR.
WARDROBE: ALFRED BERKE AND FRANK TAUSS (*UN-CREDITED*)

Ruth Hussey pretends to be a scientist in "100 Years Young."

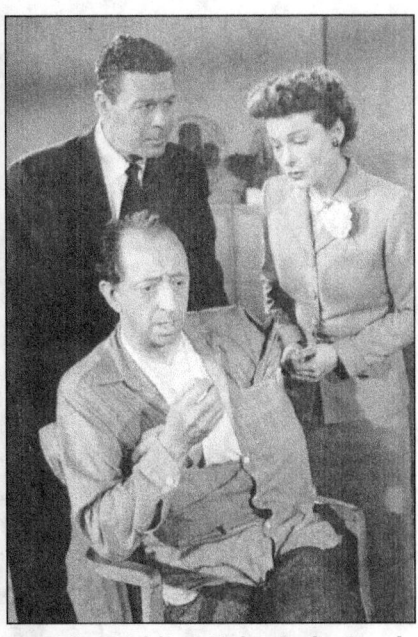

Lt. Mike Redding (John Archer) and Bernice Knight (Ruth Hussey) listen to the fascinating story told by John Bowers (John Abbott).

Rehearsal scene for John Bowers who is being led away by the police when no one believes his story.

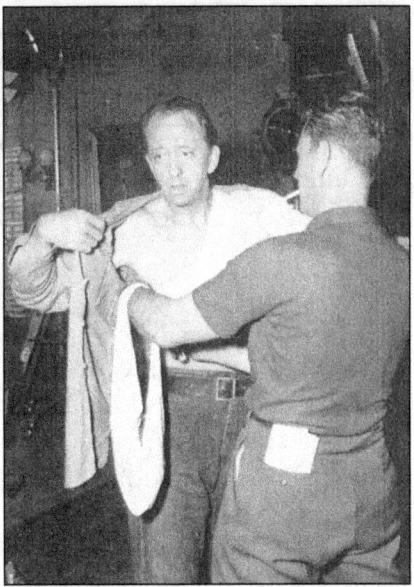

Actor John Abbott has bandages properly applied before filming commences.

Truman Bradley displays the human anatomy in "100 Years Young." The same prop hangs on the wall in "The Unexplored," "Three Minute Mile," "The Lost Heartbeat" and "Death at 2 A.M." (See photo on page 201.)

CAST: John Abbott (John Bowers, $500); John Archer (Mike Redding, $150); Larry Hudson (Dick Ganz, the chemist, $100); Ruth Hussey (Bernice Knight, $2,500); and Charles Meredith (Mr. Lyman, $125)

PLOT: Retired because of his advancing age, former chemical company employee John Bowers is captured when caught pilfering from the company. He is recognized by Bernice Knight, a young chemist, as well as by Mr. Lyman, the head of the company. Lieutenant Mike Redding of the police, cross examines Bowers and discovers he is over two hundred years old, having been kept alive by a drug inherited from the Indians. Mr. Lyman is extremely interested in the commercial possibilities of this drug and has Bowers released to work with Bernice to perfect it. Meantime, Bernice and Lt. Redding fall in love. Bernice finds that she is making no progress with Bowers and suspects that he is holding out on her because he led a horribly lonely and unhappy life for over two centuries and he does not believe people should live that long. When he realizes that Bernice intends to test the new elixir on herself, and it creates an impasse between the lovers, Bowers commits suicide and dies with his secret.

Notes
- The first day of filming was on Stage 3.
- The second day of filming was on Stage 6.
- Produced under the title "Elixir of Life," which was also the title of the script.
- The periodic table of elements hanging on the wall in this episode can also be seen hanging on the wall in a number of other episodes including "The Strange Doctor Lorenz," "Operation Flypaper" and "Are We Invaded?"
- Arthur Fitz-Richard co-wrote the first draft of the script, but since he was not involved with the final draft, he received no on-screen credit for the story.

Episode #16 "The Frozen Sound"

Production #1016 / 16B
Dates of Production: May 16 and 17, 1955
Directed by Leigh Jason

Script & Story
Final Draft by Norman Jolley, May 13, 1955
Revised pages dated May 16, 1955
Teleplay by Norman Jolley, from a story by Norman Jolley and Ivan Tors

Production Credits
1st Asst. Cameraman: Ed Nugent (*un-credited*)
1st Co. Grip: Mel Bledsoe (*un-credited*)
2nd Asst. Director: Harry Jones (*un-credited*)
2nd Cameraman: Bud Mautino (*un-credited*)

2ND CO. GRIP: TOM MATHEWS (*UN-CREDITED*)
ASSISTANT DIRECTOR: BERT CHERVIN
BOOM MAN: JIM FLANNERY (*UN-CREDITED*)
CONSTRUCTION CHIEF: ARCHIE HALL (*UN-CREDITED*)
DIRECTOR OF PHOTOGRAPHY: ROBERT HOFFMAN
FILM COORDINATOR: DONALD TAIT
FILM EDITOR: DUNCAN MANSFIELD (*UN-CREDITED*)
GAFFER: JOHN MILLMAN (*UN-CREDITED*)
MAKE-UP ARTIST: GEORGE GRAY
PRODUCTION COORDINATOR: JOE WONDER
SCIENTIFIC ADVISOR ON ELECTRONICS AND RADAR OPERATION: MAXWELL SMITH
PROPERTY MASTER: MAX PITTMAN
RECORDER: LARRY GOLDING (*UN-CREDITED*)
SCRIPT SUPERVISOR: LARRY LUND (*UN-CREDITED*) AND GUS SALVIN (*CREDITED*)
SET DECORATOR: VINCENT TAYLOR
SET DESIGNER: JACK COLLIS
SOUND MIXER: JAY ASHWORTH
SOUND SUPERVISOR: GUS GALVIN
SPECIAL EFFECTS: HARRY REDMOND, JR.
WARDROBE: ALFRED BERKE (*CREDITED*) AND FRANK TOSS (*UN-CREDITED*)

CAST: Ray Collins (Dr. Milton Otis, $750); Marilyn Erskine (Linda Otis, $1,250); Michael Fox (Dr. Gordine, $125); Elizabeth Patterson (Hannah, $300); and Marshall Thompson (Dr. David Masters, $750); Morgan Windbeil (Lester, the gardener)

PLOT: The capture of a foreign espionage agent, on whose person is found a microfilm transcript of a top-secret conference between Government Project head, Dr. Milton Otis and the Secretaries of the Air Force and Defense, leads to Otis's suspension. Dr. David Masters, a physicist from Columbia University, accepts a government assignment to investigate the case because he believes firmly in Otis' innocence. Otis' daughter, Linda, shares David's feeling. Their investigation leads to the discovery of a new kind of wire-tapping—'sonic saturation' of a slow-hardening, synthetic crystal—capable of

The Episode Guide: Season One

Ray Collins and Marilyn Erskine grab coffee and donuts before filming begins.

later reproducing complete conversations. In the process, it is also discovered that an ancient piece of lava-rock, through its natural solidifying from a molten state, has actually recorded voices from the past, opening up intriguing prospects for scientists' research into history. A hint of the future is evident in a suggested romance that grows between Masters and Linda. The guilty person proves to be Lester, the gardener, apprehended while making his pickup of the 'Living Crystal'. He was in the employ of foreign agents, including Dr. Gordine. The solution is based on an actual, startling, new discovery which introduces a new fundamental principle of science.

Marilyn Erskine displays grabs breakfast before filming.

Dr. David Masters (Marshall Thompson) discovers how secret information is smuggled.

Marilyn Erskine and Marshall Thompson clown around with the electronic equipment.

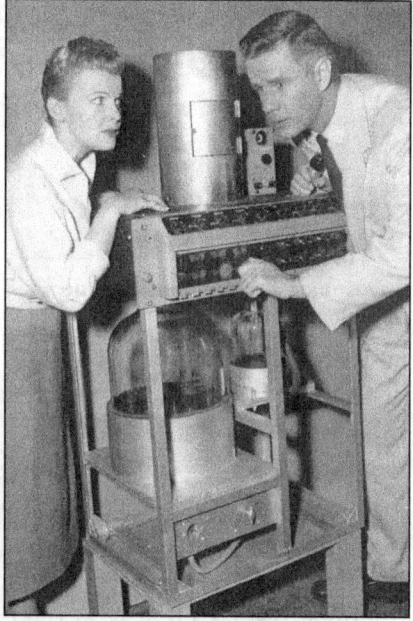

Marilyn Erskine and Marshall Thompson clown around with the electronic equipment.

Marilyn Erskine poses for a publicity shot.

Marilyn Erskine and Marshall Thompson examine a "Living Crystal." Note the *Scientific American* on the desk and the props on the bookshelves that re-appear in other episodes of *Theatre*.

NOTES

- Filmed on Stage 2 both days.
- In the original script, the government agent was referred to as a C.I.A. Agent but it was decided to be vague and not specifically disclose the name of the agency for the sake of avoiding legal clearance of the use of C.I.A. for the program.
- Produced under the title "The Living Crystals."
- The character of David Masters was originally Dr. David Loman in the original script. Dr. Gordine was originally Dr. Pataky.
- Much of the information regarding crystals in this episode originated from Robert L. Fullman's article in the March 1955 issue of *Scientific American*, titled "The Growth of Crystals."
- The photo of the rocket blasting through the Earth's atmosphere that hangs on the wall during the beginning of the second act is the same original artwork that appears on screen during the opening credits of *Gog*.

- All of the close-up insert shots of a man's hands such as Masters picking up and pouring the ant poison bottles and Otis breaking the glass bottle and removing the wax were really the hands of John Truex, a stand-in on the set. Stand-In Ann Howard was also on the set, but was not needed for filming.

The August 4, 1955 issue of *Variety* reviewed this episode:

"To find a common denominator among the home lookers, this series needs more fiction and less science. Too much lab jargon not only weighs it down for mass appeal, but creates a hazy confusion. Freezing sound is an intriguing subject and in lay terminology could have been an interest holder, but it became so involved in scientific elements that it was a challenge to normal intelligence.

"Story has to do with a scientist unjustly accused of giving up secrets to the enemy. After much probing on a high scientific level, it develops that another savant was in league with a gardener who set out vitals of ant poison to freeze the sound of classified meetings and ship them off to the Commies. As if to test the mental alertness of the lookers, a piece of lava is introduced to play off voices 'frozen' 2,000 years ago in the eruption of Pompeii. It had something to do with crystals, just to add to the mental bedlam.

"Marshall Thompson, Ray Collins and Michael Fox talk and act like scientists or the general conception thereof, and Marilyn Erskine is the heart interest and defender of the innocent. It's really not their fault if the message didn't get across. Ivan Tors, who co-authored and produced, should have lowered his sights for more understandable reaction to what he was up to. Truman Bradley's prologue was helpful, but the atmosphere soon clouded up to complicate the spy hunt."

"THE LIVING CRYSTALS"
BY IVAN TORS

A prominent scientist is accused of revealing scientific secrets to the enemy. There was a top-level conference in his house where a cabinet member and a general of the Air Force were present, and nobody else, and every word of the conversation was reported to an unfriendly country. The scientist knows that he is not guilty. Investigating every possible avenue of sabotage he finds that small bottles of liquid were planted in his house. The liquids slowly crystalized and the crystals picked up every bit of sound. All the spoken words were scribed in the crystals. The scientist finds a method to play the crystals back. It is an amazing new discovery that will enable scientists to listen to voices out of the past. In theory, the tragic cries of the perishing mob of Pompei may be scribed into the frozen lava. Amber stones may give us an account what went on in Ceasar's palace.

EPISODE #17 "THE STONES BEGAN TO MOVE"

PRODUCTION #1017 / 18B
DATES OF PRODUCTION: MAY 23 AND 24, 1955
DIRECTED BY LEW LANDERS

SCRIPT & STORY

FIRST DRAFT BY DORIS GILBERT, MAY 13, 1955
SECOND DRAFT BY DORIS GILBERT, MAY 18, 1955
TELEPLAY BY DORIS GILBERT, FROM A STORY BY IVAN TORS AND
  DORIS GILBERT

PRODUCTION CREDITS

1ST ASST. CAMERAMAN: JIM BELL (UN-CREDITED)
1ST CO. GRIP: CARL MIKSCH (UN-CREDITED)
2ND ASST. DIRECTOR: BOBBY RAY (UN-CREDITED)
2ND CO. GRIP: BUD GAUNT (UN-CREDITED)
ASSISTANT DIRECTOR: RALPH SLOSSER (UN-CREDITED)
BOOM MAN: ELMER HAGLUND (UN-CREDITED)
CAMERA OPERATOR: DICK RAWLINGS
CONSTRUCTION CHIEF: ARCHIE HALL (UN-CREDITED)
DIRECTOR OF PHOTOGRAPHY: CURT FETTERS
FILM COORDINATOR: DONALD TAIT
FILM EDITOR: DUNCAN MANSFIELD, A.C.E
GAFFER: JOHN MILLMAN (UN-CREDITED)
MAKE-UP ARTIST: GEORGE GRAY
PRODUCTION COORDINATOR: JOE WONDER

Jonathan Hale, Richard Flato and Basil Rathbone examine an ancient artifact.

SCIENTIFIC ADVISOR ON ELECTRONICS AND RADAR OPERATION: MAXWELL SMITH
PROPERTY MASTER: MAX PITTMAN
RECORDER: BOB POST (*UN-CREDITED*)
SCRIPT SUPERVISOR: LARRY LUND
SET DECORATOR: VINCENT TAYLOR
SET DESIGNER: JACK COLLIS
SOUND MIXER: GARRY HARRIS
SOUND SUPERVISOR: GUS GALVIN
SPECIAL EFFECTS: HARRY REDMOND, JR.
WARDROBE: ALFRED BERKE (CREDITED) AND FRANK TAUSS (*UN-CREDITED*)

The Episode Guide: Season One

Basil Rathbone in "The Stones Began to Move."

Jonathan Hale and Basil Rathbone perform a carbon dating experiment.

CAST: Heinie Conklin (the janitor, $70); Russ Conway (Lieutenant Crenshaw, $150); Richard Flato (Ahmed Abdullah, $225); Jonathan Hale (Morton Archer, the curator, $125); Basil Rathbone (Victor Berenson, $2,500); Robin Short (Paul Kinkaid, $100); Carol Thurston (Seja Dih's Granddaughter, $100); Helen Van Camp (the maid, $70); and Jean Willes (Virginia Kinkaid, $150)

PLOT: Paul Kinkaid, noted archeologist, is killed while making a recording that his life is being threatened because of an important scientific principle he recently stumbled upon. On the recording he asks Dr. Victor Berenson of the U.S. Scientific Research Commission to finish his research. Berenson, drawn into the matter by the New York police, finds evidence in Kinkaid's office indicating that in 'the eyes of the panther' Kinkaid believed he had found a mineral that could cancel out gravity, a mineral that can solve the age-old mystery of how the pyramids were built. Through investigation, Berenson learns that Kinkaid was murdered for this secret by an Egyptian traitor, Ahmed Abdullah, who knew of Kinkaid's arrangement with the Egyptian government to complete his experiments.

Notes

- The entire episode was filmed on Stage 6.
- Produced under the title "Eyes of the Panther."
- Actor Robin Short had to record his lines separately as the crew could not get a microphone into the recording booth where he was transcribing his voice in a message to Victor Berenson.
- The stock footage of the exterior of the observatory was reused for two other episodes, "The Human Equation" and "Postcard From Barcelona."

The August 25, 1955 issue of *Variety* reviewed this episode:

"A run-of-the-mill whodunit, 'Stones' is a strange selection for Ziv's *Science Fiction Theatre*. The scientific connection is a slight one, a pretext for tossing in a mysterioso. Basil Rathbone, as a scientist investigating the murder of a colleague, plays the role precisely as he has that of Sherlock Holmes.

"Plot is pegged on an archeologist's discovery of the secret of the building of the pyramids, for which he gets killed. Following the tack of most of these whodunits with an Egyptian flavor, the heavy turns out to be a fellow archeologist who wants to swipe rare gems which cancel out the law of gravitation. Since there was no other suspect, this was not a surprise ending. In fact, the entire half-hour is loaded down with stuffy dialog, not to mention stuffy characters.

"Rathbone fails to register because of the stet vehicle, and same goes for Robin Short, Jean Willes and others. Lew Landers' direction is as uninspired as the Doris Gilbert teleplay."

"THE EYES OF THE PANTHER"
by Ivan Tors

1. A famous archeologist is shot on the streets of New York after having made a recording of his activities. The record is mailed to a prominent member of the Atomic Energy Commission.

2. The scientist investigates why the archeologist was killed and finds that the murdered man stumbled on a new scientific discovery. When he excavated a tomb in Egypt he found a sword suspended in mid-air over the grave. Looking for a scientific explanation of

the miracle, he realized that the eyes of the panther, a golden statue inside the tomb, were directed toward the sword and at the point where the eyes converged, gravity was cancelled out.

3. The archeologist brought the eyes of the panther to the United States for further study. He believed that certain minerals had the capability of creating a force field that will cancel out gravity.

4. A group of adventurers found out about his secret and when he refused to deal with them, they murdered him in cold blood. But the eyes of the panther have not been found by the murderers.

5. Our scientists, through scientific method, finds the eyes of the panther and the scientific principle behind the secret of levitation, Indian rope trick, and how the pyramids were built without the aid of modern machinery.

EPISODE #18 "THE LOST HEARTBEAT"

PRODUCTION #1018 / 19B
DATES OF PRODUCTION: MAY 26 AND 27, 1955
DIRECTED BY HENRY S. KESLER

SCRIPT & STORY

FINAL DRAFT BY STUART JEROME, MAY 23, 1955
TELEPLAY BY STUART JEROME, BASED ON AN ORIGINAL SHORT STORY TITLED "THE MAN WHO REFUSED TO DIE" BY R. DEWITT MILLER AND ANNA HUNGER

PRODUCTION CREDITS

1ST ASST. CAMERAMAN: JIM BELL (UN-CREDITED)
1ST CO. GRIP: CARL MIKSCH (UN-CREDITED)
2ND ASST. DIRECTOR: BOBBY RAY (UN-CREDITED)
ASSISTANT DIRECTOR: DONALD VERK
BOOM MAN: ELMER HAGLUND (UN-CREDITED)
CAMERA OPERATOR: DICK RAWLINGS
CONSTRUCTION CHIEF: ARCHIE HALL (UN-CREDITED)

Director of Photography: Curt Fetters
Film Coordinator: Donald Tait
Film Editor: John B. Woelz
Gaffer: S. H. Barton (*un-credited*)
Make-up Artist: George Gray
Production Coordinator: Joe Wonder
Scientific Advisor on Electronics and Radar Operation: Maxwell Smith
Property Master: Max Pittman
Recorder: Bob Post (*un-credited*)
Script Supervisor: Larry Lund
Set Decorator: Bruce MacDonald
Set Designer: Jack Collis
Sound Mixer: Garry Harris
Sound Supervisor: Gus Galvin
Special Effects: Harry Redmond, Jr.
Wardrobe: Alfred Berke (*credited*) and Frank Tauss (*un-credited*)

Cast: Walter Kingsford (Dr. John N. Crane, $150); Pierce Lyden (the second surgeon $75); Thomas McKee (the laboratory assistant, $85); John Mitchum (Evans Munson, $75); Zachary Scott (Dr. Richard Marshall, $2,500); Jan Shepard (Joan Crane, $125); Ted Thorpe (the houseboy, $75); and Gordon Wynn (the first surgeon, $75)

Plot: Research scientist Dr. Richard Marshall is awakened one night by the strange arrival of his old friend and former teacher, Dr. John Crane, one of the world's great scientists, whom he has not seen in ten years. Crane is interested in seeing the results of Marshall's work on a new artificial heart pump. Marshall soon learns that Crane is suffering from heart disease and has only a few months to live. Crane offers himself as a human guinea pig for the operation . . . both to help Marshall and to try to prolong his own life long enough to finish his own project, a battery which transmits brain waves to the mentally afflicted, causing a return to normalcy. Marshal refuses to experiment on Crane and sends him away. But shortly afterwards, Marshal receives a clock powered by a solar battery, and knows that

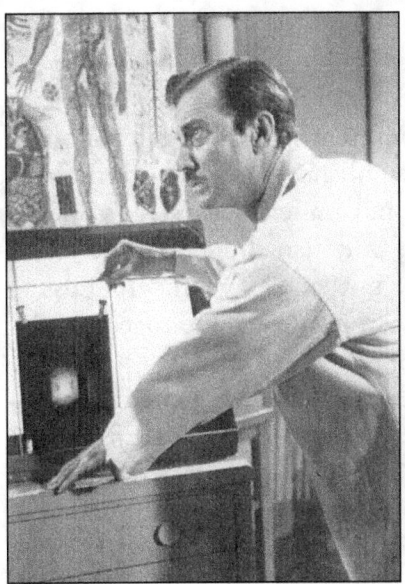

Dr. Richard Marshall (Zachary Scott) examines an x-ray in "The Lost Heartbeat."

Actors Walter Kingsford and Zachary Scott spent time with Alice in between takes.

Crane sent it. He and Crane begin work together on an artificial heart pump which will be powered by a solar battery. Before their work is completed, one of Crane's mental patients attacks him, forcing Marshall to perform the operation before they are completely ready. Crane lives but for how long nobody can say. His heroic efforts have contributed the beginning of a new field to both science and medicine.

Notes

- The entire episode was filmed on Stage 6.
- The real name of the monkey was Alice. To avoid confusing the animal during filming, it was decided to retain the monkey's name in the drama, rather than use a different name as suggested in the script.
- The first draft of the script was titled "The Man Who Refused to Die," taken from the original short story submitted to Ivan Tors by R. DeWitt Miller and Anna Hunger.
- The opening stock shot of the exterior of the house with the lights coming on was also used in "Bullet Proof," "Beyond Return," "When A Camera Fails" and "The Voice."

Script Notes

To give an idea of how much effort went into every line of dialogue in each script, Jon Epstein wrote to Ivan Tors on May 23, 1955, after reviewing the initial draft, commenting what he felt needed attention so the final draft would be polished and ready for filming. Among the comments: Epstein did not understand Crane's line on page 12, "You are my physician." He also did not understand Richard's line on page 14, "He's here in the guest room." As Epstein rationalized, Marshall and Crane were on the phone together, and it was not clear that it might be a house intercom.

"There is one major fault that I have to find with the first act—and one that I feel can be fixed very easily," remarked Epstein. "I feel that Richard and the daughter would not object to taking a chance as long as they knew Crane had to die in six months or a year. What difference would it make? Richard and the daughter must establish that Crane *could* live a long time, but, might die before the year is over, and thus not be able to finish his experiments."

Epstein also asked for clarification for Crane's line of dialogue on page 27, ". . . and open the doors of the insane asylum to many incurable cases."

Truman Bradley's narration at the closing of this episode was re-written between drafts because the producer felt it was "a little hokey." Epstein was in agreement, adding that Richard's last speech needed to be improved drastically. "The present one just scratches the surface. The idea that the operation itself worked, but, that the machinery may or may not, is the right one, but not fully explored."

The August 18, 1955 issue of *Variety* reviewed this episode:

"'The Lost Heartbeat' should more aptly have been tagged 'The Lost Ending.' Either the writer didn't know how to solve his problem, or they decided to end the episode before running over budget. Whichever it was, it left the viewer let down.

"Yarn is about a dying medico. He has a bad heart, so he goes to a young colleague and talks him into developing an artificial heart which supposedly allows old doc to live longer. Old doc has invented a solar battery to keep the artificial heart pumping. Young doc reluctantly goes along with all this, then comes the moot curtain, with young doc's careful post-operative remark that the patient may live hours or he may live long.

"Zachary Scott and Walter Kingsford do well as the medicos. Henry S. Kesler's direction is adequate. Stuart Jerome wrote this unfinished plot, from an original by R. DeWitt Miller and Anna Hunger."

EPISODE #19 "THE WORLD BELOW"

PRODUCTION #1019 / 17B
DATES OF PRODUCTION: MAY 20 AND 21, 1955
DIRECTED BY HERBERT L. STROCK

SCRIPT & STORY

FIRST DRAFT BY LEE HEWITT, MAY 3, 1955
SECOND DRAFT BY LEE HEWITT, MAY 11, 1955
REVISED PAGES DATED MAY 11 AND 16, 1955
TELEPLAY BY LEE HEWITT

PRODUCTION CREDITS

1ST ASST. CAMERAMAN: ED NUGENT (*UN-CREDITED*)
1ST CO. GRIP: CARL MIKSCH (*UN-CREDITED*)
2ND ASST. DIRECTOR: BOBBY RAY (*UN-CREDITED*)
2ND CAMERAMAN: BUD MAUTINO (*UN-CREDITED*)
ASSISTANT DIRECTOR: DONALD VERK
ASST. PROP MAN: VIC PETTROTTA (*UN-CREDITED*)
BOOM MAN: JIM FLANNERY (*UN-CREDITED*)
CONSTRUCTION CHIEF: ARCHIE HALL (*UN-CREDITED*)
DIRECTOR OF PHOTOGRAPHY: MONROE "MONK" ASKINS
FILM COORDINATOR: DONALD TAIT
FILM EDITOR: JOHN B. WOELZ
GAFFER: JOHN MILLMAN (*UN-CREDITED*)
MAKE-UP ARTIST: GEORGE GRAY
PRODUCTION COORDINATOR: JOE WONDER
SCIENTIFIC ADVISOR ON ELECTRONICS AND RADAR OPERATION:
    MAXWELL SMITH
PROPERTY MASTER: MAX PITTMAN

(LEFT TO RIGHT) **Tol Avery, Gene Barry, George Eldredge and Paul Dubov** attempt to rule out the mystery of an underwater kingdom in "The World Below."

RECORDER: LARRY GOLDING (*UN-CREDITED*)
SCRIPT SUPERVISOR: LARRY LUND
SET DECORATOR: VINCENT TAYLOR
SET DESIGNER: JACK COLLIS
SOUND MIXER: JAY ASHWORTH
SOUND SUPERVISOR: GUS GALVIN
SPECIAL EFFECTS: HARRY REDMOND, JR.
WARDROBE: ALFRED BERKE (*CREDITED*) AND FRANK TAUSS
   (*UN-CREDITED*)

CAST: Tol Avery (Professor Buck Weaver, $150); Gene Barry (Captain John Forester, $1,000); Marguerite Chapman (Jean Forester, $500); Paul Dubov (Lt. Carothers, $150); George Eldredge (Commander Stanley, $150); George Mathers (the sonar operator, $70); John Phillips (the radar operator, $70); William Stout (the TV announcer, $125); and James Waters (the bailiff, $75)

(LEFT TO RIGHT) **George Eldredge, Gene Barry and Paul Dubov discuss the possibility of an underwater kingdom in "The World Below."**

PLOT: The experimental submarine Loon collides with a reef more then two miles beneath the sea. Three of the four crewmen escape with the aid of pressure capsules. They claim to have seen and photographed a fabulous, modern city illuminated by a brilliant light just prior to the crash. Acclaimed by the country as discoverers of a fantastic city beneath the sea, they enjoy a brief rash of publicity before grappling devices fail to confirm their discovery. Captain Forester and the head of the exploration project are investigated by a joint board of inquiry. The decision of the board is that these two men are guilty of perpetrating a daring hoax and are to be so charged before a Federal Court. However, Professor Weaver, an optical expert, with the help of Captain Forester, proves to the board that the view of the city was projected under the sea by a freak picture of the harbor taken in the sub's observation bubble when the Loon was x-rayed for structural flaws. But where the strange flare of light came from, he, or no man can say until the unknown world beneath the sea is explored.

Notes

- The Hospital Ship-Cabin was originally an Emergency Hospital in the script.
- The entire episode was filmed on Stage 5.
- Produced under the title of "Beneath the Sea."
- The script called for a marine Biologist, boyish, crew cut, earnest, age thirty. His name was Bill Alexander and this character was scratched out of the script to save time for filming and the cost of what Ivan Tors felt was an unnecessary expense. Also written out of the script was the character of Mr. Lewis, a Civilian Investigation expert, legal head of the Marine Commission. Lewis's secretary was also written out. Professor Knight was an elderly, gentle scholar and was also written out.
- Tom Anthony plays the un-credited role of the TV reporter at the local hospital.
- The character of Professor Buck Weaver was originally Professor Buck Knight in the original script.
- The stock footage of the beachside house along the cliff was the same footage used in "Operation Flypaper."
- A poster mapping out the layers of Earth's atmosphere hangs on the wall in this episode, which Truman Bradley points to during his opening narration. This framed poster hangs on the wall in other episodes such as "Beyond," "Hour of Nightmare" and "Project 44."

The August 11, 1955 issue of *Variety* reviewed this episode:

"This series, which started off as promisingly, seems to have lapsed into a *Popular Mechanics* of the future. For a limited few who are up on their physics and latest technological advances, this is probably great stuff, but for the average viewer there can be nothing but frustration in the complicated scientific explanations.

"Lee Hewitt's teleplay, 'The World Below,' falls into this same category. It gets off to a fine start with Gene Barry skippering an electronically driven submarine deeper into the sea than any man had yet done. He and his partner, Tol Avery, become world heroes when they seem to have discovered a city in the ocean depths, bringing back pictures to prove their find. When the Navy can

The Episode Guide: Season One 207

> **SYNDICATION BLOOPER!**
> "THE STONES BEGAN TO MOVE" GOT SUBMERGED IN "THE WORLD BELOW" ONE TUESDAY NIGHT ON ZIV'S *SCIENCE FICTION THEATRE* OVER KTTV IN LOS ANGELES (CHANNEL 11). "STONES," WHICH GOT AN UNUSUALLY BIG ADVANCE BUILD-UP, WAS SUPPOSED TO RUN, BUT SOMEONE BLUNDERED BY PICKING UP THE PRINT OF "WORLD," ORIGINALLY SUPPOSED TO GO ON THE AIR AUG. 23, 1955. "STONES," WHICH STARRED BASIL RATHBONE, SWITCHED PLACES WITH THE DATE INTENDED FOR "WORLD."

find no signs of the city, Barry faces charges of being a party to a hoax. However, it proves to be an honest illusion, with a torturous explanation of how it all happened that must have left viewers dazedly blinking at the mumbo-jumbo.

"Performances by Barry, Avery and George Eldridge as the chairman of the naval investigating board, are all good. Paul Dubov plays a naval officer who is presenting the evidence against Barry for some reason playing him as a heavy. Marguerite Chapman is very good as Barry's wife.

"Herbert L. Strock's megging achieves an air of earnestness which at least leaves the impression the actors know what they're talking about. Camera work by Monroe "Monk" Askins is excellent. Ivan Tors produces for Ziv, with Truman Bradley intelligently narrating."

EPISODE #20 "BARRIER OF SILENCE"

PRODUCTION #1020 / 20B
DATES OF PRODUCTION: JUNE 7 AND 8, 1955
DIRECTED BY LEON BENSON

SCRIPT & STORY

FIRST DRAFT BY LOU HUSTON, JUNE 1, 1955
SECOND DRAFT BY LOU HUSTON, JUNE 3, 1955
REVISED PAGES DATED JUNE 6, 1955
FINAL DRAFT BY LOU HUSTON, JUNE 6, 1955
TELEPLAY BY LOU HUSTON

PRODUCTION CREDITS

1st Co. Grip: Mel Bledsoe (*un-credited*)
2nd Asst. Director: Jack Gertsman (*un-credited*)
2nd Cameraman: Bud Mautino (*un-credited*)
Assistant Director: Bert Chervin
Boom Man: Jim Flannery (*un-credited*)
Construction Chief: Archie Hall (*un-credited*)
Director of Photography: Robert Hoffman
Film Coordinator: Donald Tait
Film Editor: Ace Clark, a.c.e.
Make-up Artist: George Gray
Production Coordinator: Joe Wonder
Scientific Advisor on Electronics and Radar Operation: Maxwell Smith
Property Master: Max Pittman
Recorder: Larry Golding (*un-credited*)
Script Supervisor: Billy Vernon
Set Decorator: Vincent Taylor
Set Designer: Jack Collis
Sound Mixer: Jay Ashworth
Sound Supervisor: Gus Galvin
Special Effects: Harry Redmond, Jr.
Wardrobe: Alfred Berke

Cast: Phyllis Coates (Karen Sheldon, $300); John Doucette (Jerome Nielson, $150); Charles Maxwell (Robert Thornton, $100); Adolphe Menjou (Dr. Elliott Harcourt, $2,000); and Warren Stevens (Prof. Richard Sheldon, $500)

Plot: Professor Richard Sheldon, a scientist working on top secret projects, mysteriously vanishes from a city in Germany. Two weeks later he reappears, just as mysteriously, in Zurich, Switzerland. Seemingly normal except for the two-week memory lapse, Sheldon returns to America where he falls into a coma. He does not respond to any treatment. His physician, Dr. Harcourt, is forced to the conclusion that agents of an unfriendly power may have forced Sheldon to divulge information and, by an unknown means, sealed his memory. It is soon discovered, however, that Sheldon responds strangely to

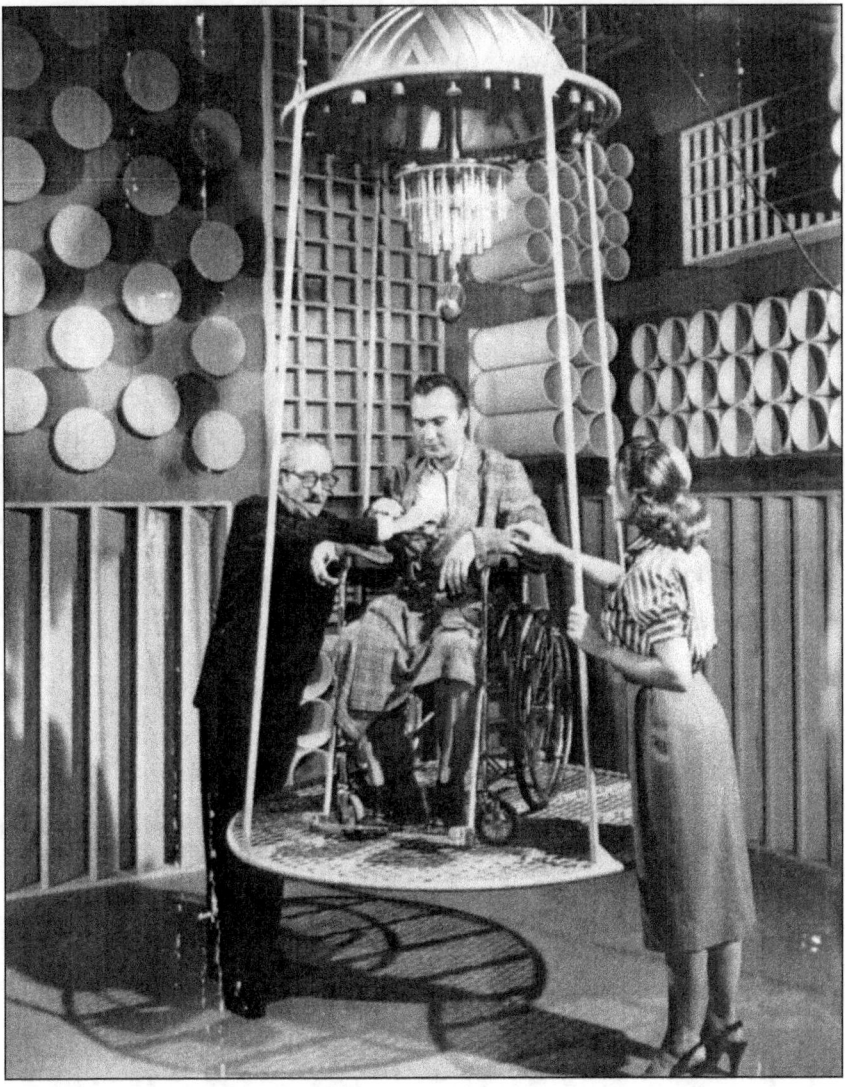

Prof. Richard Sheldon (Warren Stevens) prepares to spend time in the silence room in "Barrier of Silence."

noise. Treatment with every known sound fails to unlock Sheldon's mind. Finally it is suggested that silence rather than sound may be the key. In the scientifically-produced absolute silence room, Sheldon is able, through hypnotic suggestion, to recall the events of the lost two weeks. In the process, Dr. Harcourt learns how this psychological weapon can be used as a new technique in treating physical and mental ills.

Notes

- The entire episode was produced on Stage 6.
- Filming on the first day commenced at 9:45 a.m., after Truman Bradley's lab demonstration for episode 19b was completed.
- The stock footage of the Sheldon house was the same used in numerous episodes including "The Lost Heartbeat."
- The first draft of this episode was titled "Cone of Silence."
- The props hanging on the wall including the tubes, in the silent room, were used in "Jupitron" and "Dead Storage." To create the silent room, the audio track to the episode was removed—the actors and sound effects did not have to play make-believe on the set.

The September 1, 1955 issue of *Variety* reviewed this episode:

"What began as an interesting half-hour bogged down in technicalities and long-winded dialogue in this latest *Science Fiction* presentation. An uneven struggle against the script defeats both actors and director.

"For one thing, even a simplified explanation of sound and the effects of its absence—silence—serves to destroy whatever is left of the tale's pace. For another, narrator Truman Bradley expounds what is happening on-screen, instead of permitting the story to tell itself. So much time taken up with scientific lectures hardly makes for good television drama.

"Plot concerns a young scientist subjected to an unknown form of torture which has left him in a state of perpetual come. Adolphe Menjou eventually deduces that the scientist, played by Warren Stevens, has been subjected to utter silence over an extended period, nearly destroying his mind. Dr. Menjou manages to restore him to the attractive bosom of his family, portrayed by Phyllis Coates.

"In the past, there have been successful and interesting attempts to combine the wonders of science with the art of storytelling. This is not one of them."

EPISODE #21 "NEGATIVE MAN"

PRODUCTION #1021 / 22B
DATES OF PRODUCTION: JUNE 20 AND 21, 1955
DIRECTED BY HENRY S. KESLER

SCRIPT & STORY

FINAL DRAFT BY THELMA SCHNEE, CIRCA JUNE 15, 1955
TELEPLAY BY THELMA SCHNEE, FROM A SHORT STORY OF THE SAME NAME BY IVAN TORS

PRODUCTION CREDITS

1ST ASST. CAMERAMAN: SPEC JONES (UN-CREDITED)
1ST. CO. GRIP: CARL MIKSCH (UN-CREDITED)
2ND ASST. DIRECTOR: BOBBY RAY (UN-CREDITED)
ASSISTANT DIRECTOR: BERT CHERVIN
BOOM MAN: ELMER HAGLUND (UN-CREDITED)
CONSTRUCTION CHIEF: ARCHIE HALL (UN-CREDITED)
DIRECTOR OF PHOTOGRAPHY: MONROE "MONK" ASKINS
FILM COORDINATOR: DONALD TAIT
FILM EDITOR: DUNCAN MANSFIELD, A.C.E.
GAFFER: S.H. BARTON (UN-CREDITED)
MAKE-UP ARTIST: GEORGE GRAY
PRODUCTION COORDINATOR: JOE WONDER
SCIENTIFIC ADVISOR ON ELECTRONICS AND RADAR OPERATION: MAXWELL SMITH
PROPERTY MASTER: MAX PITTMAN
RECORDER: BOB POST (UN-CREDITED)
SCRIPT SUPERVISOR: LARRY LUND
SET DECORATOR: VINCENT TAYLOR
SET DESIGNER: JACK COLLIS
SOUND MIXER: GARRY HARRIS
SOUND SUPERVISOR: GUS GALVIN
SPECIAL EFFECTS: HARRY REDMOND, JR.
WARDROBE: ALFRED BERKE

CAST: David Alpert (Edmund Reis, $75); Dane Clark (Vic Murphy, $2,000); Tom Daly (Dr. Markell, $75); Peter Davis (Frank, $70);

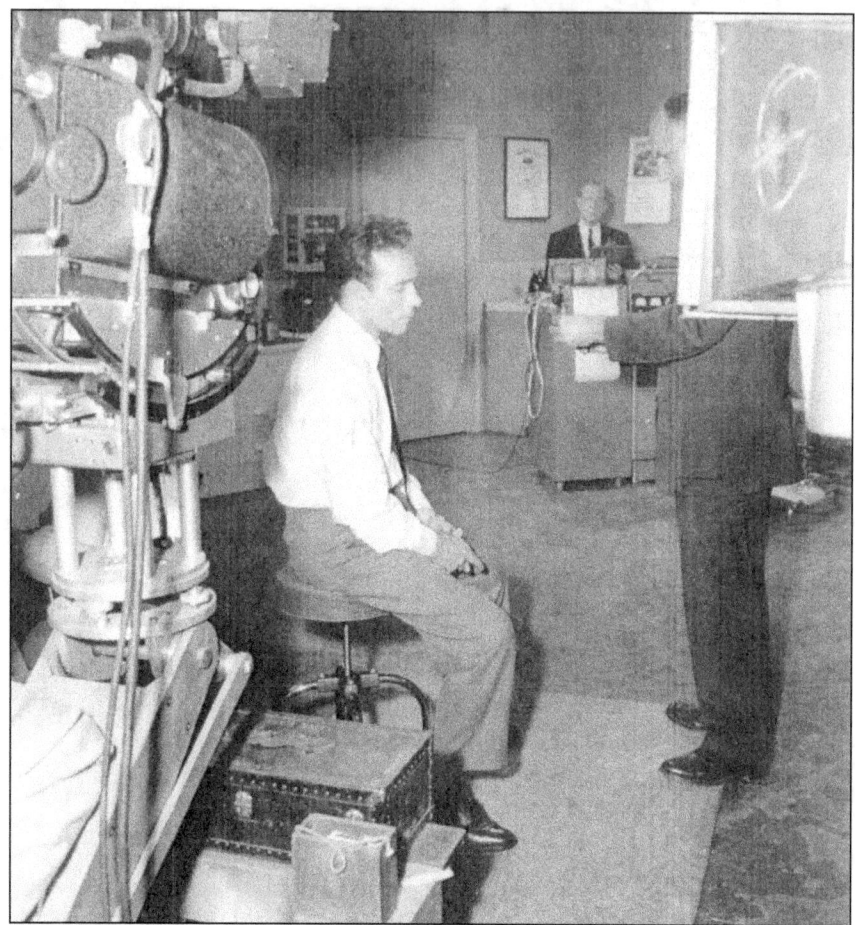

Dane Clark and Robert F. Simon in "Negative Man."

Joe Forte (Prof. Spaulding, $100); Beverly Garland (Sally Torens, $300); Pat Miller (Joe, $75); Robert F. Simon (Prof. Norman Stern, $150); and Carl "Alfalfa" Switzer (Pete, $100)

PLOT: An accidental discharge of electrical power by an "electronic brain" has a strange effect on Vic Murphy, a young electrician servicing the computer at the cybernetics research center. He is mysteriously able to solve a difficult mathematical equation with ease . . . and his physical senses are capable of unbelievable sensitivity. His acute hearing enables him to listen to both ends of a telephone conversation in a nearby phone booth and thereby, he becomes involved with Sally Torens and her rejection by her fiance. His abnormal

Robert F. Simon and Dane Clark in "Negative Man."

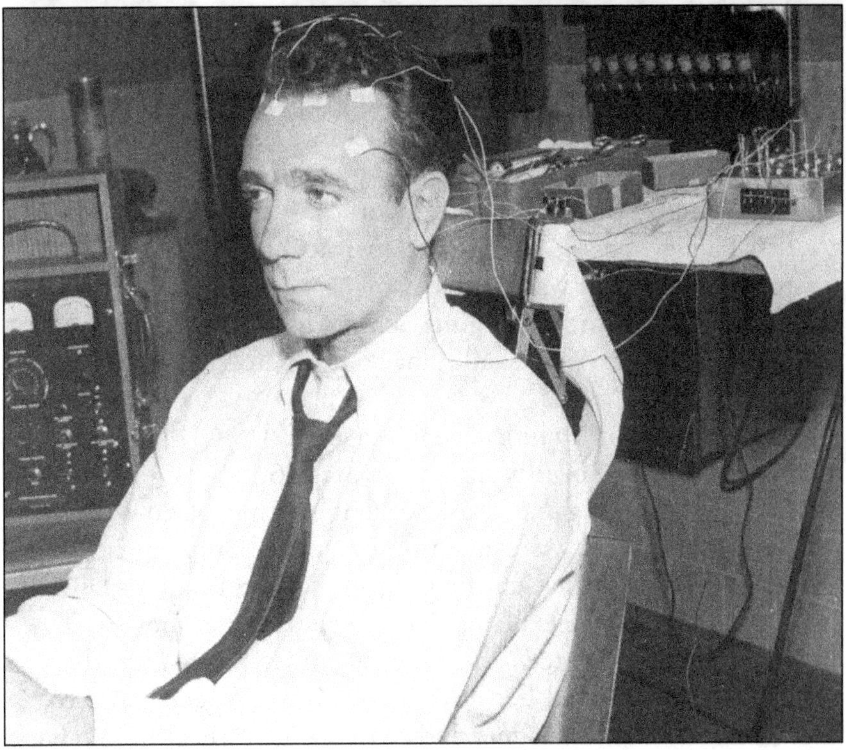

Dane Clark undergoes a series of tests in "Negative Man."

sense of smell detects gas, enabling him to foil Sally's suicide attempt. Tests at the University establish a theory advanced by Professor Stern, who attributes Vic's genius to an over supply of electrons creating a negative charge in his body and opening the way to future achievements in mental research. When Vic unexpectedly returns to normal he finds his personal life richer for having found a new love interest. He intends to equip himself to follow mental research and it appears that Sally will share his hopes and dreams of the future.

Notes

- Writer Thelma Schnee was introduced to Ivan Tors through Richard Carlson, who guest-starred in an episode of television's *Lights Out!*, which she also scripted. Months later, Schnee wrote to the actor asking if he could facilitate her employment as a staff writer for *I Led Three Lives*, which Carlson was presently the star. Carlson was unable to do so, but instead forwarded her name and contact info to Ivan Tors who, during a story conference, handed her his story outline and the premise of the series. Schnee was hired to write the first and final draft of the script.
- Schnee was later successful in selling a plot proposal to Ivan Tors less than a year later which became the second season episode, "The Throwback."
- According to production paperwork, this was Thelma Schnee's first Hollywood sale (she formerly wrote for New York television productions) and wanted her name to appear on the screen under a pen name of Virginia Sehner, but Tors explained that her career as a writer would not be hampered if she went under her real name.
- The first day of filming was on Stage 5.
- The second day of filming was on Stage 6.
- The chess board game is an excellent example of how Ivan Tors and his crew were able to use standard props to create the illusion of real scientific gadgets. During Bradley's lab demonstration, he explains that the chess pieces move as a result of a calculated "thinking machine." In reality, the chess pieces moved because the bottom of specific pieces were fitted with a magnet and someone underneath the table

Truman Bradley in casual clothing, being instructed on how to introduce the "thinking machine" to the audience, demonstrated in the form of a chess board. Sam Gilmore and Junior play with the same checkerboard in the episode, "The Long Day."

moved each chess piece as instructed in crayon underneath the table. The computers Bradley refers to as the "cybernetics research center" are prop computers (fake computers, really, just boards of lights that flash on and off) that appear in the opening pan and scan scene of all the second season episodes.

The September 8, 1955 issue of *Variety* reviewed this episode: "An electronic brain goes berserk and releases a charge of 20,000 volts into the body of a laboratory worker. His survival is hailed as a miracle but this is a mere trifle compared to what is to follow. He can think, see and hear as well as the machine, and from then on it's a series of incredibilities. It's an intriguing subject and fanciful enough to hold the tuners-in to its climatic paradox.

"In scientific jargon it is told that man uses only a small part of his mental electricity he received from the shock gave him the same abnormal powers as the 'thinking machine.' Using his extra-sensory powers, he kayoed a guy who slapped his girl far beyond his vision, smelled gas from a faraway apartment and prevented a suicide, repeated the other end of a phone conversation far from earshot, and added up a long row of figures in a flash.

"But, as the scientist said, his negative charge dissipated and he was just a plain Joe again. Truman Bradley came on to say at the close, 'Of course this was pure fiction,' which was pure superfluity. Dane Clark played the over-charged genius with dramatic tenseness and fixed expression. Beverly Garland was pert and pouty as the girl he continually dogged, and other components were Carl Switzer, Robert Simon, Joe Forte, Pat Miller, David Alpert and Tom Daly. Direction of Henry Kesler was well gaited."

"NEGATIVE MAN"

BY IVAN TORS

A young scientist is inside the giant cyclotron repairing the machine when somebody by mistake turns on the machine. The high voltage hits him but fails to kill him.

When he comes to in the doctor's office, he is apparently unharmed. The doctor sends him home to recover from the shock.

On his way home he stops in a cocktail lounge. A girl who is down and out sits at the next table waiting for somebody who does not come.

The scientist has a strange, unexplained knowledge of what goes on in the girl's mind. He tries to talk to her but the girl is scared. She thinks that he knows her and is poking fun at her plight.

When the girl walks out of the bar, the scientist knows that she is going to kill herself. Without knowing her address, he finds her apartment without any difficulty. He smells gas, carries the girl out and takes her to his doctor.

The girl's life is saved and he takes her to his home. In the meantime he reveals to the doctor his strange knowledge of what goes on inside other persons' brain. The doctor runs a test and the result is fantastic. He is in possession of incredible extra-sensory powers.

They feel that the negative charging of the brain may account for his telepathic prowess. Being exposed to high voltage must have brought on the change.

In 24 hours his extraordinary power dissipates but he saved the life of a being, found love and a new life.

EPISODE #22 "DEAD RECKONING"

PRODUCTION #1022 / 21B
DATES OF PRODUCTION: JUNE 10 AND 11, 1955
DIRECTED BY HERBERT L. STROCK

SCRIPT & STORY

FIRST DRAFT BY GENE LEVITT, JUNE 1, 1955
REVISED PAGES DATED JUNE 7 AND 8, 1955
FINAL DRAFT BY GENE LEVITT, JUNE 8, 1955
TELEPLAY BY GENE LEVITT

PRODUCTION CREDITS

1ST ASST. CAMERAMAN: JIM BELL (*UN-CREDITED*)
1ST CO. GRIP: MEL BLEDSOE (*UN-CREDITED*)
2ND ASST. DIRECTOR: BOBBY RAY (*UN-CREDITED*)
2ND CAMERAMAN: BUD MAUTINO (*UN-CREDITED*)
2ND CO. GRIP: BILL RECORD (*UN-CREDITED*)
ASSISTANT DIRECTOR: BERT CHERVIN
BOOM MAN: ELMER HAGLUND (*UN-CREDITED*)
CONSTRUCTION CHIEF: ARCHIE HALL (*UN-CREDITED*)
DIRECTOR OF PHOTOGRAPHY: ROBERT HOFFMAN
FILM COORDINATOR: DONALD TAIT
FILM EDITOR: THOMAS SCOTT
GAFFER: S.H. BARTON (*UN-CREDITED*)
MAKE-UP ARTIST: GEORGE GRAY
PRODUCTION COORDINATOR: JOE WONDER
SCIENTIFIC ADVISOR ON ELECTRONICS AND RADAR OPERATION:
    MAXWELL SMITH
PROPERTY MASTER: MAX PITTMAN
RECORDER: BOB POST (*UN-CREDITED*)

Publicity photo for "Dead Reckoning."

Script Supervisor: Larry Lund
Set Decorator: Vincent Taylor
Set Designer: Jack Collis
Sound Mixer: Garry Harris
Sound Supervisor: Gus Galvin
Special Effects: Harry Redmond, Jr.
Wardrobe: Alfred Berke

CAST: Tom Anthony (Tom, the engineer, $70); Steve Brodie (1st Lt. David Cramer, the navigator, $750); James Craig (Capt. John Perry, the pilot, $1,200); Frank Gerstle (Col. Eugene Beckwith, $100); Everett Glass (Prof. Millard Townsend, $125); Art Lewis (Tech. Sgt. Cornelius "Corny" Cooper, $75); Arleen Whelan (Evelyn Raleigh, $600); and Adam Williams (1st Lt. Frances Buchanan, the co-pilot, $300)

PLOT: A volcano erupts in the Arctic Circle, close to an American military base which is vital to the polar radar defense chain. The

Behind-the-scenes photo from "Dead Reckoning."

army doesn't want to quit the base unless it is likely that the volcano may erupt again, endangering life and property. The word of an expert geo-physicist is needed at once. The army is assigned to fly him (and his female assistant) from the University in Boston to the Arctic Circle base at once. The flight is routine, until the plane is in the Arctic Circle. Then, impenetrable weather makes instrument flying necessary. When all the instruments fail as the plane enters a magnetic storm, they discover they have passed the point of no return. The plane ascends and descends countless times, looking for a break in the weather above, or below, which will result in a chance to verify position. The process consumes great quantities of gasoline. Now it's a question of (1) sufficient fuel, and (2) clearing a mountain (which is abruptly before the base) and landing *without* a barometer. The scientist-passenger aboard solves this problem by the employment of an elementary scientific principle concerning the boiling point of water. The plane is landed safely . . . just as the last drop of gasoline is spent.

Notes

- A Ritter fan was ordered by special effects for this episode.
- The first day of production was filmed on Stage 1 and Stage 6.
- The second day of production was filmed on Stage 1.

The September 16, 1955 issue of *Variety* reviewed this episode:

"Hero of this tale of the wild, blue yonder is a geophysicist, and if that throws you, just twist the dial and come back to Earth. Stick it out and you grapple with sun spots, magnetic induction and other scraps of science that issue glibly from the professor, but must fall like a stone on the mentality of the viewer. Dramatically it has moments of suspense built up mostly from dialog in a plane fighting the elements to stay aloft.

"Crew of a scientific expedition is briefed on the peril of making a landing on an island in the Arctic, with a nearby volcano kicking up a disturbance. Caught in a magnetic storm, the instrument panel goes berserk and it's blind flying the rest of the way. But the professor traces the trouble to sun spots and the ship is righted and back on the beam.

"The real fans of this type of program must have had themselves an evening. As for the others, drawn to their sets by the magnetism, it must have been a harrowing experience. Too much science, not enough fiction and no effort made to reduce the terminology to lay understanding. Truman Bradley's explanation was helpful but it was too difficult to dig the professor. If it's the particular devotees of these fantasies they are trying to please, they'll have to settle for a relatively small audience.

"James Craig and Steve Brodie carry most of the acting load, which takes only their dialog talents. The same goes for Everett Glass, Adam Williams, Art Lewis and Frank Gerstle. Arleen Whelan goes along for the ride. Herbert Strock gives the direction exciting pace."

EPISODE #23 "A VISIT FROM DR. PLINY"

PRODUCTION #1023 / 24B
DATES OF PRODUCTION: JUNE 27 AND 28, 1955
DIRECTED BY HENRY S. KESLER

SCRIPT & STORY
FIRST DRAFT BY SLOAN NIBLEY, JUNE 21, 1955
FINAL DRAFT BY SLOAN NIBLEY, JUNE 24, 1955
TELEPLAY BY SLOAN NIBLEY

PRODUCTION CREDITS
1ST ASST. CAMERAMAN: SPEC JONES (*UN-CREDITED*)
1ST CO. GRIP: MEL BLEDSOE (*UN-CREDITED*)
2ND ASST. DIRECTOR: EDDIE MULL (*UN-CREDITED*)
2ND CAMERAMAN: HOWARD SCHWARTZ (*UN-CREDITED*)
2ND CO. GRIP: TOMMY MATHEWS (*UN-CREDITED*)
3RD GRIP: EDDIE MANRIQUEZ (*UN-CREDITED*)
ASSISTANT DIRECTOR: ED STEIN
ASST. PROP MAN: GENE STONE (*UN-CREDITED*)
BEST BOY: MIKE HUDSON (*UN-CREDITED*)
BOOM MAN: JIM FLANNERY (*UN-CREDITED*)
CONSTRUCTION CHIEF: ARCHIE HALL (*UN-CREDITED*)
DIRECTOR OF PHOTOGRAPHY: ROBERT HOFFMAN
ELECTRICIANS: ROY LEADBETTER, DICK BRIGHTMYER AND HERMAN LIPNEY (*ALL UN-CREDITED*)
FILM COORDINATOR: DONALD TAIT
FILM EDITOR: CHARLES CRAFT (*UN-CREDITED*) AND JOHN B. WOELZ (*CREDITED*)
GAFFER: BERT JONES (*UN-CREDITED*)
MAKE-UP ARTISTS: FRANK FITZ-GIBBON (*UN-CREDITED*) AND GEORGE GRAY (*CREDITED*)
PRODUCTION COORDINATOR: JOE WONDER
SCIENTIFIC ADVISOR ON ELECTRONICS AND RADAR OPERATION: MAXWELL SMITH
PROPERTY MASTER: MAX PITTMAN
RECORDER: LARRY GOLDING (*UN-CREDITED*)
SCRIPT SUPERVISOR: BILLY VERNON

Edmund Gwenn looks through a telescope in the episode, "A Visit from Dr. Pliny."

SET DECORATOR: VINCENT TAYLOR
SET DESIGNER: JACK COLLIS
SOUND MIXER: JAY ASHWORTH
SOUND SUPERVISOR: GUS GALVIN
SPECIAL EFFECTS: HARRY REDMOND, JR.
STILL PHOTOGRAPHER: HYMAN FINK (*UN-CREDITED*)
WARDROBE: ALFRED BERKE (*CREDITED*) AND FRANK TAUSS
   (*UN-CREDITED*)

CAST: Morris Ankrum (George Halsey, $100); Irvin Carroll (the news announcer); Juney Ellis (Mrs. Peterson, $100); Victoria Fox (the receptionist, $75); Edmund Gwenn (Dr. Pliny, $2,250); Marilyn Saris (Ruth Cantrell, the secretary, $75); William Schallert (Mr. Thomas, $200); and John Stephenson (Dr. Brewster, $200); and Howard Wright (Dr. Miller, $100)

Plot: At the famous Institute of Advanced Astrophysics, Dr. Brewster, the director, and Mr. Halsey, the business manager, receive a visit from the mysterious Dr. Pliny and his assistant, Mr. Thomas. Dr. Pliny has come to give him a vast scientific secret of the greatest importance, but he must work fast as his time is limited. Mr. Halsey is convinced that this is another of the typical crackpots who frequently visit the Institute, but when Dr. Pliny convinces Dr. Brewster with a fantastic demonstration that he knows what he's talking about, the director makes his own laboratory and scientific materials available. Dr. Pliny announces that he will create a machine that will create electricity from free energy . . . something that will dwarf nuclear energy. In a day he has the machine almost complete but is lacking only two small tritanium wires. This metal, he explains, has an atomic weight of three hundred, something so ridiculous that Halsey, in order to protect the good name of the Institute, sends for a psychiatrist who, after a brief interview, pronounces the little man paranoid. Warned by Ruth, the secretary, that he'll be put away for observation, Dr. Pliny and his assistant leave quietly, deeply disappointed in the turn of events. But they leave behind an unknown element known as tritanium and when Dr. Brewster completes the last component of the machine, for the first time, free energy is captured and a new age begins.

Notes

- This episode was produced under the title "The Golden Comb," which was the same title of the script.
- Production for this episode was unexpectedly held up for 20 minutes so special effects could be set up.
- The entire episode was filmed on Stage 5.
- Tritanium, referenced in this episode, is a fictional ore. It would later be referenced in episodes of *Star Trek: The Next Generation*, *Star Trek: Deep Space Nine* and *Star Trek: Voyager*.
- Truman Bradley uses a cloud chamber to create cosmic rays— electricity, in reality—and performs this same demonstration in the second-season episode, "Human Circuit."
- The cosmic ray chart hanging on the wall in this episode is the same prop that also appears in "Postcard From Barcelona,"

"Before the Beginning," "Project 44" and in the motion-picture *Gog* (1954).
- The subject of cosmic rays in this episode originate from brief passages in Bruno Rossi's article, "Where Do Cosmic Rays Come From?" originally published in the September 1953 issue of *Scientific American*.
- The gold ornament hanging on the wall in the final scene of this episode is the same prop hanging on the wall in the scientist's lab in the second-season episode, "Jupitron."
- Framed artwork that was used for the opening credit sequence of *Gog* (1954) can be seen hanging on the wall in the laboratory.

EPISODE #24 "THE STRANGE PEOPLE AT PECOS"

PRODUCTION #1024 / 25B
DATES OF PRODUCTION: JULY 5 AND 6, 1955
DIRECTED BY EDDIE DAVIS

SCRIPT & STORY
FIRST DRAFT BY DORIS GILBERT, JUNE 27, 1955
FINAL DRAFT BY DORIS GILBERT, JUNE 29, 1955
TELEPLAY BY DORIS GILBERT

PRODUCTION CREDITS
1ST ASST. CAMERAMAN: JIM BELL (*UN-CREDITED*)
1ST CO. GRIP: CARL MIKSCH (*UN-CREDITED*)
2ND ASST. DIRECTOR: EDDIE MULL (*UN-CREDITED*)
2ND CAMERAMAN: DICK RAWLINGS (*UN-CREDITED*)
ASSISTANT DIRECTOR: DONALD VERK
ASST. PROP MAN: GENE STONE (*UN-CREDITED*)
BEST BOY: MIKE HUDSON (*UN-CREDITED*)
BOOM MAN: ELMER HAGLUND (*UN-CREDITED*)
DIRECTOR OF PHOTOGRAPHY: MONROE "MONK" ASKINS
ELECTRICIANS: CHARLES STOCKWELL AND JOHN MILLMAN (*BOTH UN-CREDITED*)

FILM COORDINATOR: DONALD TAIT
FILM EDITOR: CHARLES CRAFT, A.C.E. (CREDITED) AND TOMMY SCOTT (UN-CREDITED)
GAFFER: S.H. BARTON (UN-CREDITED)
MAKE-UP ARTIST: GEORGE GRAY (1 DAY ONLY)
PRODUCTION CHIEF: ARCHIE HALL (UN-CREDITED)
PRODUCTION COORDINATOR: JOE WONDER
SCIENTIFIC ADVISOR ON ELECTRONICS AND RADAR OPERATION: MAXWELL SMITH
PROPERTY MASTER: MAX PITTMAN
RECORDER: BOB POST (UN-CREDITED)
SCRIPT SUPERVISOR: LARRY LUND
SET DECORATOR: BUD S. FRIEND (CREDITED) AND VINCENT TAYLOR (UN-CREDITED)
SET DESIGNER: JACK COLLIS
SET LABOR: SOL INVERSO (UN-CREDITED)
SOUND MIXER: GARRY HARRIS
SOUND SUPERVISOR: GUS GALVIN
SPECIAL EFFECTS: HARRY REDMOND, JR.
WARDROBE: ALFRED BERKE

CAST: Judith Ames (Amy Kern, $100); Paul Birch (Sheriff Gomez, $100); Doris Dowling (Celia Jameson, $500); Arthur Franz (Jeff Jameson, $1,250); Barry Froner (Junior Jameson, $75); Andrew Glick (Terry Jameson, $75); Dabbs Greer (Arthur Kern, $150); Hank Patterson (a farmer, $75); Beverly Washburn (Laurie Kern, $250); and James Westerfield (Dr. Conselman, $200).

PLOT: The mysterious Kerns family moves into a housing tract in New Mexico, not far from the Pecos Rocket Testing Grounds where work is being done with guided missiles. Deeply disturbed is Jeff Jameson, radar operator, who is convinced that the strange objects that have followed the rocket (known as Big Sam) every time it is tested, are flying saucers. Also learning that the Kern child is impervious to pain, talks familiarly about space and that her father behaves in an equally suspicious manner, Jameson is convinced that the Kerns are spies from another planet. One by one, each of these accusations is dis-proven and explained rationally and scientifically.

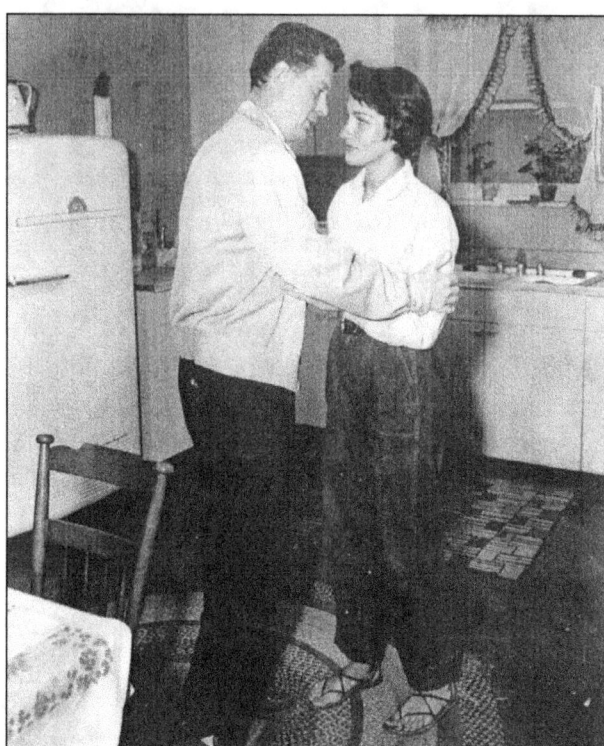

Arthur Franz and Doris Dowling comfort each other in the kitchen during rehearsals in "The Strange People at Pecos."

The kitchen set fully constructed.

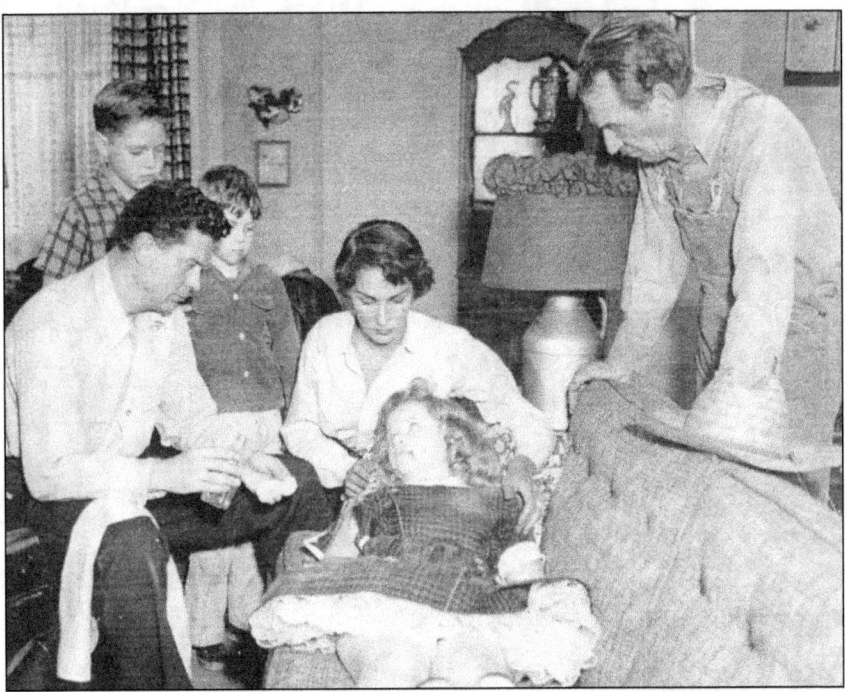

Beverly Washburn plays the role of a little girl hit by an automobile in "The Strange People at Pecos."

James Westerfield (FAR RIGHT) admirers Arthur Franz's technical skills in "The Strange People at Pecos."

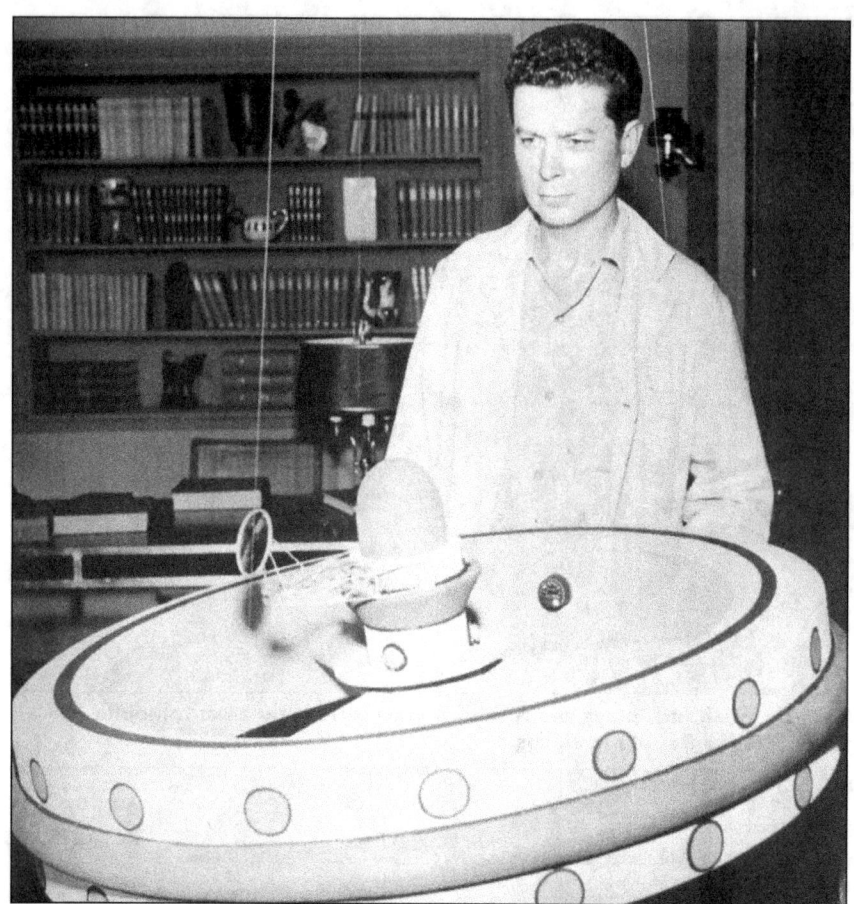

Arthur Franz examines what might be the model of a real space station in "The Strange People at Pecos."

All except one—Laurie Kern's claim that she has gone for a ride in a flying saucer.

Notes

- Beverly Washburn recalled to author/interviewer Tom Weaver: "I played a girl who people think is from another planet, because in one scene I get hit by a car and I get up and walk away and I have no pain. They had to construct this huge cut down my arm for the scene after I get hit by the car. Being in make-up was fun, because back in those days they used Hershey's Chocolate syrup for blood. I had this desire to lick it off [*laughs*]!"

- The entire first day of production was filmed on Stage 6.
- The second day of production was on Stage 6 and then on location at Plummer Park with the children.
- After principal filming was completed at the end of day one, the crew remained behind to film inserts for episode #24 from 5:40 to 6:55.
- The scene of the missile launching into the Earth's atmosphere in this episode is the same stock footage that appears in "Marked Danger" and the same footage that closed the movie *Gog* (1954).
- The model of the space station in this episode was the same model that appears in "Postcard From Barcelona" and "The Missing Waveband."

EPISODE #25 "DEAD STORAGE"

PRODUCTION #1025 / 23B
DATES OF PRODUCTION: JUNE 24 AND 25, 1955
DIRECTED BY JACK HERZBERG

SCRIPT & STORY

FIRST DRAFT BY STUART JEROME AND IVAN TORS, JUNE 17, 1955
FINAL DRAFT BY STUART JEROME, JUNE 21, 1955
TELEPLAY BY STUART JEROME, FROM AN ORIGINAL STORY BY
  IVAN TORS

PRODUCTION CREDITS

1ST ASST. CAMERAMAN: SPEC JONES (*UN-CREDITED*)
1ST CO. GRIP: MEL BLEDSOE (*UN-CREDITED*)
2ND ASST. DIRECTOR: EDDIE MULL (*UN-CREDITED*)
2ND CAMERAMAN: HOWARD SCHWARTZ (*UN-CREDITED*)
2ND CO. GRIP: TOMMY MATHEWS (*UN-CREDITED*)
3RD GRIP: EDDIE MANRIQUEZ (*UN-CREDITED*)
ASSISTANT DIRECTOR: RICHARD MCWHORTER
ASST. PROP MAN: ROBERT BENTON, SR. (*UN-CREDITED*)
BEST BOY: MIKE HUDSON (*UN-CREDITED*)
BOOM MAN: JIM FLANNERY (*UN-CREDITED*)

CONSTRUCTION CHIEF: ARCHIE HALL (*UN-CREDITED*)
DIRECTOR OF PHOTOGRAPHY: ROBERT HOFFMAN
DRIVERS: BALLARD, J. BROWN, FARMER AND RAY STODDARD [FIRST NAMES UNKNOWN] (*ALL UN-CREDITED*)
ELECTRICIANS: J. CONWALL, FRED HOUNSHELL AND WILLIAM KEILY (*ALL UN-CREDITED*)
FILM COORDINATOR: DONALD TAIT
FILM EDITOR: ACE CLARK (*UN-CREDITED*) AND CHARLES CRAFT, A.C.E. (CREDITED)
GAFFER: JOHN MILLMAN (*UN-CREDITED*)
HAIRDRESSER: PEGGY THOMPSON (*UN-CREDITED*)
MAKE-UP ARTISTS: GEORGE GRAY (*CREDITED*) AND FRANK FITZ-GIBBON (*UN-CREDITED*)
PRODUCTION COORDINATOR: JOE WONDER
SCIENTIFIC ADVISOR ON ELECTRONICS AND RADAR OPERATION: MAXWELL SMITH
PROPERTY MASTER: GENE STONE
RECORDER: LARRY GOLDING (*UN-CREDITED*)
SCRIPT SUPERVISOR: BILLY VERNON
SET DECORATOR: VINCENT TAYLOR
SET DESIGNER: JACK COLLIS
SOUND MIXER: JAY ASHWORTH
SOUND SUPERVISOR: GUS GALVIN
SPECIAL EFFECTS: HARRY REDMOND, JR.
SPECIAL EFFECTS: LOU HOPPER AND CHARLES SMITH (*BOTH UN-CREDITED*)
STILL PHOTOGRAPHY: HYMAN FINK (JUNE 25 ONLY, *UN-CREDITED*)
WARDROBE: ALFRED BERKE (CREDITED) AND FRANK TAUSS (*UN-CREDITED*)

CAST: Virginia Bruce (Dr. Myrna Griffin, $1,750); Booth Colman (Dr. McLeod, $100); Walter Coy (Warren Keith, $200); Douglas Henderson (Dr. Avery, $75); Robert Harris (Dr. Robinson, $150); and Loraine Knight (secretary for teletype)

PLOT: Members of an army project, engaged in establishing bases near the Arctic Circle, find a monstrous creature frozen in the ice. It is sent by refrigerated plane to the Institute of Scientific Research

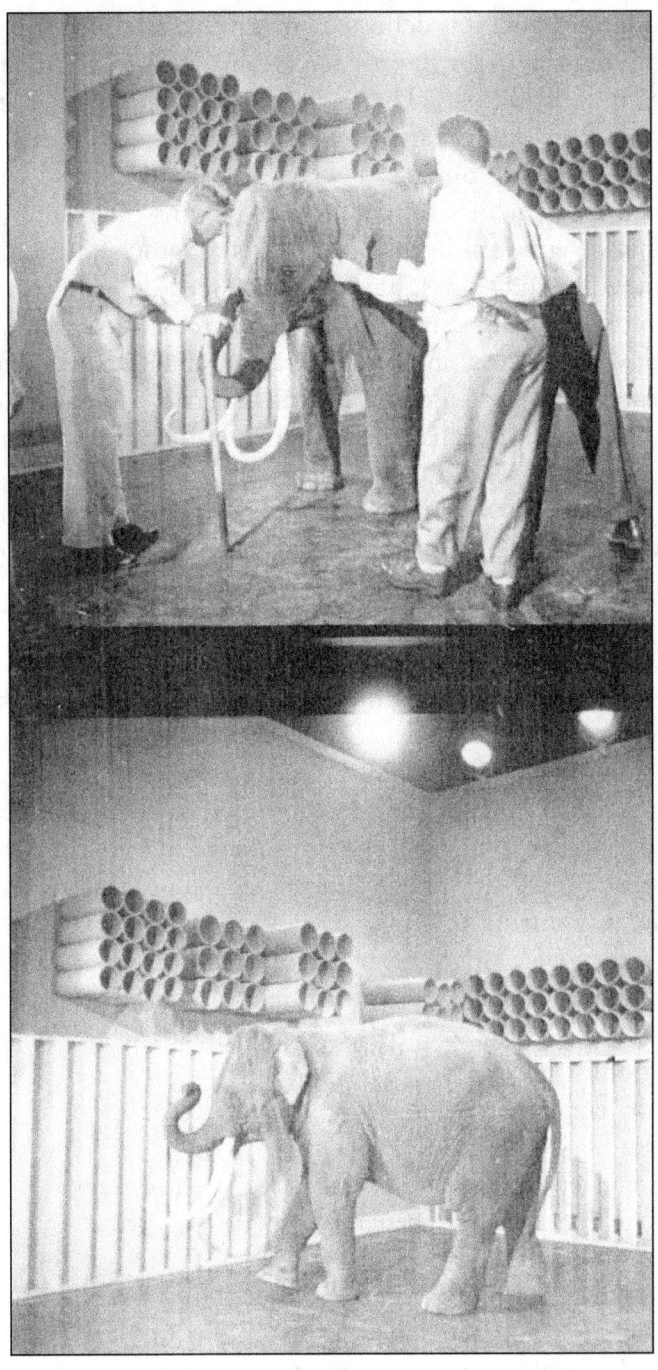

Specialized animal trainers were on the set to ensure the safety of the baby elephant.

in Washington where it is defrosted and given a treatment of galvanic shock and oxygen in an improvised steam room to see if the spark of dormant life still exists. The creature revives and for the first time in half a million years, man is face to face with a living mammoth! Dr. Myrna Griffin, one of the staff of scientists studying the mammoth, names him Toby and quickly wins his friendship. He becomes tame and healthy, but then starts outgrowing the confining room of the Institute. He is shipped off to a specially made compound in Wisconsin where he can roam at will. En route, however, traveling in a truck with Myrna, Toby becomes panicky and stampedes, breaking out of the truck and injuring Myrna. Myrna is unconscious for almost a week. During that time, Tobey pines away and finally falls victim to disease as a result of modern-day bacteria. Myrna returns to him just as he dies. But Toby's short re-life has not been in vain; thru him science has learned much about deep freezing and suspended animation.

Notes

- The entire first day of filming was devoted to interior shots on Stage 6. The second day, a Saturday, filming began on location at 7 a.m. along Mulholland Drive and the local freeway. Around 9:30 the cast and crew returned to the studio to film on Stage 6 and additional exterior shots of Stage 4 on the ramp.
- A traffic officer was paid $20 to make sure cars were kept out of the way during filming.
- Since they were unable to acquire a hairy elephant, the excuse for using a real elephant and adding as much hair as possible was for one of the scientists to remark that the ice destroyed most of his hair.
- A baby elephant was used for filming. He was bought in to the studio from the local zoo. His real name was Toby so the cast referred to him by his real name in the drama.
- The elephant trainer/keeper was Eugene Scott.
- A steam machine was set up on Stage 6 for the steam room.
- The fake steam pipes in the steam chamber were also on the wall in the second-season episode, "Jupitron."
- Stand-In Frank Hunt appears un-credited in an insert shot as the hand that lifts up the newspaper hailing: "Tobey Near Death."

- The framed map of the island on the wall in this episode also appears on the wall in "Sound of Murder."
- Actress Loraine Knight appears un-credited as the secretary operating the Teletype.

The October 6, 1955 issue of *Variety* reviewed this episode:
"Advance publicity describes 'Dead Storage' as 'a hair-raising story.' That it ain't. In fact, producer Ivan Tors' original is one of those gimmick ideas which strives for the fantastic, but trips lightly instead. Tors' modus operandi on this 'scientifiction' series is by now well established. He takes a bizarre idea and plays it for what it's worth. Sometimes it isn't worth much, as in the case of 'Storage.'

"On this outing, a prehistoric mammoth is discovered frozen in the Arctic. The half-million-year-old creature is brought to the Science Institute in Washington, brought back to life via a laboriously explained scientific process which escapes the layman viewer. And eventually it dies. To fill in are the stock ingredients—a widowed, purty femme scientist, a reporter who romances her and a male scientist who just sneers at the newsman. The mammoth (it's actually an elephant) finds in the femme scientist his momma love, and here is, inadvertently, the only fantastic note.

"Virginia Bruce and Walter Coy enact their lead roles as well as possible under the circumstances. Jack Herzberg's direction is no asset, nor is the scripting by Stuart Jerome."

"DEAD STORAGE"
A Glacier Story by Ivan Tors

A fish frozen in a block of ice may come back to life when the ice melts.

A microscopic animal called the waterbear which lives in water, may completely dry up when the lake dries out then years later come back to life when the lake bottom becomes wet again.

The navy is conducting permafrost experiments in the Artic and as they saw through the ice with electric saws, they find the well-preserved body of an ancient animal frozen in a block of ice. The animal is a baby mammoth about five feet tall and the block of ice is weighing two thousand tons.

Similar frozen mammoth were found before in the Siberian tundra, these animals bogged down in marshy plains, sinking down and froze through the glacier period. The Navy sends the block of ice with the mammoth to the Institute of Scientific Research in a refrigerator plane.

A paleontologist, a bacteriologist and a zoologist are called in for immediate consultation. The paleontologist is an old man, the bacteriologist a young scientist, the zoologist an attractive young woman who lost her husband and child in a car accident and ever since is interested only in her work. The three scientists decide to melt the block of ice and they are prepared for the following possibilities:

The animal is dead but his intestines may contain living material like grass, bacteria and bacilli from the glacier age and teach us a lot about the evolution of bacilli and bacteria and viruses.

That everything is dead but even then dead material can be studied.

That the animal is in suspended animation and with modern methods, when defrosted, can be brought back to life. These methods are galvanic shock to the heart, to the brain, different nerve centers, administration of heart-pumps and oxygen, etc.

The defrosting takes place very, very slowly in a steam chamber. When defrosted the animal is found motionless but different injections and medical experiments make his heart beat and there is a hope that the mammoth may live.

The baby mammoth is named Toby and remains in the custody of the woman zoologist and the bacteriologist. Of course, the animal must be kept in a completely sterile room, as he is vulnerable to modern day bacteria. The germs and viruses of today are slowly introduced to Toby and his custodians are watching his reactions nervously. After suffering from a few minor diseases, his health becomes consolidated and he turns into a very friendly creature.

From his behavior patterns and internal make-up, our scientists learn an awful lot about evolution and immunity. The fact that he is still alive proves that suspended animation in frozen condition is possible, that operations may be performed by putting the patients in a frozen or semi-frozen condition. That space travel may be accomplished by deep freezing the pilots and bringing them back to life after the rocket has left the gravitational pull of the Earth thus enabling them to withstand the shock and stress of the initial acceleration.

A scientific foundation donates funds to build an experimental station in Florida where the female zoologist and bacteriologist remain parents to Toby and keep observing him for the benefit of science.

EPISODE #26 "THE HUMAN EQUATION"

PRODUCTION #1026 / 26B
DATES OF PRODUCTION: JULY 12 AND 13, 1955
DIRECTED BY HENRY S. KESLER

SCRIPT & STORY

FIRST DRAFT BY NORMAN JOLLEY, JULY 1, 1955
FINAL DRAFT BY NORMAN JOLLEY, JULY 7, 1955
TELEPLAY BY NORMAN JOLLEY, BASED ON A STORY BY IVAN TORS

PRODUCTION CREDITS

1ST ASST. CAMERAMAN: JIM BELL (*UN-CREDITED*)
1ST CO. GRIP: CARL MIKSCH (*UN-CREDITED*)
2ND ASST. DIRECTOR BOBBY RAY (*UN-CREDITED*)
2ND CO. GRIP: MEL BLEDSOE (*UN-CREDITED*)
ASSISTANT DIRECTOR: JACK GERTSMAN
ASST. PROP MAN: STAN WALTERS (*UN-CREDITED*)
BEST BOY: CHARLES STOCKWELL (*UN-CREDITED*)
BOOM MAN: ELMER HAGLUND (*UN-CREDITED*)
CAMERA OPERATOR: DICK RAWLINGS
CONSTRUCTION CHIEF: ARCHIE HALL (*UN-CREDITED*)
DIRECTOR OF PHOTOGRAPHY: CURT FETTERS
ELECTRICIANS: CHARLES HANGER, FRED HOUNSHELL AND MIKE HUDSON (*ALL UN-CREDITED*)
FILM COORDINATOR: DONALD TAIT
FILM EDITOR: DUNCAN MANSFIELD (*UN-CREDITED*) AND JOHN B. WOELZ (*CREDITED*)
GAFFER: S.H. BARTON (*UN-CREDITED*)
MAKE-UP ARTIST: GEORGE GRAY

Production Coordinator: Joe Wonder
Scientific Advisor on Electronics and Radar Operation:
 Maxwell Smith
Property Master: Max Pittman
Recorder: Bob Post (*un-credited*)
Script Supervisor: Larry Lund
Set Decorator: Bruce MacDonald
Set Designer: Jack Collis
Sound Mixer: Garry Harris
Sound Supervisor: Gus Galvin
Special Effects: Harry Redmond, Jr.
Wardrobe: Alfred Berke

Cast: Peter Adams (Dr. Clements, $150); Marjorie Bennett (the woman, $75); Jean Byron (Nan Guild, $150); MacDonald Carey (Dr. Lee Seward, $2,500); Herbert Heyes (the governor, $100); Tom McKee (Dr. Henry J. Upton, $125); George Meader (Dr. Elbert Finch, $75); Elizabeth Whitney (the cleaning woman, $75); and Michael Winkelman (Ken Guild, $100)

Plot: Dr. Elbert Finch, Owen Research Foundation chief biochemist, is convicted of murder. Professing innocence, he is condemned to the gas chamber. Dr. Lee Seward, replacement for Finch at the Foundation, hopes for a quick briefing so he can proceed with Finch's extremely important anti-biotic project. He is startled to be met with resentment and hospitality by his staff, including Dr. Clements and Nan Guild, Finch's niece. The hostility increases . . . then suddenly switches to warm friendliness . . . then just as incongruously, reverts to hostility, insults by Nan and a physical attack on Seward by Clements. Just as Seward thinks he's losing his mind, he discovers that exposure to a grain fungus, employed in the lab. The anti-biotic project is actually capable of inducing insanity in a human. Experimenting on himself, Seward experiences all phases of insanity, proving that Finch was not responsible for the murder and that the staff knew nothing of their hostile actions toward Seward. Through this discovery, Finch's execution is postponed by the Governor. Mental illness is related to the chemistry of the body for the first time and a new potent weapon in science's battle against

Director Henry S. Kesler supervises production of "The Human Equation."

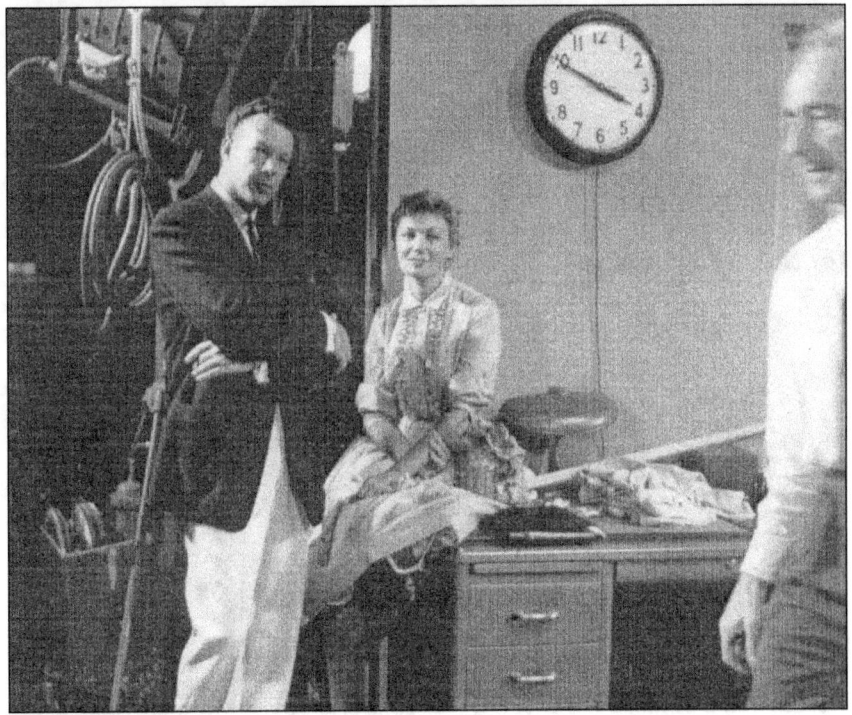
Actors take a break between takes. Director Henry S. Kesler on the far right.

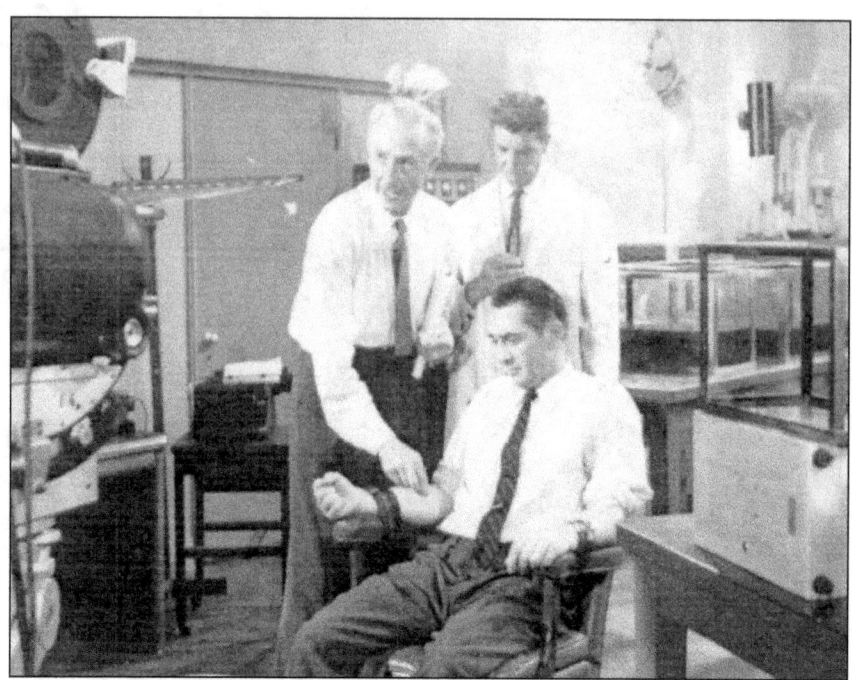

MacDonald Carey finds himself strapped down while taking direction from Henry S. Kesler.

Rehearsing a scene. Jean Byron (LEFT) comforts young Michael Winkelman (MIDDLE) when MacDonald Carey (RIGHT) comes to visit.

insanity is introduced. And in the process a warm relationship has developed between Seward and Nan and her fatherless eight-year-old son, Ken.

Notes

- The entire episode was filmed on Stage 5.
- The stock footage of the exterior of the observatory was reused for two other episodes, "The Stones Began to Move" and "Postcard From Barcelona."
- Jean Byron's casting may have been the result of her prior casting of Connie Stewart in *The Magnetic Monster* (1953).

The October 13, 1955 issue of *Variety* reviewed this episode:
"This vidpic might be labeled a why-did-he-do-it. Opening, with a scientist murdering a scrubwoman, yarn deals not with question of his guilt (there isn't any), but rather what made him kill for no apparent reason. It is interestingly told, and benefits from top thesping by Macdonald Carey, as a scientist who finds the answers.

"Carey, called in to replace the scientist-killer who is to be executed, first meets with hostility from his colleagues, then they like him very much, then they're hostile, etc. His probing uncovers fact that fumes from a new antibiotic they are working on causes temporary insanity. And with this convincer, he saves the scientist-killer from electrocution.

"Carey gives a restrained and effective performance and receives good support from Jean Byron. Peter Adams, Herbert Heyes and Michael Winkelman are okay in lesser parts. Direction by Henry S. Kesler from a well-constructed and conceived teleplay by Norman Jolley moves along at a fast tempo."

EPISODE #27 "TARGET HURRICANE"

Production #1027 / 27B
Dates of Production: June 15 and 16, 1955
Directed by Leigh Jason

SCRIPT & STORY

First draft dated July 5, 1955
Final draft dated July 11, 1955
Teleplay by Robert Schaefer and Eric Freiwald, from a story by Ivan Tors

PRODUCTION CREDIT

1st Asst. Cameraman: Spec Jones (*un-credited*)
1st Co. Grip: Mel Bledsoe (*un-credited*)
2nd Asst. Director: Eddie Mull (*un-credited*)
2nd Cameraman: Bud Mautino (*un-credited*)
2nd Co. grip: Tommy Mathews (*un-credited*)
3rd. Grip: Eddie Manriquez (*un-credited*)
Assistant Director: Donald Verk
Asst. Prop Man: Don Smith (*un-credited*)
Best Boy: Charles Stockwell (*un-credited*)
Boom Man: Jim Flannery (*un-credited*)
Cableman: Bud Alper (*un-credited*)
Construction Chief: Archie Hall (*un-credited*)
Director of Photography: Robert Hoffman
Electricians: Charles Hanger, Fred Hounshell and Hap Morley (*all un-credited*)
Film Coordinator: Donald Tait
Film Editor: Thomas Scott
Gaffer: S.H. Barton (*un-credited*)
Make-up Artist: George Gray
Production Coordinator: Joe Wonder
Scientific Advisor on Electronics and Radar Operation: Maxwell Smith
Property Master: Max Pittman
Recorder: Larry Golding (*un-credited*)
Script Supervisor: Billy Vernon

Marshall Thompson poses with Margaret Field and young Gary Marshall for a publicity photo.

SET DECORATOR: BRUCE MACDONALD
SET DESIGNER: JACK COLLIS
SOUND MIXER: JAY ASHWORTH
SOUND SUPERVISOR: GUS GALVIN
SPECIAL EFFECTS: HARRY REDMOND, JR.
STILL MAN: CHARLIE ROSE (JUNE 15 ONLY, *UN-CREDITED*)
WARDROBE: ALFRED BERKE

Marshall Thompson prepares to make an announcement in "Target Hurricane."

The Episode Guide: Season One

Margaret Field is concerned for her young son while her husband waits for the latest weather reports.

CAST: John Bryant (Lt. Collier, $80); Ray Collins (Hugh Fredericks, $300); John Doucette (Colonel Stewart, $150); Margaret Field (Julie Tyler, $500); Robert Griffin (Walter Bronson, $125); Paul Hahn (voice of the pilot, $70); Gary Marshall (Bobby Tyler, $75); Marshall Thompson (James Tyler, $1,000); and Will J. White (Non-Com, an Air Force technician, $75)

PLOT: A hurricane of unprecedented magnitude is approaching the Florida coastline with none of the tell-tale signs of an approaching hurricane having been evident until an hour before. The S.S. Arvis reports the sound of a tremendous explosion from the sea prior to the discovery of the cyclonic cloud. James Tyler, a meteorologist and local weatherman, warns the public through television and radio to dig in, be prepared and stay calm, while he and his wife are bearing down with fear. Their small son is out on a camping trip with other cub scouts and they cannot be reached. Air Rescue Helicopters fail to find them. The Flying Laboratories of the Hurricane Hunters fly into the eye of the storm to observe direction and characteristics of the wind. In the meantime, the Navy is sending a submarine with a team of scientists to the location of the reported explosion. Their finding is that a giant meteorite from outer space crashed into the ocean and was the cause of the storm. Luckily, only the outer wall of the hurricane hits the town and giving enough time to the public to prepare, averts a major disaster. Tyler is relieved when he learns that the cub scouts were safe; they had taken refuge in a cave.

Notes

- This episode was produced under the title "Hurricane Warning."
- Ivan Tors' original outline, dated Jan. 18, 1955, was titled "Hurricane." The first draft of the script re-titled the story to "Hurricane Hunters" and production notes report the episode was re-titled again as "Hurricane Warning" and assigned production number 16B, before being revised again for the version we see on film today. Tors based his story on the findings in a magazine article titled "Hurricanes" by R.H. Simpson, originally published in the June 1954 issue of *Scientific American*, which featured a weather balloon on the cover.
- The entire production was filmed on Stage 6.
- Marshall Thompson was a favorite of Ivan Tors, who, years later, hired the actor to star in another television program produced by Tors, *Daktari*.
- This was the only episode to be reviewed by the *New York Times*, who remarked: "The early evening show apparently has aimed at both the teen group and the adults, but even Tom Swift had more excitement on his old electric motorcycle than the cast did last night . . . But just at the point where science fiction usually steps in and puts nature back in its place, that's it, at the moment when the wind seems to be a best 300 yards off the beach, what does the author do? He has a prosaic high-pressure area push it out to sea. The science fiction angle comes up only when things have settled down and the submarine reports that the hurricane was caused by a meteorite hurtling into the sea. In any real science fiction story, the meteorite would have had the leading role."

- To ensure accuracy regarding the weather bureau's technical lingo, Dr. Leon Lyon was on hand during filming, according to talent contracts.
- The poster hanging on the wall behind Marshall during his telecast, warning people of the growing threat, is the same prop seen hanging on the wall in numerous episodes of the series including "Project 44."

The October 20, 1955 issue of *Variety* reviewed this episode:

"All the tension and near-panic aroused by an oncoming hurricane about to hit Florida are vividly captured in 'Target,' but just what this has to do with scientifiction is a moot point. In what appears to be an afterthought, in deference to this series' *Science Fiction Theatre* tag, writers have it that the hurricane is caused by a meteor from outer space. This is reaching way over to another planet.

"In any other anthology series, 'Hurricane' would have fit smoothly, but with Ziv ballying it as an S-and-F series, it was out of place. Yarn by Robert Schaefer and Eric Freiwald, from an original by producer Ivan Tors, is one of utter simplicity, showing how a big wind is spotted off Florida, and the precautions and warnings taken by the Weather Bureau, alerting the population of what's ahead. Stock shots of a hurricane are well integrated into the footage.

"Marshall Thompson's performance, as the weatherman in charge who is doubly concerned because his son's off on a Boy Scout hike as the wind approaches, is a very good one. While Thompson dominates, he gets good support from Margaret Field, Ray Collins, John Doucette and Gary Marshall. Leigh Jason's directing is polished."

"HURRICANE"

BY IVAN TORS

The story starts with various shots of Nevada atomic explosions. Giant four-engine flying laboratories and jet planes fly into the atomic cloud to gather important knowledge. Narrator explains the importance of flying laboratories which can cruise at high altitudes tracing radiation, testing equipment, forecasting weather, release radio sound balloons, collect samples of moisture and dust particles, etc.

Our story takes us to the Florida coast, where the Air Force has a weather station with an important function. It is their duty to fly four-engine planes into the eyes of hurricanes, register wind direction and give ample warning to the mainland. In our story, the weather plane radios back frightening information. A hurricane of usual strength is building up seven hundred miles from the coast and approaching the coastline with the unheard speed of 250 miles per hour. What is most alarming is that two ships at sea reported the sound of an explosion. The possibility prevails that an atomic bomb or a hydrogen bomb of foreign origin was dropped in the Caribbean, generating the hurricane.

The Colonel in charge calls in the mayor of the town and the manager of the local television station informing them of the imminent danger. He recommends that the TV station remain on the air all the time, warning the population of the approaching hurricane, giving instruction to board in their windows or seek shelter in basements. The population is advised not to escape the city because the roads will be clogged, traffic stopped and the danger in the open will be even greater. In the meantime, the hurricane gathers more and more momentum. Planes cannot fly into the eye of the hurricane any longer without the danger of destruction. A few matador guided missiles are shot in the hurricane's eye with radio sound equipment to register the force. The information received now is even more alarming. The speed of the hurricane reached an unprecedented 300 miles per hour. No natural hurricane ever reached that velocity.

In the meantime, scientists in cooperation with the Air Force are investigating the possibility that the source of the monstrous wind was man-made and did not originate by nature. The hurricane reaches the coast line but its full-force does not hit the city. There is a great deal of damage, some casualties, but the worst of it is over. Flying laboratories now re-enter the sector where the hurricane has originated. They find traces of metal vapor in the ocean, establishing that the hurricane was caused by a giant meteorite that hit the water and while streaking through the atmosphere, caused the atmosphere change necessary to precipitate a wind of such force. Once again, the Air Force proves itself to be worthy of any emergency.

EPISODE #28 "THE WATER MAKER"

PRODUCTION #1028 / 29B
DATES OF PRODUCTION: JULY 23, 25 AND 26, 1955
DIRECTED BY HERBERT L. STROCK

SCRIPT & STORY

FIRST DRAFT BY JERRY SACKHEIM, JUNE 20, 1955
SECOND DRAFT BY STUART JEROME, JULY 18, 1955
FINAL DRAFT BY STUART JEROME AND JERRY SACKHEIM, AUGUST 15, 1955
TELEPLAY BY STUART JEROME, FROM A STORY BY JERRY SACKHEIM

PRODUCTION CREDITS

1ST ASST. CAMERAMAN: JIM BELL (*UN-CREDITED*)
1ST CO. GRIP: CARL MIKSCH (JULY 23 ONLY, *UN-CREDITED*)
2ND ASST. DIRECTOR: BOBBY RAY (*UN-CREDITED*)
2ND CO. GRIP: TEX JACKSON (*UN-CREDITED*)
ASSISTANT DIRECTOR: ED STEIN
ASST. PROP MAN: HARRY OTT (*UN-CREDITED*)
BOOM MAN : ELMER HAGLUND (*UN-CREDITED*)
CAMERA OPERATOR: DICK RAWLINGS
CONSTRUCTION CHIEF: ARCHIE HALL (*UN-CREDITED*)
DIRECTOR OF PHOTOGRAPHY: MONROE "MONK" ASKINS
FILM COORDINATOR: DONALD TAIT
FILM EDITOR: JOHN B. WOELZ
GAFFER: S.H. BARTON (*UN-CREDITED*)
MAKE-UP ARTIST: GEORGE GRAY
PRODUCTION COORDINATOR: JOE WONDER
SCIENTIFIC ADVISOR ON ELECTRONICS AND RADAR OPERATION: MAXWELL SMITH
PROPERTY MASTER: MAX PITTMAN
RECORDER: BOB POST (*UN-CREDITED*)
SCRIPT SUPERVISOR: LARRY LUND
SET DECORATOR: BRUCE MACDONALD
SET DESIGNER: JACK COLLIS
SET LABOR: TED MCCASKEY (*UN-CREDITED*)
SOUND MIXER: GARRY HARRIS

Craig Stevens and Virginia Grey in "The Water Maker."

Producer Ivan Tors makes sure Virginia Grey is comfortable before departing for location shoots.

SOUND SUPERVISOR: GUS GALVIN
SPECIAL EFFECTS: HARRY REDMOND, JR.
WARDROBE: ALFRED BERKE

CAST: Virginia Grey (Sheila Dunlap, $750); John Mitchum (the sheriff, $80); Craig Stevens (Dr. David Brooks, $600); William Tallman (Norman Conway, $750); and Elmore Vincent (Charley, $200)

PLOT: Scientist David Brooks receives an urgent wire from his old friend, Dr. John Dunlap, asking him to come to Dunlap's isolated ranch in the Arizona desert, where he is working on a process of developing water in the desert through the chemical process of aqua crystallization. But when David arrives, he finds that Dunlap was killed a week previously in an explosion, caused by his final experiment, and that the telegram was sent by Dunlap's wife, Sheila, who was once engaged to marry David, but who broke off with him to marry the wealthier Dunlap. Bitter at Sheila's subterfuge, David wants to leave immediately . . . but two things intrigue him: The work John was doing and the mystery surrounding his death. David stays on . . . to learn that his friend had created a chemical system that creates water—and that the sheriff's cousin, Norman Conway, was the murderer. After fleeing through the desert for a spell, David and Sheila manage to trick Conway and disarm him, forcing him to the authorities who can do the investigation.

Notes
- This is one of the few episodes to be filmed in three days instead of two. The first and third day consisted of interior shots on both Stage 3 and Stage 6. The second day of filming consisted of all the exterior shots in the Arizona desert, filmed on location at the El Segundo Radio Tower located at Trask and Killgore streets.
- This episode was originally production number 25b, but re-numbered and shot at a later date than initially intended.
- The jeep featured in this episode was rented.

Episode #29 "The Unexplored"

Production #1029 / 30B
Dates of Production: July 29 and 30, 1955
Directed by Eddie Davis

Script & Story
First Draft dated July 23, 1955
Final Draft dated July 28, 1955
Teleplay by Arthur Weiss

Production Credits
1st Asst. Cameraman: Jim Bell (*un-credited*)
1st Co. Grip: Carl Miksch (*un-credited*)
2nd Asst. Director: Bobby Ray (*un-credited*)
2nd Co. Grip: Tex Jackson (*un-credited*)
3rd Grip: Walter Culp (*un-credited*)
Assistant Director: Richard McWhorter
Asst. Prop. Man: Harry Ott (*un-credited*)
Best Boy: Charles Stockwell (*un-credited*)
Boom Man: Elmer Haglund (*un-credited*)
Cableman: Gene Lloyd (*un-credited*)

Camera Operator: Dick Rawlings
Construction Chief: Archie Hall (*un-credited*)
Director of Photography: Curt Fetters
Drivers: Ray Stoddard (*un-credited*)
Electricians: Charles Hanger, Fred Hounshell and Louis Kreiger (*all un-credited*)
Film Coordinator: Donald Tait
Film Editor: Duncan Mansfield (*un-credited*) and John B. Woelz (*credited*)
Gaffer: S.H. Barton (*un-credited*)
Hairdresser: Naomi Cabin (*un-credited*)
Make-up Artist: George Gray
Production Coordinator: Joe Wonder
Scientific Advisor on Electronics and Radar Operation: Maxwell Smith
Property Master: Max Pittman
Recorder: Charles King (*un-credited*)
Script Supervisor: Larry Lund
Set Decorator: Bruce MacDonald
Set Designer: Jack Collis
Sound Mixer: Garry Harris
Sound Supervisor: Gus Galvin
Special Effects: Harry Redmond, Jr.
Wardrobe: Alfred Berke

Cast: George Crise (the college boy, $75); George Eldredge (Dean Trimble, $100); Paul Hahn (Lt. Heeley, $70); Madge Kennedy (Mrs. Canby, $150); Ruta Lee (the college girl, $75); Osa Massen (Julie Bondar, $500); Kent Smith (Prof. Alex Bondar, $1,250); and Harvey Stephens (Henry Stark, $200)

Plot: Professor Alex Bondar is seeking a clue to the nature of psychic events in the electro-chemical activity of the human brain, using Mrs. Canby as an experimental subject; she has had many psychic experiences. Prof. Bernhard Manheim, a famous biologist, is en route to the college to lecture in psychic research but he does not arrive on schedule. When Bondar's seminar is abruptly terminated on orders of the College trustee who believes such research is

Osa Massen and Kent Smith in "The Unexplored."

Producer Ivan Tors chats with actress Osa Massen.

"nonsense," Bondar resigns. His resignation triggers off a long, smoldering rift between him and his wife, a physical scientist who although she loves him, has no professional respect for his psychic research. When the police cannot find Prof. Manheim, the College trustee goads Bondar into trying to find the missing man by using the telepathic powers of Mrs. Canby. She fails but Bondar, now professionally defeated and about to lose his wife, is led to the hidden site of the mountain accident which has killed Prof. Manheim by a clairvoyant vision . . . from his wife.

Notes
- The first day of filming was on Stage 5.
- The second day of filming was on location at Bronson Canyon from 8:30 to 11:30, with filming then completed on Stage 4. The second day of filming was on a Saturday, extremely rare for ZIV-TV that normally filmed on weekdays.
- When Arthur Weiss first conceived of the plot, he titled this episode "The Brain is a Machine," which was changed by the time he wrote the first and final draft of the teleplay.

- The chart of the human body, including muscles, hanging in the wall in Bondar's classroom was also featured in "Death at 2 A.M." and "Three Minute Mile."
- The opening stock footage of the Science Hall (side and front view) is the same footage reused in five other first season episodes: "Death at 2 A.M.," "A Visit From Dr. Pliny," "Project 44," "Y..O..R..D.." and "Operation Flypaper."

The November 3, 1955 issue of *Variety* reviewed this episode:
"Clairvoyance, hypnosis, psychic research, mental telepathy and physical science are just a few of the bafflers to challenge the interest of the unscientific mind caught floundering in this channel. Those who stuck it out must still be wondering how the wife of a prof., who gave his theories short shrift, was psychic enough to lead him to the body of a lecturing biologist trapped in the wreckage of his car. Good thing, too, he didn't show up or there would have been biology to further scramble the gray cells at the sets.

"From what can be separated from the scientists, the subject of a classroom hypnotic demonstration is put under a spell to help locate the missing biologist, but it fizzed out. Caught in an occasional glare of the spotlight, the wife got some of the hypnotics on her and wouldn't you know it, she knew exactly where the body lay. At least that's what it added up to unless Truman Bradley's live eel in the opening explanation had something to do with it.

"Kent Smith and Osa Massen, who essayed the man-and-wife leads, may still be exploring each other's sub-conscious. Director Eddie Davis seemed to know what he was doing even if the rest of us didn't."

EPISODE #30 "THE HASTINGS SECRET"

PRODUCTION # 1030 / 28B
DATES OF PRODUCTION: JULY 21 AND 22, 1955
DIRECTED BY JACK HERZBERG

SCRIPT & STORY

FIRST DRAFT BY LEE HEWITT, JULY 4, 1955

Second Draft by Lee Hewitt, July 14, 1955
Final Draft by Lee Hewitt, July 20, 1955
Teleplay by Lee Hewitt

PRODUCTION CREDITS

1st Asst. Cameraman: Jim Bell (*un-credited*)
1st Co. Grip: Tex Jackson (*un-credited*)
2nd Asst. Director: Bobby Ray (*un-credited*)
2nd Cameraman: Ken Williams (*un-credited*)
2nd Co. Grip: Larry Yutronich (*un-credited*)
Assistant Director: Donald Verk
Asst. Prop Master: Harry Ott (*un-credited*)
Boom Man: Elmer Haglund (*un-credited*)
Construction Chief: Archie Hall (*un-credited*)
Director of Photography: Monroe "Monk" Askins
Film Coordinator: Donald Tait
Film Editor: Thomas Scott
Make-up Artist: George Gray
Production Coordinator: Joe Wonder
Scientific Advisor on Electronics and Radar Operation: Maxwell Smith
Property Master: Max Pittman
Recorder: Bob Post (*un-credited*)
Script Supervisor: Larry Lund
Set Decorator: Bruce MacDonald
Set Designer: Jack Collis
Set Labor: Art Sweet (*un-credited*)
Sound Mixer: Garry Harris
Sound Supervisor: Gus Galvin
Special Effects: Harry Redmond, Jr.
Wardrobe: Alfred Berke

CAST: Morris Ankrum (Dr. Clausen, $125); Barbara Hale (Pat Hastings); and Bill Williams (Bill Twining)*

---

* Both Hale and Williams (married in real life) received joint payment of $2,750 for their work on this episode.

Barbara Hale and Bill Williams on location at Bronson Canyon for the filming of "The Hastings Secret."

PLOT: Professor Hastings sends the result of his latest experiment with a surprising solvent to his employers, the Continental Telephone Company. The chemical has the property of separating many compounds into their basic molecules from its component elements. The secret of this discovery remains unknown, however, and the Professor has not been heard from for nearly three weeks. His daughter, a bio-chemist, and Bill Twining, an electronics expert requested by Hastings, journey to a termite observation outpost in Peru. They do not find the Professor but they do discover an underground termite observatory which holds the secret of Hastings' work and his fate—he was eaten by the same termites he was studying. Once they realize the peril of working with a termite that feeds on minerals instead of cellulose, they determine to recover the lost secret of the universal solvent.

On location filming "The Hastings Secret." The cast take a lunch break with director Jack Herzberg.

Barbara Hale takes a lunch break.

Notes

- The character of Bill Twining was originally Bill Cunningham in the first draft of the script.
- The first day of filming was on Stage 6. The second day of filming was shot on location, Bronson Canyon, which served as a stand-in for the Peruvian Andes.
- According to a press release issued from ZIV Television, Ivan Tors wanted to add realism to this episode about a strange kin of the termite alleged to have been responsible for the destruction of mineral deposits in the Earth. For this he imported 50,000 termites from Chicago at $15 a jar pure hokum.
- Filmed shots of termites in this episode are provided by stock footage.
- The original script called for a secretary, two or three job applicants, technicians and scientists. To cut corners in the budget, these roles were eliminated and the cast only consisted of three.
- The chart with dots on the wall in the lab in this episode also appears in "The Unguided Missile," "Three Minute Mile," "The Water Maker" and in the background of Truman Bradley's lab demonstrations in "The Voice" and "The Sound That Kills."
- Lee Hewitt wrote the teleplay based on Martin Lscher's article, "The Termite and the Cell," which appeared in the May 1953 issue of *Scientific American*.

The November 10, 1955 issue of *Variety* reviewed this episode:
"You should get a load of those termites in Peru. They eat away mountains and even ate an old professor. Of course, Truman Bradley hastens to explain, this is fiction as the little cellulose gluttons crawl off your tube. He also might have thanked those who stuck it out. Much too dreary and slow to hold still for.

"Title has apparent reference to the old Prof.'s theory that termites feed off iron ore and minerals. By the time Bill Williams and Barbara Hale get around to it, it doesn't matter anyway. It was a sight to shrink from when the army of termites started on their devastating march, just as long as they stay away from the beams holding up the old homestead.

"Not much to report on the acting of Williams or Miss Hale. They just puttered along until they found the prof.'s diary proving his theory that termites will eat up your rock garden if you let them. That is if you live in Peru. After the termites crawled away, PictSweet offered its choicest food products."

EPISODE #31 "POSTCARD FROM BARCELONA"

PRODUCTION #1031 / 31B
DATES OF PRODUCTION: AUGUST 17 AND 18, 1955
DIRECTED BY ALVIN GANZER

SCRIPT & STORY

FIRST DRAFT BY SLOAN NIBLEY, JULY 30, 1955
REVISED PAGES DATED AUGUST 5, 1955
TELEPLAY BY SLOAN NIBLEY, BASED ON TWO STORY OUTLINES BY
   TOM GRIES AND IVAN TORS

PRODUCTION CREDITS

1ST ASST. CAMERAMAN: JIM BELL (*UN-CREDITED*)
1ST CO. GRIP: CARL MIKSCH (*UN-CREDITED*)
2ND ASST. DIRECTOR: BOBBY RAY (*UN-CREDITED*)
2ND CO. GRIP: WALTER CULP (*UN-CREDITED*)
ASSISTANT DIRECTOR: DONALD VERK
AUDIO SUPERVISOR: QUINN MARTIN
BEST BOY: CHARLES STOCKWELL (*UN-CREDITED*)
BOOM MAN: ELMER HAGLUND (*UN-CREDITED*)
CAMERA OPERATOR: DICK RAWLINGS
CONSTRUCTION CHIEF: ARCHIE HALL (*UN-CREDITED*)
DIRECTOR OF PHOTOGRAPHY: CURT FETTERS
ELECTRICIANS: LOUIS KREIGER, WALTER GEDIMAN AND FRED
   HOUNSHELL (*ALL UN-CREDITED*)
FILM COORDINATOR: DONALD TAIT
FILM EDITOR: JOHN B. WOELZ
GAFFER: S.H. BARTON (*UN-CREDITED*)
MAKE-UP ARTIST: GEORGE GRAY

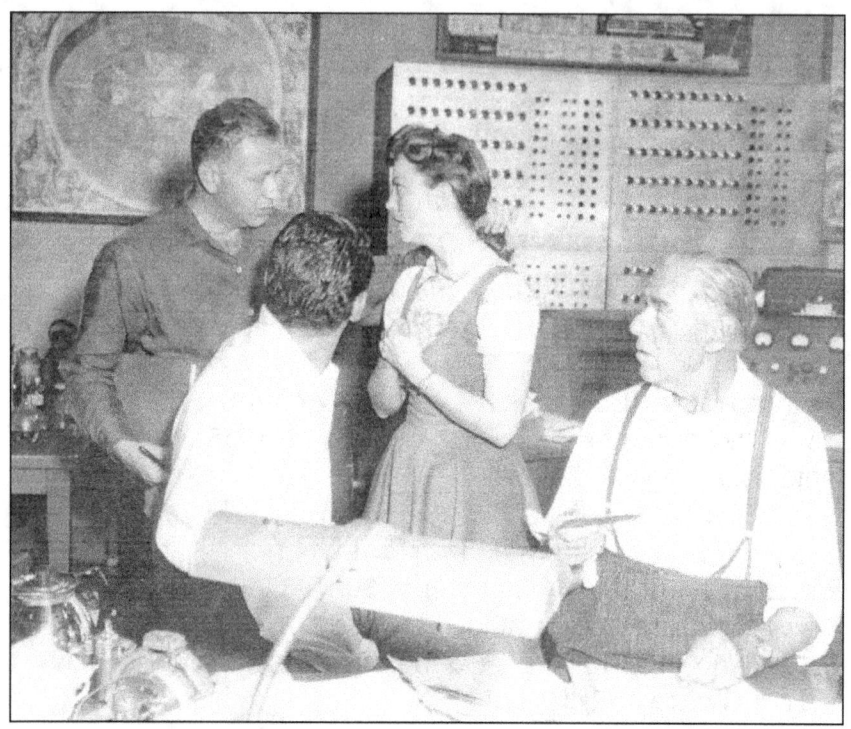

Producer Ivan Tors listens to actress Christine Larson on the set of "Postcard From Barcelona."

PRODUCTION COORDINATOR: JOE WONDER
SCIENTIFIC ADVISOR ON ELECTRONICS AND RADAR OPERATION: MAXWELL SMITH
PROPERTY MASTER: MAX PITTMAN
RECORDER: WILLIAM HANKS (*UN-CREDITED*)
SCRIPT SUPERVISOR: JANE FICKER
SET DECORATOR: BRUCE MACDONALD
SET DESIGNER: JACK COLLIS
SOUND MIXER: GARRY HARRIS
SOUND SUPERVISOR: GUS GALVIN
SPECIAL EFFECTS: HARRY REDMOND, JR.
WARDROBE: ALFRED BERKE

CAST: Keefe Brasselle (Dr. Burton, $2,500); Charles Cane (the sheriff, $100); Cyril Delevanti (Thatcher, $100); Walter Kingsford (Dr. Cole, $300); Christine Larson (Nina Keller, $300); and Hank Patterson (the taxi driver, $90)

The Episode Guide: Season One | 259

(LEFT TO RIGHT) **Keefe Brasselle, Christine Larson and Walter Kingsford try to solve the mystery of the "Postcard From Barcelona."**

Keefe Brasselle (LEFT) **and Walter Kingsford** (RIGHT) **pose for a candid shot with producer Ivan Tors** (MIDDLE).

Plot: With the death of world-renowned scientist, Dr. Charles Keller, the Crenshaw Foundation, with whom Keller had worked, assigns a young scientist, Dr. Burton, to go to Keller's secluded estate and catalogue and evaluate his papers and letters in the hopes of discovering additional facts of scientific value. Dr. Burton arrives at the Keller place and is amazed to discover an electronic telescope of fantastic efficiency, together with a collection of photographic plates taken with the instruments. More amazing than this is the discovery of two postcards from Barcelona, each one bearing only the symbols of two of Keller's earth-shaking contributions, and each one post-marked at least a year before the discoveries were given to the world. Burton meets an attractive young girl who explains that she is Keller's daughter. Burton makes arrangements with her that will pay a large sum of money for her father's life story and they, at the same time, will have access to all the pure science discovered in Keller's papers. In using the fabulous telescope, a man-made artificial asteroid is discovered, and in turn, somebody uses the wave frequency of the instrument to report that a message will arrive from Barcelona. The message finally arrives telling them that they now share Keller's secret and they'll make the same deal with him . . . silence as to the fact that someone is observing the world in return for scientific facts which will be sent every year from Barcelona.

Notes

- The entire episode was filmed on Stage 5.
- The stock footage of the exterior of the observatory was reused for two other episodes, "The Stones Began to Move" and "The Human Equation."
- The computers featured along the wall in the lab scene are the same props in the opening of every second season episode, surrounding Truman Bradley, as he turns to address the television audience.
- The model of the space station in this episode was the same model that appears in "The Strange People at Pecos" and "The Missing Waveband."
- The cosmic ray chart hanging on the wall in this episode is the same prop that also appears in "A Visit From Dr. Pliny,"

"Before the Beginning," "Project 44" and in the motion-picture *Gog* (1954).
- As seen in external shots, the house representing the Keller estate was actually the home of a Mr. Knobel, located at 1942 Laughlin Park Drive, and is the same house and driveway featured in the second-season episode "The Human Experiment."

The November 17, 1955 issue of *Variety* reviewed this episode:
"While 'Postcard' contains an intriguing premise, giving the science fiction fan much to mull over, in dramatization for the lay viewer the premise is not fully exploited. As in past episodes of this series, main fault is a plethora of static exposition, with little action to punch over points.

"In this stanza, script by Sloan Nibley from producer Ivan Tors' idea, climax is simply the decoding of a message from the unknown denizens of outer space. Message offers continuance of arrangement whereby the other-worlders will supply valuable scientific data for the betterment of mankind, provided source is kept secret. With this, story dies, as Earthlings indicate they will comply.

"Preceding this motionless climax, a leading technical brain has died. Chief (Walter Kingsford) of the foundation which has supported him dispatches foundation assistant (Keefe Brasselle) to scan the departed's papers.

"To their dismay, they find evidence scientist apparently has been suppressing valuable data and equipment. Later, though, they discover the outer-spacemen arrangement, whereby scientist has made his greatest contribution. In so doing, he had rigidly cut himself off from this world, even to neglecting his daughter (Christine Larsen).

"As indicated, the new proprietors agree to carry on the arrangements.

"Alvin Ganzer's direction does manage to point up poignancy of love-starved daughter's situation, but is unable to enliven the scientifics. Brasselle and Kingsford try hard, within the limits of the script."

"SPACE STATION"
(ORIGINALLY PLOT OUTLINE #8)
BY IVAN TORS

Professor Carlton, a prominent Astrophysicist, is requested by White Sands to take part in a program that would chart the skies segment in an attempt to find an Asteroid that could be used as a site for a space station. Carlton's telescope is trained at the sky twenty-four hours a day. The photographic plates would detect any sign of a moving object.

One day he notices a slight flash on the photographic plate. Observing that specific area of the sky, he finds a tiny speck is circling the Earth at the speed of 18,600 miles per hours. It looks like a perfect site for a space station. Carlton is elated by his discovery but being a true scientist, he is cautious and before making an announcement, he decides to call in another Astronomer, the Nobel Prize winner, Professor Langley, for consultation. While dialing his number, Professor Langley unexpectedly appears. Carlton shows his findings to Langley in a state of great excitement. Langley remains calm. He warns Carlton not to report it. He, too, knows about the object in the sky. It is not an Asteroid, but a space station—manned by beings from another Universe, observing our Earth. It is impossible for them to make a landing as they would perish in our atmosphere. They keep our planet under observation for scientific reasons, and they are anxious that the world should not know about them. The reason for it is that Earth people are not mature enough to accept such a staggering fact—it may throw our population into a panic and the space station may be attacked by our guided missiles. Carlton is stunned by these revelations. He is in doubt as to whether he should accept Langley's suggestion and not to reveal his findings. He would like to have some proof that those on the space station are peaceful friendly beings. He will play ball only if he receives such proof.

Langley assures him that these people will make him realize that he made the right choice. As the conversation goes on, Dr. Bauford steps in to interrupt the astronomers. Bauford is Carlton's best friend and head of the biology department at the same university. For seven years he tried to isolate the virus of a certain deadly disease. He succeeded five minutes ago. He invites the two other professors to dine with him and celebrate his discovery. Professor Carlton looks up at the sky where the invisible space station is circling and says, "thanks for the proof, it's a fair exchange."

"POSTCARD FROM BARCELONA"
BY TOM GRIES

When the greatest mind in the world—the final synthesis of scientific knowledge and searing imagination—dies, and the eulogies are over, and everyone once again resumes his daily routine with only a vague sense of less remaining, the doctors, who have remained in the background, quietly perform an autopsy. They find only that Doctor Max Engel died . . . because his heart stopped beating. They have no answer but old age.

Meanwhile, those close to Project L—a project not so much secret as simply unknown because its source and purpose rested largely within the mind of Dr. Engel—those people who worked with and under him are faced with a serious problem. Who would continue the work? Or, more to the point, who could continue the work?

The choice, when made public, is a surprise to many: Dr. Franklin Crisp, a young man as scientists at the top of their profession go—not yet forty but already a leader in the field of theoretical physics.

Dr. Crisp, a tall, thoughtful man, had worked briefly under Engel in the past before going on to studies of his own. Upon his return to the Institute, he is shown immediately to Engel's office, which has remained untouched since the old man's sudden death. There is the usual orderly disarray that comes of constant, diligent work. Abstruse books covering many fields of science, unopened mail from all parts of the world covering the coffee table in front of the old couch, a small pile of detective stories which the old man used for relaxation, and, most importantly, a thick legal length pad atop the desk, the first two pages of which are covered with line after line of the hieroglyphics of one of Dr. Engel's equations.

And there is something else—the only item among the thousands in the office which the staff knows nothing about, neither its spruce nor its purpose: a postcard from Barcelona.

There is no message on the card, no signature. Only the postmark and the date . . . the date of Dr. Engel's death.

Crisp begins his work faced with three important conflicts:

His welcome at the institute is not a cordial one. There are several there who worked under Engel who felt they are entitled to continue his work.

His wife feels that Crisp should continue his own work and gain recognition in his own studies, rather than work in the shadow of another man whom he couldn't possibly hope to eclipse. In addition, the strain of Engel's work was a likely factor in his death and probably killed him. She doesn't want this for Crisp.

Crisp himself is assailed with doubt. Max Engel had not been irreligious; he acknowledged the presence of a deity and was well respectful of Him rather than devout. But he felt that all things in the world, natural and otherwise, were there to be learned and known and understood. Crisp is not so sure.

Engel's subsidiary formula, and the long, unfinished end lead down a strange, uncharted, road. In the old man's notes are several references—all in connection with the long formula—to "spontaneous generation," a theory of the beginning of life held by Newton, Aristotle, William Harvey, Descartes, van Holment and even the English Jesuit Turberville, but disproved as early as the 17th Century by the Italian Francisco Redi and Abbe Lazzare Spallanzani and finally by Louis Pasteur. And open on the shelf, Engel had left a book published in 1936 by the famous Russian biochemist A.I. Oparin called *The Origin Of Life*.

Finally, in notes as yet unread even by Engel's own staff, Crisp finds what are obviously the early results of a practical experiment. This comes as a shock, since Engel was known to have left laboratory work behind him years before.

The experiment, set up in Engel's garage where, to everyone's surprise, Crisp discovers a completely equipped laboratory, is the extension of a surprisingly simple test.

In recent years Harold Urey, Nobel Prize chemist, had become interested in how electrical discharges in the upper atmosphere promoted the formation of organic compounds. Engel's notes make reference to these compounds as the first "pieces of life." Later, a student of Urey had circulated a mixture of water vapor, methane

(CH 4), ammonia (NH3), and hydrogen, all of which were glasses believed present in the early atmosphere of Earth, continuously over an electric spark. The circulation was maintained by boiling the water in one arm of the apparatus and condensed it in the other. At the end of the week, the student had analyzed the water by paper chromatography and found that it had acquired a mixture of amino acids, glycine, and alanine. Crisp repeats the experiment, traveling methodically through Engel's notes as he does so. He finds in the notes the words, "From something so simple as this . . ."

Apparently, Engel felt it possible to create organic molecules. In short, this meant the creation of life. Crisp is frightened. He hadn't bargained for something like this; it was crazy. And yet they had called the old man crazy thirty-five years before when he came up with something that was to revolutionize life and create a whole new vocabulary for newspaper headline writers and the laymen in the street. Crisp continues working on the formula, referring whenever necessary to the experiments of the old scientist. Engel's work hadn't carried him into practical applications and Crisp feels it quite possible that such applications had never entered the man's mind. Rather the knowledge of the creation of life, knowing its secret, was what seemed to interest Engel.

The strain and tension of the work became almost unbearable as Crisp progresses. In addition, there is the opposition of his wife and the conflict with the men of the Institute. Crisp seems to age years as the days go past. One day Crisp faints at his desk. His wife again refers to the work as having killed Engel, and, for the first time, Crisp is not so sure she's wrong. There suddenly seem to him to be boundaries of knowledge beyond which man was not meant to pass. One of the men in the Institute makes veiled reference to the unsolved artifact on Engel's desk: the postcard from Barcelona. Crisp asks him what he means, almost becomes violent. The man only laughs.

Crisp's wife finally takes him to a doctor. He shocks them. Unless Crisp leaves immediately, takes a vacation with complete rest, his heart will fail and he will die. No, it is not heart disease but it's obvious thatsome recent strain has been so great that Crisp's heart has been temporarily damaged.

Crisp insists upon working three more days . . . until the weekend.

Crisp's enemy at the institute is seen more often, skulking around the office. Nice he talks wildly of God's punishment and is led away to the coffee shop in the Institute by another colleague. Crisp arrives home with the news that he will leave early but will take some page and notes on his work along. His wife, glad for a partial victory, agrees and they pack to go. But that night there is a fire and explosion and the laboratory of Dr. Engel and the old white frame house go up in smoke. The Institute man with the religious obsession is taken away. Crisp and his wife leave on the plane.

A few days later, at the institute, a postcard arrives for Crisp with no message. On the front is a large cathedral facing a square, and the postmark is Barcelona.

"He left an address," says one of the men at the Institute. "Let's forward it on to him."

"No," answers the other. "I don't think we should." And he destroys it.

EPISODE #32 "FRIEND OF A RAVEN"

PRODUCTION #1032 / 32B
DATES OF PRODUCTION: AUGUST 22 AND 23, 1955
DIRECTED BY TOM GRIES

SCRIPT & STORY

"THE SEVENTH SENSE" FINAL TYPESCRIPT (ANNOTATED), BY
 RICHARD JOSEPH TUBER, AUGUST 5, 1955
MASTER MIMEO (ANNOTATED), AUGUST 5, 1955
REVISED PAGES (ANNOTATED), AUGUST 19, 1955
TELEPLAY BY RICHARD JOSEPH TUBER

PRODUCTION CREDITS

1ST ASST. CAMERAMAN: SPEC JONES (*UN-CREDITED*)
1ST CO. GRIP: MEL BLEDSOE (*UN-CREDITED*)
2ND ASST. DIRECTOR: JUD COX (*UN-CREDITED*)
2ND CAMERAMAN: AL GREEN (*UN-CREDITED*)
2ND CO. GRIP: JACK CHAMBERS (*UN-CREDITED*)
ASSISTANT DIRECTOR: EDWARD MULL

Asst. Prop Man: Charles Chicetti (*un-credited*)
Audio Supervisor: Quinn Martin
Best Boy: Del Mark (*un-credited*)
Boom Man: Jim Flannery (*un-credited*)
Construction Chief: Archie Hall (*un-credited*)
Director of Photography: Robert Hoffman
Drivers: J. Brown (*un-credited*)
Film Coordinator: Donald Tait
Film Editor: Thomas Scott
Make-up Artist: George Gray
Mixer: Jay Ashworth (*un-credited*)
Production Coordinator: Joe Wonder
Scientific Advisor on Electronics and Radar Operation:
   Maxwell Smith
Property Master: Max Pittman
Recorder: Roy Cropper (*un-credited*)
Script Supervisor: Jane Ficker
Set Decorator: Bruce MacDonald
Set Designer: Jack Collis
Set Labor: Herb Pitchard (*un-credited*)
Sound Editor: Sidney Sutherland
Sound Supervisor: Gus Galvin
Special Effects: Harry Redmond, Jr.
Wardrobe: Alfred Berke

Cast: Isa Ashdown (the little girl, $100); Virginia Bruce (Jean Gordon, $1,750); Charles Cane (Frank Jenkins, $100); William Ching (Walter Daniels, $400); Richard Eyer (Tim Daniels, $350); and Barney Phillips (Dr. Hoster, $150)

Plot: State Welfare Worker Jean Gordon comes to the farm of Steve Daniels to get him to put his ten-year-old deaf and mute son, Tim, into a school where he can learn to overcome his handicap. But Tim instinctively knows why she has come and runs off into the woods. Jean and Steve try to follow the boy, and Jean begins to realize that Tim has some sort of animal-like extra-sensory perception. This is borne out more fully when Tim saves Jean's life from the fangs of a rattlesnake. Steve doesn't want his son to become the object of

Director Tom Gries on location, answering a question from actor Richard Eyer.

scientific curiosity, and Jean obeys his wishes. But finally, Steve realizes she is right, that Tim cannot live in a human world by animal instincts, and allows the boy to be taken to a University Clinic. Three weeks later, after corrective brain surgery, his hearing is restored and he is taught to speak. But then he loses his extra-sensory perception . . . the thing the Doctor calls "The Seventh Sense." Tim becomes aware of the new world that has opened around him and even though science has failed to gain the knowledge of the Seventh Sense, a little boy has been given the chance for a happy, normal life.

Notes

- The actors and crew were each paid $2.00 in lieu of meal penalty, no lunch or dinner.
- The entire episode was produced under the title, "The Seventh Sense."
- Sound broke down 9:45 and it wasn't until afternoon that they got it fixed.
- The insert shot of the hands holding a snake is a man's hands, not the boy's.
- Actor Barney Phillips is billed in the closing credits as Bernard Phillips.
- Stand-in Ann Howard plays the un-credited role of the nurse.
- The entire first day of filming was on location at Sweetzer Canyon, and Angeles Crest at the Ranger Station, to simulate the Daniels farm. The second day of filming consisted of interior shots on Stage 4.
- The fascinating science fact about the sensitivity of a rattlesnake's senses, demonstrated in this episode, originates from an article in the October 1953 issue of *Scientific American*, titled "How A Rattlesnake Strikes."

The November 28, 1955 issue of *Variety* reviewed this episode: "Far afield in fantasy, this series wends its weekly way, and good thing, too, Truman Bradley closes with a disclaimer. The world is full of gullible, or have you forgotten the Martian invasion spearheaded by Orson Welles? But some day, he offered, this scrap of fiction may be turned to scientific fact once the unexplored or unused area of the brain is developed to its full potential. Because of the human drama caught up in this swirl of scientifics, 'Friend of a Raven' is suffered with a warmth the others in the series lacked and comes off well as an entertaining morsel of fictional fancy.

"Story is that of a youngster who suffered an injury to his brain in a fall and is stricken deaf and dumb. The father resists all efforts at correctional therapy in the belief that the boy is happier in his present state communing with denizens of the wild. He becomes friend of a raven, snakes and other beasts because of a seventh sense that can communicate basic emotions. When the truant officer father, he consents to a clinical study of the boy's case and surgery restores him to normal childhood. But his friend, the raven, now resents him and flies away.

"Direction of Tom Gries is sensitive to the dramatic values with an underplay of the scientific facets to broaden the appeal. Virginia Bruce, Richard Eyer and William Ching share top billing with equal competence."

EPISODE #33 "BEYOND RETURN"

PRODUCTION #1033 / 33B
DATES OF PRODUCTION: AUGUST 24 AND 25, 1955
DIRECTED BY EDDIE DAVIS

SCRIPT & STORY

FIRST DRAFT BY DORIS GILBERT, AUGUST 15, 1955
FINAL DRAFT BY DORIS GILBERT, AUGUST 19, 1955
TELEPLAY BY DORIS GILBERT, ADAPTED FROM THE SHORT STORY
  "THE ADAPTIVE ULTIMATE" BY JOHN JESSEL (A.K.A. STANLEY G. WEINBAUM)

PRODUCTION CREDITS

1ST ASST. CAMERAMAN: GEORGE LE PICARD (*UN-CREDITED*)
1ST CO. GRIP: MEL BLEDSOE (*UN-CREDITED*)
2ND ASST. DIRECTOR: BOBBY RAY (*UN-CREDITED*)
2ND CAMERAMAN: TOMMY MORRIS (*UN-CREDITED*)
2ND CO. GRIP: JACK CHAMBERS (*UN-CREDITED*)

Assistant Director: Erich Von Stroheim, Jr.
Asst. Prop Man: Ben Benay (*un-credited*)
Audio Supervisor: Quinn Martin
Best Boy: Charles Stockwell (*un-credited*)
Boom Man: Jim Flannery (*un-credited*)
Construction Chief: Archie Hall (*un-credited*)
Director of Photography: Robert Hoffman
Electricians: Walter Gediman, Charles Hanger and Mike Hudson (*all un-credited*)
Film Coordinator: Donald Tait
Film Editor: John B. Woelz
Gaffer: Bert Jones (*un-credited*)
Make-up Artist: George Gray
Production Coordinator: Joe Wonder
Scientific Advisor on Electronics and Radar Operation: Maxwell Smith
Property Master: Max Pittman
Recorder: Roy Cropper (*un-credited*)
Script Supervisor: Doris August
Set Decorator: Bruce MacDonald
Set Designer: Jack Collis
Set Labor: Bers Fitghard (*un-credited*)
Sound Editor: Lawrence Kaufman
Sound Mixer: Jay Ashworth
Sound Supervisor: Gus Galvin
Special Effects: Harry Redmond, Jr.
Still Man: Frankie Tanner (*un-credited*)
Wardrobe: Alfred Berke

CAST: Toni Carroll (the second nurse, $80); Tom de Graffenried (the police sergeant, $80); Kay Faylen (the first nurse, $80); Peter Hanson (Dr. Dan Scott, $150); Dennis Moore (the male cashier, $80); Alan Reynolds (the police lieutenant, $100); Zachary Scott (Dr. Erwin Bach, $2,500); James Seay (Russell, $100); Lizz Slifer (Mrs. Shay, $90); and Joan Vohs (Kyra Zelas, $400)

PLOT: Dr. Dan Scott, biochemist at a big hospital, asks permission of Dr. Erwin Bach, brilliant surgeon and head of the hospital, to

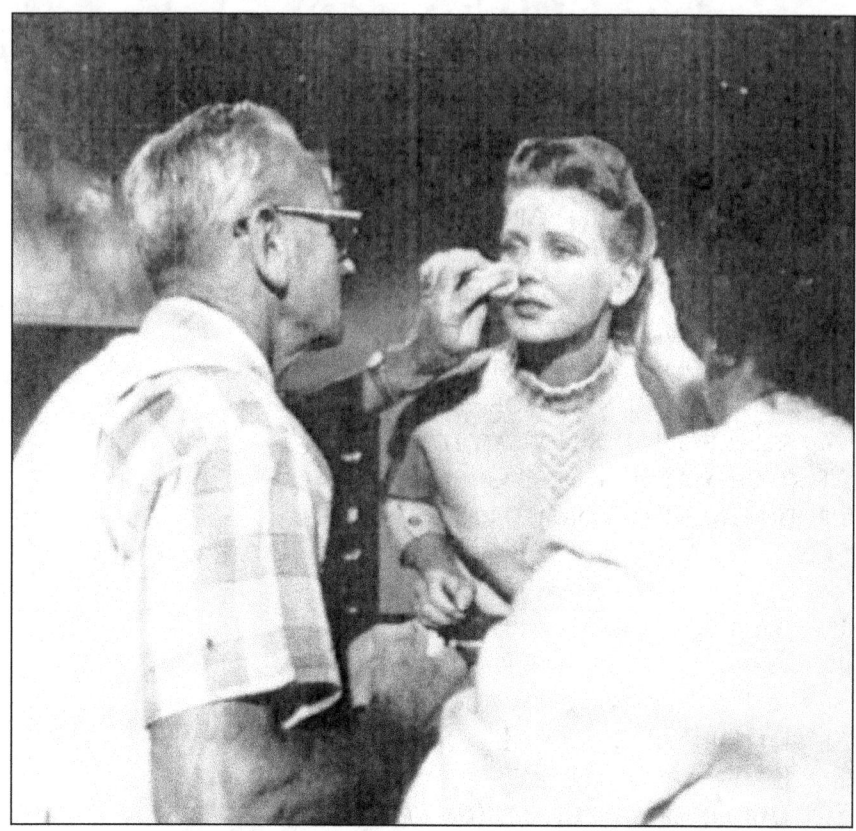

Make-up is applied to actress Joan Vohs to ensure the transformation on screen is caught on camera.

experiment on one of its patients with a new hormone he has isolated from the highly adaptive fruit fly. Dan believes that curing a disease is causing the patient to adapt to it and has already been successful with experimental animals. Bach is deeply interested, but at first refuses on the grounds of jumping the gun, then accedes when consent to the injections is given to Kyra Zelas, a pathetic, unattractive waif in the last stages of tuberculosis. Kyra has a miraculous recovery but Bach finds himself faced with a frightening situation when it is discovered that Kyra, now an ultimate adaptive, can change her physical characteristics under pressure; in revolt against her former drab existence, becoming a beautiful blonde, dangerous and immortal. Risking borderline asphyxiation, the doctors tricks Kyra into unconsciousness so they can "cure" her back to normal, for which she is grateful at the conclusion.

THE EPISODE GUIDE: SEASON ONE | 273

NOTES

Astounding Science Fiction magazine, November 1935

- The opening stock shot of the exterior of the house with the lights coming on was also used in "Bullet Proof," "The Lost Heartbeat," "When A Camera Fails" and "The Voice." A daytime shot of the same house appears in this episode—the only episode to feature a daytime shot and not the evening shot of the lights coming on.
- This episode was produced under the title of "The Girl with the Flaxen Hair."
- The first day of filming was on Stage 5.
- The second day of filming was on Stage 4.

THE ADAPTIVE ULTIMATE

This was one of two episodes adapted from a previously published short story. Stanley G. Weinbaum's short story (originally published in the November 1935 issue of *Astounding* under the pen name of John Jessel) was also the basis for a low-budget motion picture titled *She Devil*, released theatrically in April of 1957. Jack Kelly played the role of Dr. Dan Scott and Albert Dekker played the role of Dr. Richard Bach. Mari Blanchard played the role of Kyra Zelas, who faces a horrible demise in the big screen version, unlike the version dressed up for *Science Fiction Theatre*.

"The Adaptive Ultimate" had been dramatized twice. The first was on radio's *Escape* on March 26, 1949, under the original title. The second was on television's *Studio One* on September 12, 1949, titled "Kyra Zelas" (the same name as the title character).

The December 1, 1955 issue of *Variety* reviewed this episode:
"No truth could be stranger than the fiction whipped up by Doris Gilbert from John Jessel's imaginative mind for this high flight of fanciful excursion into the realm of possibility. For what it purports to prove in its magical way, the results are exhilarating and stimulating.

There's even a good run of suspense to arrest the interest and tighten the hold. In toto, the Ivan Tors-Eddie Davis creative production can stand up with the series standouts.

"Hope will rise high in the feminine heart that there yet may be isolated a hormone that can turn an ugly duckling into a group captain's princess. The fable here takes Joan Vohs from her deathbed to a ravishing thing of beauty. One shot of a serum did it, but the physical adaptation gets out of hand and it became necessary to restore her to normalcy. She is no sublimely beautiful that she's in demand as a cover girl, marries the mag publisher and attains the strength of ten women. The serum even changed her fingerprints to the utter frustration of the police. A human chameleon, she calls herself "a dangerous accident." Put to sleep, the medics perform a surgery that makes her over to what she once was.

"Miss Vohs, Zachary Scott and Peter Hanson play it for keeps with a note of pseudo-conviction that gives the tale Cinderella-like pretension. Their agreeable efforts are well seconded and director Davis keeps the pace zesty and gripping. Sponsoring Olympia Beer harps on the water rather than the hops."

EPISODE #34 "BEFORE THE BEGINNING"

PRODUCTION #1034 / 34B
DATES OF PRODUCTION: SEPTEMBER 10 AND 12, 1955
DIRECTED BY ALVIN GANZER

SCRIPT & STORY

FINAL DRAFT BY ARTHUR WEISS, SEPTEMBER 2, 1955
TELEPLAY BY ARTHUR WEISS, FROM A STORY BY ARTHUR WEISS AND IVAN TORS

PRODUCTION CREDITS

1ST ASST. CAMERAMAN: JIM BELL (*UN-CREDITED*)
1ST CO. GRIP MEL BLEDSOE (SEPT. 10 ONLY) AND CARL MIKSCH (SEPT. 12 ONLY, *UN-CREDITED*)
2ND ASST. DIRECTOR: BOBBY RAY (*UN-CREDITED*)
2ND CO. GRIP: JACK CHAMBERS (*UN-CREDITED*)

3RD GRIP: EDDIE MANRIQUEZ (*UN-CREDITED*)
ASSISTANT DIRECTOR: ERICH VON STROHEIM, JR.
ASST. PROP MAN: E. SMITH (*UN-CREDITED*)
AUDIO SUPERVISOR: QUINN MARTIN
BEST BOY: MIKE HUDSON (*UN-CREDITED*)
BOOM MAN: ELMER HAGLUND (*UN-CREDITED*)
CAMERA OPERATOR: DICK RAWLINGS
CONSTRUCTION CHIEF: ARCHIE HALL (*UN-CREDITED*)
DIRECTOR OF PHOTOGRAPHY: CURT FETTERS (SEPT. 12 ONLY) AND ROBERT HOFFMAN (SEPT. 10 ONLY)
ELECTRICIANS: HAROLD KRAUS, J. PERVELL MARLEY AND ROY SLOCUM (*ALL UN-CREDITED*)
FILM COORDINATOR: DONALD TAIT
FILM EDITOR: THOMAS SCOTT
GAFFER: BERT JONES (*UN-CREDITED*)
MAKE-UP ARTIST: GEORGE GRAY
PRODUCTION COORDINATOR: JOE WONDER
SCIENTIFIC ADVISOR ON ELECTRONICS AND RADAR OPERATION: MAXWELL SMITH
PROPERTY MASTER: MAX PITTMAN
RECORDER: WILLIAM HANES (*UN-CREDITED*)
SCRIPT SUPERVISOR: JANE FICKER
SET DECORATOR: BRUCE MACDONALD
SET DESIGNER: JACK COLLIS
SET LABOR: ART SWEET (*UN-CREDITED*)
SOUND EDITOR: MONROE MARTIN
SOUND MIXER: GARRY HARRIS
SPECIAL EFFECTS: HARRY REDMOND, JR.
STILL MAN: CHARLES RHODES (*UN-CREDITED*)
WARDROBE: ALFRED BERKE

CAST: Judith Ames (Kate Donaldson, $125); Dane Clark (Dr. Kenneth Donaldson, $2,500); Ted de Corsia (Dr. Henry Donaldson, $150); Phillip Pine (Dr. Norman Heller, $125); and Emerson Treacy (Dr. August Heinemann, $150)

PLOT: Dr. Kenneth Donaldson, a biophysicist, has constructed a Photon Gun which will duplicate, under laboratory conditions, the

Dr. Donaldson (Dane Clark) and his wife Kate (Judith Ames) celebrate when they find a cure for her fatal condition.

theoretical manner in which the first living molecule was generated on Earth. Theoretically, photons coming from the Sun traveled through the absolute zero temperature of space to a lifeless, sterilized earth, generating the first living molecules. Although Donaldson does not succeed in creating permanent life, he does succeed in creating a self-reproducing crystal. This crystal of the photon force which created it is the means by which he succeeds in curing his wife of an otherwise incurable and fatal condition of her suprarenal gland. This was a latent congenital organic condition which was aggravated and brought to the surface by Donaldson's neglect of her in favor of his scientific research.

Notes

- Produced under the title "Seed of Life," which was also the title of the teleplay.
- The cosmic ray chart hanging on the wall in this episode is the same prop that also appears in "A Visit From Dr. Pliny," "Postcard From Barcelona," "Project 44" and in the motion picture *Gog* (1954).
- The clock used to count the three minutes for Kate's medical treatment was the same prop featured prominently in numerous *Science Fiction Theatre* episodes.
- If Truman Bradley was really reading sections of Genesis direct from the Bible, he would have been on page one, not the middle of the book.
- The "creation" of the Earth during Truman Bradley's lab demonstration was stock footage Maxwell Smith had created specifically for *The Magnetic Monster* (1953)

The December 8, 1955 issue of *Variety* reviewed this episode:

"'Beginning' is a boy-meets-molecule episode, one of the better Ivan Tors entries in the *Science Fiction* series. Interest is generated throughout in the story of a biochemist working on a process to create life. Alvin Ganzer's direction is skillful, and the teleplay by Arthur Weiss a good one.

"Dane Clark is the earnest young scientist who neglects his wife to work almost 24 hours a day to find the secret of mankind. Meanwhile, his wife becomes incurably ill, but at the end it's indicated she'll live because he successfully experiments on her with his discovery. It's far-fetched, but for this type of show it doesn't detract, rather adds to it.

"Clark gives a good portrayal of the scientist so completely absorbed in his work he's unaware of everything else, including the wife. Spouse is well delineated by Judith Ames, and there's fine support from Ted de Corsia and Phillip Pine."

"SEEDS OF LIFE"
Dated: August 1, 1955
by Ivan Tors

Dr. Donaldson, leading bio-chemist, studies the secrets connected with the origin of life and living matter. In any body of water no matter how far from other—insect life will evolve. But where do these minute particles, which create life, come from?

Then how did life originate on Earth? The globe must have been completely sterilized or cauterized by heat at the time of the birth of this planet. He theorizes that life was propelled to Earth from space either by cosmic particles or photons (particles of light from the sun). But the extremely high temperatures of the sun make life impossible. But what happens if an extremely hot particle (millions of degrees) suddenly is propelled through absolute zero cold. (The temperature of space.) Is it possible that such a process may be responsible for the origin of life?

Dr. Donaldson creates such a condition on an extremely small scale. He heats a particle to extreme high temperature then accelerates it through absolute zero. The result is a new particle, a jelly-like, protoplasm-like substance that keeps on dividing itself; and the most primitive form of life has been created.

Has man got the right to create life? What will happen to this self-dividing protoplasm? Is Dr. Donaldson going to pay for tempering with nature's secret? What can we learn from this scientific principle? This is the theme of the story.

EPISODE #35 "THE LONG DAY"

Production #1035 / 35B
Dates of Production: September 15 and 16, 1955
Directed by Paul Guilfoyle

SCRIPT & STORY

Final typescript (annotated) by George and Gertrude Fass, September 7, 1955
Revised pages (annotated), September 7, 1955
Revised master mimeo (annotated), September 7, 1955
Teleplay by George and Gertrude Fass

PRODUCTION CREDITS

1st Asst. Cameraman: Jim Bell (*un-credited*)

1st Co. Grip: Carl Miksch (*un-credited*)
2nd Asst. Director Bobby Ray (*un-credited*)
2nd Co. Grip: Bud Busick (*un-credited*)
3rd Grip: Bud Busick (*un-credited*)
Assistant Director: Erich Von Stroheim, Jr.
Asst. Prop Man: Cecil Smith (*un-credited*)
Audio Supervisor: Quinn Martin
Best Boy: Mike Hudson (*un-credited*)
Boom Man: Elmer Haglund (*un-credited*)
Construction Chief: Dee Bolhius (*un-credited*)
Director of Photography: Monroe "Monk" Askins
Electricians: Wade Huff, William Kane, Roy Slocum and J. Thielman (*all un-credited*)
Film Coordinator: Donald Tait
Film Editor: John B. Woelz
Gaffer: Wade Huff (*un-credited*)
Make-up Artist: George Gray
Production Coordinator: Joe Wonder
Sound Mixer: Jay Ashworth
Property Master: Max Pittman
Recorder: William Hanks (*un-credited*)
Scientific Advisor on Electronics and Radar Operation: Maxwell Smith
Script Supervisor: Wanda Ramsey
Set Decorator: Bruce MacDonald
Set Designer: Jack Collis
Set Labor: Art Sweet (*un-credited*)
Sound Editor: Monroe Martin
Special Effects: Harry Redmond, Jr.
Wardrobe: Alfred Berke

Cast: Raymond Bailey (Dr. Edward Smiley, $200); George Brent (Sam Gilmore, $1,000); Steve Brodie (Robert Barton, $500); Jean Byron (Laura Gilmore, $200); Michael Garth (Joe Crane, $100); Bradford Jackson (Carl Eberhardt, $100); DeForest Kelley (Matt Brander, $150); Addison Richards (Howie Stevens, $125); Carol Thurston (Anne Brander, $150); and Michael Winkelman (Junior, $80)

George Gray was in charge of make-up at ZIV-TV.

PLOT: A group of scientists conducts a field test known as Operation Torch, a new type of rocket flare which can light up a wide area for any period of time—in effect, producing artificial daylight. When the test goes wrong, the "delayed" sunset doesn't last five minutes, but throughout the entire evening. The area within 100 miles radius of the town remains indefinitely in what seems to be full daylight throughout the entire evening. In spite of general alarm and panic, the scientists must accept the dictum from Washington not to reveal the cause of the phenomenon, since in so doing security would be violated. Instead, the public is given reassurances and is otherwise left to conjecture what it pleases. Meanwhile, three prosperous homeowners, outraged at the audacity of an ex-convict who dared to buy a home in their exclusive development, swear an oath to forcibly move him and his family out of town, under cover of darkness. The weight of guilt rests more and more heavily upon them as the minutes and hours of unnatural and terrifying sunlight drag on. At last, unable to bear it any longer, the conspirators unburden themselves; believing there is a direct connection between this weird extension of daylight and their plan to run their unwanted neighbor out of town. Though they decline to subscribe to a theory of supernatural intervention, they are feeling the ache of bad conscience and are only too glad to go along with the new proposal. Shortly thereafter, the artificial sun runs out of fuel and night falls once again in Springdale.

Notes

- Director Paul Guilfoyle supplies the un-credited role of the voice broadcast over the radio.

The December 15, 1955 issue of *Variety* reviewed this episode:
"Some day in the not-too-distant future, intoned Truman Bradley, physicists will have invented a substitute sun by firing a missile into the sky. Night will be turned into day, and on this peg was hung a story born of desperate device to dovetail into the thematic structure. It was so lacking in conviction that the fable was more believable. Charge this off to the writers, who suffered from stilted imagination.

"The watcher is fed such a premise as three normal men taking an oath to persecute an undesirable who moved into their diggings. Later they repudiate this oath for another, with crossed arms like they do in lodges. It's all a little silly, but for purposes of the plotted plan, it had some utility value. Asked one, 'Was it a force mightier than science that kept the skies lighted so their vengeful mission would be thwarted?' If they must know, it was the missile that got out of control when one of the gadgets stuck.

"For the fright fans, who panicked at Orson Welles' Martian invasion in radio's dim past, there was assurance from Washington of no imminent danger and to remain calm. George Brent, Steve Brodie, Jean Byron and the rest tried to make something of the fantasy, but the lighted missile blinded their efforts."

EPISODE #36 "PROJECT 44"

Production #1036 / 36B
Dates of Production: August 17 and 19, 1955
Directed by Tom Gries

SCRIPT & STORY

First Draft by Lou Huston, September 12, 1955
Revised pages dated September 15 and 16, 1955
Final Draft by Lou Huston, September 16, 1955
Teleplay by Lou Huston

PRODUCTION CREDITS

1st Asst. Cameraman: Spec Jones (*un-credited*)
1st Co. Grip: Tex Jackson (*un-credited*)
2nd Asst. Director: Bobby Ray (*un-credited*)
2nd Cameraman: Al Green (*un-credited*)
2nd Co. Grip: Darwin Anderson (*un-credited*)
Assistant Director: Bert Glazer
Asst. Prop Man: Stan Walters (*un-credited*)
Audio Supervisor: Quinn Martin
Best Boy: William Kane (*un-credited*)
Boom Man: Bill Flannery (*un-credited*)
Camera Operator: Dick Rawlings
Construction Chief: Dee Bolhius (*un-credited*)
Director of Photography: Curt Fetters
Electricians: Dick Johnson, Frank Leonetti and
    J. Thielman (*all un-credited*)
Film Coordinator: Donald Tait
Film Editor: Thomas Scott
Gaffer: Bert Jones (*un-credited*)
Make-up Artist: George Gray
Production Coordinator: Joe Wonder
Scientific Advisor on Electronics and Radar Operation:
    Maxwell Smith
Property Master: Ygnacio Sepulveda
Recorder: Roy Cropper (*un-credited*)
Script Supervisor: Wanda Ramsey

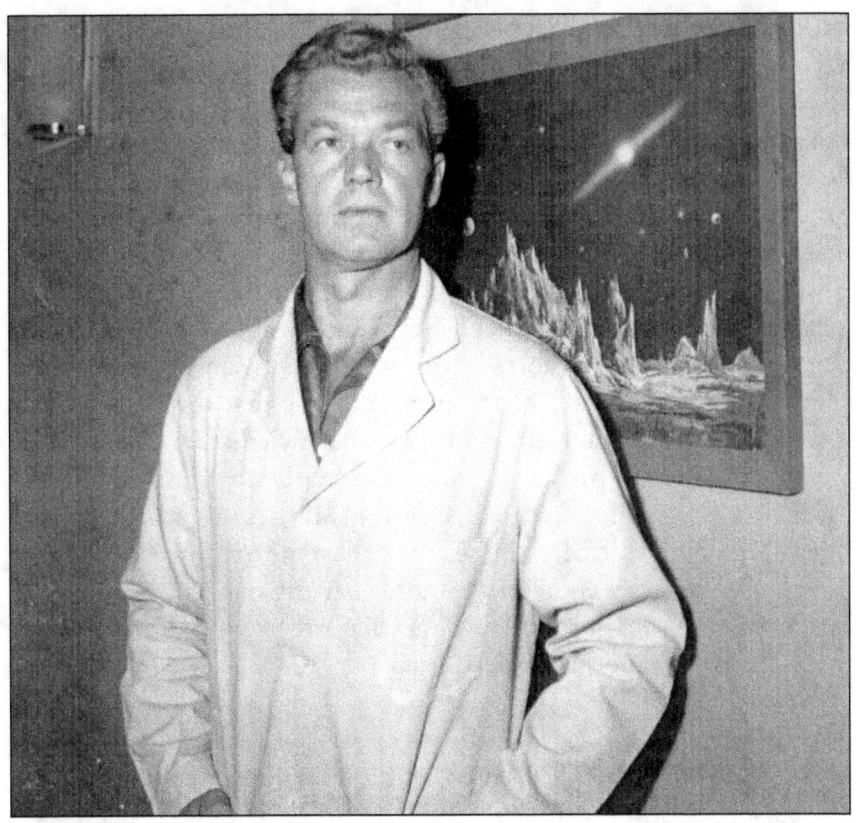

Bill Williams poses for the camera in "Project 44."

SET DECORATOR: BRUCE MACDONALD
SET DESIGNER: JACK COLLIS
SET LABOR: ART SWEET (*UN-CREDITED*)
SOUND EDITOR: MONROE MARTIN
SOUND MIXER: GARRY HARRIS
SPECIAL EFFECTS: HARRY REDMOND, JR.
WARDROBE: ALFRED BERKE

CAST: Vicki Bakken (Sylvia Weiss, $80); Tom Bernard (Elton Crane, $80); Toni Carroll (the nurse, $80); Doris Dowling (Janice Morgan, $750); Kenneth Drake (Malcolm Douglas, $80); Biff Elliot (Ed Garrett, $350); Mary Munday (Barbara Daman, $80); Robert Nelson, Jr. (Willard Hicks, $80); Patricia Parsons (Eileen Herrick, $80); Amanda Webb (Thelma Marlow, $80); Bill Williams (Dr. Arnold Bryan, $1,250); and Mack Williams (Everett Sturgis, $125)

Plot: The development of a new rocket fuel makes space travel technically possible within a few years. Dr. Arnold Bryan, an expert in aviation medicine, is put in charge of Project 44 to determine whether Man himself is physically, mentally and emotionally able to survive a long space flight. Aided by his fiancée, Janice Morgan (a psychologist), Bryan selects and trains eighty healthy young scientists who—it is hoped—will eventually explore Mars. After the group is told the true purpose of the project, they seem to deteriorate physically and mentally. After a near tragedy aboard the simulated space ship, Dr. Bryan is forced to conclude that Man is earth-bound. The only positive result of the experiment is that three couples in the project are in love and want to be married. On the verge of declaring his own project a failure, Bryan learns that one of the scientists has engineered the seeming failures to avoid making the space flight. Actually, the scientists have proven they are "space-worthy." The story ends on the note that the construction on the space ship will begin tomorrow and flight to Mars will be made—with Dr. Bryan and his bride aboard.

Notes

- Actress Toni Carroll played the role of a nurse in another episode, "Beyond Return."
- A poster mapping out the layers of Earth's atmosphere hangs on the wall in this episode, which also appears in "Beyond," "Hour of Nightmare," and the wall of Truman Bradley's laboratory during the initial opener of every episode, located behind the oscillator cone.
- The opening stock footage of the Science Hall (side and front view) is the same footage reused in five other first season episodes: "Death at 2 A.M.," "A Visit From Dr. Pliny," "The Unexplored," "Y··O··R··D··" and "Operation Flypaper."
- The two blue spacesuits used in this episode are the same used in the movie *Gog* (1954). One of those suits was used for Truman Bradley's opening introduction. The stock footage in the beginning of this episode of the two astronauts in spacesuits rotating on the spin-table and picking up speed was lifted from *Gog* (1954).
- The entire episode was produced on Stage 3 and 7.

Standard contract for actors who appeared on ZIV-TV productions. It is these contracts that were used to determine how much every actor was paid for appearing on *Science Fiction Theatre*.

- The stock footage at the closing of this episode, consisting of a rocket launch, lifted from the movie *Gog* (1954), which was the closing footage of that motion picture.
- The cosmic ray chart hanging on the wall in this episode is the same prop that also appears in "A Visit From Dr. Pliny," "Before the Beginning," "Postcard From Barcelona" and in the motion-picture *Gog* (1954).

- The man in the space suit during Truman Bradley's lab demonstration was the same actor who appeared un-credited as the fingerprint man in "Beyond Return."

DR. ROBERT S. RICHARDSON

The American astronomer of Mt. Wilson and Palomar Observatories, who appears as a guest in the beginning of this episode, discusses with Truman Bradley the realistic possibility of finding water and plant life on Mars, even with a thin atmosphere, and man's attempt to land on the planet's surface. Dr. Robert S. Richardson also wrote science fiction under the name of Philip Latham. Under his real name, Richardson wrote *Five Against Venus* (1952) and *Missing Men of Saturn* (1953). He had served as technical advisor for *The War of the Worlds* (1953) and *Conquest of Space* (1955), and wrote numerous television scripts for *Captain Video*.

The December 22, 1955 issue of *Variety* reviewed this episode:

"ZIV's *Science Fiction Theatre* which has gotten off to a slow start but has been picking up speed with regularity lately, has another good entry in 'Project 44,' a story of man's attempt to conquer space. This is right in the groove of those with an appetite for the scientifiction motif, and Lou Huston's teleplay is well written and directed with firmness by Tom Gries.

"Huston's story is of a hush-hush project wherein the government is testing eight young scientists to see if they will be able to take the hardships in a contemplated trip to Mars. All goes well until suddenly just about everybody involved begins flunking their tests and it looks as though the whole project is kaput. But the scientist in charge finds a saboteur in their midst—one of the eight, not wanting to go on the interplanetary trek because he's secretly married has rigged the tests deliberately so the venture would collapse.

"Bill Williams performs with believability as the chief scientist and receives good support from Doris Dowling, Biff Elliott, Mary Munday, Toni Carroll, Mack Williams and Vicki Bakken."

EPISODE #37 "ARE WE INVADED?"

PRODUCTION #1037 / 37B
DATES OF PRODUCTION: SEPTEMBER 20 AND 21, 1955
DIRECTED BY LEON BENSON

SCRIPT & STORY

FINAL TYPESCRIPT (ANNOTATED) BY NORMAN JOLLEY AND IVAN TORS, SEPTEMBER 15, 1955
REVISED PAGES (ANNOTATED), SEPTEMBER 19, 1955
REVISED MASTER MIMEO (ANNOTATED), SEPTEMBER 19, 1955
TELEPLAY BY NORMAN JOLLEY

PRODUCTION CREDITS

1ST ASST. CAMERAMAN: JIM BELL (*UN-CREDITED*)
1ST CO. GRIP: CARL MIKSCH (*UN-CREDITED*)
2ND ASST. DIRECTOR: WILLARD KIRKHAM (*UN-CREDITED*)
2ND CO. GRIP: BING HALL (*UN-CREDITED*)
ASSISTANT DIRECTOR: DONALD VERK
ASST. PROP MAN: STAN WALTERS (*UN-CREDITED*)
AUDIO SUPERVISOR: QUINN MARTIN
BOOM MAN: ELMER HAGLUND (*UN-CREDITED*)
CAMERA OPERATOR: DICK RAWLINGS
CONSTRUCTION CHIEF: DEE BOLHIUS (*UN-CREDITED*)
DIRECTOR OF PHOTOGRAPHY: CURT FETTERS
ELECTRICIANS: WALTER GEDIMAN, HAROLD KRAUS AND JOHN MILLMAN (*ALL UN-CREDITED*)
FILM COORDINATOR: DONALD TAIT
FILM EDITOR: THOMAS SCOTT
GAFFER: BERT JONES (*UN-CREDITED*)
MAKE-UP ARTIST: GEORGE GRAY
PRODUCTION COORDINATOR: JOE WONDER
SOUND MIXER: GARRY HARRIS
PROPERTY MASTER: MAX PITTMAN
RECORDER: WILLIAM HANKS (*UN-CREDITED*)
SCIENTIFIC ADVISOR ON ELECTRONICS AND RADAR OPERATION: MAXWELL SMITH
SCRIPT SUPERVISOR: RUTH BROWNSON

Richard Erdman and Leslie Gaye examine the same props and set used for "The Other Side of the Moon." (SEE PHOTOS FOR EPISODE 39).

Richard Erdman and Leslie Gaye pose between takes. Notice the tank on the table is the same used in a number of Truman Bradley's lab demonstrations.

SET DECORATOR: CLARENCE STEENSON
SET DESIGNER: JACK COLLIS
SET LABOR: ART SWEET (*UN-CREDITED*)
SOUND EDITOR: MONROE MARTIN
SPECIAL EFFECTS: HARRY REDMOND, JR.
WARDROBE: ALFRED BERKE

CAST: Richard Erdman (Seth Turner, $600); Antony Eustrel (Mr. Galleon, $150); Leslie Gaye (Barbara Arnold, $250); Paul Hahn (Arnold's assistant, $80); and Pat O'Brien (Dr. Arnold, $2,000)

The Episode Guide: Season One

The deserted set of "Are We Invaded?" The large poster hanging on the wall can also be seen in "Postcard From Barcelona."

Minutes before filming commences it's all quiet on the set of "Are We Invaded?"

Richard Erdman and Leslie Gaye are given instructions for the next scene. Notice the electrical wires that supply the lights and levers for the fake control panel.

PLOT: Seth Turner, brash young graduate journalism student with his fiancée, Barbara Arnold, see a UFO in the form of a fireball in the sky. A stranger, Mr. Galleon, is also present. Seth, convinced the object is a flying saucer bearing observers from another world, has a bitter argument with Barbara's father, Dr. Arnold, a distinguished astronomer, who dogmatically refuses to consider flying saucers as such. To prove his conviction to the world at large, and at the same time establish himself as a top TV news reporter, Seth films interviews and documented evidence in favor of his argument. Dr. Arnold, after viewing the film, is still adamant in his conviction and proves Seth wrong by reproducing the reported "saucer" effect in his laboratory. Seth has attempts to call in his acquaintance, Mr. Galleon, who also witnessed the fireball to corroborate his sighting and to watch the lab demonstrations, but Mr. Galleon apologizes for he will not be available. Soon after Dr. Arnold's demonstrations have completely destroyed Seth's evidence—and Seth has become more realistic and apologized—the mysterious Mr. Galleon disappears. He has left behind an envelope. Inside, Arnold finds a strange photograph which he identifies as a picture of our own solar system taken from a position originating outside the Earth's atmosphere. Authenticating it, Arnold must finally admit the picture itself is scientific proof of the fact that it could only have been taken from another system . . . or from some kind of spacecraft.

NOTES

- This episode was produced under the title "Fireball."
- The entire episode was filmed in the studio. Part of the first day was filmed on Stage 4, the remainder of the episode was filmed on Stage 5.
- The Ford convertible was among the set props, and part of the company's property for use in television and film production.
- The periodic table of elements hanging on the wall in Seth's room can also be seen hanging on the wall in a number of other episodes including "100 Years Young," "Operation Flypaper" and "The Strange Doctor Lorenz."
- Documentaries featuring eyewitnesses claiming to have seen a flying saucer were used as stock footage for Seth Turner's documentary in this episode.

The December 29, 1955 issue of *Variety* reviewed this episode:

"Those crazy dishes better known as flying saucers serve as the focal point of Norman Jolley's teleplay, 'Are We Invaded?' and it comes off the tubes a well-produced, absorbing drama dealing with invasion from another planet. Jolley is very much at home in these fanciful tales, since he for years wrote that onetime pioneer of the scientifiction tv shows, *Space Patrol*.

"When a guy and his gal are spooning, they spot a flying saucer, all of which might prove that saucers and spoons belong together. However, young guy can't sell his prospective pop-in-law, an astronomer, on it, the latter insisting it was just an optical illusion. Interesting climax sees even the expert begin to have his doubts and believe maybe there are such things as space ships. They've cut down considerably on the scientific gobbledygook in this series, and it improves it muchly. Formerly, they reeled off like scientific lectures.

"Richard Erdman turns in a good portrayal of the youth who believes in those saucers; Leslie Gaye is competent as his g.f.; Pat O'Brien is quietly efficient as the father-in-law, and Antony Eustrel good in a supporting role. Leon Benson's direction has a fine quality. Special effects rate kudos."

EPISODE #38 "OPERATION FLYPAPER"

PRODUCTION #1038 / 38B
DATES OF PRODUCTION: OCTOBER 5 AND 6, 1955
DIRECTED BY EDDIE DAVIS

SCRIPT & STORY

FINAL TYPESCRIPT (ANNOTATED) BY DORIS GILBERT, SEPTEMBER 21, 1955
REVISED PAGES, OCTOBER 3, 1955
REVISED MASTER MIMEO (ANNOTATED), OCTOBER 3, 1955
TELEPLAY BY DORIS GILBERT

PRODUCTION CREDITS

1ST ASST. CAMERAMAN: JIM BELL (*UN-CREDITED*)
1ST CO. GRIP: CARL MIKSCH (*UN-CREDITED*)

2ND ASST. DIRECTOR BOBBY RAY (*UN-CREDITED*)
2ND CO. GRIP: JACK CHAMBERS AND MEL BLEDSOE (*UN-CREDITED*)
3RD GRIP: JACK CHAMBERS (*UN-CREDITED*)
ASSISTANT DIRECTOR: ED STEIN
ASST. PROP MAN: VIC PETROTTA (*UN-CREDITED*)
AUDIO SUPERVISOR: QUINN MARTIN
BEST BOY: CHARLES STOCKWELL (*UN-CREDITED*)
BOOM MAN: ELMER HAGLUND (*UN-CREDITED*)
CABLEMAN: MR. CASEY (OCTOBER 6 ONLY, *UN-CREDITED*)
CAMERA OPERATOR: DICK RAWLINGS
CONSTRUCTION CHIEF: DEE BOLHIUS (*UN-CREDITED*)
DIRECTOR OF PHOTOGRAPHY: CURT FETTERS
ELECTRICIANS: CHARLES HANGER, FRED HOUNSHELL AND HAROLD KRAUS (*ALL UN-CREDITED*)
FILM COORDINATOR: DONALD TAIT
FILM EDITOR: CHARLES CRAFT, A.C.E.
GAFFER: S. H. BARTON (*UN-CREDITED*)
MAKE-UP ARTIST: GEORGE GRAY
PRODUCTION COORDINATOR: JOE WONDER
SOUND MIXER: GARRY HARRIS
PROPERTY MASTER: MAX PITTMAN
RECORDER: WILLIAM HANKS (*UN-CREDITED*)
SCIENTIFIC ADVISOR ON ELECTRONICS AND RADAR OPERATION: MAXWELL SMITH
SCRIPT SUPERVISOR: LARRY LUND
SET DECORATOR: CLARENCE STEENSON
SET DESIGNER: JACK COLLIS
SET LABOR: SOL INVERSO (*UN-CREDITED*)
SOUND EDITOR: SIDNEY SUTHERLAND
SPECIAL EFFECTS: HARRY REDMOND, JR.
WARDROBE: ALFRED BERKE

CAST: George Eldredge (David Vollard, $300); John Eldredge (Jonathan Vollard, $300); Dabbs Greer (Agent McNamara, $150); Mauritz Hugo (the hotel manager, $100); Kristine Miller (Alma Ford, $350); Vincent Price (Dr. Philip Redmond, $2,000); and William Vaughan (Richard Owens, $80)

Candid shot on the set of "Operation Flypaper."

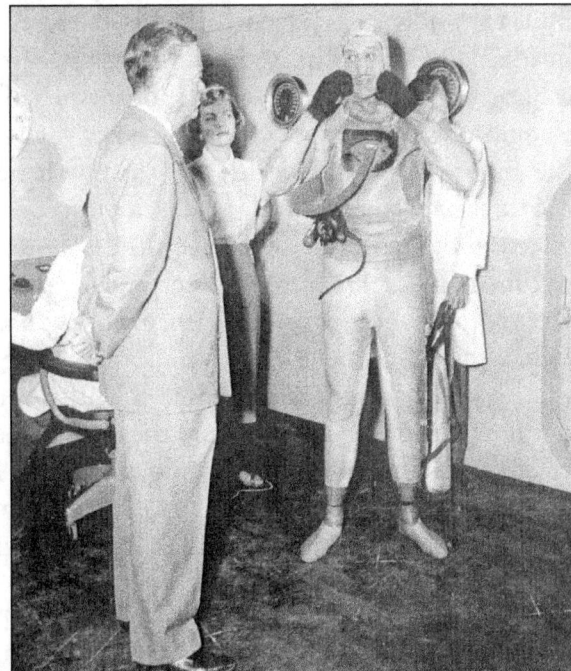

Vincent Price demonstrates the "Second Skin," an experimental diving suit for underwater exploration in "Operation Flypaper."

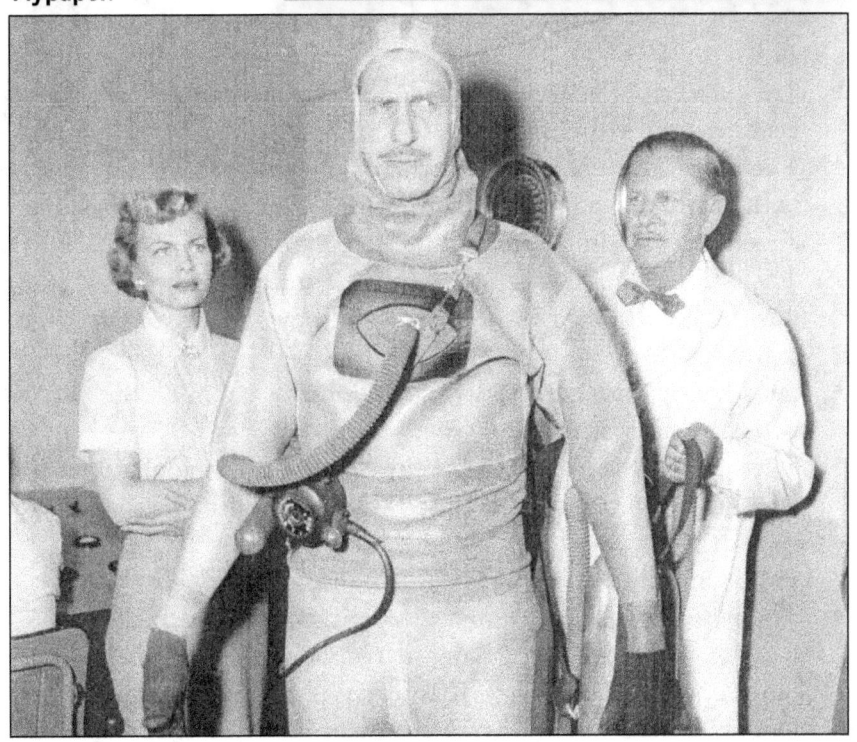

PLOT: Under heavy security guard, a secret conclave of scientists headed by Dr. Philip Redmond, a Nobel prize-winner, meets at a hotel in La Jolla. Under the sponsorship of the government, the Redmond group has met to pool its knowledge in an effort to mine the sea of its mineral wealth and thereby benefit mankind. During the meeting, three important scientific secrets are inexplicably stolen under everyone's very eyes, the only clue being that a period of time has gone unaccounted for during each robbery. None of the victims have been subjected to mass hypnosis so Redmond, his fellow-scientists and the FBI join forces to capture the elusive "time thief," a brilliant and disgruntled scientist; more than that, to find out how he does it, by a method they call Operation Flypaper. They create a fake lab rigged with hidden cameras and a new dredge to set the bait. Redmond and the FBI watch the thief in action using an invention that sends out a high frequency transmission that puts every one within hearing distance of the ultra sonic sound into a trance. Redmond and the authorities trick him into smashing the machine and they apprehend the thief.

NOTES
- The two actors who played the roles of the Vollard brothers were real-life brothers.
- The air pressure chamber in which Vincent Price is attacked is the same air pressure chamber in which two potential astronauts are almost killed in "Project 44."
- The entire episode was filmed in the studio. The first day was filmed on Stage 5 and the second day was filmed on Stage 3 and 7.
- Healthways, pioneers of diving equipment, supplied the two-man submarine footage.
- The opening stock footage of the Science Hall (side and front view) is the same footage reused in five other first season episodes: "Death at 2 A.M.," "A Visit From Dr. Pliny," "The Unexplored," "Y..O..R..D.." and "Project 44."
- The periodic table of elements hanging on the wall in this episode can also be seen hanging on the wall in a number of other episodes including "100 Years Young," "The Strange Doctor Lorenz" and "Are We Invaded?"

- The stock footage of the beachside house along the cliff was the same footage used in the opening of "The World Below."

The January 6, 1956 issue of *Variety* reviewed this episode:

"When secret documents and instruments are thefted from a hush-hush scientific project for the government, right in front of the brains working on it, it throws the entire security system into a state of consternation and the project is called off. Such is Doris Gilbert's interesting premise in 'Operation Flypaper,' a good and exciting episode in this series.

"Scientists are working on new secrets to explore the depth of the ocean when their secrets begin to vanish in an eerie manner. So Washington security bosses drop the project, but keep the scientists 'working' in a trap set up to catch the culprit. Use of TV on the room set up as a trap reveals the thief in a paranoid ex-aide of the top scientist, who has devised an instrument which causes anyone near him to go to sleep right where they are when he comes around. It's reminiscent of the 'Z-ray' concocted in other scientifictioneers. The character really flips when told he's trapped, and smashes his paralyzing invention before he's nabbed.

"Vincent Price, George and John Eldredge, Kristine Miller and Dabbs Greer acquit themselves creditably under the capable direction of Eddie Davis."

EPISODE #39 "THE OTHER SIDE OF THE MOON"

PRODUCTION #1039 / 39B

DATES OF PRODUCTION: OCTOBER 7 AND 8, 1955
DIRECTED BY EDDIE DAVIS

SCRIPT & STORY

FIRST DRAFT BY ROBERT M. FRESCO AND RICHARD JOSEPH TUBER, SEPTEMBER 26, 1955
FINAL DRAFT BY ROBERT M. FRESCO AND RICHARD JOSEPH TUBER, OCTOBER 4, 1955
TELEPLAY BY ROBERT M. FRESCO AND RICHARD JOSEPH TUBER

PRODUCTION CREDITS

1st Asst. Cameraman: Jim Bell (*un-credited*)
1st Co. Grip: Carl Miksch (*un-credited*)
2nd Asst. Director: Bobby Ray (*un-credited*)
2nd Co. Grip: Jack Chambers (*un-credited*)
3rd Grip: Mel Bledsoe (*un-credited*)
Assistant Director: Donald Verk
Asst. Prop Man: Vic Petrotta (*un-credited*)
Audio Supervisor: Quinn Martin
Best Boy: Charles Stockwell (*un-credited*)
Boom Man: Elmer Haglund (*un-credited*)
Camera Operator: Dick Rawlings
Construction Chief: Dee Bolhius (*un-credited*)
Director of Photography: Curt Fetters
Electrician: Harold Kraus, Judd LeRoy and Roy Slocum (*all un-credited*)
Film Coordinator: Donald Tait
Film Editor: John B. Woelz
Gaffer: S.H. Barton (*un-credited*)
Make-up Artist: George Gray
Production Coordinator: Joe Wonder
Sound Mixer: Garry Harris
Property Master: Max Pittman
Recorder: William Hanks (*un-credited*)
Scientific Advisor on Electronics and Radar Operation: Maxwell Smith
Script Supervisor: Larry Lund
Set Decorator: Clarence Steenson
Set Designer: Jack Collis
Set Labor: Sol Inverso (*un-credited*)
Sound Editor: Monroe Martin
Special Effects: Harry Redmond, Jr.
Still Man: Charles Rhodes (October 7 only, *un-credited*)
Wardrobe: Alfred Berke

Cast: Peter Davis (Dr. Webster, $80); Peter Dunne (Dr. Clark, $80); Beverly Garland (Kathy Kerston, $300); Paul Guilfoyle (Col. Ralph Sutton, $200); Paul Hahn (Prof. Hummell, $80); Bill Henry

Beverly Garland in "The Other Side of the Moon."

(Dean Arthur Collins, $100); Skip Homeier (Lawrence Kerston, $1,000); Philip Ober (Prof. Carl Schneider, $500); and Mack Williams (Gen. Jacob Evans, $125)

PLOT: An inquisitive young astronomer, Lawrence Kerston, develops a revolutionary electronic camera. His test photographs seem to indicate a strange halo of radioactive dust ringing the moon, unseen

Beverly Garland and Skip Homeier examine scientific apparatus in "The Other Side of the Moon."

before because no one saw the moon through the new infrared process. Labeled an over-eager upstart after Kerston publishes his claim and steals the limelight, the astronomer finds himself suspended. At the height of his depression, the Air Force evinces belief in his camera. A new series of photographs uncover the presence of alien objects landing on the moon. On the basis of this, the White House orders an unmanned rocket sent on an exploratory voyage around the satellite—a voyage with an expected, yet most satisfactory result . . . to Kerston, his nation and the world. Alien beings are using our moon as a dumping ground for atomic and nuclear waste—but depositing it only on the far side of the moon so it would not interfere with our way of living.

Beverly Garland and Skip Homeier in "The Other Side of the Moon."

Notes

- The first day of filming was on Stage 3. The second day of filming was on Stage 5.
- The plastic photo of the solar system Bradley displays in his introductory lab demonstration was the same hanging on the wall in the professor's office in the pilot episode, "Beyond."
- The observatory where Skip Homeier's character works was constructed in the studio, originally for the episode "Are We Invaded?" It was redecorated for this episode, with the hopes that the television viewers would not recognize the same set which included a huge telescope dropping down from the ceiling.
- The exterior shot of the observatory was also used in "Are We Invaded?"

The January 12, 1956 issue of *Variety* reviewed this episode:

"The moon has been so thoroughly 'explored' by television that Ivan Tors and his Ziv crew decided to see what's on the other side. What they found was a dumping ground for atomic waste material sent up from the Earth. At least that's what the unscientific mind must've deduced from this flight into space, which will need traffic patrols if the TV excursions continue at their unabated clip. But it's interesting to watch because of the current publicity attending the Government's plans for sending a satellite to the celestial body. It's also well performed by a cast topped off by Skip Homeier, grown out of brat-hood into serious acting, and Philip Ober, plus the femme touch supplied by Beverly Garland.

"When Homeier invents a new photographic principle that picks up alloy objects circulating the moon in its electronic lens, the Army brass scoffs at such space fantasy, but after a personal appeal by him, decides to send up a rocket with the camera strapped in. Radiation sends the ship plummeting but enough was picked up on the film to convince the army that the hidden side of the moon has been finally exposed.

"The mechanical gadgets in this series must have cost a pretty penny and for all the watcher knows it's the real thing unless it's done in miniature, which is a good trick of photography. Eddie Davis turns his direction to the scientific side to rev up excitement and let the actor splay along."

The Episode Guide
Season Two

EPISODE #40 "SIGNALS FROM THE HEART"

PRODUCTION #1040 / 40B
Dates of Production: February 20 and 21, 1956
Directed by Herbert L. Strock

SCRIPT & STORY
Outline by Ivan Tors (undated)
Final typescript (annotated) by Stuart Jerome, circa February 8, 1956
Master mimeo (annotated) February 8, 1956
Teleplay by Stuart Jerome, from a story by Ivan Tors

PRODUCTION CREDITS
1st Asst. Cameraman: Tod Clett (*un-credited*)
1st Co. Grip: Mel Bledsoe (*un-credited*)
2nd Asst. Director: Boby Ray (*un-credited*)
2nd Cameraman: Joe Jackman (*un-credited*)
2nd Co. Grip: Robert West (*un-credited*)
3rd Grip: Ned Labbe (*un-credited*)
Assistant Director: Erich Von Stroheim, Jr.
Asst. Prop Man: Cecil Smith (*un-credited*)
Audio Supervisor: Quinn Martin
Boom Man: Clarence Self (*un-credited*)
Cableman: Dick Smith (*un-credited*)
Construction Chief: Dee Belhius (*un-credited*)
Director of Photography: Robert Hoffman

Film Coordinator: Donald Tait
Film Editor: Duncan Mansfield, A.C.E.
Gaffer: S.H. Barton (*un-credited*)
Make-up Artist: George Gray (*un-credited*)
Production Coordinator: Joe Wonder
Production Supervisor: Barry Cohon
Property Master: Max Pittman
Recorder: John Bury (*un-credited*)
Scientific Advisor on Electronics and Radiation: Maxwell Smith
Script Supervisor: Joe Franklin
Set Decorator: Clarence Steenson
Set Designer: Jack Collis
Set Labor: Cesar Dipetre (*un-credited*)
Sound Editor: Sidney Sutherland
Sound Mixer: Phil Mitchell
Special Effects: Harry Redmond, Jr.
Wardrobe: Alfred Berke (*un-credited*)

CAST: Gordon Barnes (Chaney, $80); Michael Garth (the police sergeant, $80); Peter Hanson (Warren Stark, $350); Joyce Holden (Alma Stark, $100); Larry Kerr (Fielding, $80); Walter Kingsford (Professor Tuber, $150); Greg Moffett (Jimmy Stark, $80); Gene Roth (Tom Horton, $125); and Riza Royce (Mrs. Horton, $80)

PLOT: A terrible, unexplainable train accident has just taken place. The coroner's autopsy proves that the engineer of the train died of a heart attack just before passing a warning signal. The District Attorney and an insurance investigator go immediately to Dr. Warren Stark, a young cardiologist, who only a week before had examined the engineer and pronounced his heart normal. Their implication is that Stark was criminally negligent in not observing signs of the engineer's heart trouble. Overnight, Dr. Stark's practice disappears. Under pressure, he decides to leave town but a chance conversation with his young son about weather balloons gives him an idea for a telecardiograph, a device which can be attached to a patient's heart, so that long distance signals of the heart action can be sent to a medical center while the patient goes about his everyday life. The

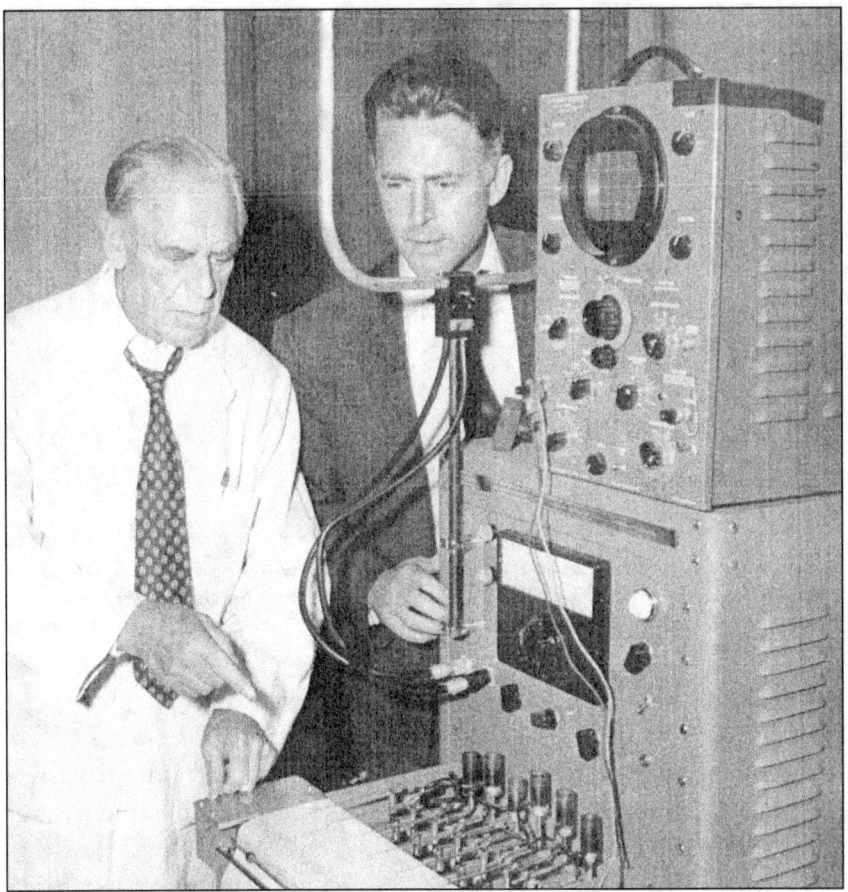

Professor Truber (Walter Kingsford) discusses technical details regarding the telecardiograph with Warren Stark (Peter Hanson).

final test for the device comes when it saves a policeman's life . . . proving the value of this new weapon in the fight against heart disease.

Notes
- The police car and station wagon featured in this episode were rented.
- Produced under the title "Message from the Heart."
- Part of the first day was devoted to filming exterior shots on the ZIV lot by the cigar store and by the incinerator.
- Troy Melton was the un-credited stuntman for this episode, paid $80 for his work.

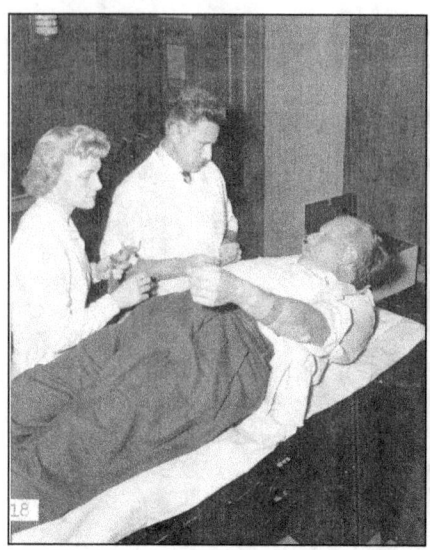 

A real nurse instructs Peter Hanson how to administer and ensure bandages are applied the proper way on Gene Roth.

Ivan Tors watches with admiration as Peter Hanson demonstrates electronic equipment with Joyce Holden.

The April 18, 1956 issue of *Variety* reviewed this episode:

"First of the new series of Ivan Tors' *Science Fiction Theatre* vidpix is an entertaining offering, but more importantly Tors has revised the structure of his series to make for considerable overall improvement.

"In the initialer—which presumably sets the pattern for upcoming frames—the former long lecture by narrator Truman Bradley is virtually done away with, and there is more time for story-telling. Also, Tors has cut down considerably on the scientific gobbledy-gook, so that the layman can understand what's going on, even if he can't fathom some of the mysteries posed in the world of science.

"'Heart' depicts Peter Hanson as a medico discredited because a week after he examined a train engineer and said his heart was okay, the engineer has a heart attack, is involved in an accident in which 24 are killed. The doc develops a radio cardiograph—a cardiograph strapped to the person—which helps considerably to track down the No. 1 killer—heart disease. Bradley came on at the end to say that while the story is fiction, such an invention is actually being developed. Plot was interestingly unfolded, and well directed by Herbert Strock.

Director Herbert L. Strock instructs actor Walter Kingsford how to operate the controls in "Signals from the Heart."

"Peter Hanson, Joyce Holden, Walter Kingsford and Gene Roth all contribute good performances. Stuart Jerome teleplay, from a Tors original, is a good one. Olympia Beer pitches were okay, but bragging has more to do with the water used in the brew rather than the beer itself."

"MESSAGE FROM THE HEART"
BY IVAN TORS

At one of the great medical centers, a new electrocardiograph device is in experimental operation. It works as follows:

A small telemetering gadget is attached to the heart of the patient and his heart impulses are being radioed back through a miniature transmitter to the medical center. As the patient works, or drives his car, keeps busy at his office, plays tennis, argues with his wife, carries on with his children, his heart action is automatically monitored miles away.

A new patient is being examined at this medical center. The examining physician is convinced that the patient's heart complaints are due to excessive nervous strain. The patient refuses to admit to the Doctor the cause of this pressure. The truth about him is that early in his youth, he spent two years in prison somewhere in Canada for car theft. Now he is a successful businessman and a good family man. He is about to enlarge his business and he requested permission to sell stock of his new company. He is afraid that if the truth comes out about his past, the Security Commissioner will refuse the stock issue. He had seen a man in town who was in jail with him and he is afraid of being recognized and blackmailed by this person and his fears are the factor bringing on his heart condition.

The patient leaves the hospital with the telemetering gadget attached to his heart and his heart activity is recorded at the medical center throughout the day. Suddenly the stylus pen of the monitoring device shows great excitement. The activity is so strong that the Doctor realizes that his patient will die unless he can administer tranquilizing drugs to him without delay. An ambulance drives to his home where he is supposed to be at this hour but they do not find him there. His wife cannot tell the Doctor where her husband is. He was due at home at 5 o'clock and now it is 7:00. They call his office and he is not in the office. The electronic expert who rigged up the gadget gets an idea. They can track him down by triangulation following the impulses which still keep coming through. Two separate ambulances with monitoring equipment follow the track of the radio emission and they locate him in a garage where the blackmailer ex-cellmate holds him at gun point threatening to kill him unless he complies with his blackmail. The Doctor and the electronic expert save the patient from the felon and they save him from an eminent heart attack by immediate medical attention.

The patient wakes up next morning in the hospital in a much improved condition and decides to tell the truth about himself to his wife, the Doctor and the Security Commissioner. He finds out, much to his relief, that nobody holds against him the juvenile crime he committed 30 years ago. From here on he can live without fear. In the meantime, medical science learns a lot from this experience and a new electro-cardiographic gadget proves itself to be great new medical instrument and a life saver.

Truman Bradley material should be based on a demonstration of telemetering devices. How Rocket Flights, weather balloon ascents, test planes and so on are being telemetered.

EPISODE #41 "THE LONG SLEEP"

PRODUCTION #1041 / 42B

DATES OF PRODUCTION: FEBRUARY 27 AND 28, 1956
DIRECTED BY PAUL GUILFOYLE

SCRIPT & STORY

SYNOPSIS BY IVAN TORS, JAN. 10, 1956
FINAL TYPESCRIPT (ANNOTATED) BY ARTHUR WEISS, FEBRUARY 17, 1956
REVISED MASTER MIMEO, FEBRUARY 23, 1956
TELEPLAY BY ARTHUR WEISS, FROM A STORY BY IVAN TORS

PRODUCTION CREDITS

1ST ASST. CAMERAMAN: BILL RANALDI (*UN-CREDITED*)
1ST CO. GRIP: BUD GAUNT (*UN-CREDITED*)
2ND ASST. DIRECTOR: BOBBY RAY (*UN-CREDITED*)
2ND CO. GRIP: EARL MUSSEY (*UN-CREDITED*)
3RD GRIP: BOB DAUDETTE (*UN-CREDITED*)
ANIMAL TRAINER: MR. RICHARDS (*UN-CREDITED*)
ASSISTANT DIRECTOR: MAC WRIGHT
ASST PROP MAN: JOHN GENGIA (*UN-CREDITED*)
AUDIO SUPERVISOR: QUINN MARTIN
BOOM MAN: CLARENCE SELF (*UN-CREDITED*)
CAMERA OPERATOR: DICK RAWLINGS
CONSTRUCTION CHIEF: DEE BOHLIUS (*UN-CREDITED*)
DIRECTOR OF PHOTOGRAPHY: MONROE "MONK" ASKINS
ELECTRICIANS: DIXIE DUNBAR, FRED HOUNSHELL, MIKE HUDSON AND LOUIS KREIGER (*ALL UN-CREDITED*)
FILM COORDINATOR: DONALD TAIT
FILM EDITOR: DUNCAN MANSFIELD, A.C.E.
GAFFER: S.H. BARTON (*UN-CREDITED*)
MAKE-UP ARTIST: GEORGE GRAY

Production Coordinator: Joe Wonder
Production Supervisor: Barry Cohon
Property Master: Max Pittman
Recorder: John Bury (*un-credited*)
Scientific Advisor on Electronics and Radiation: Maxwell Smith
Script Supervisor: Jeanne Lippman
Set Decorator: Clarence Steenson
Set Designer: Jack Collis
Set Labor: Herb Pritchard (*un-credited*)
Sound Editor: Sidney Sutherland
Sound Mixer: Phil Mitchell
Special Effects: Harry Redmond, Jr.
Wardrobe: Alfred Berke

CAST: John Doucette (John Barton, $300); William Erwin (Mike Weldon, $100); Dick Foran (Dr. Samuel Willard, $600); Barry Froner (Gene Willard, $100); Eddie Gallagher (Al Hall, $80); Nancy Hale (Ruth Taney, $200); and Helen Mowery (Alma Willard, $150)

PLOT: Dr. Samuel Willard, a young researcher in experimental medicine who has been working in the field of animal hibernation, saves the life of an apparently incurable sick orangutan by putting him into artificial hibernation. After the local papers herald the story as a medical miracle, the crazed John Barton brings his dying son from the hospital to Dr. Willard with a plea to save the boy with the new hibernation procedure. Barton brushes aside the doctor's argument that neither morals nor ethics justify trying the procedure on a human being. Willard is forced to comply because Barton has kidnapped Willard's wife and child and will kill them if the doctor refuses. One week later the procedure is a success and Dr. Willard wonders if he succeeded or if a higher force did it for the sake of his family.

NOTES

- The poster hanging on the wall in Dr. Willard's laboratory of the human nervous system makes an appearance in the next

Production supervisor Barry Cohon on the set of "The Long Sleep."

episode, when Truman Bradley holds up the poster, when questioning how man handles the complications of hypnotism. It's also hanging in the background in "End of Tomorrow" as Bradley demonstrates the numerous ways nature ensures protection from harmful outside interference.

- One of the un-credited electricians for this television production was Dixie Dunbar, formerly a child star of the 1930s who retired from acting for a career on stage, who is perhaps best known for her legs in the now-famous television commercials that featured totally covered from hips to head by a giant Old Gold cigarette box (also performed later by Mary Tyler Moore). She retired from the entertainment industry shortly after her brief career at ZIV as an electrician for a number of television productions (and at least three known *Science Fiction Theatre* episodes).

"THE LONG SLEEP"
Dated: Jan. 10, 1956
by Ivan Tors

A professor of experimental medicine working with animals who hibernate through the winter finds that under hibernation the animals remain miraculously healthy. No viruses or bacteria attack them, they suffer no colds or infectious disease.

He starts to apply artificial hibernation to animals, which ordinarily don't hibernate. He takes a sick monkey who suffers of virus pneumonia whose temperature is so high that it cannot possibly live more than ten to fifteen minutes. He packs the monkey on ice, reducing his body temperature to 70 degrees. (First administering sedation that will keep him asleep for a period of two weeks.) After two weeks he brings the body temperature of the monkey back to normal and the monkey who had no chance to live is healthy.

He publishes scientific articles on his experiments but he does not even speculate on the possibility for humans. So much more research has to be done before an experiment with human beings can be undertaken.

One night he is in his laboratory when he hears a car stopping outside. He opens the door and sees a man carrying a bundle in his arms and depositing the bundle on his lab-table. As the shape on the lab-table is uncovered he sees that the shape is the shape of a girl. The girl has a 107 degree temperature and is dying. The man tells the doctor that he stole the girl from her hospital bed. The doctors told him that she has only an hour to live. He insists that he should try the same experiment on her he tried on the monkey. When the doctor refuses to comply, the man tells him that the doctor is in no condition to bargain, his wife and son were abducted from his home and if this girl dies, they will also die. The doctor has no choice. He packs the girl in ice after administering sedation. A suspense of two weeks follow. The man who is with him in the lab forces him not to admit anyone while he refuses to help unless he produces proof that his wife and child are okay. He succeeds to overcome the intruder by hypnosis but now the experiment went too far and nothing can be gained by stopping.

The two weeks are over, the girl comes to, the wife and child are released but soon after that the girl dies and the man is taken away by police. But without the act of this crazed man, the doctor never had dared to try his experiment on a human being and the fact that the girl who didn't have a chance lived for more than two weeks proves that hibernation may be a very important factor in saving lives.

EPISODE #42 "WHO IS THIS MAN?"

PRODUCTION #1042 / 45B

DATES OF PRODUCTION: MARCH 5 AND 6, 1956
DIRECTED BY WILLIAM CASTLE

SCRIPT & STORY

SYNOPSIS BY CHARLES B. SMITH, N.D.
FINAL TYPESCRIPT (ANNOTATED), FEBRUARY 27, 1956
TELEPLAY BY CHARLES B. SMITH

PRODUCTION CREDITS

1ST ASST. CAMERAMAN: BILL RANALDI (*UN-CREDITED*)
1ST CO. GRIP: MEL BLEDSOE (*UN-CREDITED*)
2ND ASST. DIRECTOR: BOBBY RAY (*UN-CREDITED*)
2ND CAMERAMAN: BOB JOHANNES (*UN-CREDITED*)
2ND CO. GRIP: KENNETH DAY (*UN-CREDITED*)
3RD GRIP: JACK CHAMBERS (*UN-CREDITED*)
ASSISTANT DIRECTOR: BERT GLAZER
ASST PROP MAN: EVERETT RICHARDSON (*UN-CREDITED*)
AUDIO SUPERVISOR: QUINN MARTIN
BEST BOY: MIKE HUDSON (*UN-CREDITED*)
BOOM MAN: BILL FLANNERY (*UN-CREDITED*)
CABLEMAN: DICK SMITH (*UN-CREDITED*)
CONSTRUCTION CHIEF: DEE BOHLIUS (*UN-CREDITED*)
DIRECTOR OF PHOTOGRAPHY: ROBERT HOFFMAN
ELECTRICIANS: [FIRST NAME UNKNOWN] BROOKS AND CHARLES HANGER (*BOTH UN-CREDITED*)
FILM COORDINATOR: DONALD TAIT
FILM EDITOR: DUNCAN MANSFIELD, A.C.E.
GAFFER: S.H. BARTON (*UN-CREDITED*)

Make-up Artist: George Gray (*un-credited*)
Production Coordinator: Joe Wonder
Production Supervisor: Barry Cohon
Property Master: Max Pittman
Recorder: Roy Cropper (*un-credited*)
Scientific Advisor on Electronics and Radiation: Maxwell Smith
Script Supervisor: Jeanne Lippman
Set Decorator: Bruce MacDonald
Set Designer: Jack Collis
Set Labor: Sol Inverso (*un-credited*)
Sound Editor: Monroe Martin
Sound Mixer: Jay Ashworth
Special Effects: Harry Redmond, Jr.
Still Man: Charles Rhodes (*un-credited*)
Wardrobe: Alfred Berke (*un-credited*)

CAST: David Alpert (Dr. Porter Gwen, $100); Bruce Bennett (Dr. Hugh Bentley, $1,000); Tom Bernard (Joe Ellison, $100); Maureen Cassidy (Judy, $100); Lisa Davis (Alice Cooper, $100); Don Eitner (Henry Richards, $80); Tom Pittman (Willis, $80); Sam Scar (the waiter, $80); Charles Smith (Tommy Cooper, $100); and Harlow Wilcox (Dr. Karl Krauss, $100)

PLOT: Hugh Bentley, a psychologist specializing in hypnotherapy, teaching at a major university, is prevailed upon by Alice Cooper, one of his students, to take on her brother who displays a series of personality problems that affects not only his personal life, but his studies as well. Bentley, by placing Tommy in a state of hypnosis, hopes to find the reason for the young man's condition. Bentley hypnotizes the youth and tells him to go as far back as his memory can. Tommy relates details of a prior life which Bentley cannot believe since he does not believe in prior life regression. While Bentley digs deeper under hypnosis, his colleagues are mystified as the boy claims to be a man named Jack Welsh who was executed for murder in Harper, Kansas, 1887. After giving him a post hypnotic suggestion to carry on the character traits of the murder, they discover Tommy is greatly changed—even getting into a fight with

Truman Bradley proudly demonstrates a hypnotized chicken.

Truman Bradley throws the chicken into the air. Note the specialized trainer handling the alligator.

Dr. Hugh Bentley (Bruce Bennett) poses for a publicity shot in "Who Is This Man?"

Tommy Cooper (Charles Smith) is about to be picked on by the other students in "Who Is This Man?"

Director William Castle.

a bully and almost commits murder. Bentley again hypnotizes Tommy and by using hypnosis and post-hypnotic suggestion has the youth forget all that has happened. A meeting of the teaching staff follows. Dr. Gwen comes in with proof that a man named Jack Welsh did live and was executed in Harper, Kansas in 1887. Science apparently has much more to learn about the human brain.

Notes

- Triangle flags hanging on the wall in the cafeteria say "Fairfax," "Denison," "Darwin" and "Colman." A number of these same flags appear on the wall as background props in a number of *Meet Corliss Archer* television episodes, also produced by ZIV-TV.

> **Blooper!**
> When the doctors verify the facts from a historical society, they claim Jack Welsh was murdered in September of 1888, but when Tommy Cooper is under hypnosis earlier in the episode, he claims the year is 1887.

The May 2, 1956 issue of *Variety* reviewed this episode:

"Inevitably, the reincarnation fad was due for a going-over on the *Science Fiction Theatre*, but even those viewers mesmerized by the current craze of purported age regression must have found this treatment pedestrian. Charles B. Smith's teleplay has but little imagination; is actually merely an attempt to capitalize on the Bridey Murphy bit.

"Seems there's a shy, introverted young student, and the prof puts him in a state of hypnosis to try to help him. Well, gee, turns out in the last century he was a different guy, who killed another, and hanged for it. Just why this made him shy in his second life is never explained. Mebbe he felt 'no noose is good noose.' The profs all come to the conclusion there's little they know about age regression. Vehicle is static, with most of the footage being of the young guy in his chair telling of his other life, and of the profs discussing same.

"Bruce Bennett, Charles Smith, David Alpert and Harlow Wilcox turn in routinish performances. Direction by William Castle is uninspired."

"THE OTHER SELF"
by Charles B. Smith

Hugh Bentley, a professor of psychology at a major university, has hypnotized a student during class to illustrate the value of hypnotherapy. He clearly states that he does not believe in reincarnation. Later that day, Alice Cooper, one of his students, prevails upon him to help her younger brother, Tommy Cooper. Tommy is a waiter in the school cafeteria. He is terribly shy, nervous, afraid of animals.

At Bentley's laboratory that afternoon, Tommy fills out a medical history card for Bentley. Tommy is *right* handed. Bentley hypnotizes Tommy and asks him to go as far back in his memory as he can. Tommy tells him that the year is 1881. He is working in a livery stable in a Western town. His name is Jack Welsh. He is 35 years old! He was a runaway from his home in the East because he killed a man in a fight! He lost his temper and used a particularly vicious and individual wrestling hold on the man. Coming forward a few years he tells of being caught and executed. Bentley is taking all of this on a tape recorder. Bentley is sure that Tommy must have read or seen a picture with a similar plot. He plants post-hypnotic suggestions in Tommy's mind and carefully awakens him. Tommy appears greatly changed. He is confident, alert, not shy. While he answers a couple of questions from Bentley he uses his *left* hand to doodle with pencil. Bentley cautiously asks him if he has seen Western picture or read book about West. He answers in negative. A lad comes in with a cat. Tommy is not afraid of the cat. Tommy leaves. Bentley looks at doodling. Tommy has written in a different hand the name Jack Welsh!

Bentley has three faculty members listen to tape. They can only offer explanation Bentley has been given. One of them doesn't seem so sure but does not speak up at this time.

Tommy is back on the job at cafeteria. Bluffs down bully who thought he was still old, shy Tommy. He makes a date with girl for school dance. Faculty member who heard tape sends to the town Tommy told of being executed in for information. Relative there was found in old records. Forwarded photostatic copy of handwritten confession of executed man. It tallies with the new Tommy's handwriting. The personality of Jack Welsh has spanned two lives!

Phone call from Alice. Tommy, at the dance, in fight with boy, had almost killed him, using Jack Welsh's wrestling hold. Bentley again puts Tommy in trance. Bentley tells Tommy to forget what happened. He carefully awakens Tommy who is himself again although he retains a touch of the stronger personality. Tommy does not remember days during which he was "Jack Welsh." In time, working with Bentley, he will be completely cured of personality problem.

Meeting of scientists to discuss and possibly find explanation. They state that there are many things about brain they do not know. Memory is one of them. Where memory comes from—how it is retained in brain. They will continue working, hoping to find the answer.

EPISODE #43 "THE GREEN BOMB"

PRODUCTION #1043 / 418
DATES OF PRODUCTION: FEBRUARY 22 AND 23, 1956
DIRECTED BY TOM GRIES

SCRIPT & STORY
TYPESCRIPT (ANNOTATED) BY TOM GRIES, FEBRUARY 14, 1956
MASTER MIMEO (ANNOTATED) FEBRUARY 14, 1956
TELEPLAY BY TOM GRIES, FROM A STORY BY IVAN TORS

PRODUCTION CREDITS
1ST ASST. CAMERAMAN: RALPH KING (*UN-CREDITED*)
1ST CO. GRIP: MEL BLEDSOE (*UN-CREDITED*)
2ND ASST. DIRECTOR: BOBBY RAY (*UN-CREDITED*)
2ND CAMERAMAN: JOE JACKMAN (*UN-CREDITED*)
2ND CO. GRIP: KENNETH DAW (*UN-CREDITED*)
ASSISTANT DIRECTOR: BERT GLAZER
ASST. PROP MAN: JOHN CENGIA (*UN-CREDITED*)
AUDIO SUPERVISOR: QUINN MARTIN
BOOM MAN: CLARENCE SELF (*UN-CREDITED*)
DIRECTOR OF PHOTOGRAPHY: ROBERT HOFFMAN
FILM COORDINATOR: DONALD TAIT
FILM EDITOR: DUNCAN MANSFIELD, A.C.E.
PRODUCTION COORDINATOR: JOE WONDER
PRODUCTION SUPERVISOR: BARRY COHON
PROPERTY MASTER: MAX PITTMAN
RECORDER: JOHN BURY (*UN-CREDITED*)
SET DECORATOR: CLARENCE STEENSON
SET DESIGNER: JACK COLLIS
SOUND EDITOR: LAWRENCE KAUFMAN
SOUND MIXER: PHIL MITCHELL
SPECIAL EFFECTS: HARRY REDMOND, JR.

CAST: Whit Bissell (Maxwell Carnevan, $200); Robert Griffin (Ralph Scott, $250); George Huerta (Raphael, $80); Charles Maxwell (Jonathan Shaw, $80); Eve McVeagh (Ann Page, $125); Leo Needham (Officer Bishop, $80); Melville Ruick (Dr. Selwyn Frake, $100);

(LEFT TO RIGHT) **Robert Griffin, Whit Bissell and Kenneth Tobey confront the truth in "The Green Bomb."**

Robert Sherman (Ken Clayton, $100); and Kenneth Tobey (Frank Davis, $400).

PLOT: Frank Davis, head of security at Pacific Division of the International Electric Corporation (an atomic reactor breeder plant), worries because Dr. Maxwell Carnevan and his assistant, Ann Page, have the privilege of free access to the plant without thorough checking by security guards. Ralph Scott, administrative head of the institution, tells Davis to lay off because of Carnevan's great knowledge and value, and the fear of losing the man. The situation is brought to a head when one of the radioactive dogs, used for testing, escapes. Carnevan objects to the use of scintillometers in the search but Davis, with Scott's permission, goes ahead. The dog is found in the company with a youngster named Raphael, but after the animal and the boy are returned the indications of radiation continue. They seem to come from Carnevan's house. Spurred by the discovery that four pounds of fissionable material are missing, Davis and Scott go to Carnevan's house. They find a nuclear device there which the doctor has personally built himself. But it's not a bomb in the regular sense. It's a "benevolent bomb" made of chloroplasm, to be used to make desert lands fertile.

Notes
- The beagle featured in Truman Bradley's lab demonstration scene in this episode is the same Gene Lockhart holds in "Miracle of Doctor Dove."
- Filming was delayed 45 minutes while the cast and crew waited for dog cage to arrive with the dog.
- The tumbler tube featured in the lab demonstration from which Truman Bradley removes the beagle is the same prop used for "The Last Barrier."
- Two un-credited stand-ins were used for this episode: Grant Davis and Joe Zeoran. Both men doubled for more than one role since their on-screen appearances were oblivious. These included the security officer at the television screen, two security guards and a man in a radioactive suit.
- The first half of the second day was filmed on location at Bronson Canyon followed by filming at Nichols Canyon before the cast and crew returned to the studio for the rest of the interior shots.

"THE SPY"
Dated: January 27, 1956
by Ivan Tors

A radioactive dog disappears from a research institute. To touch this dog may be dangerous to humans and a Geiger counter search is on for the beagle. One of the security officers who are looking for the dog detects a great amount of radiation. He thinks he is on the track of the beagle but instead his scintillation counter leads him to the desert home of Dr. Canover who is in charge of one of the great plutonium breeding plants. Dr. Canover treats the searching officer rudely and orders him off his land. He assures him that the dog is not there. The officer knows enough that the source of radiation coming from the Doctor's home must be a thousand times stronger than anything coming from the experimental hound.

Getting back to the reservation, the officer begins to think. There was some talk that some of the thermo-nuclear weapons which were exploded at some of the latest tests didn't have the power that the mathematics of fission anticipated. Besides, Dr. Canover was the only person who was allowed to leave the reservation without being searched. The officer becomes suspicious of Dr. Carnover and decides on a one man campaign to observe his activities.

The result of this investigation is shattering. It looks as if Dr. Canover would be stealing material from the reservation and transporting it to his home. In as much as he is in complete charge and he is the only one who knows every aspect of the operation nobody else is in position to find out what he is doing. Canover looks to the officer as a disloyal person who is absconding with enough critical material to assemble a thermo-nuclear weapon strong enough to explode the nation's capital.

When the officer has enough proof, he reports his findings to his superior. A special investigating staff arrives from Washington and Dr. Canover is taken by surprise. They find a new type of fission bomb at the home he constructed. It is different from any other radioactive weapon ever constructed. Out of the stolen material he built a chlorophyll bomb: a weapon that if exploded over a desert area, its radioactive ashes will make the land fertile. Dr. Canover is a deeply religious man and he feels that he can give his scientific mind to bomb building only if he invests the same amount of time and scientific thinking in something constructive. With this new weapon, if completed, this nation could win the friendship of all the other nations and underprivileged areas and gain world leadership by construction rather that destruction.

EPISODE #44 "WHEN A CAMERA FAILS"

PRODUCTION #1044 / 44B
DATES OF PRODUCTION: MARCH 12 AND 13, 1956
DIRECTED BY HERBERT L. STROCK

SCRIPT & STORY
"IMAGES OF THE PAST" FINAL TYPESCRIPT BY NORMAN JOLLEY, FEBRUARY 27, 1956
REVISED PAGES (ANNOTATED), MARCH 6, 1956
MASTER MIMEO, FEBRUARY 27, 1956
TELEPLAY BY NORMAN JOLLEY, FROM A STORY BY IVAN TORS

PRODUCTION CREDITS
1ST ASST. GEORGE LE PICARD (*UN-CREDITED*)
1ST CO. GRIP: CARL MIKSCH (*UN-CREDITED*)
2ND ASST. DIRECTOR: BRUCE SATTERLEE (*UN-CREDITED*)
2ND CAMERAMAN: BOB JOHANNES (*UN-CREDITED*)
2ND CO. GRIP: ROBERT DABKE (*UN-CREDITED*)
ASSISTANT DIRECTOR: WILLARD KIRKHAM
ASST. PROP MAN: WALTER BRODFOOT (*UN-CREDITED*)
AUDIO SUPERVISOR: QUINN MARTIN
BEST BOY: MIKE HUDSON (*UN-CREDITED*)
BOOM MAN: BILL FLANNERY (*UN-CREDITED*)
CONSTRUCTION CHIEF: DEE BOHLIUS (*UN-CREDITED*)
DIRECTOR OF PHOTOGRAPHY: CURT FETTERS
ELECTRICIANS: FRED HOUNSHELL AND JOHN MILLMAN
   (*BOTH UN-CREDITED*)
FILM COORDINATOR: DONALD TAIT
FILM EDITOR: DUNCAN MANSFIELD (*UN-CREDITED*) AND JOHN B. WOELZ (CREDITED)
GAFFER: S.H. BARTON (*UN-CREDITED*)
MAKE-UP ARTIST: GEORGE GRAY (MARCH 13 ONLY)
PRODUCTION COORDINATOR: JOE WONDER
PRODUCTION SUPERVISOR: BARRY COHON
PROPERTY MASTER: MAX PITTMAN
RECORDER: ROY CROPPER (*UN-CREDITED*)
SCIENTIFIC ADVISOR ON ELECTRONICS AND RADIATION:

Dr. Richard Hewitt (Gene Lockhart) is heart-broken to learn that no one can see the biggest scientific discovery in decades in "When A Camera Fails."

MAXWELL SMITH
SCRIPT SUPERVISOR: JEANNE LIPPMAN
SET DECORATOR: BRUCE MACDONALD
SET DESIGNER: JACK COLLIS
SET LABOR: BILL BENTHAN (*UN-CREDITED*)
SOUND EDITOR: SIDNEY SUTHERLAND
SOUND MIXER: JAY ASHWORTH
SPECIAL EFFECTS: HARRY REDMOND, JR.
STILL MAN: CHARLES RHODES (*UN-CREDITED*)
WARDROBE: ALFRED BERKE (*UN-CREDITED*)

Dr. Richard Hewitt (Gene Lockhart) faces the possibility that he suffers delusions in "When A Camera Fails."

CAST: Lewis Auerbach (Don Kaiser, $80); Opal Euard (Martha Hewitt, $100); Byron Kane (Dr. Brady, $125); Gene Lockhart (Dr. Richard Hewitt, $2,000); Mack Williams (Dr. Johnston, $125); and Than Wyenn (Dr. Herbert, $125)

PLOT: Dr. Richard Hewitt, geophysics professor at a Midwestern University, has found a way of amplifying light within the range of his ultra microscope. He looks at a piece of green glass sent to him by the Nuclear Research Commission under his microscope and is amazed to see an exact image of the atom bomb blast that fused the rock itself. Believing that the evolution of the Earth can be found within other rocks, he sees images of dinosaurs, the glacial age and ancient Egypt. He is convinced he has discovered something that may confirm or shatter the historical records of the evolution of the Earth. No one else can see them, however, and Dr. Brady, head of the University's psychiatric department, believes that overwork and fatigue have caused Hewitt to have delusions. His wife, Martha, is deeply hurt that he will be unable to get the recognition he deserves. Hewitt is replaced at the University by his assistant professor, Dr. Herbert, who, out of curiosity, checks into the microscope and the image theory. He inadvertently uses a pair of Hewitt's glasses and sees what no one else was able to. It is soon discovered that Hewitt had a special prescription calling for polarized lenses. It is deduced that the images are actually present but invisible unless seen through polarization. Hewitt is released from the sanitarium and reinstated after it is evident that he has discovered a new source of knowledge of the world's evolution . . . his "images of the past."

Notes

- Produced under the title "Images of the Past."
- Two stand-ins were un-credited for playing background roles: Evelyn Cherry and Andrew Roud.
- The opening stock shot of the exterior of the house with the lights coming on was also used in "Bullet Proof," "The Lost Heartbeat," "Beyond Return" and "The Voice."
- The entire episode was filmed on Stage 3.
- Production for this episode did not run smoothly. There was a 25-minute delay in production on the morning of the first day because the crab dolly that was rented was broken. It had to be exchanged and the camera switched to the new dolly. On the second day of production, there was a 45-minute delay due to the animals not cooperating, a 32-minute delay spent making the insert shot for the diamond ring (the light was reflecting too brightly for the texture of the diamond to be seen on the screen) and a 25-minute delay due to electrical effects not working.
- Cesar Depite was originally scheduled to supply set labor for this episode.
- On March 12, Truman Bradley filmed a number of lab demonstrations from 4:15 to 8:25 p.m. for a number of episodes, including retaking scenes for production 40b which had to be thrown away and started again from scratch. According to one inter-office memo, he was wearing the wrong tie and to make sure it matched the season two opener, the lab demonstrations had to be re-filmed.

The May 16, 1956 issue of *Variety* reviewed this episode:

"Rock strata formed since civilization's dawn carries images—or photographs—of that civilization, and a new, powerful microscope is developed which brings those images to light. Such is the premise of this excursion into fantasy, but it's carried out so unimaginatively it becomes pretty dreamy.

"The characters just talk, talk and talk—compounding the immobility of the vehicle. The scientist who discovers the images is sent to a 'sanitarium' because his confreres think he's daft. However, it develops they weren't wearing polarized glasses as was he, so he's released, vindicated.

"Gene Lockhart, in the lead, does adequately with the material given him. Not the same can be said for Opal Euard, as his wife, who robotly reads her lines. Mack Williams, Than Wyenn and Byron Kane are okay; same can't be conceded direction by Herbert L. Strock."

"EXPLORING TIME"
(A.K.A. "IMAGES OF THE PAST")
BY IVAN TORS

Dr. Hewitt has found a way of amplifying light within the range of his ultra microscope by feeding electric currents to the terminals of a sine-sulphide-phospher screen.

Dr. Hewitt receives from the Atomic Energy Commission a piece of green glass which is a composite of desert sand fused together by the force of a fusion-bomb at the time of an explosion test. He examines a fragment of this green glass under his new microscope. To his amazement, he sees the image of the exploding bomb. He realizes he has come upon a stupendous discovery. Certain crystals will take pictures just like emulsion on a film if exposed to a tremendous light-effect. This leads Dr. Hewitt to believe that lightning, in a similar manner, might have taken pictures to be found in the geological strata around us.

He collects crystal from all over the world—Rome, Greece, Ancient Egypt and tests thousands of them under his microscope. He sees images out of the past. They are vague but nevertheless there. He can see the giant dinosaur, faint pictures of the Great Deluge when lightning was frequent as well as some great evolutionary developments—

images out of the Pliocene, the Glacier Age and the recent past. He thinks that his discovery will shatter the world but he is greatly disappointed when he presents it to the President of his University. Nobody else seems to see the images but he. He sees them clearly but everybody else says that they can see nothing under his microscope. He almost loses his mind. A psychiatrist declares him insane. He is replaced and a new professor takes over his position at the University.

One day the new professor leaves his own glasses at home and finds a pair of Dr. Hewitt's in his desk. He tries on Hewitt's glasses and looks into his ultra microscope. Now he too can see the images of the past. Hewitt was not insane. The small crystals did take the pictures of the past. He examines Hewitt's glasses and finds out that they are polarized. It took polarized glasses to see the image. He had a particular eye-weakness that required polarized light for correction.

Dr. Hewitt is rehabilitated, restored to his job and the faint images of the past are now available to mankind. A new scientific principle was born that will enable us to re-evaluate history, geology and evolution in the light of a new source of knowledge which has now been discovered.

EPISODE #45 "BULLET PROOF"

PRODUCTION #1045 / 46B

DATES OF PRODUCTION: MARCH 15 AND 16, 1956
DIRECTED BY PAUL GUILFOYLE

SCRIPT & STORY

FINAL TYPESCRIPT (ANNOTATED) BY LEE HEWITT, MARCH 5, 1956
TELEPLAY BY LEE HEWITT

PRODUCTION CREDITS

1ST ASST. CAMERAMAN: JIM BELL (*UN-CREDITED*)
1ST CO. GRIP: MEL BLEDSOE (*UN-CREDITED*)
2ND ASST. DIRECTOR: BOB TEMPLETON (*UN-CREDITED*)
2ND CO. GRIP: NORMAN HESS (*UN-CREDITED*)
ASSISTANT DIRECTOR: WILLARD KIRKHAM

Asst. Prop Man: Stan Walter (*un-credited*)
Audio Supervisor: Quinn Martin
Best Boy: Charles Stockwell (*un-credited*)
Boom Man: Elmer Haglund (*un-credited*)
Camera Operator: Dick Rawlings
Construction Chief: Dee Bolhius (*un-credited*)
Director of Photography: Robert Hoffman
Electricians: Dixie Dunbar and Fred Hounshell (*both un-credited*)
Film Coordinator: Donald Tait
Film Editor: Duncan Mansfield (*un-credited*) and John B. Woelz (credited)
Gaffer: Al Ronso (*un-credited*)
Make-up Artist: George Gray (*un-credited*)
Production Coordinator: Joe Wonder
Production Supervisor: Barry Cohon
Property Master: Max Pittman
Recorder: Lloyd Hanks (*un-credited*)
Scientific Advisor on Electronics and Radiation: Maxwell Smith
Script Supervisor: Larry Lund
Set Decorator: Bruce MacDonald
Set Designer: Jack Collis
Set labor: Sol Inverso (*un-credited*)
Sound Editor: Monroe Martin
Sound Mixer: Garry Harris
Special Effects: Harry Redmond, Jr.
Still Man: Joe Walters (March 15 only, *un-credited*)
Wardrobe: Alfred Berke

CAST: Christopher Dark (Ralph Parr, $175); John Eldredge (Prof. Rudman, $150); Jacqueline Holt (Jean Rudman, $100); John Mitchum (Sgt. Reynolds, $80); Gene Roth (George Martin, $125); and Marshall Thompson (Jim Connors, $750)

PLOT: An escaped criminal named Ralph Parr tries to sell Prof. Rudman a fantastically lightweight and very nearly indestructible foil metal. While testing the material, Rudman is accidentally killed

Marshall Thompson takes instructions from the cameraman. Also pictured is director Paul Guilfoyle.

Marshall Thompson in "Bullet Proof."

Marshall Thompson examines the mysterious metal under Christopher Dark's threatening and watchful eye.

Escaped criminal Ralph Parr introduces himself to Jim Connors.

by a ricochet bullet that strikes the metal. While the police investigate Rudman's death with the aid of Jim Conners, the professor's assistant and Rudman's daughter Jean; a mysterious holdup man defies police bullets in a series of daring robberies. His exploits earn him the name of the "Bulletproof Man." When the police cannot capture the bulletproof man, Jim convinces a wealthy steel manufacturer to offer a reward for a sample of the strange metal. He is contacted by the bulletproof man and agrees to pay fifty thousand dollars demanded. Jim meets up with the bulletproof killer and discovers a seared area of glass fused into the sand, indicating that a spacecraft landed and blasted off, leaving behind the mysterious metal foil. Parr is promptly arrested for the daring holdups.

Notes
- The isolated part of the highway in the desert was filmed on location at Bronson Canyon on the morning of the first day. After which the cast and crew returned to the studio and filmed the rest of the episode on Stage 3 for the remainder of the first day of filming and the entire second day.
- Paul Guilfoyle supplies the un-credited voice of the radio announcer which appears twice in this episode. After principal filming was completed on the second day at 5 p.m., the director remained on the set to read his lines so the recording could be looped into the sound track during editing. As a member of the guild, he was paid $80 for the talent work.
- The sheriff's car featured at the end of the story was owned by the studio, not rented like many of the automobiles that appeared on ZIV-TV productions. The same car can be seen in a number of first season episodes of *Highway Patrol*.
- The opening stock shot of the exterior of the house with the lights coming on was also used in "The Lost Heartbeat," "Beyond Return," "When A Camera Fails" and "The Voice."
- The un-credited role of the police officer in this episode is played by Frank Hunt.

The May 23, 1956 issue of *Variety* reviewed this episode: "There isn't much to Ivan Tors' latest excursion into fantasy and the only sympathy engendered in Lee Hewitt's vidplay is for the heavy.

It probably wasn't meant that way, but the 'villain' seems to get the dirty end of the stick.

"Christopher Dark plays an escaped con who brings to a noted prof a piece of flexible, bulletproof metal heretofore unknown to science. He wants to sell it, which doesn't seem unreasonable. But the prof pulls a gun on him and kills himself as the bullet ricochets. Then the con tries to sell it elsewhere, but is nabbed by the cops and never does get anything for the metal. Develops he found it in an isolated spot. Apparently left behind by a flying saucer.

"Dark is fine in his role, despite the fuzzy script; Marshall Thompson, who has top billing but less to do, is satisfactory, and so is Jacqueline Holt. Paul Guilfoyle's directing is hampered by the script."

EPISODE #46 "THE FLICKER"

PRODUCTION #1046 / 43B

DATES OF PRODUCTION: MARCH 19 AND 20, 1956
DIRECTED BY HERBERT L. STROCK

SCRIPT & STORY

NARRATIVE BY ROBERT E. SMITH, N.D.
FINAL TYPESCRIPT (ANNOTATED) BY LOU HUSTON, FEBRUARY 22, 1956
REVISED PAGES (ANNOTATED), MARCH 14, 1956
REVISED MASTER MIMEO (ANNOTATED), MARCH 14, 1956
TELEPLAY BY LOU HUSTON, FROM A STORY BY ROBERT E. SMITH

PRODUCTION CREDITS

1ST ASST. CAMERAMAN: JIM BELL (*UN-CREDITED*)
1ST CO. GRIP: CARL MIKSCH (*UN-CREDITED*)
2ND ASST. CAMERAMAN: GLEN GALLAGHER (MARCH 19 ONLY, *UN-CREDITED*)
2ND ASST. DIRECTOR: BOB TEMPLETON (*UN-CREDITED*)
2ND CO. GRIP: ROBERT DABKE (*UN-CREDITED*)
3RD CO. GRIP: NORMAN HESS (*UN-CREDITED*)
ASSISTANT DIRECTOR: DONALD VERK

Asst. Prop Man: Vic Petrotta (*un-credited*)
Audio Supervisor: Quinn Martin
Best Boy: Charles Stockwell (*un-credited*)
Boom Man: Elmer Haglund (*un-credited*)
Cableman: Dick Smith (*un-credited*)
Camera Operator: Dick Rawlings
Construction Chief: Dee Bolhius (*un-credited*)
Director of Photography: Monroe "Monk" Askins
Electricians: Jimmy Field and Mike Hudson (*both un-credited*)
Film Coordinator: Donald Tait
Film Editor: Duncan Mansfield, A.C.E.
Gaffer: S.H. Barton (*un-credited*)
Make-up Artist: George Gray (*un-credited*)
Production Coordinator: Joe Wonder
Production Supervisor: Barry Cohon
Property Master: Max Pittman
Recorder: Lloyd Hanks (*un-credited*)
Scientific Advisor on Electronics and Radiation: Maxwell Smith
Script Supervisor: Larry Lund
Set Decorator: Clarence Steenson
Set Designer: Jack Collis
Set Labor: Sol Inverso (*un-credited*)
Sound Editor: Sidney Sutherland *
Sound Mixer: Garry Harris
Special Effects: Harry Redmond, Jr.
Wardrobe: Alfred Berke (*un-credited*)

CAST: Judith Ames (Jane Morris, $100); Irene Bolton (the girl, $80); Michael Fox (Dr. James Kinkaid, $300); Bradford Jackson (Steve Morris, $125); and Victor Jory (Det. Lt. Kiel, $1,000)

PLOT: Steve Morris, from all appearances a jobless denizen of skid row, kills a girl—a complete stranger—with absolutely no motive. He has no recollection of the crime or the three hours duration. Dr.

---

* Spelled Sydney Sutherland in the closing credits of this episode.

Michael Fox looks on as Truman Bradley renewed his friendship with Victor Jory on the set of "The Flicker." Both men had appeared together on the set of *Charlie Chan in Rio* in 1941.

Kinkaid, a police psychiatrist, becomes interested in the case. Routine police work establishes the truth of Steve's claim that he is a reputable student of sociology—which makes his crime all the more baffling. Dr. Kinkaid thinks that Steve's behavior and memory lapse indicate post-hypnotic suggestion. To the practical Det. Lt. Kiel, Steve is a typical "psychopathic killer." Both investigators, learning that Steve may have visited a cheap movie house during his three-hour blackout, attend the theatre to obtain data for a lie-detector test. They see enacted on the screen a duplicate—or prototype—of the crime Steve has committed—strangling a girl in a phone booth. The psychiatrist conducts a series of tests that prove that a freak "flicker" in the theatre projector, in exact phase with Steve's individual brain-wave pattern, induced a trance state. This made him helplessly susceptible to later stimuli that "key-in" the murderous suggestion of the movie and Det. Lt. Kiel almost murders his partner until the trance is broken. These tests also establish that the "flicker" effect holds promise of beneficial results in speeding up the learning process and reaching unexplored areas of the human mind.

THE EPISODE GUIDE: SEASON TWO | 335

(LEFT) **Det. Lt. Kiel (Victor Jory) discovers that a flicker can create a subconscious impulse to murder, thanks to Dr. James Kinkaid (Michael Fox).**

(ABOVE) **Michael Fox tries to memorize scientific language as scientific advisor Maxwell Smith takes notes.**

Dr. James Kinkaid (Michael Fox) attempts to "key-in" the murderous suggestion of murder to Det. Lt. Kiel (Victor Jory).

(LEFT TO RIGHT) **Michael Fox, Herbert L. Strock and Victor Jory discuss the filming of "The Flicker."**

Victor Jory examines the equipment in "The Flicker."

Notes

- Robert E. Smith's 19 page plot synopsis titled "Flicker" included the following note on the final page as the author's suggestion to the producer: "An effective bit of business might be to have the home-viewer's screen develop a peculiar but distinctive flicker while the story credits are being shown." This was not taken into consideration. Director Herbert L. Strock had attempted to make this episode a bit varied from most of the *Theatre* productions by filming a ceiling view of numerous rooms, and during routine police questioning, zooming the camera back. After Victor Jory attempts to smash a chair on actor Michael Fox, the camera catches a view from below.
- The slow motion film of the bullet shattering the glass was also featured in the series premiere, "Beyond," also as part of Truman Bradley's lab demonstration.
- On the afternoon of the second day, Jory and Fox finished their scenes at 4:40 p.m. and Truman Bradley filmed his opening and closing lab demonstrations until 6:20 and voice narration from 6:20 to 6:35 p.m.

Episode #47 "The Unguided Missile"

Production #1047 / 49B

Dates of Production: March 28 and 29, 1956
Directed by Herbert L. Strock

Script & Story

First Draft by Arthur Weiss, March 22, 1956
Revised Pages dated March 26 and 27, 1956
Final Draft by Arthur Weiss, March 27, 1956
Teleplay by Arthur Weiss

Production Credits

1st Asst. Cameraman: Jim Bell (*un-credited*)
1st Co. Grip: Carl Miksch (*un-credited*)
2nd Asst. Director: Bob Templeton (*un-credited*)
2nd Co. Grip: Mel Bledsoe (*un-credited*)

3RD GRIP: KENNETH DAY (*UN-CREDITED*)
ASSISTANT DIRECTOR: ED STEIN
ASST PROP MAN: VIC PETROTTA (*UN-CREDITED*)
AUDIO SUPERVISOR: QUINN MARTIN
BEST BOY: CHARLES STOCKWELL (*UN-CREDITED*)
BOOM MAN: ELMER HANKS (*UN-CREDITED*)
CAMERA OPERATOR: DICK RAWLINGS
CONSTRUCTION CHIEF: DEE BOLHIUS (*UN-CREDITED*)
DIRECTOR OF PHOTOGRAPHY: CURT FETTERS
ELECTRICIANS: WALTER GEDIMAN, FRED HOUNSHELL AND JUDD LEROY (*ALL UN-CREDITED*)
FILM COORDINATOR: DONALD TAIT
FILM EDITOR: DUNCAN MANSFIELD, A.C.E.
GAFFER: AL RONSO (*UN-CREDITED*)
MAKE-UP ARTIST: GEORGE GRAY
PRODUCTION COORDINATOR: JOE WONDER
PRODUCTION SUPERVISOR: BARRY COHON
PROPERTY MASTER: YGNACIO SEPULVEDA
RECORDER: LLOYD HANKS (*UN-CREDITED*)
SCIENTIFIC ADVISOR ON ELECTRONICS AND RADIATION: MAXWELL SMITH
SCRIPT SUPERVISOR: LARRY LUND
SET DECORATOR: BRUCE MACDONALD
SET DESIGNER: JACK COLLIS
SET LABOR: SOL INVERSO (*UN-CREDITED*)
SOUND EDITOR: MONROE MARTIN
SOUND MIXER: GARRY HARRIS
SPECIAL EFFECTS: HARRY REDMOND, JR.
WARDROBE: ALFRED BERKE

CAST: Morris Ankrum (Martin Campbell, $125); Peter Hanson (Dr. Henry Maxton, $350); Tom Browne Henry (Dr. Haley, $100); Ruth Hussey (Janice O'Hara, $2,500); Francis McDonald (Prof. Bernini, $125); and Lizz Slifer (Millie, $80)

PLOT: Jan O'Hara, magazine editor, innocently publishes a top-secret mathematical calculation which reveals the work of the inter-continental ballistic missile project at State University. Under

Truman Bradley demonstrates microwave transmitters in "The Unguided Missile."

questioning, she honestly denies knowing how or where she got the calculation. But that night she is again disturbed by a dream—one of a series of dreams during the past month in which she becomes aware of certain other abstruse mathematical information. Knowing that this information is somehow related to the ICBM project, she presents it to Henry Maxton, the project physicist. He is faced with the impossible fact that secret data which he received only last night and wrote only temporarily on a blackboard is now known by Mrs. O'Hara. With her help, he tries to solve the enigma by scientific investigation and testing the possibility of mental telepathy. All efforts fail until he discovers that a microwave passing from one relay tower to another passes through his office and then through Miss O'Hara's penthouse apartment. In passing through him, the beam was modulated by the electronic impulses of his brain; and on passing through Miss O'Hara, the Modulated beam was translated back into thoughts inside her head. She is cleared of any wrongdoing.

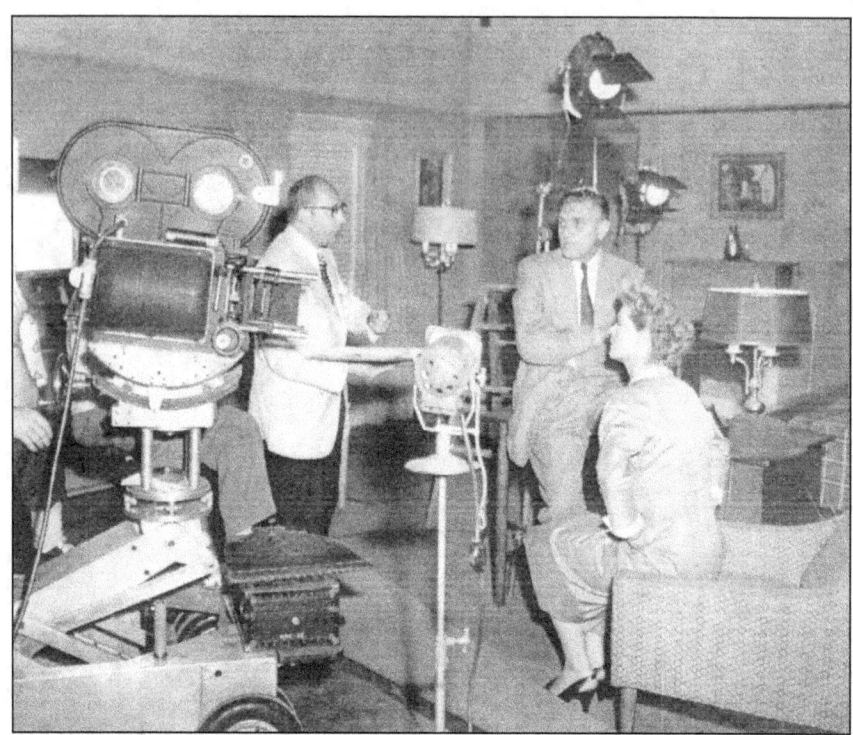

Director Herbert L. Strock discusses the scene with Moriss Ankrum and Ruth Hussey.

Notes

- Produced under the title "Two of a Kind." The film was later re-titled "Miracle at Midnight" before changing to "The Unguided Missile."
- The entire episode was filmed on Stage 3.
- Stand-ins Evelyn Cherry and Tom Anthony are featured in this episode for the insert shots. It is Cherry's hand that writes on the card, and Anthony's hand that writes on the chalkboard.
- The magazine Ruth Hussey reviews at her desk is fictional. *Communique* was a non-existent magazine at the time and artwork depicting a missile launching from the Earth's atmosphere graces the cover—the same artwork that was framed and hanging on the wall in numerous episodes of *Science Fiction Theatre*, and appeared as background matting on the opening credits of *Gog*.

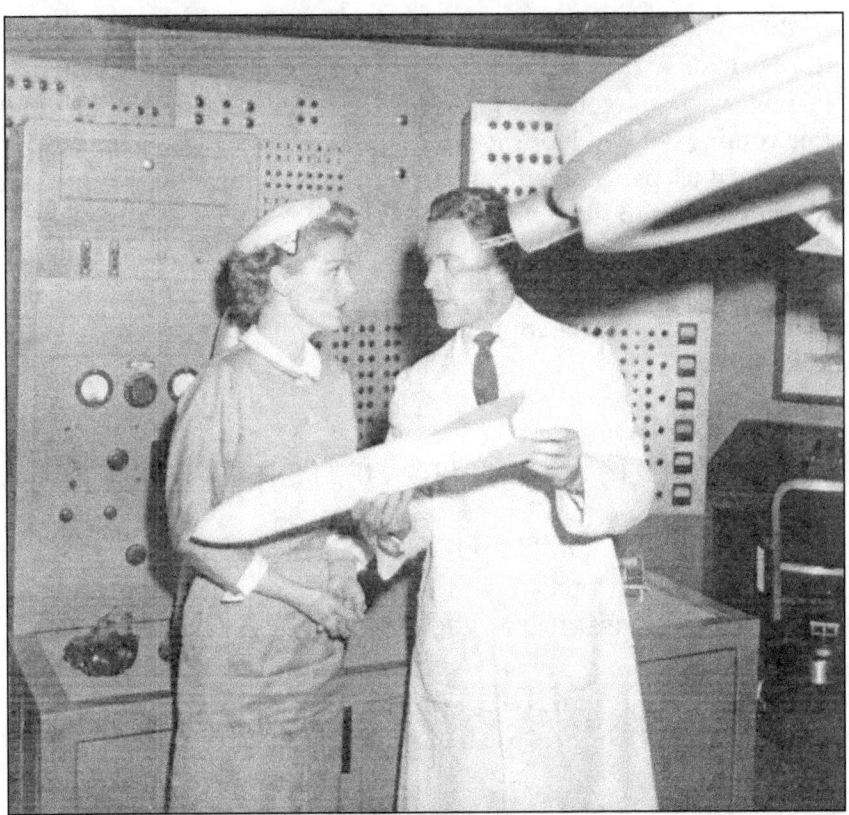

Peter Hanson explains the inter-continental ballistic missile project to actress Ruth Hussey in "The Unguided Missile."

- The chart with dots on the wall also appears in "The Hastings Secret," "The Water Maker" and in the background of Truman Bradley's lab demonstrations in "The Voice" and "The Sound That Kills."
- Director Paul Guilfoyle was originally assigned to direct this episode, but the directing chore was re-assigned the night before filming to Herbert L. Strock.

The June 7, 1956 issue of *Variety* reviewed this episode:
"Once again this series falls into the unhappy habit of extensive use of jargon which bewilders the layman. At times 'Missile' is much like a scientific lecture, but while it would be apropos in such a class it's dull for the tviewer. Also, there are few sets used, so that the vidpic has a static, talky quality.

"Ruth Hussey, a mag editor, has some top secret info about guided missiles in an article. When the scientists and security men demand to know where she got it she professes not to know. Eventually—a long time coming—it develops she received thought waves from a scientist a la mental telepathy, the thoughts bouncing off a microwave antenna into her little noodle. Simple?

"Miss Hussey's portrayal meets the not-too-high demands of her role, while Peter Hanson, Francis McDonald and Morris Ankrum offer good support. There is a sluggish tempo in Herbert Strock's direction."

EPISODE #48 "END OF TOMORROW"

PRODUCTION #1048 / 478
DATES OF PRODUCTION: APRIL 3 AND 4, 1956
DIRECTED BY HERBERT L. STROCK

SCRIPT & STORY
FINAL TYPESCRIPT (ANNOTATED) BY PETER BROOKE, MARCH 28, 1956
MASTER MIMEO (ANNOTATED), MARCH 30, 1956
TELEPLAY BY PETER R. BROOKE

PRODUCTION CREDITS
1ST ASST. CAMERAMAN: JIM BELL (*UN-CREDITED*)
1ST CO. GRIP: MEL BLEDSOE (*UN-CREDITED*)
2ND ASST. DIRECTOR: BOB TEMPLETON (*UN-CREDITED*)
2ND CO GRIP: CARL MIKSCH (*UN-CREDITED*)
3RD GRIP: NORMAN HESS (*UN-CREDITED*)
ASSISTANT DIRECTOR: DONALD VERK
ASST. PROP MAN: YGNACIO SEPULVEDA (*UN-CREDITED*)
AUDIO SUPERVISOR: QUINN MARTIN
BEST BOY: CHARLES STOCKWELL (*UN-CREDITED*)
BOOM MAN: ELMER HAGLUND (*UN-CREDITED*)
CABLEMAN: RICHARD SMITH (*UN-CREDITED*)
CAMERA OPERATOR: DICK RAWLINGS
CONSTRUCTION CHIEF: DEE BOLHIUS (*UN-CREDITED*)

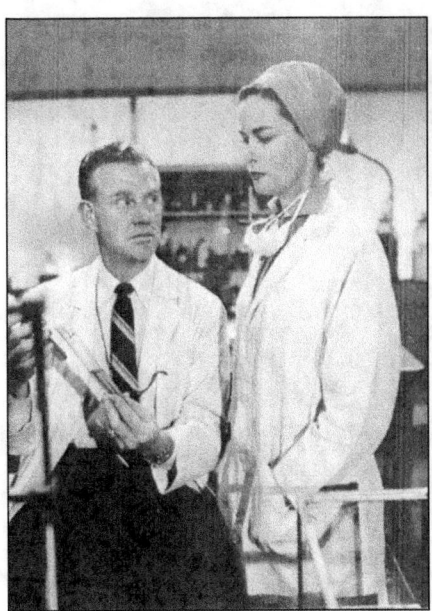

Jane Brandon (Diana Douglas) keeps a close eye on Prof. Horace Reimers (Dabbs Greer), who should not be trusted.

Keith Brandon (Christopher Dark) has his suspicions while Professor Horace Reimers (Dabbs Greer) reveals his universal antibiotic.

DIRECTOR OF PHOTOGRAPHY: ROBERT HOFFMAN
ELECTRICIANS: MIKE HUDSON, JUDD LEROY AND HERMAN LIPNEY (*ALL UN-CREDITED*)
FILM COORDINATOR: DONALD TAIT
FILM EDITOR: THOMAS SCOTT
GAFFER: AL RONSO (*UN-CREDITED*)
MAKE-UP ARTIST: GEORGE GRAY (*UN-CREDITED*)
PRODUCTION COORDINATOR: JOE WONDER
PRODUCTION SUPERVISOR: BARRY COHON
PROPERTY MASTER: MAX PITTMAN
RECORDER: LLOYD HANKS (*UN-CREDITED*)
SCIENTIFIC ADVISOR ON ELECTRONICS AND RADIATION: MAXWELL SMITH
SCRIPT SUPERVISOR: LARRY LUND
SET DECORATOR: BRUCE MACDONALD
SET DESIGNER: JACK COLLIS
SET LABOR: SOL INVERSO (*UN-CREDITED*)
SOUND EDITOR: SIDNEY SUTHERLAND

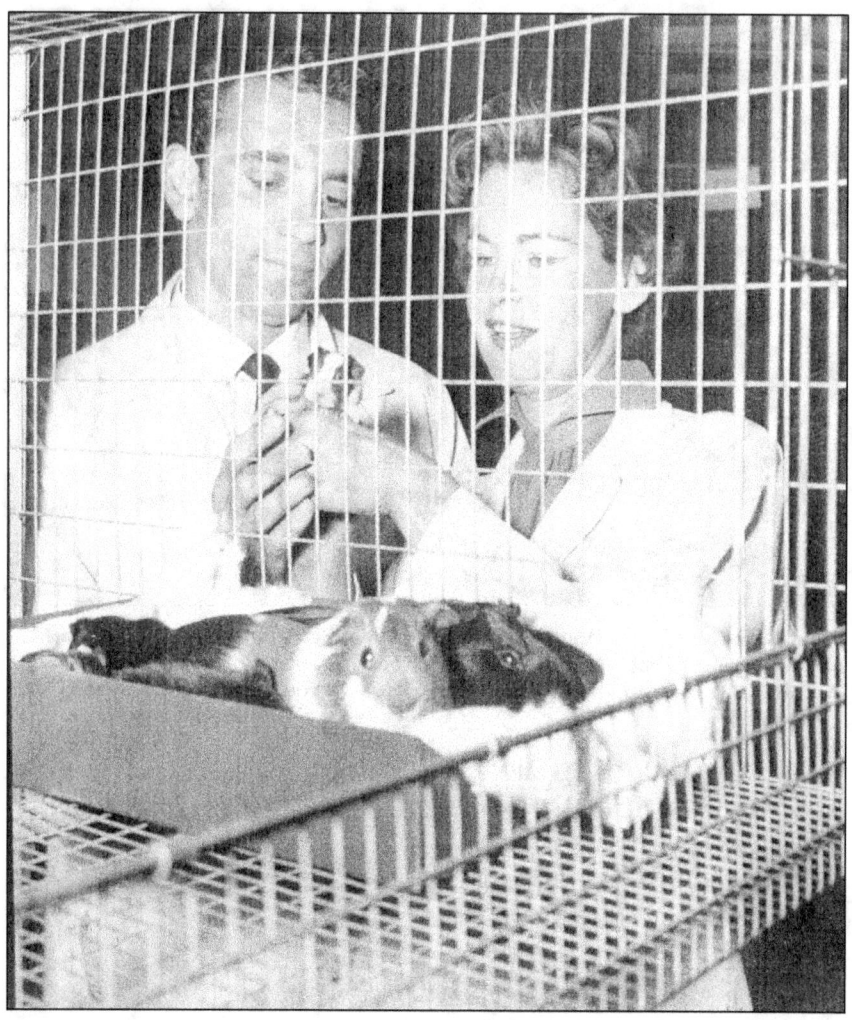

Keith Brandon and his wife Jane examine the guinea pigs in "End of Tomorrow."

SOUND MIXER: GARRY HARRIS
SPECIAL EFFECTS: HARRY REDMOND, JR.
STILL MAN: CHARLES RHODES (*UN-CREDITED*)
WARDROBE: ALFRED BERKE

CAST: Christopher Dark (Keith Brandon, $400); Diana Douglas (Jane Brandon, $150); Michael Garth (Lt. Ruskin, $100); Dabbs Greer (Prof. Horace Reimers, $150); Walter Kingsford (Rudyard Parker, $150); and Arthur Marshall (the scientist, $80)

The Episode Guide: Season Two | 345

> **BLOOPER!**
> IN THE OPENING OF THE SECOND ACT, A STACK OF NEWSPAPERS IS TOSSED ON THE STREET CORNER, HERALDING "INNOCULATIONS START TODAY." THE WORD INOCULATION IS MISSPELLED.

PLOT: Dr. Keith Brandon, a government bacteriologist, is summoned by the Scientific Research Division in the middle of the night to meet a newly arrived scientist named Professor Reimers. The latter claims to have discovered a universal antibiotic which is capable of eradicating all virus diseases. Parker, the chief of the Scientific Research Division, has made it Keith's sole priority to verify the validity of said anti-biotic. According to experiments which Keith witnesses, the serum appears to be valid. However, Keith's laboratory assistant and wife, Jane, discovers that the drug has a decomposing effect on the genes of the injected animals. This effect manifests itself in the sole regeneration of the female species, which will cause the human race to die out within 100 years. Since Congress has already passed a bill approving general inoculation, it becomes Keith's and Jane's responsibility to bring their findings to the attention of the government, over the many hurdles placed by Reimers himself. After they succeed in breaking red tape and proving the side effect of the antibiotic, Reimers mysteriously disappears without a trace . . . after almost succeeding to sabotage the survival of the human race.

NOTES
- The microscope Truman Bradley uses in the beginning of this episode is the same Gene Lockhart uses in his lab in the episode "When A Camera Fails."
- The entire episode was filmed on Stage 3.
- This episode was produced under the title of "100 Years From Now."
- Un-credited stand-ins supplied the hands that appeared in insert shots. The hands that demonstrate the mini amplified listening device actually belong to Tom Anthony. Evelyn Cherry's hands were used for the close-up of the wrist watch.

The June 13, 1956 issue of *Variety* reviewed this episode:

"The beings from another planet, faced with an increasingly rarified atmosphere, might like to colonize Earth and therefore wouldn't be sorry to see the human race extinguished is a challenging proposition. However, the theme, the whole point of the accompanying charade, is laid out by narrator Truman Bradley, as an epilogue, surely a hind-forward method of scene-setting.

"Until that time, a mysterious scientist, played by Dabbs Greer, has been acting so oddly that it's surprising that anyone trusts him. Yet on his say-so, with comparatively skimpy research, the entire world is ready to be inoculated with a serum he's discovered. Trouble is that while the serum is effective against all virus diseases, it also alters the reproductive processes so that only females will be born. Thus, if intrepid scientists Christopher Dark and Diana Douglas hadn't become suspicious and exposed the plot, the human race would gradually have become no more.

"Herbert L. Strock's direction isn't able to do much with the Peter R. Brooke script, for which he can't be overly criticized. Dark and Miss Douglas are fittingly intense as the young researchers, but Walter Kingsford, as their dense superior, and Greer are too hampered by the method of presentation to achieve any plausibility."

EPISODE #49 "MIND MACHINE"

PRODUCTION #1049 / 488

Dates of Production: March 26 and 27, 1956
Directed by Paul Guilfoyle

SCRIPT & STORY

Final typescript (annotated), by Ellis Marcus, March 15, 1956
Revised pages (annotated), March 19, 1956
Revised master mimeo (annotated), March 23, 1956
Teleplay by Ellis Marcus

PRODUCTION CREDITS

1st Asst. Cameraman: Jim Bell (*un-credited*)
1st Co. Grip: Carl Miksch (*un-credited*)

2ND ASST. DIRECTOR: BOB TEMPLETON (*UN-CREDITED*)
2ND CO. GRIP: MEL BLEDSOE (*UN-CREDITED*)
3RD GRIP: ROBERT DABKE (*UN-CREDITED*)
ASSISTANT DIRECTOR: DONALD VERK
ASST. PROP MAN: VIC PETROTTA (*UN-CREDITED*)
AUDIO SUPERVISOR: QUINN MARTIN
BEST BOY: CHARLES STOCKWELL (*UN-CREDITED*)
BOOM MAN: ELMER HAGLUND (*UN-CREDITED*)
CAMERA OPERATOR: DICK RAWLINGS
CONSTRUCTION CHIEF: DEE BOLHIUS (*UN-CREDITED*)
DIRECTOR OF PHOTOGRAPHY: CURT FETTERS
ELECTRICIANS: FRED HOUNSHELL AND JOHN MILLMAN (*BOTH UN-CREDITED*)
FILM COORDINATOR: DONALD TAIT
FILM EDITOR: THOMAS SCOTT
GAFFER: AL RONSO (*UN-CREDITED*)
MAKE-UP ARTIST: GEORGE GRAY (*UN-CREDITED*)
PRODUCTION COORDINATOR: JOE WONDER
PRODUCTION SUPERVISOR: BARRY COHON
PROPERTY MASTER: MAX PITTMAN
RECOERDER: LLOYD HANKS (*UN-CREDITED*)
SCIENTIFIC ADVISOR ON ELECTRONICS AND RADIATION: MAXWELL SMITH
SCRIPT SUPERVISOR: LARRY LUND
SET DECORATOR: CLARENCE STEENSON
SET DESIGNER: JACK COLLIS
SET LABOR: SOL INVERSO (*UN-CREDITED*)
SOUND EDITOR: SIDNEY SUTHERLAND
SOUND MIXER: GARRY HARRIS
SPECIAL EFFECTS: HARRY REDMOND, JR.
STILL MAN: CHARLES RHODES (MARCH 26 ONLY, *UN-CREDITED*)
WARDROBE: ALFRED BERKE (*UN-CREDITED*)

CAST: Lonie Blackman (Joyce McLain, $80); Fred Coby (Capt. Landry, $100); Cyril Delevanti (Dr. Lewis Milton, $275); Helen Jay (the nurse, $80); Sydney Mason (Charlie Olsen, $100); Jim Sheldon (Corp. Dodd, $80); Brad Trumbull (Dr. Cook, $100); and Bill Williams (Dr. Alan Cathcart, $800)

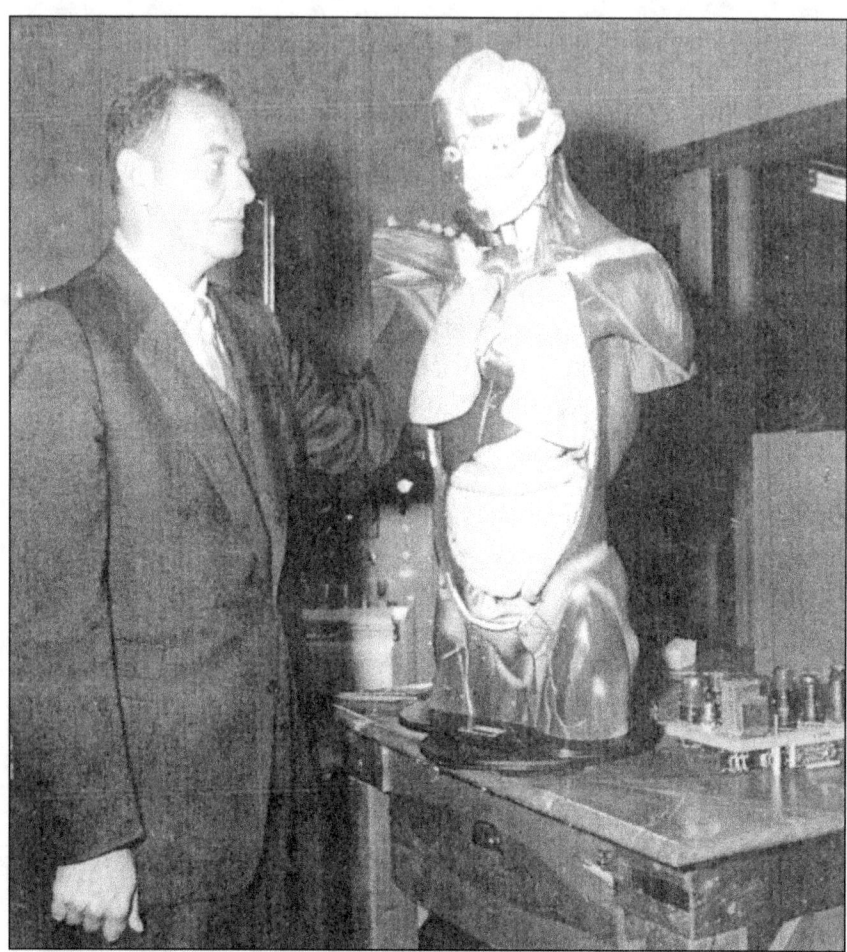

Producer Ivan Tors on the set of "Mind Machine."

PLOT: Doctor Lewis Milton, an aging scientist who has developed a device for picking up individual brain impulses, hopes to be able to convert and decode them so they can be fed into an electric typewriter. He learns, however, that he has high blood pressure and cannot stand up under the grueling work required of him. After convincing Doctor Alan Cathcart to take over the project, Milton suffers a stroke. As the old man lies completely paralyzed, a victim of a cerebral hemorrhage and unable to speak, Cathcart realizes it may take months to understand the working of the Mindwriter, Doctor Milton's device. Suddenly Cathcart discovers that Doctor Milton can move the index finger of one hand. With this the dying

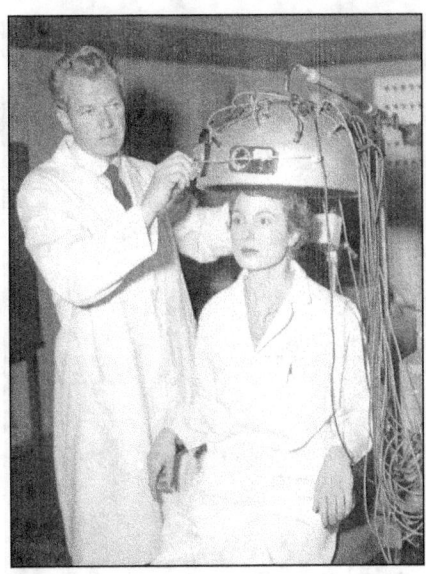

Bill Williams and Lonie Blackman testing the equipment in "Mind Machine."

Bill Williams and Lonie Blackman pauses between takes on the set of "Mind Machine."

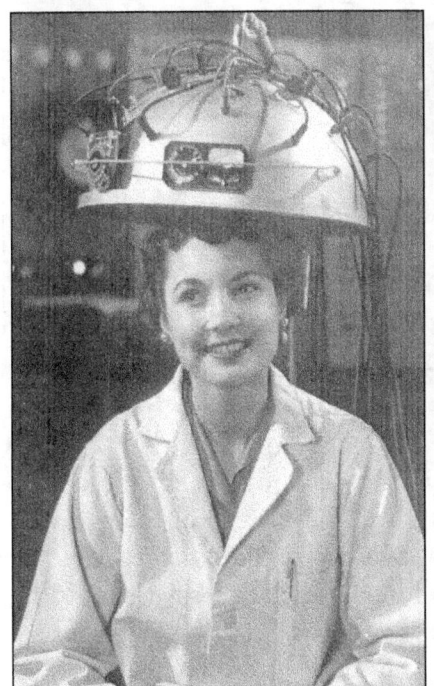

Lonie Blackman poses for a candid photo.

Bill Williams examines the results.

```
                    CIPHER KEY

A   B   C   D   E   F   G   H   I   J   K   L   M   N   O   P   Q   R   S   T
#   N   B   X   C   V   ∅   7   4   A   M   5   R   Z   2   9       L   D   J
XXXXXXWXXXXXXXXZX

U   V   W   X   Y   Z
8   E   W       G
```

                    COMPLETE FREQUENCY CHART
                         (The Lord's Prayer)

E (C) - 33	V (E) - 8
T (J) - 21	F (V) - 6
A (#) - 21	G (∅) - 6
O (2) - 21	M (R) - 6
S (D) - 21	W (W) - 6
I (4) - 18	Y (G) - 6
R (L) - 18	B (N) - 4
N (Z) - 16	P (9) - 4
H (7) - 15	C (B) - 1
D (X) - 10	K (M) - 1
L (5) - 9	Q - 0
	X - 0
U (8) - 9	Z - 0

This cipher key was pulled from the ZIV archives, created by script writer Ellis Marcus specifically to make sure the accurate code was featured on the chalk board in this episode.

man manages to convey instructions to Cathcart using the binary system of numbers, the language of the electronic computers. Following Milton's instructions, Cathcart uses his own experiments to keep the old man's brain alive long enough to find a key to the code—the word "heaven" within the Lord's Prayer—which makes the old man's invention succeed. This accomplishment opens the door to the mysteries of the human brain and the process of deciphering a hidden text.

Notes
- Produced under the title "The Mind Writer."

The June 21, 1956 issue of *Variety* reviewed this episode:
"This one might be a hit at Caltech, but it's a miss on TV. So much scientific mumbo-jumbo is scattered throughout 'Mind' a viewer tuning in in the middle might get the impression it was partly dubbed in Pakistani. A wholly contrived gimmick didn't make it more palatable.

"Seems the scientists are on the verge of inventing a mind machine, which, in effect, reads the mind. Messages emanating from the mind via the machine are unintelligible, and a dying scientist tells 'em to use his brain after he dies. They do and solve their little mystery. However, it's painfully clear they could have done the same thing with just anybody's mind—living people especially—but tossed in the dead-man's-brain to hoke it up.

"Actors doing the best they can with thankless material include Bill Williams, Cyril Delevanti, Brad Trumbull, Sydney Mason, Lonnie Blackman, Helen Jay. Paul Guilfoyle's directing is unimaginative."

Episode #50 "The Missing Waveband"

Production #1050 / 50B
Dates of Production: April 5 and 6, 1956
Directed by Jack Herzberg

Script & Story
First Draft by Lou Huston, March 27, 1956
Final Draft by Lou Huston, March 30, 1956
Teleplay by Lou Huston, from the short story "Operation M-3" by Ivan Tors

Production Credits
1st Asst. Cameraman: Jim Bell (*un-credited*)
1st Co. Grip: Mel Bledsoe (*un-credited*)
2nd Asst. Director: Bob Templeton (*un-credited*)
2nd Co. Grip: Carl Miksch (*un-credited*)

3rd Grip: Norman Hess (*un-credited*)
Assistant Director: Ed Stein
Asst. Prop: Walter Bradfoot (*un-credited*)
Audio Supervisor: Quinn Martin
Best Boy: Charles Stockwell (*un-credited*)
Boom Man: Elmer Haglund (*un-credited*)
Camera Operator: Dick Rawlings
Construction Chief: Dee Bolhius (*un-credited*)
Director of Photography: Robert Hoffman
Electricians: Mike Hudson, Louis Kreiger and Victor Pizanti (*all un-credited*)
Film Coordinator: Donald Tait
Film Editor: Duncan Mansfield, A.C.E.
Gaffer: Al Ronso (*un-credited*)
Make-up Artist: George Gray (*un-credited*)
Production Coordinator: Joe Wonder
Production Supervisor: Barry Cohon
Property Master: Max Pittman
Recorder: Lloyd Hanks (*un-credited*)
Scientific Advisor on Electronics and Radiation: Maxwell Smith
Script Supervisor: Larry Lund
Set Decorator: Bruce MacDonald
Set Designer: Jack Collis
Set Labor: Sol Inverso (*un-credited*)
Sound Editor: Sidney Sutherland
Sound Mixer: Garry Harris
Special Effects: Harry Redmond, Jr.
Still Man: Charles Rhodes (*un-credited*)
Wardrobe: Alfred Berke (*un-credited*)

CAST: Dick Foran (Dr. Vincent Millhurst, $600); Michael Fox (Dr. Maxwell, $125); George Leigh (General Rayburn, $100); Charles Maxwell (the voice, $80); Tom McKee (the newscaster, $125); Stafford Repp (Prof. Van Doorne, $125); and Gene Roth (Dr. Lawrence, $125)

PLOT: In the very near future, three man-made satellites circle the Earth, thanks to a magnificent mathematical equation credited to a

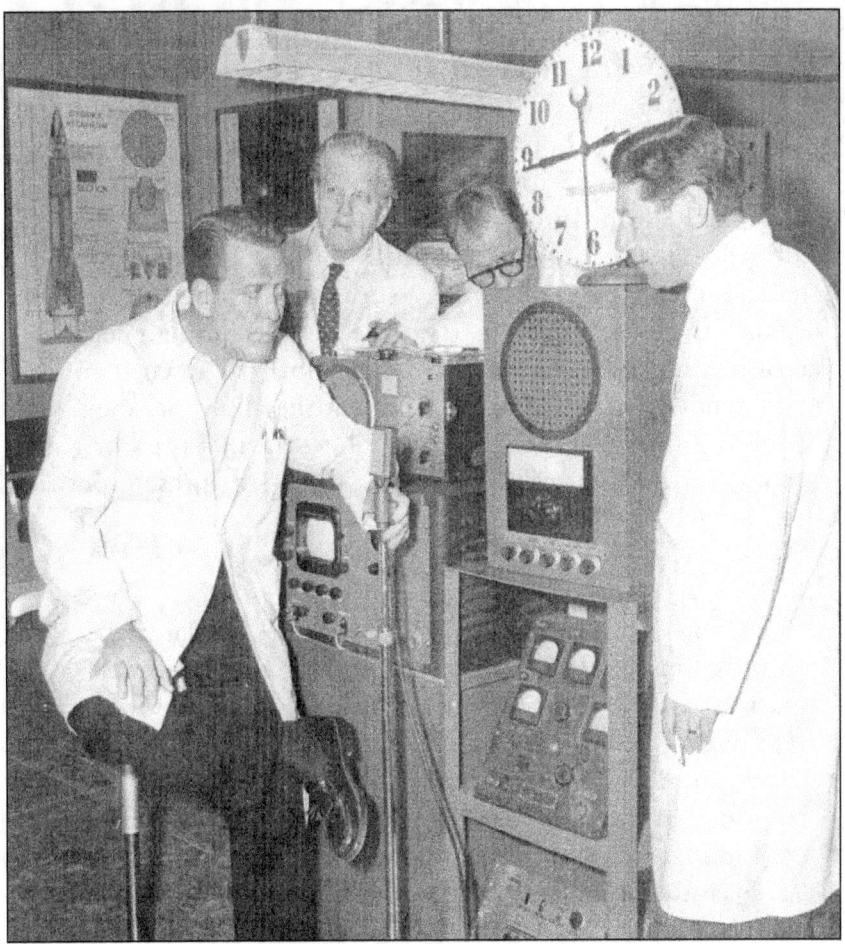

(LEFT TO RIGHT) **Dick Foran, Gene Roth, Stafford Repp and Michael Fox attempt to discover the origin of the mysterious voice in "The Missing Waveband."**

prominent scientist, Dr. Millhurst. But Millhurst confides later to three other distinguished scientists that the equation was conceived by another man—a scientist evidently unable to leave a totalitarian country. Millhurst was contacted by the foreigner while experimenting on a previously unknown and secret wave-length. Millhurst and his associates contact the mysterious voice and obtain much valuable information. Among these, he tells them how inter-continental ballistic missiles can be rendered totally useless as an offensive weapon. The mysterious scientist, however, continues to refuse to reveal his identity or his location. Following instructions from the voice, the

American scientists construct a device that can detect supersonic objects by the vortex they create when passing rapidly through the Earth's magnetic field. They test the device by pin-pointing the satellites, even though they are on the opposite side of the globe. The threat of attack by long-range rockets and fast jet planes is ended, for intercepting rockets can be launched in time to destroy the missiles before they are half way to the target. After the free world is safe from a sneak attack, the scientists use the same tracking device to try to locate the foreign scientist's transmitter, hoping it may be possible eventually to rescue him from the unfriendly power. To their amazement they find that the signals do not originate on Earth at all. The transmissions originate from a point millions of miles out in space—the present position of the planet Jupiter.

Notes

- Some of the computers against the wall are the same as featured in "Mind Machine" and a few are the ones that surround Truman Bradley in the opening signature for each episode.
- The capsule model on Dr. Millhurst's desk is the same residing on the shelf that Truman Bradley walks past in the beginning of every episode during the signature opening.
- This episode was produced under the title "The Missing Wave Length."
- The entire episode was filmed on Stage 3.
- Actor Charles Maxwell supplied the mysterious voice. Known as Special Agent Joe Carey, a recurring character on Ziv's *I Led Three Lives* program, his voice was recorded the day before production began—Wednesday, April 4.
- The model of the space station in this episode was the same model that appears in "The Strange People at Pecos" and "Postcard From Barcelona."
- The character of Dr. Maxwell may have been a tip-of-the-hat to Dr. Maxwell Smith, the technical advisor on the series since the first episode.

The June 27, 1956 issue of *Variety* reviewed this episode:

"Like most of the entries in this series, 'Waveband' has a gimmick and surrounds the gimmick with scientists speaking in terms only an Einstein could comprehend. Thus this vidpic has a certain amount of interest via the gimmick, but it fails to overcome the general lassitude and immobility caused by the excess verbiage in the two-set pic.

"A scientist stumbles on a new wave length unknown to anyone, he thinks—and a voice comes over it, giving him all kinds of secret info and displaying a vast knowledge of science. The voice even gives him the secret of defense against the 5,000-mile-an-hour guided missile, but in such verbiage only a science fiction player could understand it. Scientists think this unknown voice is from behind-the-iron-curtain, but it develops it's from Jupiter, way off in outer space.

"Dick Foran, Stafford Repp, Gene Roth and Michael Fox rate credit for handling those king-sized words, but little else, since this particular series requires very little emoting. Jack Herzberg direction, like Lou Huston's teleplay, is so-so."

"OPERATION M-3" (A.K.A. "MAN-MADE MOON")

Dated: March 5, 1956
By Ivan Tors

A young scientist receives worldwide acclaim as the man responsible for the functioning of man-made satellites. Previous attempts to put up satellites did not succeed until he came up with a new equation that made it possible to calculate the orbit of such satellites correctly. He receives the greatest scientific awards and is celebrated as the man having the greatest powers of reasoning and logic since the death of Einstein.

The young scientist remains very humble. He arranges an unpublicized meeting with three other scientists who all have contributed, by their great discoveries, to the welfare of this world. At this meeting our scientist reveals that it wasn't his power of logic to which he could attribute his discovery, but that foreign land. He explains that, while looking for a missile wave length, he succeeded in finding a heretic unknown wave band, and on this wave length he made contact with this foreign scientist who had discovered the same wave length. The foreign scientist, who spoke excellent English, did not reveal who he was or where he lived. The impression of our scientist is that he is working in a totalitarian country from which he is withholding his full scientific knowledge but that he is willing to pass it on to the scientists of a free nation. At a certain time of the evening, the foreign scientist communicates with him and reveals scientific knowledge that is staggering. Our side is very lucky that his scientific know-how is not turned against us, as it might be in the hands of aggressive forces. It was this foreign scientist who had given him the equation which is responsible for the success of the satellite stations. Our scientist explains that he couldn't reveal the real origin of his knowledge as he was afraid to endanger the safety of the foreign scientist.

The other scientists find it difficult to believe that a brain could exist that it was so far in advance of anything we know in science. But there is proof. At the designated hour the voice makes contact with our group and reveals wisdom of immense proportions. His suggestions help to answer many scientific mysteries. Our three scientists would like to know whether there is a way to eliminate aggression and whether a counter-weapon could be found to cancel out the destructive power of the intercontinental ballistic missile. The answer is yes. Any object moving with a greater speed than 1,000 miles per hour will create a vortex in the magnetic field of the Earth and the vibrations can be recorded on a seismograph-like instrument. Then a counter-weapon can be fired that will be guided to these vibrations and destroy the missile. In other words, an electronic map of the world can be created where the firing of every missile, the flying of every plane, which, exceeds the speed of 1,000 miles, can be traced and intercepted. Such a weapon can eliminate aggression from the face of the world.

Our scientists try to construct such an instrument and they succeed. They are tremendously grateful to the voice from the foreign land but the voice remains silent from hereon. Through an electronic tracking device, our scientists try to locate the origin of the transmitter that carried the benevolent voice. They succeed to pinpoint the origin. The voice came from space.

EPISODE #51 "THE HUMAN EXPERIMENT"

PRODUCTION #1051 / 51B
Dates of Production: April 10 and 11, 1956
Directed by Paul Guilfoyle

SCRIPT & STORY
First Draft by Doris Gilbert, circa April 4, 1956
Revised pages dated April 5, 1956
Teleplay by Doris Gilbert, from the story of the same name by Ivan Tors

PRODUCTION CREDITS
1st Asst. Cameraman: Jim Bell (April 11, *un-credited*) and Ed Wade (April 10, *credited*)
1st Co. Grip: Carl Miksch (*un-credited*)
2nd Asst. Director: Lynn Parsons (April 10, *credited*) and Bob Templeton (April 11, *un-credited*)
2nd Co. Grip: Kenneth Daw (*un-credited*)
Assistant Director: Ed Stein
Assistant Prop Man: Stan Walters (*un-credited*)
Audio Supervisor: Quinn Martin
Best Boy: Charles Stockwell (*un-credited*)
Boom Man: Elmer Haglund (April 11) and W.C. Smith (April 10) (*both un-credited*)
Camera Operator: Dick Rawlings (April 10, *credited*) and Jack Rawlings (April 11, *un-credited*)
Construction Chief: Dee Bolhius (*un-credited*)
Director of Photography: Monroe "Monk" Askins
Electricians: Fred Hounshell, Harold Kraus, Louis Kreiger and Al Ronso (*all un-credited*)
Film Coordinator: Donald Tait
Film Editor: Tommy Scott (*un-credited*) and John B. Woelz (*credited*)
Gaffer: Al Ronso (*un-credited*)
Make-up Artist: George Gray (*un-credited*)
Production Coordinator: Joe Wonder
Production Supervisor: Barry Cohon

Property Master: Max Pittman
Recorder: Lloyd Hanks (April 11) and Howard Wohlman (April 10) (*both un-credited*)
Scientific Advisor on Electronics and Radiation: Maxwell Smith
Script Supervisor: Jeanne Lippman (April 10) and Larry Lund (April 11)
Set Decorator: Clarence Steenson
Set Designer: Jack Collis
Set Labor: Bill Bentham (*un-credited*)
Sound Editor: Monroe Martin
Sound Mixer: Garry Harris (April 11) and Herman Lewis (April 10)
Special Effects: Harry Redmond, Jr.
Still Man: Charles Rhodes (April 11, *un-credited*)
Wardrobe: Alfred Berke

CAST: Claudia Barrett (Jean Richardson, $125); George D. Barrows (Adam, $80); Virginia Christine (Dr. Eleanor Ballard, $125); Gloria Clark (Ruth, the maid, $80); Alan Paige (the gardener, $80); Marshall Thompson (Dr. Tom MacDouggal, $750); Julie Van Zandt (Wanda Ballard, $80)

PLOT: Biochemist Dr. Eleanor Ballard believes that through an insect serum that pre-determines the development of the egg in the insect society, the same adjustment to his surroundings can be given to the psychological misfit, the mentally ill, unable to cope with life around them. Dr. Tom McDouggal, a young Canadian scientist, goes to visit Dr. Ballard in order to see her work in progress and finds that she is being held captive, a veritable slave by the very misfits she has turned into a queen, a soldier and workers, according to the pattern of an insect society. The rescue of Dr. Ballard and the problem of what to do with the cases, now far out of hand, constitutes the crux of the story when Dr. McDouggal sneaks into the house late one night to sabotage the lab and kidnap Dr. Ballard. When the serum wears off, the human guinea pigs revert to their original conditions.

Actress Julie Van Zandt takes a lunch break on the set of "The Human Experiment."

Actress Julie Van Zandt takes direction from director Paul Guilfoyle in "The Human Experiment."

Notes

- The first day of filming was all done in the studio. While the cast and crew were at lunch, the studio was used to record sound effects for production 37b of *Highway Patrol*.
- The second day of filming consisted of exteriors shot on location. Two directors were on hand. Paul Guilfoyle directed drive-way shots at the home of Mr. Knobel, located at 1942 Laughlin Park Drive, and at 5241 Franklin Ave. for exterior scenes of the ranch and house for this production. Herbert Strock filmed scenes at Bronson Canyon with actors Wayne Morris, Frank Gerstle and Harlan Warde for production 52b. Mr. Knobel's house was also used for a drive-way shot for the first-season episode "Postcard From Barcelona."

"THE HUMAN EXPERIMENT"
by Ivan Tors

The scientific introduction demonstrates that, among social insects, a completely different form of life will evolve from the very same egg, if, the egg is fed by different chemicals or hormones. A soldier termite looks like a lobster and has no resemblance to a worker termite at all. He is fifteen times the size of the ordinary termite and is equipped with giant claws. A queen bee or a queen ant looks very different from the other species though the egg is the same.

Is it possible that chemical science will develop a hormone that will change the characteristics of a human being, making one hard working and diligent like a worker insect, aggressive and ferocious like a soldier insect and regal and maternal like the queen? This is the theme of our story.

A young Canadian scientist was very impressed by a scientific paper published by a Miss Eleanor Ballard, a famous biochemist. He decides to visit her to discuss his own research work along the very same lines. Her home and private laboratory is situated in a remote area in the country and not readily accessible. When the young doctor presents himself at the door, he finds himself forcibly ejected by an aggressive servant who tells him that Miss Ballard will not see anyone. Upon his insistence, a very young woman appears who professes to be Ballard's daughter, but the young scientist had seen Miss Ballard's photograph and sees no resemblance. He notices two other persons on the premises—two servants who remain quiet and work in and around the house incessantly. The young scientist returns to his hotel completely puzzled. There is an unexplained mystery about the house. The people he had contact with showed definite paranoid tendencies. As he inquires about, he finds that nobody had seen Miss Ballard for a long time and no one has any knowledge of the existence of a daughter.

Our young scientist steals back at night to the house, climbs in through the window and finds Miss Ballard in the lab. He identifies himself to her and she asks him to keep in hiding. She explains that she is kept a prisoner in her own house and if her captors were to discover his presence, they would definitely kill him. Then she tells her story. She was working on a certain hormone, learning from the social insects which hormone could change the mental make up of a human being. She tried her hormone first on animals, which experiments yielded amazing results. Ferocious animals injected by worker hormones became docile and tamable; timid animals turned into ferocious species when injected by soldier hormones.

She decided to carry her experiment to humans and selected four mentally inflicted people with personality disorders who she injected with these hormones. The results were amazing. A painfully shy young woman takes on the poise and determination of a queen; a catatonic patient turns into an aggressive soldier-type and two manic-depressives who were in the manic stages of insanity became peaceful and docile, and these were the servants working incessantly around the house. But the instincts of the soldier and the queen went far beyond her expectations. As soldier insects keep slaves in their hives, she is now kept as a hostage by the girl and the soldier, forced to produce the hormones they need for their existence. The queen has the intelligence to know whether she produces the right hormones and she is threatened with death in case she disobeys them. She lives in a house of nightmare of her own making.

The young scientist frees the woman chemist from her predicament. When they again return to the house, they find that the inhabitants, without the hormones, have reverted to their original state. The soldier is no longer dangerous—he is back to his catatonic stage; the queen is painfully shy and the workers are as they were before the experiment. The days of horror are over for Miss Ballard but science profited by her experiment.

EPISODE #52 "MAN WHO DIDN'T KNOW"

PRODUCTION #1052 / 53B
DATES OF PRODUCTION: MAY 2 AND 3, 1956
DIRECTED BY HERBERT L. STROCK

SCRIPT & STORY
FIRST DRAFT BY RIK VOLLAERTS, APRIL 18, 1956
FINAL DRAFT BY RIK VOLLAERTS, APRIL 26, 1956
TELEPLAY BY RIK VOLLAERTS

PRODUCTION CREDITS
1ST ASST. CAMERAMAN: JIM BELL (*UN-CREDITED*)
1ST CO. GRIP: CARL MIKSCH (*UN-CREDITED*)
2ND ASST. DIRECTOR: BRUCE BILSON (*UN-CREDITED*)
2ND CO. GRIP: TOMMY MATHEWS (*UN-CREDITED*)
3RD GRIP: JACK CHAMBERS (*UN-CREDITED*)
ASSISTANT DIRECTOR: ED STEIN
ASST. PROP: VIC PETROTTA (*UN-CREDITED*)
AUDIO SUPERVISOR: QUINN MARTIN
BOOM MAN: ELMER HAGLUND (*UN-CREDITED*)
CAMERA OPERATOR: DICK RAWLINGS
CONSTRUCTION CHIEF: ARCHIE HALL (*UN-CREDITED*)
DIRECTOR OF PHOTOGRAPHY: CURT FETTERS
FILM COORDINATOR: DONALD TAIT
FILM EDITOR: DUNCAN MANSFIELD, A.C.E.
GAFFER: CHARLES STOCKWELL (*UN-CREDITED*)
MAKE-UP ARTIST: GEORGE GRAY (*UN-CREDITED*)
PRODUCTION COORDINATOR: JOE WONDER
PRODUCTION SUPERVISOR: BARRY COHON
PROPERTY MASTER: MAX PITTMAN
RECORDER: LLOYD HANKS (*UN-CREDITED*)
SCIENTIFIC ADVISOR ON ELECTRONICS AND RADIATION:
  MAXWELL SMITH

Script Supervisor: Larry Lund
Set Decorator: Clarence Steenson
Set Designer: Robert Kinoshita
Set Labor: Claude Means (*un-credited*)
Sound Editor: Sidney Sutherland
Sound Mixer: Garry Harris
Special Effects: Harry Redmond, Jr.
Wardrobe: Alfred Berke (*credited*) and Lou Palfy (*un-credited*)

CAST: Susan Cummings (Peggy Kendler, $125); Granville Dixon (Pat Johnson, Ph.D., $80); Bill Erwin (Harold Lewis, M.D., $80); Arthur Franz (Mark Kendler, $750); Joe Hamilton (Sven Bergstrom, $80); Paul Lukather (the radio operator, $80); Voltaire Perkins (Jim Woodward, $80); Guy Rennie (Sam Gilman, Ph.D., $80); and Bruce Wendell (Al Mitchell, $80)

PLOT: Mark Kendler, physicist and pilot in Project Icarus (the development of a nuclear powered plane), is lost at sea when one of the early attempts at getting a reactor airborne fails. He disappears for six months, finally showing up at Singapore with no memory of the past six months. He has had apparent major surgery to repair injuries he suffered from the crash. Aside from loss of hearing in one ear and occasional headaches, he is physically and mentally well again. After careful screening by the Bureau of Scientific Security (BSS), he is allowed to return to work. After some months, the BSS gets evidence from overseas that a foreign power is getting information from Project Icarus. Careful checkup of the Project and Kendler reveals nothing. Then a tape recording is intercepted from a courier in West Berlin, with a conversation that took place in Kendler's office. At the end of the tape, Kendler is alone, speaking his thoughts. Mark listens to the tape and finds evidence that it was not made by recording instruments, but by a radio transmitter. A monitoring arrangement is set up to locate the spy broadcast. Finally, in the highest part of the radio spectrum, a broadcast is heard coming from Kendler himself. A search of his clothing reveals nothing. But x-rays locate the transmitter—in his ear cavity, the size of a walnut, powered by a mercury solar power battery in his neck. It is removed through careful surgery, and then cleverly used to broadcast false information on Icarus to the agents of the foreign power.

Notes
- The names of the fictional characters vary between the first and final draft of the script. The character of Al Mitchell was originally Al Wendling, changed to Al Clark and then changed a third time before filming began. The character of Pat Johnson, Ph.D was originally Pat Warner in the first draft. The character of John Bergstrom, Ph.D was Sven Bergstrom in the first draft.
- Produced under the title "The Broadcast," which was the same title of the teleplay.
- Bradley talks about the process of miniaturization through science, and comments how one day airplanes will be fueled by atomic energy.
- Actor Tom Anthony plays the un-credited role of the Western Union messenger boy.
- The insert shots of the hands with the reel-to-reel tape player belong to stand-in Frank Hunt.

Episode #53 "The Phantom Car"

Production #1053 / 54B
Dates of Production: April 30 to May 2, 1956
Directed by Herbert L. Strock

Script & Story
Final Draft by Lee Hewitt, April 26, 1956
Teleplay by Lee Hewitt

Production Credits
1st Asst. Cameraman: Jim Bell (*un-credited*)
1st Co. Grip: Carl Miksch (*un-credited*)
2nd Asst. Director: Bruce Bilson (*un-credited*)
2nd Co. Grip: Tommy Mathews (*un-credited*)
3rd Grip: Jack Chambers (*un-credited*)

ASSISTANT DIRECTOR: ED STEIN
ASST. PROP MAN: VIC PETROTTA (*UN-CREDITED*)
AUDIO SUPERVISOR: QUINN MARTIN
BOOM MAN: ELMER HAGLUND (*UN-CREDITED*)
CAMERA OPERATOR: DICK RAWLINGS
CONSTRUCTION CHIEF: ARCHIE HALL (*UN-CREDITED*)
DIRECTOR OF PHOTOGRAPHY: CURT FETTERS
FILM COORDINATOR: DONALD TAIT
FILM EDITOR: THOMAS SCOTT
GAFFER: CHARLES STOCKWELL (*UN-CREDITED*)
MAKE-UP ARTIST: GEORGE GRAY (*UN-CREDITED*)
PRODUCTION COORDINATOR: JOE WONDER
PRODUCTION SUPERVISOR: BARRY COHON
PROPERTY MASTER: MAX PITTMAN
RECORDER: LLOYD HANKS (*UN-CREDITED*)
SCIENTIFIC ADVISOR ON ELECTRONICS AND RADIATION:
   MAXWELL SMITH
SCRIPT SUPERVISOR: LARRY LUND
SET DECORATOR: CLARENCE STEENSON
SET DESIGNER: ROBERT KINOSHITA
SET LABOR: CLAUDE MEANS (*UN-CREDITED*)
SOUND EDITOR: SIDNEY SUTHERLAND
SOUND MIXER: GARRY HARRIS
SPECIAL EFFECTS: HARRY REDMOND, JR.
WARDROBE: ALFRED BERKE (*CREDITED*) AND LOU PALFY
   (*UN-CREDITED*)

CAST: Judith Ames (Reggie Gress, $100); John Archer (Arthur Gress, $600); Joe Colbert (Dr. Phil Avery, $80); Pat Donahue (Miss Sloan, the nurse/secretary, $80); William Fawcett (Mort Woods, $250); Herbert C. Lytton (Doc Lloyd, $100); Tyler McVey (Sheriff Barney Cole, $225); and Troy Melton (Joe, the medic, $320)

PLOT: While vacationing in the Mesa Flat desert, Professor Gress' wife, Reggie, is the victim of a mysterious hit and run car that has no driver. Adding to the mystery is the manner in which a brain surgeon is brought to the little desert hospital where Reggie is prepared for emergency surgery. While Reggie recovers under the care of Doctor Lloyd, a small town doctor, and the specialist, Doctor Avery, Gress is asked by the local Sheriff to investigate the strange hit and run case when the Sheriff's attempts to chase the car have failed. Using scientific detection methods, Gress proves the car is an experimental radar controlled, electronically guided vehicle. A tracer chemical tracks the car to its inventor, Doctor Avery, who becomes a victim of his own device. Wounded, Avery explains that the controls are jammed and the vehicle is headed straight for Mesa City. The doctor meant no harm, but Reggie was hit because the car's guidance system failed to pick up humans or animals. The men race to the city and, finding the controls, shut the automobile off before any harm can come to the community.

Notes

- Produced under the title "Ghost Car."
- To accomplish the illusion of the driverless car, the crew fashioned a cloth over the driver and passenger seat hiding the driver contained from within. A special mirror was added to the vehicle so the driver could see where he was going. The cloth covering the driver is noticeable on screen, but excused during the conclusion when the heroes pull the cover off to reveal the guidance system underneath.
- For a number of close-up shots the automobile was attached to a tow truck with the camera attached to its back end, so the car was being dragged by the tow truck and thus giving the audience a front hood view of the car with no driver in the seat.
- Filmed simultaneously with "The Man Who Didn't Know," but this episode was filmed on location at Mirror Lake near Palmdale and the Antelope Motel. The third and final day of this episode concluded on location, then the crew began with the next cast for the other episode, which concluded at the studio the next day.
- The cast and crew suffered from a 15 minute meal penalty due to the driver getting lost.
- The role of Mort Woods was originally intended for Tyler McVey and the role of Barney Cole was originally intended for Herbert C. Lytton.

- Actor Harry Wilson plays the un-credited role of the pedestrian who, towards the end of the drama, witnesses the phantom car come to a stop in the middle of the road.
- Stand-In Joe De Angelo plays two roles in the beginning of this episode: the man putting gas into his car and the mechanic looking under the hood of another car.

EPISODE #54 "BEAM OF FIRE"

PRODUCTION #1054 / 52B

DATES OF PRODUCTION: APRIL 11, 12 AND 13, 1956
DIRECTED BY HERBERT L. STROCK

SCRIPT & STORY

FINAL DRAFT BY STUART JEROME, MARCH 30, 1956
TELEPLAY BY STUART JEROME, FROM THE SHORT STORY "THE BEAM" BY IVAN TORS

PRODUCTION CREDITS:

1ST ASST. CAMERAMAN: ED WADE (UN-CREDITED)
1ST CO. GRIP: MEL BLEDSOE (UN-CREDITED)
2ND ASST. DIRECTOR: LYNN PARSONS, JR. (UN-CREDITED)
2ND CAMERAMAN: JACK MARQUETTE (UN-CREDITED)
2ND CO. GRIP: GEORGE HILL (UN-CREDITED)
ASSISTANT DIRECTOR: ED STEIN
ASST. PROP MAN: STAN WALTER (UN-CREDITED)
AUDIO SUPERVISOR: QUINN MARTIN
BEST BOY: CHARLES STOCKWELL (UN-CREDITED)
BOOM MAN: W.C. SMITH (UN-CREDITED)
CABLEMAN: DICK SMITH (UN-CREDITED)
CONSTRUCTION CHIEF: DEE BOLHIUS (UN-CREDITED)
DIRECTOR OF PHOTOGRAPHY: MONROE "MONK" ASKINS
ELECTRICIANS: CHARLES HANGER, LOUIS KREIGER AND VICTOR PIZANTI (ALL UN-CREDITED)
FILM COORDINATOR: DONALD TAIT
FILM EDITOR: DUNCAN MANSFIELD, A.C.E.
GAFFER: AL RONSO (UN-CREDITED)

Make-up Artist: George Gray (*un-credited*)
Production Coordinator: Joe Wonder
Production Supervisor: Barry Cohon
Property Master: Max Pittman
Recorder: John Powers (*un-credited*)
Scientific Advisor on Electronics and Radiation: Maxwell Smith
Script Supervisor: Joe Franklin
Set Decorator: Clarence Steenson
Set Designer: Jack Collis
Set Labor: Bill Bentham (*un-credited*)
Sound Editor: Gus Galvin
Sound Mixer: Herman Lewis
Special Effects: Harry Redmond, Jr.
Still Man: Charles Rhodes (April 13 only, *un-credited*)
Wardrobe: Alfred Berke

CAST: Ed Chandler (the voice, $80); John Dennis (Dr. Charles Hayes, $80); Frank Gerstle (Davis, $125); Paul Harber (Jennings, $80); Wayne Morris (Steve Conway, $1,000); Leonard Mudie (Dr. Bellow, $125); Bruce Payne (Dr. Hunter, $80); George Pembroke (Dr. Benton, $80); William Vaughan (the wiretapping expert, $80); and Harlan Warde (Dr. Lindstrom, $125)

PLOT: Famed scientist Dr. John Bellow, working on a top-secret government project to develop a new propellant capable of launching rockets for inter-planetary travel, is mysteriously killed in his lab by a fireball that incinerates the lab, his papers and himself. Security Agent and fellow scientist Steve Conway, assigned to guard Bellow, has nothing to go on except a strange phone call which he received for Bellow immediately before the scientist's death. Conway is immediately sent to Dr. Charles Hayes, the second most important man on the project. Despite every precaution, Hayes, too, is killed. Investigation determines that an unknown form of sound vibration, directed and intensified by the rays of the sun, is the weapon being used. But modern science is powerless to stop it. Conway evolves a dangerous plan to force the beam into action again, tricking the criminals. It works. By devising a system of parabolic mirrors, the rays

Wayne Morris takes direction from Herbert L. Strock on the set of "Beam of Fire."

Wayne Morris looks over the script with producer Ivan Tors.

are reflected back to the point of origin. When they reach the spot on the side of a mountain, nothing remains but a burned spot on the rocky landscape and a melted piece of metal of unknown origin. Wherever the saboteur came from, he wanted to prevent man from attempting travel into space.

Notes
- The sound chart hanging on the wall in Bellow's lab is the same Bradley uses to demonstrate signals in the beginning of "The Unguided Missile."
- The un-credited role of the security guard is played by stand-in Jack Krupnick.
- Actor Tom Anthony assists Truman Bradley with the fluoroscope for this episode.

"THE BEAM"
Dated circa March 30, 1956
by Ivan Tors

A famous scientist is working on a new chemical that will revolutionize rocket flights and may make space travel possible within our lifetime.

The scientist works in a secluded laboratory under the protection of security guards. In spite of all precautions, a mysterious ball of fire enters his laboratory and burns him to cinders. The head of the security guards is afraid that another scientist, who is working in conjunction with this new project at a different location, may meet with the same fate, so he flies to the second location to enforce even stricter security regulations. In spite of all these efforts, the second scientist is murdered by a mysteriously directed beam which turns out to be a high decibel sound wave of mysterious origin. The sound vibrations destroy the nerve tissues of the scientist's brain.

A group of scientists analyze the situation and come to the conclusion that the group responsible for interfering with the completion of this project must be determined to sabotage space travel and that their weapon is a system of mirrors which can direct high frequency sound beams anywhere desired. An idea is set forth at this meeting. What if a system of mirrors were to be built which could reflect these beams back to the point of origin?

A trap is laid for the unknown saboteur. It is announced that another scientist took the inventor's place in research. Then, a system of mirrors is set up which, in conjunction with a computing machine and thermostat, analyzes the origin of the death ray, and returns it to the point of generation. A ball of fire is visible from the top of a mountain twenty miles from the desert laboratory. When the scientists reach the spot, they find molten metal in the place where the death beam had originated. Analyzing the metal, they find it heavier than anything that exists on Earth.

EPISODE #55 "THE LEGEND OF CRATER MOUNTAIN"

PRODUCTION #1055 / 55B

DATES OF PRODUCTION: MAY 9 AND 10, 1956
DIRECTED BY PAUL GUILFOYLE

SCRIPT & STORY

"THE CHILDREN'S GAME" FINAL TYPESCRIPT (ANNOTATED) BY LUE HALL AND BILL BUCHANAN, LATER RETITLED "THE CHILDREN" ON APRIL 19, 1956.
REVISED PAGES (ANNOTATED), APRIL 27 AND MAY 25, 1956
REVISED MASTER MIMEO, MAY 25, 1956
TELEPLAY BY LUE HALL AND BILL BUCHANAN

PRODUCTION CREDITS

1ST ASST. CAMERAMAN: DAVID CURLAND (*UN-CREDITED*)
1ST CO. GRIP: CARL MIKSCH (*UN-CREDITED*)
2ND ASST. DIRECTOR: EDDIE MULL (*UN-CREDITED*)
2ND CAMERAMAN: ROB TELMIE (*UN-CREDITED*)
2ND CO. GRIP: WALTER CULP (*UN-CREDITED*)
3RD GRIP: TOMMY MATHEWS (*UN-CREDITED*)
ASSISTANT DIRECTOR: ED STEIN
ASST. PROP MAN: EVERETT RICHARDSON (*UN-CREDITED*)
AUDIO SUPERVISOR: QUINN MARTIN
BEST BOY: MIKE HUDSON (*UN-CREDITED*)
BOOM MAN: MARTIN STELLE (*UN-CREDITED*)

CABLEMAN: DICK SMITH (*UN-CREDITED*)
CONSTRUCTION CHIEF: ARCHIE HALL (*UN-CREDITED*)
DIRECTOR OF PHOTOGRAPHY: CURT FETTERS
ELECTRICIANS: DIXIE DUNBAR AND WALTER GEDIMAN
  (*BOTH UN-CREDITED*)
FILM COORDINATOR: DONALD TAIT
FILM EDITOR: CHARLES CRAFT, A.C.E.
GAFFER: JIMMY FIELD (*UN-CREDITED*)
MAKE-UP ARTIST: GEORGE GRAY (*UN-CREDITED*)
PRODUCTION COORDINATOR: JOE WONDER
PRODUCTION SUPERVISOR: BARRY COHON
PROPERTY MASTER: MAX PITTMAN
RECORDER: DON VALENTINE (*UN-CREDITED*)
SCIENTIFIC ADVISOR ON ELECTRONICS AND RADIATION:
  MAXWELL SMITH
SCRIPT SUPERVISOR: JEANNE LIPPMAN
SET DECORATOR: LOU HAFLEY
SET DESIGNER: ROBERT KINOSHITA
SET LABOR: TED MCCASKEY (*UN-CREDITED*)
SOUND EDITOR: GUS GALVIN
SOUND MIXER: JAY ASHWORTH
SPECIAL EFFECTS: HARRY REDMOND, JR.
STILL MAN: JOE WALTERS (MAY 9 ONLY, *UN-CREDITED*)
WARDROBE: ALFRED BERKE

CAST: Nadine Ashdown (Susan Avitor, $100); Marilyn Erskine (Marian Brown, $1,250); Paul Guilfoyle (Mr. Avitor, $100); Bradford Jackson (Dr. Jim Harris, $125); Jo Ann Lilliquist (Rosellen Avitor, $100); and Freddy Ridgeway (Bobby Avitor, $100)

PLOT: Near an isolated desert community in Arizona, there is a meteor crater which the older, more superstitious inhabitants claim, was the landing place of a space ship some two hundred years ago. Within the community itself is a one-room elementary school. Marian Brown, the teacher, is aided in her observation and study of three of her students by Dr. Jim Harris, a friend of Marian's during their University days. The three students in question are the Avitor children, members of the strange and quiet Avitor family. The

Truman Bradley discovering how playful the baby leopard can be when the cameras are not rolling for "The Legend of Crater Mountain."

Producer Ivan Tors admiring the baby leopard with Truman Bradley.

(LEFT TO RIGHT) **Jo Ann Lilliquist, Freddy Ridgeway and Nadine Ashdown as the Avitor children in "The Legend of Crater Mountain."**

children have a marked ability to exercise telekinesis, moving objects without touching them, a subject which Jim is presently investigating back at the University. As the children exhibit their strange power in the form of active opposition to their teacher, Jim realizes that Marian's life may be in danger, and he encourages her to come back to "civilization" with him. Marian refuses the offer, however, and is soon seriously hurt by one of the children's "tricks" of telekinesis. Realizing their destruction, the children are quickly sorry of their actions and their feelings are reiterated by their curiously gentle father. He sincerely apologizes for his children and explains that his family had, for the past two hundred years, produced mind-readers, magicians and gifted people—but are certainly not space aliens. Jim realizes that it was two hundred years ago when the meteor landed—or was it a spaceship?

Notes

- The closing scene in this episode differs greatly from the original script, in which Mr. Avitor apologizes to the school teacher for his children's actions and promises their future acts will be only constructive, as an aid to mankind. As the Avitor family passes the meteor crater in their Jeep, Mr. Avitor tells his children that to help the human race is their reason for being here on Earth. As seen in the film, the ending was revised to add the question of whether or not the children were from another planet.
- Production under the title of "The Children."
- Actress Nadine Ashdown, billed as Nadene Ashdown in the closing credits, was a child actor who appeared in half a dozen television shows such as *The Lone Ranger* and *The Adventures of Wild Bill Hickok*, and nine motion pictures. This was her final screen appearance. Freddy Ridgeway and Jo Ann Lilliquist were also child actors who appeared in a small handful of television programs in the fifties and then never pursued a screen career. Ridgeway appears in numerous episodes of *Science Fiction Theatre*.
- The television script instructed the set designers to make sure the interior of the elementary school appeared as "a dilapidated one-room country school. The rough, practical structure has a general rundown appearance; the walls are streaked, a heavy wooden beam over the door is creaked. There are several desks for children, a large desk for the teacher, a blackboard, a wall map, a globe, a coal heater with coal scuttle beside it. The teacher's quarters are concealed by a curtain at one side. Small touches—curtains, pot of flowers, etc. – show Marian's attempt to make the classroom more attractive."

EPISODE #56 "LIVING LIGHTS"

PRODUCTION #1056 / 56B

DATES OF PRODUCTION: MAY 25 AND 28, 1956
DIRECTED BY HERBERT L. STROCK

SCRIPT & STORY
FIRST DRAFT BY ELLIS MARCUS, CIRCA APRIL 25, 1956
FINAL DRAFT BY ELLIS MARCUS, MAY 14, 1956
TELEPLAY BY ELLIS MARCUS, BASED ON SEPARATE SHORT STORIES BY ELLIS MARCUS AND IVAN TORS

PRODUCTION CREDITS

1ST ASST. CAMERAMAN: JIM BELL (*UN-CREDITED*)
1ST CO. GRIP: CARL MIKSCH (*UN-CREDITED*)
2ND ASST. DIRECTOR: JAY SANDRICH (*UN-CREDITED*)
2ND CO. GRIP: MEL BLEDSOE (*UN-CREDITED*)
ASSISTANT DIRECTOR: DONALD VERK
ASST. PROP MAN: YGNACIO SEPULVEDA (*UN-CREDITED*)
AUDIO SUPERVISOR: QUINN MARTIN
BEST BOY: CHARLES STOCKWELL (*UN-CREDITED*)
BOOM MAN: ELMER HAGLUND (*UN-CREDITED*)
CAMERA OPERATOR: DICK RAWLINGS
CONSTRUCTION CHIEF: ARCHIE HALL (*UN-CREDITED*)
DIRECTOR OF PHOTOGRAPHY: MONROE "MONK" ASKINS AND CURT FETTERS
ELECTRICIANS: CHARLES HANGER, MIKE HUDSON AND GLEN KNIGHT (*ALL UN-CREDITED*)
FILM COORDINATOR: DONALD TAIT
FILM EDITOR: DUNCAN MANSFIELD, A.C.E.
GAFFER: AL RONSO (*UN-CREDITED*)
MAKE-UP ARTIST: GEORGE GRAY (*UN-CREDITED*)
PRODUCTION COORDINATOR: JOE WONDER
PRODUCTION SUPERVISOR: BARRY COHON
PROPERTY MASTER: MAX PITTMAN
RECORDER: LLOYD HANKS (*UN-CREDITED*)
SCIENTIFIC ADVISOR ON ELECTRONICS AND RADIATION: MAXWELL SMITH

Actress Joan Sinclair panics when the living lights savagely attack her in "Living Lights."

SCRIPT SUPERVISOR: JEANNE LIPPMAN (MAY 28) AND LARRY LUND (MAY 25)
SET DECORATOR: BRUCE MACDONALD
SET DESIGNER: ROBERT KINOSHITA
SET LABOR: BILL BENTHAM (*UN-CREDITED*)
SOUND EDITOR: SIDNEY SUTHERLAND
SOUND MIXER: GARRY HARRIS
SPECIAL EFFECTS: HARRY REDMOND, JR.
STILL MAN: CHARLES RHODES (MAY 28, *UN-CREDITED*)
WARDROBE: ALFRED BERKE (*UN-CREDITED*)

CAST: Darlene Albert (Elaine Foster, $200); Michael Garth (Charles Irwin, $80); Skip Homeier (Bob Lurie, $1,000); Jason Johnson (Prof. Adams, $200); Joan Sinclair (Grace Lurie, $200); and Robert Weston (Doctor Bane, $80)

PLOT: Young college instructor Bob Lurie and his wife, Grace, steal a number of supplies from the college laboratories to create a synthesized atmosphere of the planet Venus in a bell jar. Their homemade science project was designed in the hopes of proving that living organisms can adapt themselves to such a hostile environment, as he grows a small crop of lichens in the bell jar. To his surprise late one evening, a ball of light appears in the jar. It moves about, consumes the lichen as though feeding on them, causing chemical changes in the atmosphere of the jar which seems to help the lichens grow. When the living light leaves the bell jar and travels around the lab, Bob realizes it is alive. This theory is confirmed with surprising repercussions in which mankind and all living inhabitants of the Earth are endangered. Bob and Grace call for the assistance of friends to help. Soon after the threat is discovered, the living lights decide to eliminate their existence before they can be studied.

NOTES

- The stock footage of the college is the same featured in the episode "Who is This Man?"
- The entire episode was filmed on Stage 5 at the studio.
- On the afternoon of April 6, 1956, Ellis Marcus had a story conference with Ivan Tors and after working out the details of the story, agreed to change the title to "The Living Lights" and Marcus was assigned to do the teleplay based on the two original story outlines.
- Years after this episode aired, *The Outer Limits* would feature a premise not too different from this episode. "Wolf 359" (original telecast November 7, 1964) concerned a scientist's efforts to speed the evolution of an alien culture under glass. Working on behalf of corporate interests, scientist Jonathan Meridith creates a miniature version of a remote planet in his laboratory. When a mysterious life form evolves along with

the developing experiment, Meridith must weigh the value of his experiment versus the possible dangers. *The Outer Limits* version was based on an original story treatment by Richard Landau titled "Greenhouse." This same idea had been explored through numerous other science-fiction stories, including Theodore Sturgeon's "Microscopic God," originally published in the April 1941 issue of *Astounding Science Fiction*.

- The female assisting Truman Bradley in the beginning of this episode is actress Bek Nelson, making her screen debut. Her credits immediately following this production included television commercials and background walk-ins until she appeared in an acting role in 1957 on *Tales of the Texas Rangers*. Afterwards, she appeared in supporting roles for dozens of television programs and would later play the recurring role of Dru Lemp on *Lawman* and Phyllis Sloan on television's *Peyton Place*.

The August 8, 1956 issue of *Variety* reviewed this episode:

"In the vicinity of Cal Tech this series must be avidly devoured. Surely where more beer is sold, on the East Side (not the brand of the sponsoring brew), they'd flee these excursions into biochemistry like a fallen meteor.

"Patently inspired by what narrator Truman Bradley called the 'Lubbock Lights,' which apparently created some stir among Texans and headline writers, this episode concerns a ball of light which breaks out of its glassed-in-confinement to befuddle the scientists and almost blind a girl student with its ultra violet intensity. What it proved is for more scholarly minds than those unscientifically inclined. Bradley did open his thesis on some such explanatory note as 'The Earth is the only place suitable for life' and epilogged that 'it's a step forward into the unknown.' The atmosphere of Venus is more like our own, the viewer is told, so it must be assumed that planet will receive the first caller from this could sod of ours.

"Skip Homeier, for a change, is cast in a sympathetic role and plays the experimenting young scientist as if he had come out of MIT. Joan Sinclair and Darlene Albert act their way through the esoteric fog with agreeable pretense, and the male supporters snap to their assigned auxiliaries. Ivan Tors and Herbert Strock knew what they were doing as producer-director team or so the impression prevailed. Narrator Bradley's voice sounds much like that of KRCA's top newscaster, Jack Latham."

"LIFE FORMS FROM VENUS"
Dated: April 6, 1956
by Ellis Marcus

Professor Arthur B. Lurie, astrophysics department of State University, has been devoting every moment of his spare time to his pet side interest . . . forms of life which exist on Earth without oxygen, light, etc. These include sea creatures which exist in the depths of the oceans. It has occurred to Lurie that these crystalline forms of life exist under conditions of temperature, pressure and lack of breathable atmosphere similar to those found on other planets

He compares their chemical components with chemical data obtained by spectroscope from Venus and discovers marked similarities. In a large bell jar he synthesizes the atmosphere of Venus complete with temperature and pressure conditions and introduces the deep-sea crystalline forms of primitive life into the bell jar.

After a time he observes a strange glow in the bell jar. This glow behaves in a very odd way—it moves out of the bell jar, consumes leaves from a plant, floats around the lab. It generates a small amount of heat, which fluctuates arbitrarily from ten to ninety degrees centigrade. Periodically, it returns to the ball jar and seems to "feed" on the atmosphere and chemicals there.

POSSIBLE PLOT LINE: Lurie calls in a colleague to show this Venusian beast, but the beast has disappeared. Later it returns to the lab and the bell jar to "feed," but to Lurie's astonishment it brings three other fellow light blobs with it.

Investigation reveals these light blobs came from the sea. Lurie's original beast somehow propagated them there. There is a threat that these beasts will multiply uncontrolled on Earth.

Danger—they create a gas which is part of Venus's atmosphere and which is poisonous to animal life on Earth. Lurie and colleague are in a sweat. They finally trap all beasts by placing the bell jar in a large, light absorbent box. The beasts go in there to feed and Lurie closes the box on them. Days later when the box is opened the beasts are gone. The atmosphere in the bell jar has been consumed and the black velvet lining of the box is encrusted with chemical deposits which turn out to be the "remains" of the beasts.

Their light energy was "sucked" out of them. Now that he is able to control the light blobs, Lurie sets out to create and study more of them. He has proved that forms of life, not dependant on oxygen, can exist on other planets.

"LIFE FORM"
Dated: April 2, 1956
by Ivan Tors

A young scientist refuses to believe that life can exist only in the presence of oxygen. He observes how life can exist under the most difficult conditions, like 30,000 feet under the sea. Crystals are life forms which do not require oxygen.

He creates, in a bell jar, conditions which are identical to the surface of the planet Venus, by filling the jar with gases exactly like those which compose the atmosphere of that planet. After a period of waiting, new life forms appear. These are globes of light. Whether they can think is the question our story will tell.

Episode #57 "Jupitron"

Production #1057 / 58B
Dates of Production: May 31 and June 1, 1956
Directed by Paul Guilfoyle

Script & Story
First Draft by Arthur Weiss, circa May 10, 1956
Revised pages dated May 24 and 25, 1956
Final Draft by Arthur Weiss, May 25, 1956
Teleplay by Arthur Weiss

Production Credits
1st Asst. Cameraman: Jim Bell (*un-credited*)
1st Co. Grip: Carl Miksch (*un-credited*)
2nd Asst. Director: Jay Sandrich (*un-credited*)

2ND CO. GRIP: MEL BLEDSOE (*UN-CREDITED*)
ASSISTANT DIRECTOR: ED STEIN
ASST. PROP MAN: STAN WALTERS (*UN-CREDITED*)
AUDIO SUPERVISOR: QUINN MARTIN
BEST BOY: CHARLES STOCKWELL (*UN-CREDITED*)
BOOM MAN: ELMER HAGLUND (*UN-CREDITED*)
CAMERA OPERATOR: DICK RAWLINGS
CONSTRUCTION CHIEF: ARCHIE HALL (*UN-CREDITED*)
DIRECTOR OF PHOTOGRAPHY: CURT FETTERS
ELECTRICIANS: CHARLES HANGER, FRED HOUNSHELL AND MIKE HUDSON (*ALL UN-CREDITED*)
FILM COORDINATOR: DONALD TAIT
FILM EDITOR: THOMAS SCOTT
GAFFER: AL RONSO (*UN-CREDITED*)
MAKE-UP ARTIST: GEORGE GRAY (JUNE 1 ONLY)
PRODUCTION COORDINATOR: JOE WONDER
PRODUCTION SUPERVISOR: BARRY COHON
PROPERTY MASTER: MAX PITTMAN
RECORDER: LLOYD HANKS (*UN-CREDITED*)
SCIENTIFIC ADVISOR ON ELECTRONICS AND RADIATION: MAXWELL SMITH
SCRIPT SUPERVISOR: JEANNE LIPPMAN
SET DECORATOR: CLARENCE STEENSON
SET DESIGNER: ROBERT KINOSHITA
SET LABOR: BILL BENTHAM (*UN-CREDITED*)
SOUND EDITOR: GUS GALVIN
SOUND MIXER: GARRY HARRIS
SPECIAL EFFECTS: HARRY REDMOND, JR.
WARDROBE: ALFRED BERKE

CAST: Michael Fox (Dr. Norstad, $125); Toni Gerry (Nina Barlow, $350); Lowell Gilmore (August Wykoff); Paul Guilfoyle (the voice, $80); Arthur Marshall (Frank, the lab technician, $80); and Bill Williams (Dr. John Barlow, $800)

PLOT: When a scientist, Dr. John Barlow and his wife, Nina, fall asleep on the beach late one evening, a strange mist envelops them. They awaken to find themselves in a laboratory on one of the

> **BLOOPER!**
> WHEN THE MIST FIRST ENTERS THE PICTURE, IT'S SHOWN PREMATURELY FROM BEHIND NINA BARLOW.

moons of Jupiter. The only human occupant of the laboratory is August Wykoff, a scientist who disappeared from Earth without a trace ten years previous. He has brought Dr. Barlow here in order to tell him what direction his research in photosynthesis should take, since the synthetic creation of food will be a life and death problem for the Earth within (by Barlow's calculations) fifty years. Wykoff explains that he helped solve a life and death problem for a foreign life form situated on another planet and in return they offer Jupitron—a catalyst that would solve Earth's similar problem. Armed with this knowledge, Barlow and his wife are then returned to Earth. But upon awakening they don't know whether they have merely dreamed their experience or lived it . . . until Barlow discovers that he has an over-concentration of argon in his blood stream. The strong concentration is such that he could not have gotten it on Earth.

NOTES

- Principle filming for this episode was the shortest of the 78 episodes. It was completed in a day and a half, a total of 10 hours, 45 minutes.
- Two un-credited stand-ins/extras were on hand for this episode. Jack Ramstead and Lois James.
- From 12:30 to 8:00 p.m. on June 1, Truman Bradley was filmed for lab demonstrations for the opening and closings of productions 55, 56 and 57.
- The fake steam pipes in the steam chamber were also on the wall in the first-season episode "Dead Storage."
- The gold ornament hanging on the wall in this episode is the same prop hanging on the wall in the first-season episode, "A Visit from Dr. Pliny."
- Arthur Weiss wrote his teleplay based on two *Scientific American* magazine articles: "The Chemistry of Jupiter" by

Francis Owen Rice, originally published in the June 1956 issue, and "Progress in Photosynthesis" by Eugene I. Rabinowitch in the November 1953 issue.

The August 15, 1956 issue of *Variety* reviewed this episode:
"Producer Ivan Tors' flights into fantasy seem to become more fanciful and flighty each passing week. In 'Jupitron,' a scientist and his wife are in some mysterious manner transported to Jupiter, given a 'secret' formula to benefit Earth, and sent back to this planet. It's interesting—up to a point—but yarn's greatest oversight is its failure to explain the 'how' of it all.

"On Jupiter they meet another Earth scientist who had vanished ten years ago and somehow landed on Jupiter because they needed the brains. He's happy there, and he arranged the interplanetary abduction in order to help Earth via a food-making formula to take care of our increasing population. Obviously, writer Arthur Weiss didn't attempt to explain the 'how' of this yarn, since this would tax the most vivid imagination.

"Bill Williams, Toni Gerry, Lowell Gilmore are adequate in the undemanding roles. Paul Guilfoyle's direction is okay."

EPISODE #58 "THE THROWBACK"

PRODUCTION #1058 / 59B
DATES OF PRODUCTION: JUNE 14 AND 15, 1956
DIRECTED BY PAUL GUILFOYLE

SCRIPT & STORY
FIRST DRAFT BY THELMA SCHNEE, CIRCA MAY 23, 1956
FINAL DRAFT BY THELMA SCHNEE, JUNE 11, 1956
TELEPLAY BY THELMA SCHNEE, BASED ON HER ORIGINAL STORY "NOBODY DIES"

PRODUCTION CREDITS
1ST ASST. CAMERAMAN: JIM BELL (*UN-CREDITED*)
1ST CO. GRIP: MEL BLEDSOE (*UN-CREDITED*)
2ND ASST. DIRECTOR: JAY SANDRICH (*UN-CREDITED*)

2ND CO. GRIP: TOMMY MATHEWS (*UN-CREDITED*)
ASSISTANT DIRECTOR: EDDIE STEIN
ASST. PROP MAN: STAN WALTERS (*UN-CREDITED*)
AUDIO SUPERVISOR: QUINN MARTIN
BEST BOY: CHARLES STOCKWELL (*UN-CREDITED*)
BOOM MAN: ELMER HAGLUND (*UN-CREDITED*)
CAMERA OPERATOR: DICK RAWLINGS (SECOND CAMERAMAN)
CONSTRUCTION CHIEF: ARCHIE HALL (*UN-CREDITED*)
DIRECTOR OF PHOTOGRAPHY: ROBERT HOFFMAN (FIRST CAMERAMAN)
ELECTRICIANS: JIMMY FIELD, MIKE HUDSON, JAMES HUNTER AND HERMAN LIPNEY (ALL *UN-CREDITED*)
FILM COORDINATOR: DONALD TAIT
FILM EDITOR: JOHN B. WOELZ
GAFFER: AL RONSO (*UN-CREDITED*)
MAKE-UP ARTIST: UNKNOWN
PRODUCTION COORDINATOR: JOE WONDER
PRODUCTION SUPERVISOR: BARRY COHON
PROPERTY MASTER: MAX PITTMAN
RECORDER: LLOYD HANKS (*UN-CREDITED*)
SCIENTIFIC ADVISOR ON ELECTRONICS AND RADIATION: MAXWELL SMITH
SCRIPT SUPERVISOR: LARRY LUND
SET DECORATOR: CLARENCE STEENSON
SET DESIGNER: ROBERT KINOSHITA
SET LABOR: BILL BENTHAM (*UN-CREDITED*)
SOUND EDITOR: SIDNEY SUTHERLAND
SOUND MIXER: GARRY HARRIS
SPECIAL EFFECTS: HARRY REDMOND, JR.
STILL MAN: BILL CARY (JUNE 14 ONLY, *UN-CREDITED*)
WARDROBE: UNKNOWN

CAST: Tom Bernard (Alec Dawes, $80); Virginia Christine (Prof. Anna Adler, $150); Tris Coffin (Joe Castle Sr., $150); Peter Hanson (Asst. Prof. Norman Hughes, $350); Edward Kemmer (Joe Castle, $150); Jan Shepard (Marie Adler, $225); and Bill Welsh (the television announcer, $80)

Truman Bradley poses for the camera.

PLOT: Assistant Professor Norman Hughes battles with his superior, Professor Anna Adler, over his startling hypothesis: that genes and chromosomes carry memories from generation to generation. Through the Professor's daughter, Marie, Norman meets Joe Castle, a brilliant fencer whose family of extremely long pedigree has always shown a marked talent for fencing or dueling. Norman discovers in the Castle genealogy that a remote ancestor whose physical traits and personality characteristics bear a striking resemblance to the present Joe Castle. His excitement turns to horror when he realizes that the ancestor died at the age of 22, as the result of a fall from his favorite race horse, Esmeralda, and almost immediately thereafter learns that Joe Castle is going to race his foreign sports car which he has christened . . . Esmeralda. Marie persuades Joe not to race—and they learn that the car which is racing in Joe's position has had a terrible smash-up. Joe, who had scoffed bitterly at Norman's hypothesis, is a chastened man who decides to abandon his reckless pursuits in an effort to help Norman establish his theory on a sound scientific basis.

NOTES

- The scenes in the park were shot on location at Poinsettia Park (located at Romaine & Fuller Streets) and the exterior of the garage was filmed on the studio lot. Location filming commenced on the first half of the first day, June 14. The cast and crew then reported back to the studio for the remainder of filming.
- On June 14, approximately one hour of filming was lost due to overhead aircraft during exterior shooting. The sound was so loud that the voices of the actors were being drowned out. And take after take had to be shot until the sound of the airplanes was not caught on camera.
- The scenes of the exterior of the garage were filmed in the garage on the studio lot.
- Actor Bill Welsh, who played the role of the television announcer, returned to the studio two weeks after filming was completed, on June 29, to record the audio track for this episode.
- On the second day of filming, the interior of the laboratory was filmed on Stage 6, which also served as Truman Bradley's demonstration workshop.
- The sports car that Joe Castle drives in the beginning of this episode was rented for this production.
- The insert shot featuring a close-up of Prof. Adler's hand with the mouse being removed from the screened cage was un-credited stand-in Ann Howard's hand.
- The hands that hold the sketch of Ed Kemmer's face are not Peter Hanson's. The hands were un-credited stand-in Frank Hunt.

The August 22, 1956 issue of *Variety* reviewed this episode:

"Thelma Schnee's teleplay, another go-round at the Bridey Murphy cycle, is one of the better science fiction entries of the season. Attempting neither to affirm nor deny the reincarnation theory, Miss Schnee nonetheless presents her problem in an interesting, engrossing manner.

"Her story deals with a young scientist in genetics and his researching into a theory that memory genes are carried on through generations of a family. In this search he comes up with a young man who has all the characteristics of an ancestor who was killed on a certain date in a (horse) race, he talks his descendant out of entering a (car) race the same date, only 400 years later. Sure 'nuf, there's a bad crash and the descendant would have died in the crash, judging from the post position he had been assigned. It's all on the bizarre side, but well enacted and produced. Footage of the auto race accident is exciting.

"Peter Hanson, Ed Kemmer, Virginia Christine, Tris Coffin and Jan Shepard register in their roles, and Paul Guilfoyle provides good direction."

EPISODE #59 "MIRACLE OF DOCTOR DOVE"

PRODUCTION #1059 / 57B
DATES OF PRODUCTION: MAY 23, 24 AND JUNE 19, 1956
DIRECTED BY HERBERT L. STROCK

SCRIPT & STORY
FIRST DRAFT BY GEORGE ASNESS, MAY 9, 1956
REVISED PAGES DATED MAY 15 AND 24, 1956
FINAL DRAFT BY GEORGE ASNESS, MAY 24, 1956
TELEPLAY BY GEORGE ASNESS, FROM A 3-PAGE STORY BY GEORGE ASNESS AND A 2-PAGE STORY BY IVAN TORS

PRODUCTION CREDITS
1ST ASST. CAMERAMAN: JIM BELL (*UN-CREDITED*)
1ST CO. GRIP: CARL MIKSCH (*UN-CREDITED*)
2ND ASST. DIRECTOR: JAY SANDWICH (*UN-CREDITED*)
2ND CO. GRIP: MEL BLEDSOE (*UN-CREDITED*)
ASSISTANT DIRECTOR: ED STEIN
ASST. PROP MAN: EVERETT RICHARDSON (*UN-CREDITED*)
AUDIO SUPERVISOR: QUINN MARTIN
BEST BOY: CHARLES STOCKWELL (*UN-CREDITED*)
BOOM MAN: ELMER HAGLUND (*UN-CREDITED*)
CAMERA OPERATOR: DICK RAWLINGS
CONSTRUCTION CHIEF: ARCHIE HALL (*UN-CREDITED*)

DIRECTOR OF PHOTOGRAPHY: MONROE "MONK" ASKINS
ELECTRICIANS: CHARLES HANGER, MIKE HUDSON AND GLEN
  KNIGHT (ALL UN-CREDITED)
FILM COORDINATOR: DONALD TAIT
FILM EDITOR: JOHN B. WOELZ
GAFFER: AL RONSO (UN-CREDITED)
MAKE-UP ARTIST: GEORGE GRAY (UN-CREDITED)
PRODUCTION COORDINATOR: JOE WONDER
PRODUCTION SUPERVISOR: BARRY COHON
PROPERTY MASTER: YGNACIO SEPULVEDA
RECORDER: LLOYD HANKS (UN-CREDITED)
SCIENTIFIC ADVISOR ON ELECTRONICS AND RADIATION:
  MAXWELL SMITH
SCRIPT SUPERVISOR: LARRY LUND
SET DECORATOR: BRUCE MACDONALD
SET DESIGNER: ROBERT KINOSHITA
SET LABOR: BILL BENTHAM (UN-CREDITED)
SOUND EDITOR: LAWRENCE KAUFMAN
SOUND MIXER: GARRY HARRIS
SPECIAL EFFECTS: HARRY REDMOND, JR.
STILL MAN: JOE WALTERS (MAY 23 ONLY, UN-CREDITED)
WARDROBE: ALFRED BERKE

CAST: Cyril Delevanti (Dr. Kenneth White, $150); Kay Faylen (Alice Kinder, $200); Gene Lockhart (Dr. Elward Dove, $2,000); Virginia Pohlman (Nora Lester, $80); Rhodes Reason (Sean Daly, $200); Robin Short (Jeff Spencer, $100); Gretchen Thomas (Hanna Macy, $80); and Charles Wagenheim (Ed Gorman, $100)

PLOT: Three elderly scientists have disappeared. Jeff Spencer of the Office of Scientific Security learns that another researcher, old Dr. White, sold his house, has withdrawn his money from the bank and is leaving on a trip; and like the others, he is a patient of Dr. Elward Dove. Dove plans to send White out of the country on a false passport, thanks to the work of forger Ed Gorman, who supposedly died in prison 18 years before. Spencer tracks down the mysterious doctor and, faced with arrest, Dove reveals to Spencer that he has discovered the "clock" present in all living organisms,

Truman Bradley poses for the camera in between takes.

which controls body cell regeneration. He has developed a serum which adds many years to man's life. But an ever-increasing population without equally increasing food supply might bring disaster so the three scientists kept alive by the serum are working secretly to solve the Earth's food problem so Dove's miracle serum can be introduced to the world. Gorman, whom Dove had brought back to life with his serum, overhears this and thinking he can make a fortune peddling the serum, tries to steal it; he is killed accidentally. Dove helps Dr. White escape and join the other scientists, but is himself arrested. Deprived of the serum, he ages and dies overnight in his cell. But his secret lives in the minds of the four vanished scientists. Some day man will have the gift of long life.

NOTES

- Un-credited stand-ins were Jack Jackson, Ellen Kilsten and Kenneth MacLeod.
- There was an automatic arbitration regarding story credit for this episode, since Ivan Tors, whose name was on the story, was a producer. The three-page story outline by George Asness was dated March 16, 1956. Ivan Tors' outline was dated April 2. On April 3, Asness was then commissioned to write the teleplay, dated May 10, 1956.
- Location shots were filmed on the morning of the first day at the corner of Romaine and Fuller Streets for approximately 45 minutes. The cast and crew then returned to the studio to film the remainder of the episode on Stage 5.
- Produced under the title of "The Clock."
- Weeks after principal filming was completed, it was decided to film a revised scene to improve the story. On June 19, 1956, pickup shots with Robin Short and Rhodes Reason were filmed from 4 to 7:07 p.m.. This is the scene set in the interior of the Office of Scientific Security. Herbert Strock directed the sequence on Stage 5. Assistant Director Erich von Stroheim Jr. and Second Assistant Director Bruce Satterlee were involved with the pickup shots, but were not credited on screen for their participation.
- The opening stock shot is the same opening stock shot used for "Sun Gold."
- The beagle Gene Lockhart holds in this episode is the very same dog Truman Bradley featured in the lab demonstration scene of "The Green Bomb."

The August 29, 1956 issue of *Variety* reviewed this episode:

"Skimpy production budgets are the real heavies in Ivan Tors' scientifiction series. Typical is 'Dove,' an interesting enough story but unspooled in static, talky fashion obviously to conserve on sets and shooting time. The viewer is told about the most bizarre happenings, not shown them. Consequently, the entire stanza lacks punch in a presentation that might be okay for radio.

"George Asness' teleplay concerns a scientist who apparently has discovered a secret serum to prolong man's life. In fact, the scientist involved is almost 100, but doesn't look a day over Gene Lockhart. The government's scientist security spies get into the act, and the scientist is tossed in the clink, where he suddenly becomes a feeble old man and dies. They jailed him because he was using the help of a criminal executed 18 years previous, but just howcum this guy is still around isn't explained in the talkathon.

"Gene Lockhart, Cyril Delevanti, Robin Short, Charles Wagenheim and Kay Faylen plod through their routinish roles without distinction, hampered as they are by the construction, which also hampered Herbert L. Strock's direction."

"THE CLOCK"
Date: March 16, 1956
by George Asness

Old General Barker, who has just begun to inquire after the health of a V.I.P. engaged in important international negotiations, is walking home. He accosts Dr. Frederick Ballard and addresses him as Dr. Paul Copeland, whom he had known thirty years ago. He says the doctor hasn't changed a bit. Dr. Ballard disclaims being Copeland, and points out that Copeland would now be an old man like the general himself, instead of in his early forties, as Ballard. The general remembers that Copeland had disappeared mysteriously. He apologizes and goes home.

The F.B.I. contacts the general and asks him about his meeting with Dr. Ballard. He tells them what had happened.

At his home, Ballard and his beautiful wife, to whom he is deeply devoted, are reading the newspaper. The headlines tell of the death of Osgood Keller in a distant state. Keller had died in an explosion in his laboratory in an obscure village. Ballard, who was supposed to have gone to a movie with his wife, claims a headache and asks her to go alone. When she leaves, he starts packing a bag.

The F.B.I. finds that Keller's prints match those of Dr. Davis, who had disappeared 22 years ago. Strangely, though, the dead Keller does not look any older than Dr. Davis when he disappeared. The F.B.I. also finds Ballard's fingerprints in the explosion-torn laboratory.

They decide to question Ballard. They go to his house and find that his wife had just called the Missing Persons Bureau—Ballard had disappeared. Knowing how devoted Ballard was to his wife, the

F.B.I. arrest her and let it be known that she is being held for his murder. The ruse works and Ballard gives himself up to prove that his wife was innocent. He is charged with complicity in the disappearance and death of Dr. Davis, alias Keller, and with being involved in the disappearance of several other well known scientists within the last 25 years.

Ballard claims that he is about 160 years old; that he had discovered the mysterious clock within every living organism which regulates its growth and decline from birth to death, and has learned to both slow and speed up this clock. In his laboratory, he injects a newly born rabbit with a serum, and the rabbit goes from babyhood to full growth and then dies of old age, within the space of one hour. Dr. Ballard then claims that he is disappointed in man; that with longer life and an ever-increasing birth rate, human life would still come cheaper. He himself has had to disappear periodically, and reappear under a different name lest people become suspicious of his seeing agelessness; and that Dr. Keller actually was Dr. Davis—that he and Ballard had been working on further research and that Davis had disappeared for the same reason, and had reappeared at that laboratory, where he had continued to work in research along the same lines. Dr. Ballard occasionally visited him for conferences. He states that he is deeply disappointed in the way man has applied his newfound knowledge to destroy his fellowman, and is unfortunately not quite ready for long life. He has greatly unhappy and lonely, as one after another, he saw his friends and family grow old and die. He had never permitted himself any close ties for that reason; but in spite of everything, he had fallen deeply in love with the woman to whom he was now married, and was determined not to treat himself any further—but to grow old with her in the normal way.

Ballard begs them not to reveal any of this to his wife, but the Government officials to whom the F.B.I. pass on their information, agree to this only on condition that he will share his secret with the world. Very reluctantly he promises to do so, but, when the government scientists with whom he is supposed to work arrive at his laboratory, they find that this time both he and his wife have disappeared. A search proves fruitless. Then Dr. Quenton Green, an eminent Washington surgeon, reveals that Dr. Ballard is a patient in his private clinic; that he had made a bargain with him, whereby in return for prolonging the life of the V.I.P. who was greatly needed by our people at the moment to carry on those delicate international negotiations, he had performed an operation on Dr. Ballard which had completely wiped out his memory. He hands over a letter written by Dr. Ballard, in which he claims that he had put himself and his scientific knowledge of the mysterious clock beyond anyone's reach, but that he had attained that knowledge and so others who follow would doubtless again attain it some day, when man more ready for the gift of longevity; that he and his wife would live out their normal days as normal human beings.

"THE CLOCK"
Dated: April 2, 1956
by Ivan Tors

There is a meeting in the offices of Scientific Security. The mysterious disappearances of three scientists are discussed. Professor McCardell, age 67, Professor DuVal, age 62, and Professor Johnson, age 66, all disappeared within the past five years. There is no explanation for their disappearances. It is suggested by somebody, that it may have been political but that doesn't make much sense inasmuch as McCardell was a marine biologist, DuVal a meteorologist and Johnson an agriculturist, and their work was never connected with defense. The Pattern was always the same. They sold their homes and belongings, withdrew their bank account and suddenly and inexplicably, disappeared. There is only one clue that the investigation has to go on. All these men were the patients of Dr. Vincent Dove, a well-known physician and expert on glandular functions.

Spencer, the chief investigator for the office, suspects that Dr. Dove organized their disappearance and that he may be a foreign agent who recruited these scientists for work in a totalitarian country. He plants an attractive young woman undercover agent, Alice Kinder, in Dr. Dove's office, where she takes a job as a receptionist. When Miss Kinder checks in at Dr. Dove's office, she meets with many surprises. According to the diploma on the wall, Dr. Dove must be at least 75 years old, though he is vigorous and has great strength. Then she finds the pedigree of Dr. Dove's favorite dachshund, and according to that, the animal is 34 years old, impossibly long for a dog. She plants a tape machine in the Doctor's inner-office and

Spencer poses as her fiancé. He picks her up after hours and finds opportunities to meet the doctor.

Soon there are two mysterious visitors in the office, one being Professor White, a nutritional expert nearly 70 years old. The tape recorder proves that Dr. Dove and Dr. White came to an agreement that Dr. Dove would secure a passport under a fictitious name for Dr. White and that Dr. White would leave the country after selling all his belongings and liquidating his bank account. Then another old man appears at the office. His name is Gorman and Spencer, upon investigation, finds that this Gorman was a famous counterfeiter thirty years ago and that he spent most of his early life in Federal prisons. The tape recording reveals that Gorman is reluctant to forge another passport but Dr. Dove tells him he is not going to give him any more medicine unless he complies with his request.

Dr. White is packing in his apartment when Dr. Dove appears with a forged passport and hands it to Dr. White. At this time, Spencer and Alice Kinder appear and arrest the two aged men. Spencer demands to know the purpose of shipping Dr. White out of the country and the reason for a successful doctor purchasing a forged passport from a criminal. He cannot conceive of anything else but subversive activity. Dr. Dove breaks down and tells the truth.

About 10 years ago, Dr. Dove arrived at a great medical discovery. The human body is composed of cells and, in a young body, the cells divide and multiply at regular intervals. When the multiplying process slows down, the body begins to age. When it stops, the body dies. There is a built-in clock in the human cell tissue that regulates this procedure. Dr. Dove found a chemical that could delay the stopping of the cell divisions, thus giving another fifty years to anybody's life. But he couldn't turn it over to the world because, if this discovery would have been announced, every human being would have asked for the serum, thus over-populating the world, causing great famines and maybe wars for the possession of this elixir. He decided that he would give it only to a few scientists whose work would make it possible for the Earth to support a much larger population. The work Professor McCardell was to find a way to harvest the ocean; Dr. DuVal was working on an experiment that eventually would make the climate in arid countries beneficial to agriculture and Dr. Johnson was working on a method by which the radio-active isotope treatment of the soil could increase the fertility 8 to 10 times. Dr. White had developed nutritional value. The three missing professors, with false passports and under assumed names were working somewhere in Switzerland with the understanding that, as soon as they solved the problems of feeding the population of the world, they would turn their findings over to the United Nations.

Spencer is staggered by this revelation, but he has no choice. Dr. Dove broke the law when he forged the passports. But Dr. Dove tells him that he is living on borrowed time anyhow and in the minute when he doesn't administer the serum to himself, he will die. If the secret is made known to the world, panic will follow, as everybody will want the serum. They are not ready yet for mass production. It is better that everything be forgotten.

The next morning, they find him dead in his cell. And the whereabouts of the other scientists are still unknown to us. We can only hope that one day the results of their work will be made available to the whole world.

EPISODE #60 "ONE THOUSAND EYES"

PRODUCTION #1060 / 62B

DATES OF PRODUCTION: JUNE 20 AND 21, 1956
DIRECTED BY PAUL GUILFOYLE

SCRIPT & STORY

FIRST DRAFT BY STUART JEROME, JUNE 11, 1956
REVISED PAGES DATED JUNE 15, 18 AND 22, 1956
FINAL DRAFT BY STUART JEROME, JUNE 22, 1956
TELEPLAY BY STUART JEROME

PRODUCTION CREDITS

1ST ASST. CAMERAMAN: ED NUGENT (*UN-CREDITED*)
1ST CO. GRIP: MEL BLEDSOE (*UN-CREDITED*)
2ND ASST. DIRECTOR: BRUCE SATTERLEE (*UN-CREDITED*)
2ND CAMERAMAN: HOWARD SCHWARTZ (*UN-CREDITED*)
2ND CO. GRIP: TOMMY MATHEWS (*UN-CREDITED*)

3rd Grip: Eddie Manrique (*un-credited*)
Assistant Director: Bert Chervin
Asst. Prop Man: Everett Richardson (*un-credited*)
Audio Supervisor: Quinn Martin
Best Boy: Charles Stockwell (*un-credited*)
Boom Man: Bill Flannery (*un-credited*)
Construction Chief: Archie Hall (*un-credited*)
Director of Photography: Robert Hoffman
Electricians: Fred Hounshell, James Hunter and Herman Lipney (*all un-credited*)
Film Coordinator: Donald Tait
Film Editor: Duncan Mansfield, A.C.E.
Gaffer: Al Ronso (*un-credited*)
Make-up Artist: George Gray (*un-credited*)
Production Coordinator: Joe Wonder
Production Supervisor: Barry Cohon
Property Master: Max Pittman
Recorder: Charles King (*un-credited*)
Script Supervisor: Jeanne Lippman
Set Decorator: Clarence Steenson
Set Designer: Robert Kinoshita
Set Labor: Ted McCaskey (*un-credited*)
Sound Editor: Sidney Sutherland
Sound Mixer: Jay Ashworth
Special Effects: Harry Redmond, Jr.
Still Man: Joe Walters (June 20 only, *un-credited*)
Wardrobe: Alfred Berke (*un-credited*)

CAST: Jean Byron (Ada March, $400); Tom Dillon (the mail file clerk, $80); David Hughes (Dr. Robert March, $200); Vincent Price (Gary Williams, $2,000); and Bruce Wendell (Lt. Jules Moss, $90)

PLOT: Police Crime Lab expert Gary Williams believes that one day all crimes will be solved within the laboratory. One afternoon, Gary receives a surprise visit from his ex-fiancée, Ada March, who ten years ago jilted him to marry wealthy scientist Robert March. Now Ada reveals that her husband's life has been threatened by an

Vincent Price and Jean Byron pose for publicity photos with director Paul Guilfoyle in "One Thousand Eyes."

Vincent Price holds the image of a ghost in his hand, unaware that it is the solution to a murder mystery.

unknown person who wants to get possession of an important new invention March is working on. Gary agrees to see about the installation of special police equipment in March's lab, including a burglar alarm. But that night Ada and Gary find Dr. March dead. He has been murdered, shot in the back. Evidence points to the killer being March's lab assistant, who was himself killed in an auto accident immediately afterwards. The police feel the case is closed, but Gary suspects otherwise. By discovering what Dr. March's secret invention was (a camera that can take pictures in the dark), he uncovers the real murderer, Ada, and at the same time adds a great contribution to the prevention of crime.

NOTES
- Beginning with this episode of the series, ZIV-TV ceased crediting Maxwell Smith (or anyone for that matter) as "Scientific Advisor" during the closing credits.
- Four stand-ins and five extras were hired for non-speaking roles consisting of one photographer, two members of the press, two medical staff, two detectives and two police officers.
- The first draft of the teleplay was titled "Invention of Dr. March."

EPISODE #61 "BRAIN UNLIMITED"

PRODUCTION #1061 / 608
DATES OF PRODUCTION: JUNE 18 AND 19, 1956
DIRECTED BY TOM GRIES

SCRIPT & STORY
FIRST DRAFT BY SLOAN NIBLEY, CIRCA MAY 29, 1956
FINAL DRAFT BY SLOAN NIBLEY, JUNE 19, 1956
TELEPLAY BY SLOAN NIBLEY, BASED ON ORIGINAL STORIES BY SLOAN NIBLEY AND IVAN TORS

PRODUCTION CREDITS
1ST ASST. CAMERAMAN: ED NUGENT (*UN-CREDITED*)
1ST. CO. GRIP: MEL BLEDSOE (*UN-CREDITED*)

2ND ASST. DIRECTOR: BRUCE SATTERLEE (*UN-CREDITED*)
2ND CAMERAMAN: HOWARD SCHWARTZ (*UN-CREDITED*)
2ND CO. GRIP: TOMMY MATHEWS (*UN-CREDITED*)
ASSISTANT DIRECTOR: ERICH VON STROHEIM, JR.
ASST. PROP MAN: VIC PETROTTA (*UN-CREDITED*)
AUDIO SUPERVISOR: QUINN MARTIN
BEST BOY: CHARLES STOCKWELL (*UN-CREDITED*)
BOOM MAN: BILL FLANNERY (*UN-CREDITED*)
CABLEMAN: DICK SMITH (*UN-CREDITED*)
CONSTRUCTION CHIEF: ARCHIE HALL (*UN-CREDITED*)
DIRECTOR OF PHOTOGRAPHY: ROBERT HOFFMAN
ELECTRICIANS: FRED HOUNSHELL, JAMES HUNTER AND HERMAN LIPNEY (*ALL UN-CREDITED*)
FILM COORDINATOR: DONALD TAIT
FILM EDITOR: JOHN B. WOELZ
GAFFER: AL RONSO (*UN-CREDITED*)
MAKE-UP ARTIST: GEORGE GRAY (*UN-CREDITED*)
PRODUCTION COORDINATOR: JOE WONDER
PRODUCTION SUPERVISOR: BARRY COHON
PROPERTY MASTER: MAX PITTMAN
RECORDER: GEORGE ANDERSON (*UN-CREDITED*)
SCRIPT SUPERVISOR: JEANNE LIPPMAN
SET DECORATOR: CLARENCE STEENSON
SET DESIGNER: ROBERT KINOSHITA
SET DRESSER: CLARENCE STEENSON
SET LABOR: TED MCCASKEY (*UN-CREDITED*)
SOUND EDITOR: MONROE MARTIN
SOUND MIXER: JAY ASHWORTH
SPECIAL EFFECTS: HARRY REDMOND, JR.
STILL MAN: JOE WALTERS (JUNE 19 ONLY, *UN-CREDITED*)
WARDROBE: ALFRED BERKE

CAST: George Becwar (the doctor, $80); Diana Douglas (Elaine Conover, $150); Arthur Franz (Dr. Jeff Conover, $750); Thomas B. Henry (Dr. McKenzie, $100); Burt Mustin (Mr. Stevenson, $100); Melinda Plowman (Alice, $100); Bob Wehling (Henry Mason, the patient, $80); and Doug Wilson (Ralph Marken, $200)

Arthur Franz and Diana Douglas in "Brain Unlimited."

PLOT: Dr. Jeff Conover, a young scientist, bails out of a plane in an attempt to prove the usefulness on an untried "anti-blackout" serum. Something goes wrong and the trial is not a success, but, in the few seconds before blacking out, Conover relives in complete detail, several months of his life. He becomes fascinated with the idea that something, either electrical or chemical, can release the brakes on the human mind, making it many thousand times more powerful, and, in spite of violent objections from his boss, Dr. McKenzie, and his wife, Elaine, deserts his job to devote that time. His scientific enquiries into the tremendous acceleration of the brain, he tells them, are much more important than the anti-blackout serum. Working with fanatical dedication and assisted by Ralph Marken, his regular assistant, he collects case histories similar to his own, then experiments with chemicals—first on animals, then on himself. The results are not satisfactory until electro-shock is added and, in the final experiment, demonstrates the soundness of his theory by solving the anti-blackout problems in a matter of moments . . . at the cost of a severe convulsion and a cracked vertebra.

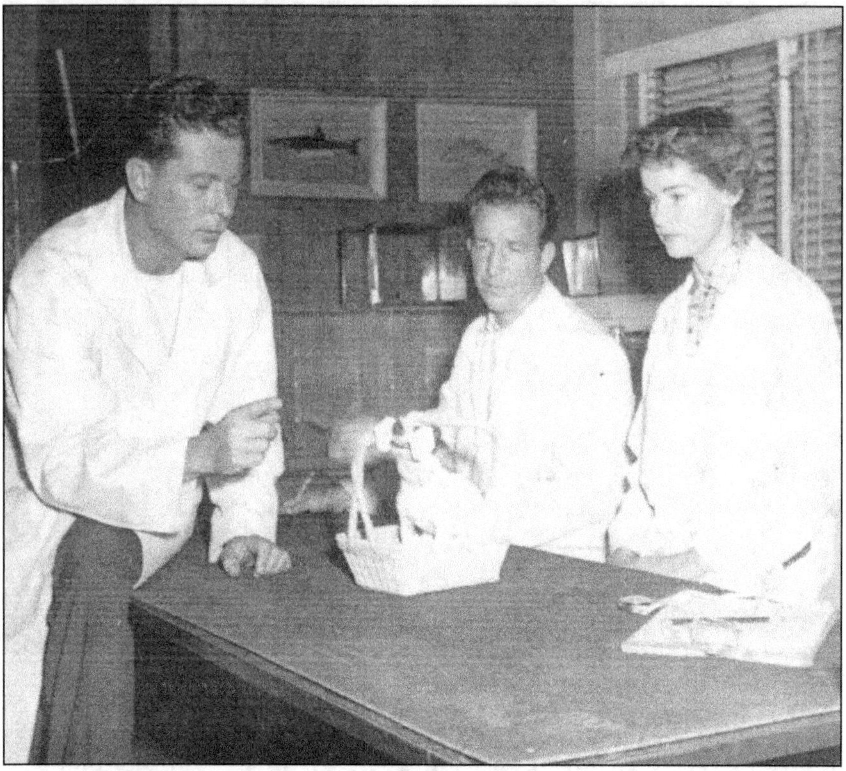

Arthur Franz and Diana Douglas in "Brain Unlimited."

Even the dog takes time out to nurse her babies.

NOTES

- Actor Bob Wehling was not only a character actor for a dozen television programs including Ziv's *Harbor Command*, but spent much of his time as a script writer. His contributions included *Cheyenne, Bronco, The Richard Boone Show* and seven episodes of Walt Disney's *Zorro*.
- The entire episode was filmed on Stage 5.
- This episode was produced under the title of "The Last Second."
- The character of Mr. Stevenson was originally Mr. Sorenson in the first draft of the script.

"THE LAST SECOND"
DATED: APRIL 2, 1956
BY IVAN TORS

A medical scientist takes part in an aviation medicine experiment. He has to bail out using a special parachute. He knows that the parachute will open one second after the jump. He jumps and within the second he can see his whole life, from boyhood to maturity, and everything that ever happened to him, flash through his mind.

After the jump, he analyzes this phenomenon that so many people have talked about. Under stress, the activity of the human brain can multiply a million times. Is it possible to find a drug that can bring on this tremendous capacity of the brain? He finds a key to the unlocked compartment of the human mind. Under shock, with a new medicine, the brain can retain everything it sees, hears or experiences. While under the effect of the drug, our scientist reads a book in a foreign language and his mind retains every word.

He demonstrates miraculous mental feats to other scientists and it looks like his discovery will be the greatest boon to education. But one day he loses his memory completely and experiments have to come to a stop until science can find out how this drug can be applied safely.

"THE LAST SECOND"

by Sloan Nibley

Dr. Jeff Conover, a young scientist, is working on a revolutionary approach to air and space travel for one of America's largest companies. Problem: Instead of overcoming the forces of gravity with more force, discover what it is by searching the unified field theory of electromagnetism for a formula that will give us an 'anti-gravity' solution.

His wife, Elaine, herself a biologist, is interested in his work but her fears are justified when he is forced to bail out of a rocket ship at a tremendous height. However, he lands unharmed and with additional valuable information.

He is now deeply impressed with a phenomena that happened to him during the first few seconds of the jump; in his mind he relived, clearly, several years of his childhood, remembering in detail incidents long forgotten. He analyzes this phenomenon that many people have talked about and experienced and a fascinating idea occurs to him. Is it possible that through a drug or some other external stimulus, the human brain can be accelerated a million fold?

Obsessed with the thought of such possibilities, Dr. Conover neglects his actual work for the company to explore what he considers a much greater possibility for the human race. Elaine is particularly useful to him with her knowledge of biology and he is soon in the midst of experimenting on white mice and their speed of learning, influenced by strychnine and other drugs.

Sure that the solution to his problem lies in the discovery and isolation of some kind of super-adrenalin, manufactured by the ductless gland during supreme stress or fright, he and his wife subject themselves to various experiments, running all possible biological tests in their quest for the elusive body chemical.

Examining every possibility avenue, Dr. Conover interviews and runs tests on mathematical freaks, memory wizards, psychologists who are experimenting in time perception under hypnotics, memory under hypnotics, sodium amytal interviews with psychotic, time element in dreams, teaching during sleep via the sub-conscious, time distortion induced by drugs, unconscious thinking, motivation in learning, time perception and all other facets relating to the subject. He feels that he is making progress.

Dr. Janoff, his boss, is becoming annoyed at what he considers Jeff's dereliction to duty and, in an interview with Elaine, expresses fears that this obsession is not only hurting the company but doing Jeff no good. She admits that he sleeps only an hour or two a night, has lost weight and is at a state bordering on exhaustion and promises Janoff that she'll try and straighten him out.

In attempting to persuade her husband to drop his experimenting for a while, get back to the company project and catch up on some sleep, Elaine only succeeds in making Jeff highly annoyed with her and forcing him into greater activity. So *she* has left him now! He'll show them all how wrong they have been!

Jeff's countless experiments and indefatigable investigations are beginning to pay off . . . he has finally isolated the drug that will allow the brain to race like a wild motor, disengaged from the body. The moment is at hand and he subjects himself to its influences and effects. In a few blinding moments of brilliant clarity his mind is able to deduce from the thousands of scientific facts stored in its vast recesses, the final equation needed in the anti-gravity experiment.

It is an hour or so before Jeff is recovered partially from his experience and is able to discuss it with Elaine and Dr. Janoff. They are, of course, more than elated at the discovery of the equation and the fact that Jeff has demonstrated something that will sure prove of even more value. However, something has happened to Jeff. As is the case of human beings being subjected to metrazol, insulin and electro shock, all memory of recent things and events has been blacked out. His shock having been much deeper, the memory of events since his parachute jump is completely gone, and with it much of the information relative to his experiment, as he worked too fast to record everything. However it is now established that there *is* a key to the human mind and somehow it will again be found.

EPISODE #62 "DEATH AT MY FINGERTIPS"

PRODUCTION #1062 / 638
DATES OF PRODUCTION: JUNE 29, JULY 2 AND 3, 1956
DIRECTED BY TOM GRIES

SCRIPT & STORY
FIRST DRAFT BY JOEL MALCOLM RAPP, CIRCA JUNE 22, 1956
FINAL DRAFT BY JOEL MALCOLM RAPP, JUNE 27, 1956
TELEPLAY BY JOEL MALCOLM RAPP

PRODUCTION CREDITS
1ST ASST. CAMERAMAN: ED NUGENT (*UN-CREDITED*)
1ST CO. GRIP: MEL BLEDSOE (*UN-CREDITED*)
2ND ASST. DIRECTOR: BRUCE SATTERLEE (*UN-CREDITED*)
2ND CAMERAMAN: CHARLES WHEELER (*UN-CREDITED*)
2ND CO. GRIP: TOMMY MATHEWS (*UN-CREDITED*)
ASSISTANT DIRECTOR: ERICH VON STROHEIM, JR.
ASST. PROP MAN: BOB BENTON, SR. (*UN-CREDITED*)
AUDIO SUPERVISOR: QUINN MARTIN
BEST BOY: CHARLES STOCKWELL (*UN-CREDITED*)
BOOM MAN: BILL FLANNERY (*UN-CREDITED*)
CONSTRUCTION CHIEF: ARCHIE HALL (*UN-CREDITED*)
DIRECTOR OF PHOTOGRAPHY: MONROE "MONK" ASKINS
ELECTRICIANS: FRED HOUNSHELL, KEN HUNTER AND HERMAN LIPNEY (*ALL UN-CREDITED*)
FILM COORDINATOR: DONALD TAIT
FILM EDITOR: JOHN B. WOELZ
GAFFER: AL RONSO (*UN-CREDITED*)
MAKE-UP ARTIST: GEORGE GRAY (*UN-CREDITED*)
PRODUCTION COORDINATOR: JOE WONDER
PRODUCTION SUPERVISOR: BARRY COHON
PROPERTY MASTER: MAX PITTMAN
RECORDER: JOE KEENER (*UN-CREDITED*)
SCRIPT SUPERVISOR: JEANNE LIPPMAN
SET DECORATOR: CLARENCE STEENSON
SET DESIGNER: ROBERT KINOSHITA
SET LABOR: TED MCCASKEY (*UN-CREDITED*)

SOUND EDITOR: CHARLES OVERHULSER
SOUND MIXER: JAY ASHWORTH
SPECIAL SCIENTIFIC EFFECTS: HARRY REDMOND, JR.
STILL MAN: JOE WALTERS (*UN-CREDITED*)
WARDROBE: ALFRED BERKE AND FRANK CARDINALI (*UN-CREDITED*)

CAST: David Alpert (George Warren, $100); Lonie Blackman (Judith Rogers, $80); Dick Foran (Dr. Donald Stewart, $600); Michael Granger (Larry Evans, $100); June Lockhart (Eve Patrick, $1,250); Charles Postal (Dr. Leonard Mills, $80); John Stephenson (Inspector Mark Davis, $300); and William Vaughan (Stanley Barnes, $80)*

PLOT: Dr. Leonard Mills, Dean of Barker Medical College, is stabbed to death and a fingerprint check of the murder weapon reveals the killer to be Dr. Donald Stewart, a respectable faculty member at Barker. Although six perfect fingerprints are found, Stewart denies the murder and even passes a lie-detector test. Inspector Mark Davis is baffled further when the fingerprint department reveals that *more* of Dr. Stewart's prints have been found but they were definitely left by sometime after Dr. Stewart was taken into custody. Inspector Davis is distraught to think that there might be two people with identical fingerprints. The entire system of identification through fingerprints will become worthless and obsolete if this contingency is true. Davis' fears are alleviated, however, and the mystery is solved when Eve Patrick, Stewart's fiancée and Mills' lab assistant, discovers that Dr. Mills had perfected a synthetic skin which had enabled Stanley Barnes, a revenge-bent neurotic young man, to force Dr. Stewart's fingerprints and frame him by leaving the prints on the scalpel he drove into Dr. Mills' back. The boy's error was in not knowing that the synthetic skin was permanent. Dr. Stewart and Eve express their delight in the discovery of the skin, realizing its great potential value as an aid in plastic surgery and treatment of skin disease.

---

* William Vaughn appeared on *Science Fiction Theatre* three times but his name was mis-spelled Vaughan in the closing credits for this episode.

Truman Bradley in a lab demonstration.

NOTES
- The character of Stanley Barnes was originally Stanley Roberts in the first draft of the script. The character of Al Jonas was originally Harry Jonas in the first draft.
- The episode was filmed entirely on Stage 2.
- The first draft of this teleplay, dated June 22, 1956, was titled "Second Skin."

EPISODE #63 "SOUND THAT KILLS"

PRODUCTION #1063 / 69
DATES OF PRODUCTION: JULY 11 AND 12, 1956
DIRECTED BY HERBERT L. STROCK

SCRIPT & STORY
FIRST DRAFT BY MEYER DOLINSKY, DATE UNKNOWN
REVISED PAGES DATED JULY 10, 1956
FINAL DRAFT BY MEYER DOLINKSY, JULY 11, 1956
TELEPLAY BY MEYER DOLINKSY

PRODUCTION CREDITS
DIRECTOR OF PHOTOGRAPHY: CURT FETTERS
1ST ASST. CAMERAMAN: ED NUGENT (UN-CREDITED)
1ST CO. GRIP: CARL MIKSCH (UN-CREDITED)
2ND ASST. DIRECTOR: BRUCE SATTERLEE (UN-CREDITED)
2ND CAMERAMAN: JOHN WEILER (UN-CREDITED)
2ND CO. GRIP: JACK CHAMBERS (UN-CREDITED)
ASSISTANT DIRECTOR: ERICH VON STROHEIM, JR.
ASST PROP MAN: STAN WALTERS (UN-CREDITED)
AUDIO SUPERVISOR: QUINN MARTIN
BEST BOY: CHARLES STOCKWELL (UN-CREDITED)
BOOM MAN: BILL FLANNERY (UN-CREDITED)
CONSTRUCTION CHIEF: ARCHIE HALL (UN-CREDITED)
ELECTRICIANS: FRED HOUNSHELL, HAROLD KRAUS AND HERMAN LIPNEY (ALL UN-CREDITED)
FILM COORDINATOR: DONALD TAIT
FILM EDITOR: THOMAS SCOTT (CREDITED) AND JOHN B. WOELZ (UN-CREDITED)
GAFFER: AL RONSO (UN-CREDITED)
MAKE-UP ARTIST: GEORGE GRAY
PRODUCTION COORDINATOR: JOE WONDER
PRODUCTION SUPERVISOR: BARRY COHON
PROPERTY MASTER: MAX PITTMAN
RECORDER: JOHN BURY (UN-CREDITED)
SCRIPT SUPERVISOR: JEANNE LIPPMAN
SET DECORATOR: BRUCE MACDONALD

Set Designer: Robert Kinoshita
Set Labor: Bill Bentham (UN-CREDITED)
Sound Editor: Gus Galvin
Sound Mixer: Jay Ashworth
Special Effects: Harry Redmond, Jr.
Wardrobe: Alfred Berke (CREDITED) AND Frank Cardinali (UN-CREDITED)

CAST: Cynthia Baer (the girl desk clerk, $80); Ray Collins (Dr. Paul Sinclair, $300); David Dwight (the waiter, $80); Paul Hahn (Johnson, the security officer, $80); Jean G. Harvey (the maid, $80); Larry Hudson (Peters, the security officer, $80); Ludwig Stossel (Dr. Wissman, $400); and Charles Victor (Ed Martin, $250)

PLOT: Dr. Richard Wissman, a world-renowned atomic physicist who has been denied top-secret clearance because he was once forced to work in a labor camp and because of some unfortunate family connections, is anxious to prove his loyalty so he can work in atomic research. He visits an old friend of his, Dr. Paul Sinclair, who is in the city presiding over a convention of top government physicists. Dr. Wissman wants to show his old friend a new device he has developed that is able to photograph breaks and cracks in pipelines while they are still underground. During Dr. Wissman's visit at the Fairmount Hotel, where the convention is taking place, Dr. Swanson, head of research for guidance systems of atomic missiles, is found murdered in his hotel suite. Dr. Wissman is able to show Dr. Sinclair and the Chief Security Officer, Ed Martin, that the murder was committed through an ultrasonic sound oscillator. His knowledge of the crime and the fact that he is a poor security risk brings Dr. Wissman under the scrutiny of the very suspicious Security Chief. However, Dr. Wissman is allowed to bring his special camera into play to capture the actual foreign agent operating at the convention. Both Dr. Sinclair and Security Chief, Ed Martin, now assure Richard Wissman that he will receive his top-secret clearance.

NOTES
- The first draft of the script did not feature the maid or the

drugstore clerk. Instead, the characters were Dr. Frederick Coleman and Dr. Swanson. The scene was replaced with a different scene instead.
- This episode was produced under the title of "Camera X1," also the title of the teleplay during filming.
- The developed film footage shown towards the end of the drama was accomplished by means of a negative-reversal effect.
- The desk in the hotel lobby in the opening scene is the same desk Truman Bradley sits behind during the lab demonstrations in the opening of the first season episodes.
- Actress Dolores Michaels played the role of the drugstore clerk for a scene that was filmed, but never made it to the final cut.

EPISODE #64 "SURVIVAL IN BOX CANYON"

PRODUCTION #1064 / 61B

Dates of Production: June 28 and 29, 1956
Directed by Herbert L. Strock

SCRIPT & STORY

First Draft by Lou Huston, circa May 15, 1956
Final Draft by Lou Huston, June 24, 1956
Teleplay by Lou Huston, based on the short story "The Incredible Dr. Tovac" by Ivan Tors

PRODUCTION CREDITS

1st Asst. Cameraman: Ed Nugent (*un-credited*)
1st. Co. Grip: Mel Bledsoe (*un-credited*)
2nd Asst. Director: Bruce Saterlee (*un-credited*)
2nd Cameraman: Charles Wheeler (*un-credited*)
2nd Co. Grip: Tommy Mathews (*un-credited*)
Assistant Director: Bert Chervin
Asst Prop Man: Bob Benton, Sr. (*un-credited*)
Audio Supervisor: Quinn Martin

Best Boy: Charles Stockwell (*un-credited*)
Boom Man: Bill Flannery (*un-credited*)
Construction Chief: Archie Hall (*un-credited*)
Director of Photography: Monroe "Monk" Askins
Drivers: J. Brown and T. Garber (*both un-credited*)
Electricians: Fred Hounshell, Ken Hunter and Herman Lipney (*all un-credited*)
Film Coordinator: Donald Tait
Film Editor: John B. Woelz
Gaffer: Al Ronso (*un-credited*)
Make-up Artist: George Gray (*un-credited*)
Production Coordinator: Joe Wonder
Production Supervisor: Barry Cohon
Property Master: Max Pittman
Recorder: Joe Keener (*un-credited*)
Script Supervisor: Jeanne Lippman
Set Decorator: Clarence Steenson
Set Designer: Robert Kinoshita
Set Labor: Ted McCaskey (*un-credited*)
Sound Editor: Sidney Sutherland
Sound Mixer: Jay Ashworth
Special Effects: Harry Redmond, Jr.
Still Man: Joe Walters (June 28 only, *un-credited*)
Wardrobe: Frank Cardinali

CAST: Bruce Bennett (Dr. Sorenson, $1,000); Paul Birch (Raymond Michaels, $150); Susan Cummings (Ellen Barton, $125); Dale Hutchinson (Ed Clayborn, $80); DeForest Kelley (Dr. Milo Barton, $150); Freddy Ridgeway (Donald Barton, $100); Bing Russell (the operator, $80); Bob Sherman (Frederick Reiner, $100); and Harlan Warde (Everett Prescott, $125)

PLOT: The advancement of computer technology has proven to do the job where human life could not. An important scientist, Dr. Milo Barton, is visiting his family in Southern California prior to participating in a nuclear test at an atomic Energy Commission test base in Nevada. An electronic computer predicts a storm, necessitating setting the test ahead several hours. Dr. Barton takes off in

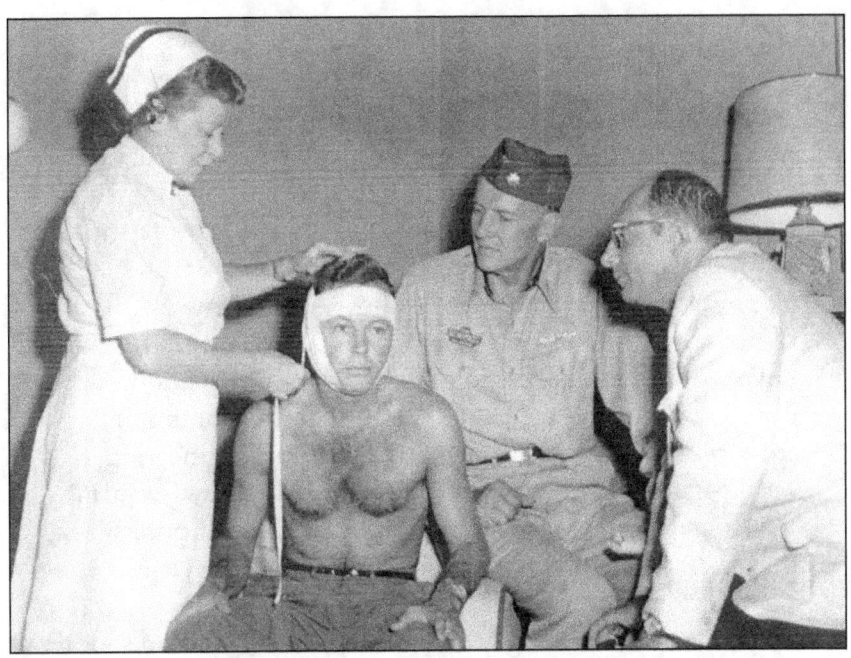

A real nurse applies bandages on DeForest Kelley in the presence of Bruce Bennett and director Herbert L. Strock.

his private plane for Las Vegas. When radio and radar contact with Barton are lost, the Civil Air Patrol is called out to search for the missing scientist. Fifty planes cover a vast area without result. Finally, Dr. Sorenson, a major in the CAP, finds a fragment of the tail section of Barton's plane, but nothing else. Frederick Michaels, AEC scientist in charge of the test, calls off the bomb drop until Barton is found, since he may have parachuted into the blast-area. The approaching storm will not only mean grounding the research planes, but result in a costly delay in the atomic test. Michaels calls on the computer for help. Thousands of bits of data are fed into the computer known as "Dr. Tovac." The data includes Barton's last known position, the location of the tail fragment, and wind velocity and direction at various levels. The computer indicates Barton's probable landing spot—a rugged mountaintop. The air search concentrates on this area, but finds no trace of Barton. Dr. Sorenson, confident that the computer is right, makes a parachute jump to search the area on foot. He finds Barton, injured in a crevasse. Barton is flown to the hospital, and the atomic test proceeds as scheduled, thanks to the courage of the Civil Air Patrol and the brains of a giant computer.

NOTES

- All of the interior shots were filmed on the first day on Stage 4 and 5.
- All of the exterior shots were filmed on the second day. The exterior shots of the rough terrain were filmed at Bronson Canyon. After the cast and company returned to the studio at 4:20, the camera crew continued on to the Bendix Corporation (located at 5630 Arbor Vitae in Los Angeles) to film all the computer scenes until 6:20. The Computer Division of Bendix Aviation Corporation was acknowledged during the closing credits for supplying the computer equipment. David C. Evans, Supervisor of Engineering, was assigned to help assist Ivan Tors and his crew, ensuring that footage of computers were not just any computers—they were data-processing equipment and electronic information-processing machines.
- Dr. Tovac, the thinking computer featured in this episode, was partially constructed from footage from the Bendix Corporation and original footage using the same computers that Truman Bradley is surrounded by in the opening sequence of every episode.
- This episode has perhaps the most narration from Truman Bradley for a single episode, due to the overuse of stock footage.
- To ensure the accuracy of the U.S. Air Force when it came to the procedures of the Civil Air Patrol, Major Martin was hired as the technical advisor.
- During the closing credits of this episode, the following was stated: "Our gratitude to Major General Walter R. Agee, U.S.A.F., National Commander of the Civil Air Patrol and to the senior and cadet members of the C.A.P. for their technical assistance."
- Four stand-ins and one extra were on hand to play the roles of rescue searchers at the base of operations, radio operators and a radio operator technician. While most of those in individual roles cannot be identified, Andrew Roud, Murray Yeats and Bonnie Clark are among them.

"THE INCREDIBLE DR. TOVAC"
Dated: April 2, 1956
by Ivan Tors

A very important scientist, whose presence at a nuclear fission test is imperative, decides to visit his family before taking off with a scientific expedition. The plane crashes at 20,000 feet altitude over rugged mountains in Nevada.

The approach of a storm forecast will make an aerial search impossible in six hours. The Civil Air Patrol and the Air Rescue Service have six hours to find this vitally important man before search has to be abandoned. Fifty civilian planes and two helicopters comb the area without finding a trace of the missing scientist. Finally, a light plane sights a piece of shiny metal on a dry lake. The plane lands and the pilot verifies that the piece of aluminum is from the missing plane. They have only a few hours left for search. Suddenly, somebody gets the idea of feeding all the available information to a computer. The name of the computer is Dr. Tovac (Transistor Operative Variable Automatic Computer). The question is, if a 2-pound metal object fell from 20,000 feet altitude, passing through specific wind velocities at specific altitudes, where did a 180-pound man float with a parachute?

The Weather Department supplies a great deal of data on different atmospheric pressures, wind directions and velocities at the time of the accident. An Air Force radar station supplies the data of the altitude of the plane and its location at the time of the accident. Dr. Tovac goes to work and figures out the exact location of the missing man. The search continues but now, all of the fifty planes comb a smaller area for the missing man.

They don't find a trace of him but one of the flyers, a doctor, decides that he has sufficient faith in the judgment of the computer to jump over the exact spot designated by Dr. Tovac. And Dr. Tovac was right! He finds the scientist badly injured in a cave on the very same spot where he was supposed to have fallen. The terrain is too rugged for even a helicopter landing. The doctor is not a surgeon but he has to perform immediate surgery to save the life of this important scientist.

Through his walkie-talkie, he contacts one of the search planes flying overhead. The plane in turn contacts a surgeon who gives instructions on the radio as to the procedure to be followed by the doctor. Next morning, the search party arrives and the injured scientist is now in good enough condition to be moved. His life will be saved, thanks to the courage of the members of the Civil Air Patrol and the brains of a giant computer.

EPISODE #65 "THE VOICE"

PRODUCTION #1065 / 64B

DATES OF PRODUCTION: JULY 9 AND 10, 1956
DIRECTED BY PAUL GUILFOYLE

SCRIPT & STORY

FIRST DRAFT BY DORIS GILBERT, DATE UNKNOWN
REVISED PAGES DATED JULY 10, 1956
FINAL DRAFT BY DORIS GILBERT, JULY 11, 1956
TELEPLAY BY DORIS GILBERT

PRODUCTION CREDITS

1ST ASST. CAMERAMAN: ED NUGENT (*UN-CREDITED*)
1ST CO. GRIP: CARL MIKSCH (*UN-CREDITED*)
2ND ASST. DIRECTOR: BRUCE SATTERLEE (*UN-CREDITED*)
2ND CAMERAMAN: BUD WILDER (*UN-CREDITED*)
2ND CO. GRIP: JACK CHAMBERS (*UN-CREDITED*)
3RD GRIP: EDDIE MANRIQUEZ (*UN-CREDITED*)
ASSISTANT DIRECTOR: JAY SANDRICH
ASST PROP MAN: STAN WALTERS (*UN-CREDITED*)
AUDIO SUPERVISOR: QUINN MARTIN
BOOM MAN: BILL FLANNERY (*UN-CREDITED*)
CONSTRUCTION CHIEF: ARCHIE HALL (*UN-CREDITED*)
DIRECTOR OF PHOTOGRAPHY: CURT FETTERS
DRIVERS: ART HOUSTON, CONRAD RADICE, ALLEN REED AND RAY STODDARD (*ALL UN-CREDITED*)
ELECTRICIANS: FRED HOUNSHELL, HAROLD KRAUS, HERMAN LIPNEY AND CHARLES STOCKWELL (*ALL UN-CREDITED*)
FILM COORDINATOR: DONALD TAIT
FILM EDITOR: CHARLES CRAFT, A.C.E

Gaffer: Al Ronso (*un-credited*)
Make-up Artist: George Gray (*un-credited*)
Production Coordinator: Joe Wonder
Production Supervisor: Barry Cohon
Property Master: Max Pittman
Recorder: Joe Keener (*un-credited*)
Script Supervisor: Jeanne Lippman
Set Decorator: Clarence Steenson
Set Designer: Robert Kinoshita
Set Labor: Ted McCaskey (*un-credited*)
Sound Editor: Charles Overhulser
Sound Mixer: Jay Ashworth
Special Effects: Harry Redmond, Jr.
Still man: Charles Rhodes (July 10 only, *un-credited*)
Wardrobe: Alfred Berke

CAST: Morris Ankrum (Dr. MacDermott, $150); Beverly Barnes (the phone receptionist, $80); Julian Burton (the rancher's son, $80); Donald Curtis (Roger Brown, $300); Antony Eustrel (Mendoza, $150); Billy Griffith (the rancher, $80); Hal Hoover (the condemned man, $80); Kristine Miller (Anna Brown, $300); Anna Navarro (the nurse, $80); Bruce Payne (Edward Stevens, the lawyer, $80); Bill Phipps (Dr. Stockton, $150); and Roland Varno (the scientist, $80)*

PLOT: Roger Brown, a successful and cogent trial lawyer, who only the night before scoffed at a mentalist on a television program, is en route to San Diego on an errand of mercy to save the life of a condemned man with new evidence. En route, his plane goes over a mountain and he finds himself paralyzed as a result, unable to move or talk. Through the accident he learns that he is able to send for help and accomplishes his purpose without any physical means of communication—only by the sheer power of transmitting his thought to others whose help is urgently needed. After the surgery,

---

* Anthony Eustrel was spelled Antony in the closing credits for this episode and "Are We Invaded?" The exact spelling of his name remains elusive, since his name was Antony, Anthony and Tony throughout numerous television productions.

he is no longer paralyzed but his telepathic ability is gone. Thanks to his temporary and unexplained ability, the right messages were delivered to the right people and the condemned man's life is saved.

NOTES

- The chart with dots on the wall behind Truman Bradley also appears in "The Unguided Missile," "Three Minute Mile," "The Water Maker" and "The Hastings Secret."
- Produced under the title of "The Silent Voice."
- Stock footage of the exterior of a house with the lights on was used for the opening shot featuring the title of the drama superimposed on the screen. This served as the outside of Roger Brown's house in this episode and was also used in the opening of "When A Camera Fails," which also served as the house of Dr. Richard Hewitt. The same footage appears in "Bullet Proof" and "The Lost Heartbeat."
- The jeep driven by the old rancher was rented for the purpose of this production.
- The entire production was filmed on Stage 6 except for the exterior scenes which were shot on location at Bronson Canyon during the first half of the second day.
- The solo scenes with the condemned man behind prison bars was filmed separately on July 3.

EPISODE #66 "THREE MINUTE MILE"

PRODUCTION #1066 / 66B

DATES OF PRODUCTION: JULY 20 AND 23, 1956
DIRECTED BY EDDIE DAVIS

SCRIPT & STORY

FINAL DRAFT BY GEORGE ASNESS, JULY 12, 1956
TELEPLAY BY GEORGE ASNESS

PRODUCTION CREDITS

1ST ASST. CAMERAMAN: JIM BELL (*UN-CREDITED*)
1ST CO. GRIP: CARL MIKSCH (*UN-CREDITED*)
2ND ASST. DIRECTOR: JAY SANDRICH (*UN-CREDITED*)
2ND CO. GRIP: MEL BLEDSOE (*UN-CREDITED*)
ASSISTANT DIRECTOR: DONALD VERK
ASST PROP. MAN: YGNACIO SEPULVEDA (*UN-CREDITED*)
AUDIO SUPERVISOR: QUINN MARTIN
BEST BOY: CHARLES STOCKWELL (*UN-CREDITED*)
BOOM MAN: ELMER HAGLUND (*UN-CREDITED*)
CAMERA OPERATOR: DICK RAWLINGS
CONSTRUCTION CHIEF: ARCHIE HALL (*UN-CREDITED*)
DIRECTOR OF PHOTOGRAPHY: MONROE "MONK" ASKINS
DRIVERS: DALSTRUM, T. GARBER AND MYNEAR [FIRST NAMES UNKNOWN] (*ALL UN-CREDITED*)
ELECTRICIANS: JIMMY FIELD, FRED HOUNSHELL AND MIKE HUDSON (*ALL UN-CREDITED*)
FILM COORDINATOR: DONALD TAIT
FILM EDITOR: CHARLES CRAFT, A.C.E. (*CREDITED*) AND TOMMY SCOTT (*UN-CREDITED*)
GAFFER: AL RONSO (*UN-CREDITED*)
MAKE-UP ARTIST: GEORGE GRAY
PRODUCTION COORDINATOR: JOE WONDER
PRODUCTION SUPERVISOR: BARRY COHON
PROPERTY MASTER: MAX PITTMAN
RECORDER: LLOYD HANES (*UN-CREDITED*)
SCRIPT SUPERVISOR: LARRY LUND
SET DECORATOR: CLARENCE STEENSON
SET DESIGNER: ROBERT KINOSHITA
SET LABOR: BILL BENTHAM (*UN-CREDITED*)
SOUND EDITOR: CHARLES OVERHULSER
SOUND MIXER: GARRY HARRIS
SPECIAL EFFECTS: HARRY REDMOND, JR.
WARDROBE: ALFRED BERKE

CAST: Robert Bice (Ted Shane, $80); John Eldredge (Carter Paige, $125); Bill Henry (Jim Dale, $80); Gloria Marshall (Jill Paige, $125); Martin Milner (Brit, $400); Leonard St. Leo (the photographer,

Jill Paige attempts to learn her fiancé's secret of super-power strength.

$17.85); and Marshall Thompson (Dr. Nat Kendall, $750)

PLOT: Nat Kendall, Biology Professor at Haverlee College, finds a way to speed up bodily processes electronically with the result that his best student, Brit, can now lift a 1000-pound weight and run a mile in three minutes. Kendall and Brit keep their work a secret until an ambitious newspaperman accidentally learns the facts about their project. The owner of the paper, Carter Paige, is determined to publish the news. Kendall implores him not to print it . . . a premature announcement could do a lot of harm as such an experiment is dangerous to the human body unless it is done under controlled conditions. Paige refuses to play ball but when Kendall saves his daughter's life at the risk of his own, playing human guinea pig with his own discovery, the publisher agrees to keep the experiment a secret and even offers to finance it to a successful conclusion.

> Leonard St. Leo was perhaps the most popular "extra" on the set. Most episodes required a few extras on hand in case there was a need to have pedestrians walking in the background or simulate background crowd noises. The minimum scale was $17.85 per day, regardless of whether or not the actor appeared on camera. For this episode, two extras were available for each day of filming, one man and one woman, and Leonard St. Leo is the only person to appear on the film—playing the un-credited role of the photographer. Of all the extras that appeared on *Science Fiction Theatre* and never received on-screen credit, Leonard St. Leo averaged 50 percent of those roles.

NOTES

- The chart with dots on the wall in Dr. Kendall's lab in this episode also appears in "The Unguided Missile," "The Water Maker," "The Hastings Secret" and in the background of Truman Bradley's lab demonstrations in "The Voice" and "The Sound That Kills."
- The poster hanging on the wall in this episode, displaying the human anatomy including blood vessels and muscles, appear in two other episodes, "Death at 2 A.M." and "The Unexplored." Truman Bradley displayed the same poster in "100 Years Young."
- The episode was produced under the title "The Strong in Heart," the original title of George Asness' final draft of this script.
- All of the interior shots of the lab were filmed on Stage 5 for both days except for the afternoon of day two, where the exterior scenes at the sports field, the opening scene outside the research building and the public park were filmed on location at Poinsettia Park, 936 North Poinsettia.
- After Bradley completed his work at 8 p.m., the technical crew remained behind to shoot a complicated window insert for Production 37 of another television series, *The Man Called X*.

EPISODE #67 "THE LAST BARRIER"

PRODUCTION #1067 / 658
DATES OF PRODUCTION: JULY 18 AND 19, 1956
DIRECTED BY PAUL GUILFOYLE

SCRIPT & STORY
FIRST DRAFT BY RIK VOLLAERTS, JUNE 25, 1956
REVISED PAGES DATED JULY 10, 1956
FINAL DRAFT BY RIK VOLLAERTS, JULY 12, 1956
TELEPLAY BY RIK VOLLAERTS

PRODUCTION CREDITS
1ST ASST. CAMERAMAN: ED NUGENT (*UN-CREDITED*)
1ST CO. GRIP: MEL BLEDSOE (*UN-CREDITED*)
2ND ASST. DIRECTOR: BRUCE SATTERLEE (*UN-CREDITED*)
2ND CO. GRIP: TOMMY MATHEWS (*UN-CREDITED*)
ASSISTANT DIRECTOR: JAY SANDRICH
ASST. PROP MAN: VIC PETROTTA (*UN-CREDITED*)
AUDIO SUPERVISOR: QUINN MARTIN
BEST BOY: CHARLES STOCKWELL (*UN-CREDITED*)
BOOM MAN: BILL FLANNERY (*UN-CREDITED*)
CAMERA OPERATOR: DICK RAWLINGS
CONSTRUCTION CHIEF: ARCHIE HALL (*UN-CREDITED*)
DIRECTOR OF PHOTOGRAPHY: ROBERT HOFFMAN
ELECTRICIANS: FRED HOUNSHELL, JAMES HUNTER AND GLEN KNIGHT (*ALL UN-CREDITED*)
FILM COORDINATOR: DONALD TAIT
FILM EDITOR: THOMAS SCOTT
FILM EDITOR: CHARLES CRAFT (*UN-CREDITED*)
GAFFER: AL RONSO (*UN-CREDITED*)
MAKE-UP ARTIST: GEORGE GRAY
PRODUCTION COORDINATOR: JOE WONDER
PRODUCTION SUPERVISOR: BARRY COHON
PROPERTY MASTER: MAX PITTMAN
RECORDER: JOHN BURY (*UN-CREDITED*)
SCRIPT SUPERVISOR: JEANNE LIPPMAN
SET DECORATOR: JAMES WALTERS

SET DESIGNER: ROBERT KINOSHITA
SET LABOR: BILL BENTHAM (*UN-CREDITED*)
SOUND EDITOR: CHARLES OVERHULSER
SOUND MIXER: JAY ASHWORTH
SPECIAL EFFECTS: HARRY REDMOND, JR.
STILL MAN: BILL CARY (JULY 19 ONLY, *UN-CREDITED*)
WARDROBE: ALFRED BERKE

CAST: George Barrows (Boatswain's Mate, $80); William Ching (Dr. Robert Porter, $500); Jason Johnson (Ray Cordell, $80); Sydney Mason (Dr. Stephen Dorian, $200); Tom McKee (Wayne Masters, $125); Lee Millar (Ned, $80); Jim Sheldon (the radio operator, $80); and Bruce Wendell (Daniel Borden, $100)

PLOT: A U.S. naval task force far out in the Pacific, presumably to fire a nuclear test shot, is actually there to launch a new type of space ship. Observatories across the country and the Federal Bureau of Scientific Security are asked to cover up any flying saucer reports that might be observed. The XR-1 is successfully launched and it leaves the atmosphere. Once in space, its new hydrogen ion booster reactor propels the ship, permitting it to save rocket fuel. When the XR-1 is about to start for the moon so photographs can be taken, two unidentified objects are noticed on the radar screen accompanying the XR-1. Four more flying objects follow. Various explanations are put forth but the fact remains that the objects cannot be thrown off by maneuvers of the XR-1. During the moon circuit, one after another, the television cameras black out, the regular motion picture cameras, and finally part of the controls. It's decided that whatever the flying objects are, they might destroy the XR-1, so the experimental craft is flown back to Earth. Over White Sands, it finally crashes. Analysis of the components of the XR-1 shows that the disabled parts of the ship were burned out by some high powered ray, unknown to scientists, which acted selectively to 'blind' the XR-1. Whatever the flying objects around the XR-1 were, they wanted to avoid being photographed.

NOTES

- The character of Daniel Borden was originally Daniel Blake in the script.
- The name of the rocket, XR-1 was originally XM-1 in the final script.
- Stan Walters was originally scheduled to be the assistant prop man for Max Pittman, but Walters fell ill the morning of the first day of filming and Vic Petrotta took over the job.
- The lab demonstration hosted by Truman Bradley was a bit misleading, but reveals just how many times props were reused on the program, simulating a number of different electronic equipment that normally went over-noticed by the casual viewer. Here, Bradley asks the audience to take a peek in the viewer of a tube to witness air friction on an airplane—which was really stock footage. The same tumbler prop was used previously in "The Green Bomb" (sans viewer) when Bradley removed a Beagle from within the container, and later when Dr. Neville asks his mother to look inside a viewer attached to a tube in "The Human Circuit," with added control knobs.
- Footage of the observatory and the XR-1 was stock footage provided courtesy of UFA film. According to an article published in the November 1989 issue of *Filmfax* magazine, columnist Charles Lee Jackson, II suggested the extensive footage featured in this episode may well have been lifted from an unfinished German sci-fi film (pre-WWII), the title of which is translated as Rocketflight to the Moon.
- On October 24, 1946, a V-2 rocket with a motion picture camera was launched from the White Sands Proving Grounds. It recorded images from 65 miles above the Earth, covering 40,000 square miles. White Sands footage was responsible for much of the stock footage for this episode including the rocket to Earth shot, the establishing shot of White Sands Missile station and the rocket crash landing towards the end of the episode.
- All of the interior shots were filmed on the first day on Stage 5. The second day of filming was on location at the

Pacific Division of the Bendix Aviation Corporation, located at Sherman Way and Lankershim Blvd. Bendix also provided the technical equipment seen in the exterior shots and the personnel who properly operated (or pretended to operate) the equipment.
- While the cast and crew were on location on the second day of production, Truman Bradley was on the set to film the lab demonstrations for the opening and closing scenes of episodes 64, 65 and 69, under the direction of Paul Guilfoyle.
- Actress Barbara Knudsen and actor Leonard St. Leo were on the same set an hour before Bradley to film a Bromo Seltzer commercial, under the direction of Eddie Davis.
- The title of the first draft of the teleplay, dated June 25, 1956, is "Breakthrough."

COMMENTARY

"The Last Barrier," originally produced under the title "Breakthrough," underwent considerable amount of research by scripter Rik Vollaerts, his fourth and final contribution to the series, but with assistance of Ivan Tors, who provided the scriptwriter with numerous magazine articles regarding the past endeavors of the U.S. Air Force and the development of two-stage rockets.

This episode may be dated when compared to present NASA programs, space shuttles and man-made satellites circling around the globe. But since the film was produced in the summer of 1956 and dramatizes in documentary fashion the first rocket to break through the Earth's atmospheric envelope and beyond, courtesy of a new ion booster, this episode can only be enjoyed when placed between historical timelines.

The first American-built rocket to leave the Earth's atmosphere (the WAC) was launched on March 22, 1946. It was launched from White Sands, New Mexico and attained 50 miles of altitude. It wasn't until October 4, 1957, months after this television episode aired on American television, that the Soviet Union stunned the world by placing the first satellite, Sputnik, into space.

EPISODE #68 "SIGNALS FROM THE MOON"

PRODUCTION #1068 / 67B
Dates of Production: August 15 and 16, 1956
Directed by Paul Guilfoyle

SCRIPT & STORY
First Draft by Tom Gries, circa July 17, 1956
Final Draft by Tom Gries, July 23, 1956
Revised pages dated August 14, 1956
Teleplay by Tom Gries

PRODUCTION CREDITS
1st Asst. Cameraman: Jim Bell (*un-credited*)
1st Co. Grip: Carl Miksch (*un-credited*)
2nd Asst. Director: Jay Sandrich (*un-credited*)
2nd Cameraman: John Weiler (*un-credited*)
2nd Co. Grip: Jack Chambers (*un-credited*)
Assistant Director: Ed Stein
Asst Prop Man: Stan Walters (*un-credited*)
Audio Supervisor: Quinn Martin
Boom Man: Elmer Haglund (*un-credited*)
Construction Chief: Archie Hall (*un-credited*)
Director of Photography: Robert Hoffman
Electricians: Walter Gediman, Mike Hudson, Harold Kraus and Louis Kreiger (*all un-credited*)
Film Coordinator: Donald Tait
Film Editor: Thomas Scott
Gaffer: Calman Bassin (*un-credited*)
Make-up Artists: George Gray (*credited*) and John Sweeeney (Aug. 15 only, *un-credited*)
Production Coordinator: Joe Wonder
Production Supervisor: Barry Cohon
Property Master: Max Pittman
Recorder: Lloyd Hanks (*un-credited*)
Script Supervisor: Larry Lund
Set Decorator: Clarence Steenson
Set Designer: Robert Kinoshita

SET LABOR: BILL BENTHAM (*UN-CREDITED*)
SOUND EDITOR: LAWRENCE KAUFMAN
SOUND MIXER: GARRY HARRIS
SPECIAL SCIENTIFIC EFFECTS: HARRY REDMOND, JR.
WARDROBE: ALFRED BERKE

CAST: Bruce Bennett (Gen. Frank Terrance, $1,000); Don Brodie (Ward Baxter, $100); Michael Fox (Dr. Paul Edwards, $125); Bhupesh Guha (the bell boy, $80); Alfred Linder (Pandit Chandra Singh, $125); Steven Ritch (Dr. Richard Patterson, $125); and Bob Shield (Dr. Robert Werth, $100)*

PLOT: Recently in the United States on an important diplomatic mission, Pandit Chandra Singh is shot in an assassination attempt and every effort is being made to save his life. The bullet lodged in his brain must be removed and there is only one man who can perform the operation. His name is Dr. Robert Werth. General Frank Terrance, presidential aide, and Dr. Paul Edwards, superintendent and chief surgeon of Georgetown Hospital in the nation's capitol, attempt to reach Dr. Werth at his home in San Francisco only to find that he is halfway across the Pacific, on his way to Hawaii on the Lurline. Dr. Edwards informs General Terrance and Ward Baxter, State Department representative, that he will have to perform the operation himself, but that he doesn't think he can save Pandit Singh. Dr. Edwards once saw the operation performed on closed circuit television. General Terrance suggests a hookup to the Lurine by both television and radiotelephone, so that Dr. Werth can guide him. Because TV signals travel in a straight line and not with the curvature of the Earth, a unique arrangement has to be made. For the first time in history, a television picture will be bounced off the Moon. Dr. Richard Patterson, electronics and astronomy expert is called in and ordered by General Terrance to use a new atomic-reactor turbine to provide the necessary million watts of power. The signal is relayed from the operating room to the

---

* Bob Shield, credited as Robert Shield on a few TV productions, was listed as Bob Franklin on his salary contract with ZIV.

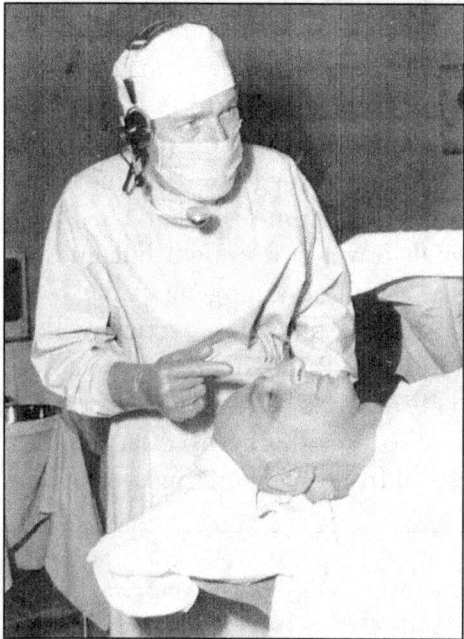

Producer Ivan Tors (LEFT) observes a quick make-up job applied to actor Alfred Linder in front of actor Bruce Bennett in "Signals from the Moon."

Dr. Paul Edwards (Michael Fox) prepares for surgery in "Signals from the Moon."

turbine, then up to the Moon and back down to the ship where Dr. Werth watches and guides Dr. Edwards in the operation. Pandit Singh is on the operating table within the necessary four hours, and the operation is completed during the 15 to 20 minutes that the signal can be sustained.

NOTES

- The entire episode was shot on Stage 5, including the scenes at the Atomic Turbine Plant.
- Shooting was scheduled to begin 8:15 on the second day of production but was delayed 30 minutes because of generator failure. Because he was able to resolve the problem within 30 minutes instead of an expected hour, the cableman was rewarded a full hour lunch break instead of 30 minutes like the rest of the cast and crew (who normally would have had an hour).
- Un-credited actors in this episode include Stewart Newmark and Robert Davison. Davison was formerly a costume designer for numerous motion pictures and whose biggest claim to fame was Charles Laughton's *Leben des Galilei* in 1947.
- The first draft of this teleplay, dated July 17, 1956, is titled "Surgery on Channel 3."

EPISODE #69 "DOCTOR ROBOT"

PRODUCTION #1069 / 72B

DATES OF PRODUCTION: AUGUST 6 AND 7, 1956
DIRECTED BY EDDIE DAVIS

SCRIPT & STORY

FINAL DRAFT BY ELLIS MARCUS, CIRCA JULY 26, 1956
TELEPLAY BY ELLIS MARCUS

PRODUCTION CREDITS

1ST ASST. CAMERAMAN: JIM BELL (*UN-CREDITED*)
1ST CO. GRIP: JACK CHAMBERS (AUG. 6) AND CARL MIKSCH (AUG. 7) (*BOTH UN-CREDITED*)

2ND ASST. DIRECTOR: LYNN PARSONS (AUG. 6) AND BOB
   TEMPLETON (AUG. 7) (*BOTH UN-CREDITED*)
2ND CAMERAMAN: JOHN WEILER (*UN-CREDITED*)
2ND CO. GRIP: EDDIE MANRIQUEZ (*UN-CREDITED*)
ASSISTANT DIRECTOR: JAY SANDRICH
ASST. PROP. MAN: BOB BENTON, SR. (*UN-CREDITED*)
AUDIO SUPERVISOR: QUINN MARTIN
BEST BOY: CHARLES STOCKWELL (*UN-CREDITED*)
BOOM MAN: ELMER HAGLUND (*UN-CREDITED*)
CONSTRUCTION CHIEF: ARCHIE HALL (*UN-CREDITED*)
DIRECTOR OF PHOTOGRAPHY: ROBERT HOFFMAN
ELECTRICIANS: WALTER GEDIMAN, FRED HOUNSHELL AND LOUIS
   KREIGER (*ALL UN-CREDITED*)
FILM COORDINATOR: DONALD TAIT
FILM EDITOR: THOMAS SCOTT
GAFFER: CALMAN BASSIN (*UN-CREDITED*)
MAKE-UP ARTIST: GEORGE GRAY (*UN-CREDITED*)
MUSIC EDITOR: HAYES PAGEL
PRODUCTION COORDINATOR: JOE WONDER
PRODUCTION SUPERVISOR: BARRY COHON
PROPERTY MASTER: MAX PITTMAN
RECORDER: LLOYD HANKS (*UN-CREDITED*)
SCRIPT SUPERVISOR: NORMAN CANTRELL (AUG. 6 ONLY, *CREDITE*D)
   AND LARRY LUND (AUG. 7 ONLY, *UN-CREDITED*)
SET DECORATOR: CLARENCE STEENSON
SET DESIGNER: ROBERT KINOSHITA
SOUND EDITOR: MONROE MARTIN
SOUND MIXER: GARRY HARRIS
SPECIAL SCIENTIFIC EFFECTS: HARRY REDMOND, JR.
WARDROBE: ALFRED BERKE

CAST: Whit Bissell (Fred Lopert, $200); Elizabeth Flournoy (Eleanor Lopert, $80); Esther Furst (the nurse, $80); Peter Hanson (Dr. Edgar Barnes, $350); John Stephenson (Philip Colson, $150); Robert Weston (Roger Paulson, $80); and Doug Wilson (Douglas Hinkle, $80)

PLOT: The latest and most interesting computer machine to come

Whit Bissell tinkers with the fake computers on the set of "Doctor Robot." Notice the fake computers are set on top of wooden crates marked for ZIV TV Studios, which never appear on camera during the episode.

of age is designed to translate languages. As it is being assembled and fed with its polyglot vocabulary, the head of the project, Dr. Barnes, discovers that someone is tampering with the machine. Since it will eventually handle secret government materials, Barnes contacts the FBI. With help from Barnes, Agent Colson makes an investigation. They soon discover that the guilty man is Fred Lopert, one of the top scientists on the project. They suspect him of espionage, but eventually discover his motives are blameless.

Peter Hanson (PICTURED) **and Whit Bissell** (BEHIND THE CAMERA ON THE RIGHT) **prepare for their next scene.**

They also discover that Lopert is putting the machine to a far better use than translating languages. He was using the machine to analyze all the facts and data and provide statistics for diagnosis and possible treatment of his wife's critical illness, a severe case of Endocarditis and inflamed heart lesion. He was formulating his wife's problem in mathematical terms and hoped his wife would make her decision based on the digital computer. When the truth becomes known, understanding that the nation's security is not at risk, Barnes and Colson help him finish his task.

NOTES

- The insert shot of Dr. Barnes' hand holding the wires next to the terminals was indeed actor Peter Hanson's. The same footage is used twice. Once when he discovers the possibility that someone soldered the wires to the terminals and the second time when he shows Colson the yet unfinished computer. The reuse of the same footage, however, creates a blooper when the footage is shown the second time. Dr. Barnes is holding the wires in his left hand but it's clearly his right hand that holds them.
- The thinking computer in this episode is based on the same principal of M.A.N.I.A.C. (Mathematical, Analytical, Numerical Integrator And Computer) which was demonstrated in the same fashion in Ivan Tors' *The Magnetic Monster* (1953). While the concept of the thinking computer was revisited for this episode, it does remain probable that stock footage from the movie was considered for use on this program, but obviously never used.
- The first draft of the teleplay, dated July 26, 1956, is titled "The Consulting Machine."

EPISODE #70 "THE HUMAN CIRCUIT"

PRODUCTION #1070 / 68B

Dates of Production: August 21 and 22, 1956
Directed by Eddie Davis

SCRIPT & STORY

First Draft by Joel Malcolm Rapp, circa August 7, 1956
Final Draft by Joel Malcolm Rapp, August 14, 1956
Teleplay by Joel Malcolm Rapp

PRODUCTION CREDITS

1st Asst. Cameraman: Jim Bell (*un-credited*)
1st Co. Grip: Carl Miksch (*un-credited*)
2nd Asst Director: Bruce Satterlee (*un-credited*)

2ND CO. GRIP: MEL BLEDSOE (*UN-CREDITED*)
3RD GRIP: JACK CHAMBERS (*UN-CREDITED*)
ASSISTANT DIRECTOR: ED STEIN
ASST. PROP MAN: YGNACIO SEPULVEDA (*UN-CREDITED*)
AUDIO SUPERVISOR: QUINN MARTIN
BEST BOY: CHARLES STOCKWELL (*UN-CREDITED*)
BODY MAKE-UP WOMAN: ANN GILLIAM (AUG. 21 ONLY, *UN-CREDITED*)
BOOM MAN: ELMER HAGLUND (*UN-CREDITED*)
CAMERA OPERATOR: DICK RAWLINGS
CONSTRUCTION CHIEF: ARCHIE HALL (*UN-CREDITED*)
DIRECTOR OF PHOTOGRAPHY: CURT FETTERS
ELECTRICIANS: CALMAN BASSIN, CHARLES HANGER AND FRED HOUNSHELL (*ALL UN-CREDITED*)
FILM COORDINATOR: DONALD TAIT
FILM EDITOR: JAMES DYER
GAFFER: AL RONSO (*UN-CREDITED*)
MAKE-UP ARTIST: GEORGE GRAY
PRODUCTION COORDINATOR: JOE WONDER
PRODUCTION SUPERVISOR: BARRY COHON
PROPERTY MASTER: MAX PITTMAN
RECORDER: LLOYD HANKS (*UN-CREDITED*)
SCRIPT SUPERVISOR: LARRY LUND
SET DECORATOR: CLARENCE STEENSON
SET DESIGNER: ROBERT KINOSHITA
SET LABOR: BILL BENTHAM (*UN-CREDITED*)
SOUND EDITOR: MONROE MARTIN
SOUND MIXER: GARRY HARRIS
SPECIAL SCIENTIFIC EFFECTS: HARRY REDMOND, JR.
STILL MAN: JOE WALTERS (AUG. 21 ONLY, *UN-CREDITED*)
WARDROBE: ALFRED BERKE

CAST: Thomas Anthony (the man answering the phone, $80); Phil Arnold (Chet Arnold, $100); William Ching (Dr. George Stoneham, $500); Joyce Jameson (Nina La Salle, $300); Leo Needham (Captain Bob Stanton, $80); Renee Patryn (Rosie, $80); Gretchen Thomas (Mary Neville, $80); Marshall Thompson (Albert Neville, $750); and James Waters (Harry, $80)

William Ching in make-up before filming commences on "The Human Circuit."

William Ching and Marshall Thompson look over Joyce Jameson at a nightclub in "The Human Circuit."

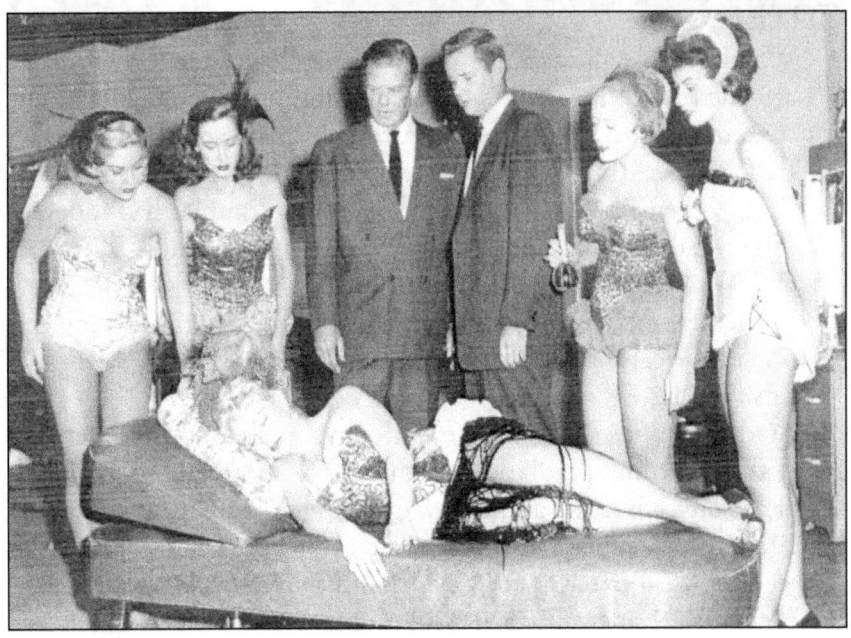

PLOT: A young brain specialist named Dr. George Stoneham learns from a patient, Nina LaSalle, a nightclub dancer, that she has 'seen' an atomic explosion. Attributing this 'hallucination' to an optic-nerve pressure condition, Stoneham relates the incident to a friend, Dr. Albert Neville, a young, brilliant physicist who affirms the girl's vision as a reality. An accidental explosion in the Pacific was kept a secret, but since she saw it at the same time and was hundreds of miles away, he doesn't suspect her as an espionage agent. Instead, Neville is convinced the girl is possessed with clairvoyant powers, and seeks to scientifically explain the phenomenon, which he does by means of tuning her in to another vision, utilizing the principles of television. Electrically, he causes her to see a plane crash as if she was watching live television and because he reports to the Air Control that there is a survivor, a man's life is saved. The pilot, Bob Stanton, learns of his benefactor and a romance is begun between him and Miss LaSalle, now billed as "Saturday Knight" as the star of her club's new revue. Stoneham and Neville, admitting that their experiments have really proved nothing conclusively, are glad that they have opened the way to further experimentation and belief in "borderline phenomena."

NOTES

- When Dr. Neville asks his mother to look inside a viewer attached to a tube, this is the same tumbler prop Bradley used to demonstrate air friction on airplanes in the episode "The Last Barrier," and which Bradley removed a Beagle from in "The Green Bomb." For this episode, the tumbler has added (fake) dials on the side so Marshall Thompson could adjust for his mother, who takes a peak inside.
- The exterior shot of the medical facility building was filmed outside a real medical facility located at 1400 Grand Street in Los Angeles.
- Bradley supposedly creates cosmic rays in a cloud chamber, with help from a radiation chamber, which is really bolts of electricity—but the audience never knew the difference. Bradley also explained that cosmic rays were never known to exist until enterprising scientists discovered 30 years previous. Numerous scientists and physicists tend to watch

the show and spot mistakes, forgetting that the series was accurate at the time it was broadcast. This episode, for example, some debate that Bradley's statement should be 40, not 30. Cosmic rays were discovered in 1912 by Austrian-American physicist Victor Hess, when he found that an electroscope discharged more rapidly as he ascended in a balloon. He attributed this to a source of radiation entering the atmosphere from above, and in 1936 was awarded the Nobel prize for his discovery. Bradley was not referring to the 1912 date of discovery, but rather American physicist Robert A. Millikan who named these energy particles "cosmic rays" in 1925. Add thirty years to 1925 and Bradley's statement of 30 years is accurate.

- Truman Bradley uses a cloud chamber to create cosmic rays—electricity, in reality—and performs this same demonstration in the first-season episode, "A Visit From Dr. Pliny."
- The first draft of this teleplay, dated August 7, 1956, is titled "Station M.I.N.D."

EPISODE #71 "SUN GOLD"

PRODUCTION #1071 / 71B

DATES OF PRODUCTION: SEPTEMBER: 5 AND 6, 1956
DIRECTED BY EDDIE DAVIS

SCRIPT & STORY

FIRST DRAFT BY PETER R. BROOKE, CIRCA JULY 13, 1956
SECOND DRAFT BY PETER R. BROOKE, JULY 23, 1956
FINAL DRAFT BY PETER BROOKE, JULY 24, 1956
TELEPLAY BY PETER R. BROOKE

PRODUCTION CREDITS

1ST ASST. CAMERAMAN: JIM BELL (*UN-CREDITED*)
1ST CO. GRIP: CARL MIKSCH (*UN-CREDITED*)
2ND ASST. DIRECTOR: DON SCHIFF (*UN-CREDITED*)
2ND CAMERAMAN: JOHN WEILER (*UN-CREDITED*)
2ND CO. GRIP: JACK CHAMBERS (*UN-CREDITED*)

3RD GRIP: JACK CHAMBERS (*UN-CREDITED*)
ASSISTANT DIRECTOR: ED STEIN
ASST. PROP MAN: STAN WALTERS (*UN-CREDITED*)
AUDIO SUPERVISOR: QUINN MARTIN
BOOM MAN: BILL FLANNERY (*UN-CREDITED*)
CONSTRUCTION CHIEF: ARCHIE HALL (*UN-CREDITED*)
DIRECTOR OF PHOTOGRAPHY: CURT FETTERS
ELECTRICIAN: CHARLES HANGER (*UN-CREDITED*)
FILM COORDINATOR: DONALD TAIT
FILM EDITOR: JIM DYER (*UN-CREDITED*) AND JOHN B. WOELZ (*CREDITED*)
GAFFER: CALMAN BASSIN (*UN-CREDITED*)
MAKE-UP ARTIST: ARMAND DELMAR
PRODUCTION COORDINATOR: JOE WONDER
PRODUCTION SUPERVISOR: BARRY COHON
PROPERTY MASTER: MAX PITTMAN
RECORDER: RUSS SCHULTZ (*UN-CREDITED*)
SCRIPT SUPERVISOR: LARRY LUND
SET DECORATOR: BRUCE MACDONALD
SET DESIGNER: ROBERT KINOSHITA
SET LABOR: BILL BENTHAM (*UN-CREDITED*)
SOUND EDITOR: MONROE MARTIN
SOUND MIXER: JAY ASHWORTH
SPECIAL SCIENTIFIC EFFECTS: HARRY REDMOND, JR.
STILL MAN: JOE WALTERS (*UN-CREDITED*)
WARDROBE: BERT OFFORD

CAST: Ross Elliot (Howard Evans, $400); Marilyn Erskine (Dr. Susan Calvin, $1,250); Paul Fierro (Padre Xavier, $250); and Julian Rivero (Tawa, $125)

PLOT: Fragments of green glass, a by-product of atomic explosion, have been reportedly found in the isolated regions of the Andes in Peru, indicating an atomic explosion in ancient times. Howard Evans, a nuclear scientist, is commissioned by the Defense Department to look into this phenomenon for reasons of scientific interest as well as world security. Evans presents the fragments to an archeologist, Doctor Susan Calvin, who is an expert on Peru and Inca culture.

(LEFT TO RIGHT) **Ross Elliot, Marilyn Erskine, director Eddie Stein and producer Ivan Tors** on location at Iverson Ranch for the episode "Sun Gold."

Ross Elliot and Marilyn Erskine take direction from director Eddie Stein while filming on location at Bronson Canyon.

 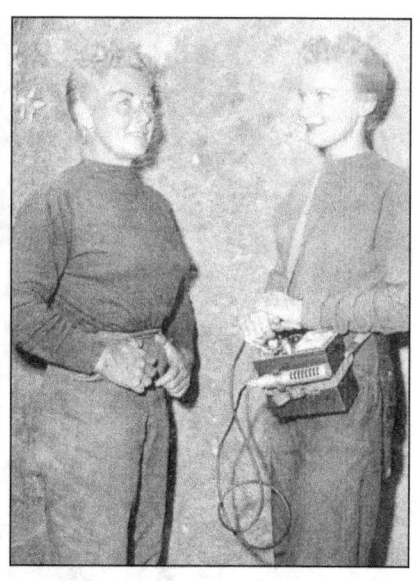

Marilyn Erskine and Ross Elliot enjoy a hot cup of coffee before the sun sets.

Marilyn Erskine (RIGHT) **poses next to her stunt woman** (LEFT).

Joining forces, both scientists set out on an expedition into the "forbidden territory" of Red Ghost Valley. Even the superstition-ridden Inca tribes have no plausible explanation for the fact that up to this date only one man managed to return alive from the obscure valley's grip of death. This man is an Inca by the name of Tawa, who is promptly enlisted as the couple's guide into the unknown. After several close escapes from death, the trio finally reaches the threshold of the valley's secret—a secret that has been well guarded through centuries by the remnants of an ancient, unorthodox and highly superior civilization. The mystery of the "Green Glass" is solved when they discover the ancient race developed solar heat rays strong enough to produce the glass, as well as the additional discovery that once upon a time the vanquished people of said valley possessed the scientific and ingenious means to fabricate gold because of a visitor from outer space. A skull that does not resemble a human being is found to support the hieroglyphics on the walls.

NOTES

- The initial teleplay featured the character of Col. Higgins, described as a leathery war-horse, representing the Defense Department. In order to cut costs that Tors felt were

unnecessary, the scene with that character recruiting Howard Evans and Susan Calvin was revised so Evans would introduce and recruit Susan, thus setting the stage for the drama.
- The opening stock shot with the title "Sun Gold" super imposed on the screen is the same opening stock shot used for "Miracle of Doctor Dove."
- The map of the solar system with a glowing sun in the center, on the wall with Truman Bradley in the beginning of this episode, was the same map displayed with Bradley in "The Miracle Hour," and the same map pointed out during Bradley's closing remarks in "Stranger in the Desert."
- The stock airplane shot in the beginning of this episode was used in a number of ZIV-TV productions including *The Man Called X*.
- Part of this episode was filmed on location in Bronson Canyon and the Iverson Ranch.
- Director Eddie Davis took on the challenge of filming two episodes at the same time. "Killer Tree" was also filmed on location on the same days.

EPISODE #72 "FACSIMILE"

PRODUCTION #1072 / 75B

DATES OF PRODUCTION: AUGUST 23 AND 24, 1956
DIRECTED BY EDDIE DAVIS

SCRIPT & STORY

FINAL DRAFT BY JOHN BUSHNELL, CIRCA AUGUST 15, 1956
REVISED PAGES DATED SEPTEMBER 12, 1956
TELEPLAY BY JOHN BUSHNELL AND STUART JEROME, FROM AN ORIGINAL STORY BY JOHN BUSHNELL

PRODUCTION CREDITS

1ST ASST. CAMERAMAN: JIM BELL (*UN-CREDITED*)
1ST CO. GRIP: CARL MIKSCH (*UN-CREDITED*)
2ND ASST. DIRECTOR: JAY SANDRICH (*UN-CREDITED*)
2ND CO. GRIP: MEL BLEDSOE (*UN-CREDITED*)

3RD GRIP: JACK CHAMBERS (*UN-CREDITED*)
ASSISTANT DIRECTOR: DONALD VERK
ASST. PROP MAN: VICTOR PETROTTA (*UN-CREDITED*)
AUDIO SUPERVISOR: QUINN MARTIN
BEST BOY: CHARLES STOCKWELL (*UN-CREDITED*)
BOOM MAN: ELMER HAGLUND (*UN-CREDITED*)
CABLEMAN: BARRY THOMAS (*UN-CREDITED*)
CAMERA OPERATOR: DICK RAWLINGS
CONSTRUCTION CHIEF: ARCHIE HALL (*UN-CREDITED*)
DIRECTOR OF PHOTOGRAPHY: CURT FETTERS
ELECTRICIANS: CALMAN BASSIN, CHARLES HANGER AND LOUIS KREIGER (*ALL UN-CREDITED*)
FILM COORDINATOR: DONALD TAIT
FILM EDITOR: JOHN B. WOELZ
GAFFER: AL RONSO (*UN-CREDITED*)
MAKE-UP ARTIST: GEORGE GRAY (*UN-CREDITED*)
PRODUCTION COORDINATOR: JOE WONDER
PRODUCTION SUPERVISOR: BARRY COHON
PROPERTY MASTER: MAX PITTMAN
RECORDER: LLOYD HANKS (*UN-CREDITED*)
SCRIPT SUPERVISOR: LARRY LUND
SET DECORATOR: BRUCE MACDONALD
SET DESIGNER: ROBERT KINOSHITA
SET LABOR: BILL BENTHAM (*UN-CREDITED*)
SOUND EDITOR: MONROE MARTIN
SOUND MIXER: GARRY HARRIS
SPECIAL EFFECTS: HARRY REDMAN (*UN-CREDITED*)
SPECIAL SCIENTIFIC EFFECTS: HARRY REDMOND, JR.
STILL MAN: JOE WALTERS (AUG. 23 ONLY, *UN-CREDITED*)
WARDROBE: LOU PALFY

CAST: Lynn Cartwright (the nurse at the desk, $80); Fred Coby (Dr. Stone, $100); Donald Curtis (Hugh Warner, $300); Arthur Franz (George Bascomb, $750); Thomas B. Henry (Dr. Hargrove, $250); Aline Towne (Barbara Davis, $300); and Than Wyenn (Dr. Schiller, $150)

PLOT: Two scientists, working on a new type of transistor to be

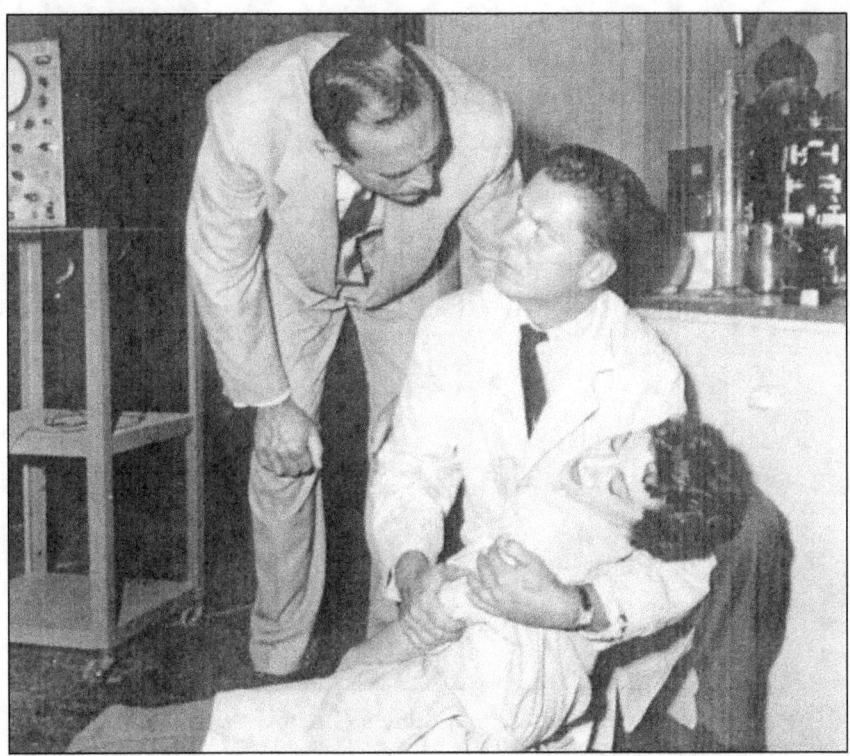

Arthur Franz holds an unconscious Aline Towne while Donald Curtis inquires if something is wrong in "Facsimile."

used for the U.S. Government's Earth satellite project, are suddenly stricken within a few hours of each other; one with appendicitis, the other with inflamed ileum. Shortly afterwards, a third lab worker, Barbara Davis, is found unconscious with symptoms of a brain injury. George Bascomb, a young scientist and head of the project, suspects sabotage but is unable to prove anything. When the first two scientists are operated on, the surgeons learn the operations were needless—both men were perfectly well and healthy. George staves off impending surgery on Barbara while he makes a complete check of the lab. They eventually discover that their new transistor is picking up radio waves and, like cosmic rays, these waves could be the cause of the ailments. They trace the waves to the point of origin—the hospital where Barbara is confined. There they make an accidental discovery that the transistor is sensitive enough to pick up the electronic impulses created by pain from the surgical room overhead.

(LEFT TO RIGHT) **Donald Curtis, Fred Coby and Arthur Franz investigate the source of Aline Towne's ailments.**

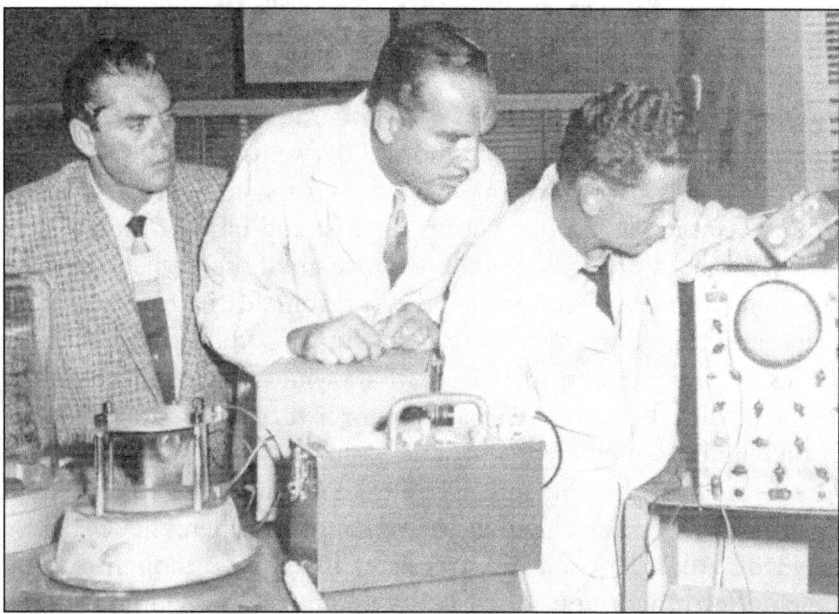

(LEFT TO RIGHT) **Fred Coby, Donald Curtis and Arthur Franz in "Facsimile."**

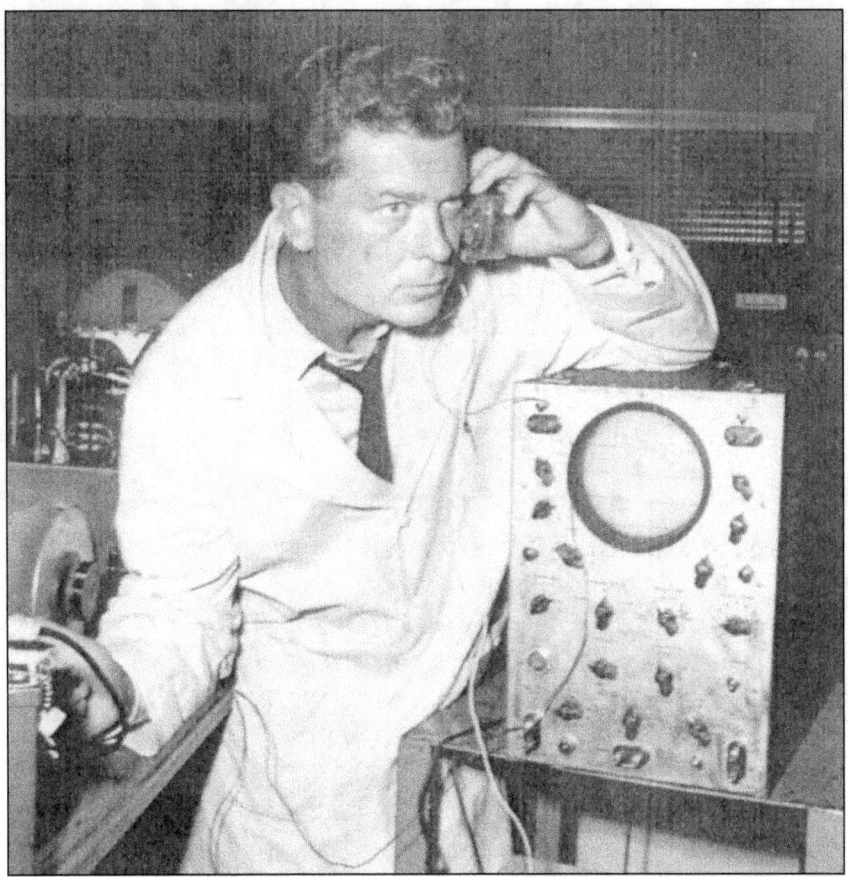

Arthur Franz performs an experiment in "Facsimile."

NOTES
- When George analyzed the room air for foreign gas elements, the prop creating electricity was the same prop used by Truman Bradley during his demonstrations in the beginning of this episode and in the beginning of "Sun Gold."
- First part of the first day was filmed on location at the exterior rear gate to the studio, on Poinsetta, next to Jack Rabin's special effects department. Rabin was responsible for special effects for numerous television productions including *Men Into Space* and *The Adventures of Superman*. The rest of the production was filmed in the studio.
- The station wagon driven by Curtis, Coby and Franz in this episode was rented.

EPISODE #73 "KILLER TREE"

PRODUCTION #1073 / 708
DATES OF PRODUCTION: SEPTEMBER 5 AND 6, 1956
DIRECTED BY EDDIE DAVIS

SCRIPT & STORY
FIRST DRAFT BY ROBERT E. SMITH, JULY 23, 1956
REVISED PAGES BY LOU HUSTON, DATED AUGUST 22, SEPTEMBER 4 AND 12, 1956
FINAL DRAFT BY LOU HUSTON SEPTEMBER 12, 1956
TELEPLAY BY LOU HUSTON, FROM A STORY BY ROBERT E. SMITH

PRODUCTION CREDITS
1ST ASST. CAMERAMAN: JOHN WEILER (*UN-CREDITED*)
1ST CO. GRIP: CARL MIKSCH (*UN-CREDITED*)
2ND ASST. DIRECTOR: DON SCHIFF (*UN-CREDITED*)
2ND CAMERAMAN: JOHN WEILER (*UN-CREDITED*)
2ND CO. GRIP: JACK CHAMBERS (*UN-CREDITED*)
3RD GRIP: JACK CHAMBERS (*UN-CREDITED*)
ASSISTANT DIRECTOR: ED STEIN
ASST. PROP MAN: STAN WALTERS (*UN-CREDITED*)
AUDIO SUPERVISOR: QUINN MARTIN
BOOM MAN: BILL FLANNERY (*UN-CREDITED*)
CONSTRUCTION CHIEF: ARCHIE HALL (*UN-CREDITED*)
DIRECTOR OF PHOTOGRAPHY: CURT FETTERS
ELECTRICIANS: CHARLES HANGER (*UN-CREDITED*)
FILM COORDINATOR: DONALD TAIT
FILM EDITOR: JAMES DYER
GAFFER: CALMAN BASSIN (*UN-CREDITED*)
MAKE-UP ARTIST: ARMAND DELMAR
PRODUCTION COORDINATOR: JOE WONDER
PRODUCTION SUPERVISOR: BARRY COHON
PROPERTY MASTER: MAX PITTMAN
RECORDER: RUSS SCHULTZ (*UN-CREDITED*)
SCRIPT SUPERVISOR: LARRY LUND
SET DECORATOR: BRUCE MACDONALD
SET DESIGNER: ROBERT KINOSHITA

Actress Bonita Granville relaxing between takes.

SET LABOR: BILL BENTHAM (*UN-CREDITED*)
SOUND EDITOR: MONROE MARTIN
SOUND MIXER: JAY ASHWORTH
SPECIAL SCIENTIFIC EFFECTS: HARRY REDMOND, JR.
STILL MAN: JOE WALTERS (*UN-CREDITED*)
WARDROBE: BERT OFFORD

CAST: Terry Frost (Deputy Terry, $80); Bonita Granville (Barbara Cameron, $750); Hank Patterson (Mr. Skinner, the old prospector, $80); Keith Richards (Clyde Bishop, $300); and Bill Williams (Paul Cameron, $800).

On location at Bronson Canyon for "Killer Tree," (LEFT TO RIGHT) **Bonita Granville, Bill Williams, Eddie Davis, Keith Richards and script supervisor Larry Lund.**

Bill Williams and Bonita Granville taking a lunch break between scenes while filming on location.

The Episode Guide: Season Two

Bill Williams, Bonita Granville and Keith Richards admire Eddie Davis' personal shooting script.

PLOT: Scientist Paul Cameron and his wife, Barbara, go exploring in the desert near the Sierra, Nevada mountains and stumble upon a native superstition about a killer tree that stands guard over a treasure buried beneath it, and seeks death to all those who come near. The intelligent seismologists ignore the legend until a delirious old prospector mumbles a strange story about the same tree that brings sudden death to all who rests beneath its boughs. At first the scientists theorize the tree attracts lightning bolts, so they camp nearby the tree overnight so they can make tests in the morning. When the sun breaks dawn, Barbara finds Paul unconscious beneath the tree and pulls him to safety. Further tests reveal an odorless gas that remains low to the ground. The tree, once a great Sequoia, dug thousands of feet below the surface and as the roots decay, the gas produced by underground petroleum leaks to the surface. The tree that once stood there, known as ignorance and death, has now become the center of a promising new future and scientists have barely scratched the surface.

Mr. Skinner, the old prospector (Hank Patterson) is discovered by the cast of "Killer Tree."

NOTES

- The actor playing the role of Deputy Terry was Terry Frost, owner and operator of Terry Gene's, a coffee shop on Wilshire Blvd. in Los Angeles during WWII. He was classified a 4F draft rating due to a club foot.
- The electronic equipment featured in the tent towards the end of the episode is the same equipment featured in laboratories in other episodes.
- Closing credits acknowledged that the X-Ray Television System used by Truman Bradley was developed by the X-Ray Division of General Electric.
- Part of this episode was filmed on location in Bronson Canyon and the Iverson Ranch.
- Director Eddie Davis took on the challenge of filming two episodes at the same time. "Sun Gold" was also filmed on location and on the same days.
- Tom Anthony appears un-credited as Truman Bradley's lab assistant in the beginning of this episode.

EPISODE #74 "GRAVITY ZERO"

PRODUCTION #1074 / 73B

DATES OF PRODUCTION: SEPTEMBER 20 AND 21, 1956
DIRECTED BY PAUL GUILFOYLE

SCRIPT & STORY

FINAL TYPESCRIPT (ANNOTATED) BY DONALD CORY, CIRCA
 AUGUST 14, 1956
REVISED MASTER MIMEO (ANNOTATED), SEPTEMBER 6, 1956
OPENING PAGES (ANNOTATED), SEPTEMBER 13, 1956
TELEPLAY BY DONALD CORY

PRODUCTION CREDITS

1SR ASST. CAMERAMAN: JIM BELL (*UN-CREDITED*)
1ST CO. GRIP: CARL MIKSCH (*UN-CREDITED*)
2ND ASST. DIRECTOR: JIM ENGLE (*UN-CREDITED*)
2ND CAMERAMAN: JOHN WEILER (*UN-CREDITED*)
2ND CO. GRIP: JACK CHAMBERS (*UN-CREDITED*)
ASSISTANT DIRECTOR: ED STEIN
ASST. PROP MAN: STAN WALTERS (*UN-CREDITED*)
AUDIO SUPERVISOR: QUINN MARTIN
BOOM MAN: BILL FLANNERY (*UN-CREDITED*)
CONSTRUCTION CHIEF: ARCHIE HALL (*UN-CREDITED*)
DIRECTOR OF PHOTOGRAPHY: CURT FETTERS
ELECTRICIANS: CHARLES HANGER, MIKE HUDSON, WILLIAM KANE
 AND JUDD LeROY (*ALL UN-CREDITED*)
FILM COORDINATOR: DONALD TAIT
FILM EDITOR: JAMES DYER
GAFFER: CALMAN BASSIN (*UN-CREDITED*)
MAKE-UP ARTIST: GEORGE GRAY
MUSIC EDITOR: JOE INGE
PRODUCTION COORDINATOR: JOE WONDER
PRODUCTION SUPERVISOR: BARRY COHON
PROPERTY MASTER: MAX PITTMAN
RECORDER: RUSS SCHULTZ (*UN-CREDITED*)
SCRIPT SUPERVISOR: JEANNE LIPPMAN
SET DECORATOR: BRUCE MacDONALD

SET DESIGNER: ROBERT KINOSHITA
SET LABOR: BILL BENTHAM (*UN-CREDITED*)
SOUND EDITOR: MONROE MARTIN
SOUND MIXER: JAY ASHWORTH
SPECIAL SCIENTIFIC EFFECTS: HARRY REDMOND, JR.
STILL MAN: JOE WALTERS (*UN-CREDITED*)
WARDROBE: ALFRED BERKE (*UN-CREDITED*)

CAST: Lisa Gaye (Elizabeth Wickes, $150); Percy Helton (Dr. John Hustead, $150); William Hudson (Ken Waring, $125); Walter Kingsford (Dean Howard Menzies, $150); and Lizz Slifer (the girls' dorm supervisor, $80)

PLOT: Doctor John Hustead, a professor at Mannering Institute of Technology, has for some time been working to perfect his experiment in the relativity of weights and masses. Now the money for the project is almost used up, and he must produce a concrete, practical result, or he and his assistant, Elizabeth Wickes, will be hunting for new jobs. The pressure comes at just the wrong time for they are on the brink of discovery. Dean Menzies warns Hustead that a Board of Regents meeting, which is to take place the end of the week, will determine his future. Hustead makes the deadline, however, by discovering a method for changing the value of g—the attraction due to gravity—and is able to move huge objects such as a 2,000 lb thermal unit as if it weighed only pounds. After burning up numerous resistance coils, he discovers the project is subject to environmental conditions and temperature control. Thus, in addition to saving his own reputation and assuring Elizabeth's future happiness, he brings a new meeting of forces between theoretical and applied science. The Hustead equation will be used in the next missile launch and perhaps future launches.

NOTES
- On the second day of production, filming began at Joe's Rowe Commissary for the first shot, then the cast and crew moved to Stage 3.
- The chart of electromagnetic waves hanging on the wall in Dr. Hustead's lab is the same one that appears on the wall in other

William Hudson and Lisa Gaye in "Gravity Zero."

Percy Helton and Lisa Gaye observe the anti-gravity device.

Soon after *Science Fiction Theatre* concluded, ZIV-TV began producing *Men Into Space*, reusing many of the same props seen on *Theatre*.

(LEFT TO RIGHT) **Percy Helton, Lisa Gaye and director Paul Guilfoyle share a laugh on the set of "Gravity Zero."**

scientists' labs such as "Three Minute Mile," "The Strange Lodger," and "The Missing Waveband." Truman Bradley also introduced the same chart to the television audience during the lab demonstration in "The Missing Waveband."
- On September 20, Bill Kane, electrician, and prop men Pittman and Stanley took a half hour lunch break instead of an hour so they could be available for publicity stills.
- On the second day of production, production was halted for 30 minutes due to camera motor and a faulty sound cable.
- Un-credited extras on the set included S. Brown, L.L. True and stunt man H. Kerns.
- The first draft of the teleplay, dated circa August 14, 1956, was titled "The Value of 'G'"

EPISODE #75 "THE MAGIC SUITCASE"

PRODUCTION #1075 / 74B
Dates of Production: September 18 and 19, 1956
Directed by Paul Guilfoyle

SCRIPT & STORY
First Draft by Lou Huston, circa August 22, 1956
Final Draft by Lou Huston, September 12, 1956
Teleplay by Lou Huston, from a story by William R. Epperson

PRODUCTION CREDITS
1st Co. Grip: Carl Miksch (*un-credited*)
1st Asst. Cameraman: Jim Bell (*un-credited*)
2nd Asst. Director: Jim Engle (*un-credited*)
2nd Cameraman: John Weiler (*un-credited*)
2nd Co. Grip: Jack Chambers (*un-credited*)
Assistant Director: Ed Stein
Asst. Prop: Stan Walters (*un-credited*)
Audio Supervisor: Quinn Martin
Boom Man: Bill Flannery (*un-credited*)

Construction Chief: Archie Hall (UN-CREDITED)
Director of Photography: Curt Fetters
Electricians: Charles Hanger, Mike Hudson, William Kane and Judd LeRoy (ALL UN-CREDITED)
Film Coordinator: Donald Tait
Film Editor: John B. Woelz
Gaffer: Calman Bassin (UN-CREDITED)
Key Grip: Carl Miksch
Make-up Artist: George Gray
Music Editor: Joe Inge
Production Coordinator: Joe Wonder
Production Supervisor: Barry Cohon
Property Master: Max Pittman
Recorder: Russ Schultz (UN-CREDITED)
Script Supervisor: Jeanne Lippman
Set Decorator: Bruce MacDonald
Set Designer: Robert Kinoshita
Set Labor: Bill Bentham (UN-CREDITED)
Sound Editor: Monroe Martin
Sound Mixer: Jay Ashworth
Special Scientific Effects: Harry Redmond, Jr.
Still Man: Joe Walters (UN-CREDITED)
Wardrobe: Alfred Berke (UN-CREDITED)

CAST: Judith Ames (Eileen Scott, $125); George Douglas (Dr. Jorgenson, $100); Ian Fulton (the lab assistant); Theodore Lehmann (Mr. Jackson, $80); Arthur Marshall (the tall, thin scientist, $80); Freddy Ridgeway (Terry Scott, $100); Andrew Roud (the lab assistant); James Seay (Security Chief Miller, $125); Leonard St. Leo (the lab assistant); William Vaughan (John Scott, $100); and Charles Winninger (Grandpa Scott, $750).

PLOT: On their way to a mountain cabin, Grandpa Scott and his grandson Terry, age 9, pick up a hitch-hiker who has apparently taken the wrong road. He stays all night with them, but the next morning the stranger has disappeared and he left his suitcase in the room. Terry discovers that the suitcase has an electric outlet. Experimenting, the boy plugs in the transformer cord of his electric

Preparing to film an exterior scene with Grandpa Scott (Charles Winninger) behind the wheel.

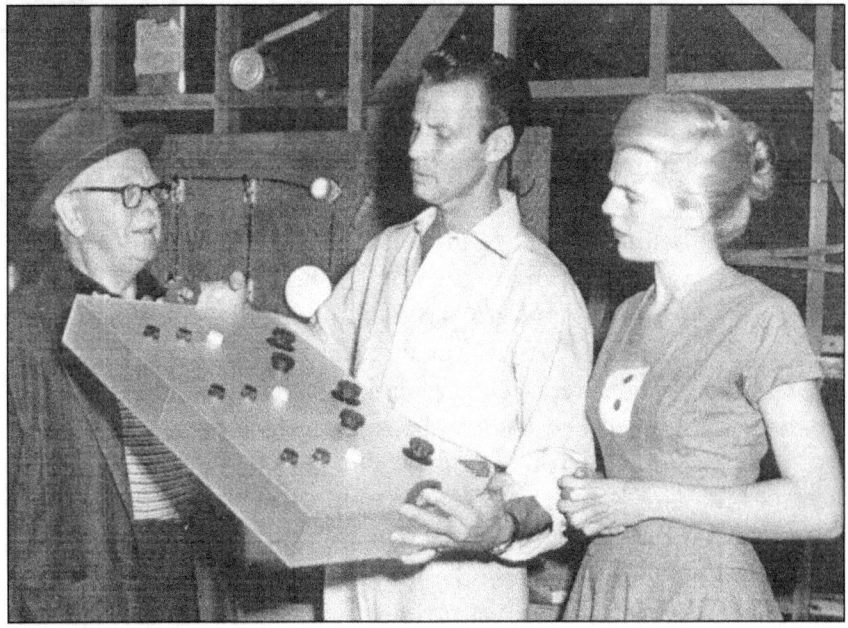

(LEFT TO RIGHT) **The cast examines a prop created for "The Magic Suitcase."**

train. The train runs. Grandpa scolds the boy for tampering with someone else's property, but is, himself, intrigued. Opening the suitcase, Scott finds a thin transparent tray, containing no batteries or any visible source or power. That night the old man finds that the device is capable of lighting the entire cabin. Cutting short their vacation, Scott takes the boy back home. Scott's son, John, an electronics engineer, takes the suitcase to his lab. John and his superior, Dr. Jorgenson, make extensive tests. They are unable to learn how the vast amount of energy is produced. Attempts to dismantle the device are futile. The metal resists cutting tools and torches. Grandpa Scott suggests that the power of the device itself be used to focus a heat-producing induction current on the shell. When this is done the device disintegrates. Chemical analysis shows that, by some means unknown to science, hydrogen gas has been compressed into an almost indestructible metal. The power source is determined to be an electric current flowing indefinitely at a temperature of Absolute Zero—a phenomenon our science has been able to produce only on a small scale under critical conditions. Dr. Jorgenson—taking confidence from the demonstrated fact that power *can* be produced on a vast scale—optimistically resolves to continue research to uncover the secret.

NOTES

- On the second day of filming, the cast and crew had to wait 25 minutes due to a blown out fuse in the sound equipment.
- During Truman Bradley's introductory lab demonstration, there is a photo of an atomic bomb going off, hanging on the wall. This same photo was hanging on the wall in the opening scene of "Survival in Box Canyon."
- George Douglas replaced actor John Zaremba, who was originally scheduled to play the role of Dr. Jorgenson.
- The fictitious roads mentioned by name by Grandpa Scott are Pine Crest Road and Rock Canyon Road, after Pine Crest Lake and a famous rock canyon, both located in Upper Franklin Reservoir where the location shots were filmed.
- The role of John Scott was originally intended for actor James Seay.

- Truman Bradley visited the set on Monday, September 17 for lab demonstrations for productions 70b, 71b, 73b, 74b and 75b. Herbert L. Strock was the director.

THE UPPER FRANKLIN RESERVOIR

The first day of filming consisted of exterior shots on location at Upper Franklin Reservoir beginning at 8:30 a.m. (the cast and crew left studio at 8). Mountain roads within the vicinity were filmed, consisting of the scenes where Grandpa meets the stranger with the suitcase. Later that afternoon, there followed scenes of the interior and exterior of the garage. At the end of the first day of filming, the company returned to the studio to work on Stage 5 around 3 p.m. The rest of episode was filmed at the studio on the same stage during the second day of production.

Franklin Canyon Reservoir was a small three-acre lake located just north of Beverly Hills in the Santa Monica Mountains. In the 1930s, the movie industry discovered Franklin Canyon's unspoiled beauty and lack of palm trees and began making arrangements with the Department of Water and Power to use the area for filming. Claudette Colbert's famous hitchhiking scene in *It Happened One Night* was filmed there in 1935. It was also used for the North Carolina lake where Andy Griffith and Ron Howard walked to go fishing in the opening credits of *The Andy Griffith Show*.

EPISODE #76 "BOLT OF LIGHTNING"

PRODUCTION #1076 / 78B

DATES OF PRODUCTION: OCTOBER 17, 18 AND 19, 1956
DIRECTED BY EDDIE DAVIS.

SCRIPT & STORY

FIRST DRAFT BY MEYER DOLINSKY, CIRCA AUGUST 11, 1956
FINAL DRAFT BY MEYER DOLINSKY, AUGUST 16, 1956
TELEPLAY BY MEYER DOLINSKY

PRODUCTION CREDITS

1ST ASST. CAMERAMAN: BILL MCGOWAN (*UN-CREDITED*)

1st Co. Grip: Carl Miksch (*un-credited*)
2nd Asst. Director: Don Schiff (*un-credited*)
2nd Cameraman: Brick Marquard (*un-credited*)
2nd Co. Grip: Jack Chambers (*un-credited*)
Assistant Director: Ed Stein
Asst. Prop Man: Harry Ott (*un-credited*)
Audio Supervisor: Quinn Martin
Boom Man: Doug Grant (*un-credited*)
Construction Chief: Archie Hall (*un-credited*)
Director of Photography: Curt Fetters
Electricians: Calman Bassin, [first name unknown] Brooks, Mike Hudson, Judd LeRoy and [first name unknown] Reiser (*all un-credited*)
Film Coordinator: Donald Tait
Film Editor: James Dyer
Gaffer: Calman Bassin (*un-credited*)
Key Grip: Carl Miksch
Make-up Artist: George Gray
Production Coordinator: Joe Wonder
Production Supervisor: Barry Cohon
Property Master: Max Pittman
Recorder: Ken Corson (*un-credited*)
Script Supervisor: Betty Leven
Set Decorator: Clarence Steenson
Set Designer: Robert Kinoshita
Set Labor: Owen Davis (*un-credited*)
Sound Editor: Bill Naylor
Sound Mixer: Roy Meadows
Special Scientific Effects: Harry Redmond, Jr.
Wardrobe: Alfred Berke (*un-credited*)

CAST: Bruce Bennett (Dr. Sheldon Thorpe, $1,000); Connie Buck (Madame Di Cosa, $80); Kristine Miller (Cynthia Blake, $150); Steve Mitchell (Mr. Denby, $100); Bruce Payne (Mr. Adams, $80); Sydney Smith (Doctor Franklin, $125); and Lyle Talbot (General Dodsworth, $125)

PLOT: Dr. Blake's mysterious death was more than just headlines;

Bruce Bennett plays around with the electricity on the set of "Bolt of Lightning."

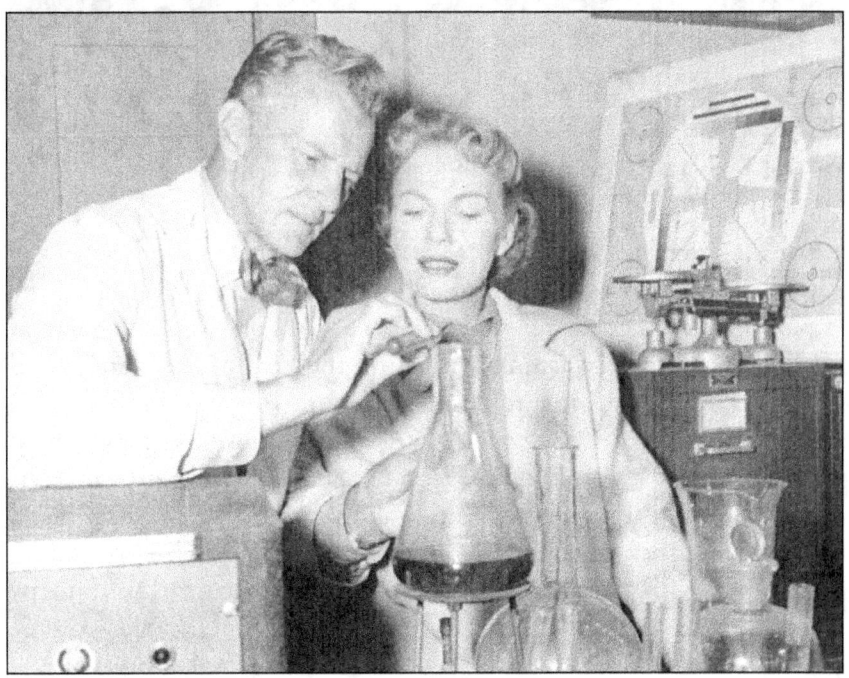

Kristine Miller observes Bruce Bennett's experiment.

Actress Kristine Miller panics in "Bolt of Lightning."

the famous scientist and his laboratory were destroyed by a heat source twice the intensity of the sun. Reputable scientists and officials were seriously considering the rumors that a flying saucer had caused the explosion. A former partner with Dr. Blake years previous, Dr. Sheldon Thorpe is hired by Washington to find the heat source that caused the explosion. Gaining reluctant cooperation from Dr. Blake's daughter, Cynthia, Dr. Thorpe methodically interviews people who had contact with Dr. Blake before his death. It isn't until he finds faint depressions in a plastic tablecloth on which Blake had scribbled and, using chemicals and infra-red film, uncovers blueprints to a complex electro-vanadium. In his own laboratory, Dr. Thorpe duplicates the electrical circuit and, in reproducing the strange glowing ball of intense heat, is himself almost killed. Thorpe lives, however, to demonstrate that the strange glowing ball was crystallized lightning that could successfully be harnessed in a magnetic field controlled by two parabolic reflectors. While General Dodsworth and Dr. Franklin, President of the University, looked on, Dr. Thorne explained with a miniature model how the crystallized ball of lightning can build canals and destroy enemy aircraft in the defense of our cities. The General shakes the scientist's hand in gratitude as Cynthia Blake, who was initially prejudiced against the lab work that killed her father, finds her faith rekindled.

NOTES

- The first day of filming was on Stages 2 and 6. Second day of filming was on Stages 6 and 3. Third day of filming was on Stage 3 for only two hours. On the evening of October 19, the same production company went to Poinsetta Park to film evening shots of the park for the *West Point* series.
- The stock footage of the laboratory explosion in the beginning of this episode was from the 1934 German film, *Gold*.
- According to the production sheets and the shooting script, there was a park scene shot on location, with Guy Buccola in a supporting role. This scene never made it to the finished film. Buccola was also un-credited as one of the giant leeches in *Attack of the Giant Leeches* (1959).

EPISODE #77 "THE STRANGE LODGER"

PRODUCTION #1077 / 77B

Dates of Production: October 4 and 5, 1956
Directed by Eddie Davis

SCRIPT & STORY

First Draft by Arthur Weiss, September 20, 1956
Revised pages dated October 3 and 16, 1956
Final Draft by Arthur Weiss, October 16, 1956
Teleplay by Arthur Weiss

PRODUCTION CREDITS

1st Asst. Cameraman: Dick Batcheller (*un-credited*)

1st Co. Grip: Glen Harris (*un-credited*)
2nd Asst. Director: Don Schiff (*un-credited*)
2nd Cameraman: Frank Dugis (*un-credited*)
2nd Co. Grip: Bill Jones (*un-credited*)
Assistant Director: Ed Stein
Asst. Prop Man: Stan Walters (*un-credited*)
Audio Supervisor: Quinn Martin
Construction Chief: Archie Hall (*un-credited*)
Director of Photography: Curt Fetters
Film Coordinator: Donald Tait
Film Editor: Jim Dyer (*un-credited*) and Thomas Scott (*credited*)
Gaffer: Calman Bassin (*un-credited*)
Make-up Artist: George Gray (*un-credited*)
Music Editor: Joe Inge
Production Coordinator: Joe Wonder
Production Supervisor: Barry Cohon
Property Master: Max Pittman
Recorder: Chuck King (*un-credited*)
Script Supervisor: Wanda Ramsey
Set Decorator: Bruce MacDonald
Set Designer: Robert Kinoshita
Set Labor: Bill Bentham (*un-credited*)
Sound Editor: Monroe Martin
Sound Mixer: Roy Meadows
Special Scientific Effects: Harry Redmond, Jr.
Still Man: Tom Morrison (*un-credited*)
Wardrobe: Alfred Berke (*un-credited*)

CAST: Cyril Delevanti (Mr. Rohrbach, $150); George Gilbreath (Bob Wilson, $80); Peter Hanson (Dr. Jim Wallaby, $350); Hugh Lawrence (Mr. Ross, $125); Charles Maxwell (Bill North, $80); Frances Pasco (Mrs. Garby, the landlady, $80); Jan Shepard (Maggie Dawes, $225); Daniel White (Bud, the truck driver, $80); and John Zaremba (Mr. Brunner of the FCC, $100)

PLOT: Dr. Jim Wallaby, a research engineer, has developed the Poll-O-Meter, a mobile electronic machine that takes TV polls by

The Episode Guide: Season Two

The cast poses before the Poll-O-Meter.

Jan Shepard discusses the Strange Lodger with Peter Hanson.

Peter Hanson, Jan Shepard and Charles Maxwell relazing between takes.

Cyril Delevanti and Peter Hanson play out their roles in "The Strange Lodger," with director Eddie Davis looking over their shoulders.

Charles Maxwell, Jan Shepard and Peter Hanson look over the Poll-O-Meter in a publicity photo.

scanning housetop TV antennas as it goes along the street. In the course of a TV survey, the machine indicates that "Channel 84" is being received by a certain antenna atop a boarding house. The antenna feeds into the TV set of Mr. Henry Rohrbach, an innocent looking little man who is in reality not receiving Channel 84, but is sending a report on this Channel, possibly to a spaceship a thousand miles from the Earth. The substance of the report—sent in code—is merely the content of an encyclopedia. By the time Wallaby breaks the code, and gets back to Mr. Rohrbach's boardinghouse room accompanied by a Federal investigator of UFOs (Unidentified Flying Objects), the little gentleman has completed his report and taken himself off to his spaceship by means of teleporting himself there the same way images are projected to television screens. As Rohrbach explains before he vanishes, the teleportation is no more than a logical extension of a now mundane formula: $E = mc^2$.

NOTES
- The character of Bill North was originally Bill West in the final teleplay, but changed before filming began.
- The original story for which this episode was based on was titled "Channel 84."
- This episode was titled "Calculex" during filming and production.
- Tape reels in Wilson's office are from the same stock footage shown in "Doctor Robot."
- The Poll-O-Meter truck was rented for this episode, and dressed up with signage to fit the purpose of the story.
- The exterior of Mr. Rohrbach's residence was filmed on location on the first day of filming, located at 4423 Kingswell Avenue in Los Angeles. The house was owned by Mr. Werner who gave permission to ZIV-TV to use the exterior of his house for filming. In the episode, the name of the street and city was never referenced, but the house number was given, 4423—not a fictitious number! Shots of Kingswell Avenue were also used, hence the palm trees that were exposed—something the crew purposely avoided for most of the productions such as *I Led Three Lives*, which supposedly took place in New England.

- The script originally featured a scene at the local zoo, with Jim Wallaby, Bill North and Maggie Dawes trying to find a connection with the zebras that was mentioned in the mysterious transmission. Actor Troy Melton was paid $80 to play the role of the zoo attendant but filming at the entrance of the Griffith Park Zoo, and the zebra pen, was cancelled on account of rain. The scene was ultimately never shot. Harry LeRoy and Leonard St. Leo, extras on hand to play the role of citizens enjoying the zoo, were never used.
- Wallaby's laboratory, used for the opening scene, was in reality the Curtis Laboratory, located at 2718 Griffith Park Blvd. in Los Angeles, California.

EPISODE #78 "THE MIRACLE HOUR"

PRODUCTION #1078 / 76B

DATES OF PRODUCTION: SEPTEMBER 28 AND OCTOBER 1, 1956
DIRECTED BY PAUL GUILFOYLE

SCRIPT & STORY

"NONE SO BLIND" FINAL TYPESCRIPT (ANNOTATED), CIRCA SEPTEMBER 17, 1956
OPENING (ANNOTATED), OCTOBER 16, 1956
REVISED PAGES (ANNOTATED), SEPTEMBER 27, 1956
REVISED MASTER MIMEO (ANNOTATED), SEPTEMBER 27, 1956
TELEPLAY BY STANLEY H. SILVERMAN

PRODUCTION CREDITS

1ST ASST. CAMERAMAN: ED NUGENT (*UN-CREDITED*)
1ST CO. GRIP: MEL BLEDSOE (*UN-CREDITED*)
2ND ASST. DIRECTOR: JIM ENGLE (*UN-CREDITED*)
2ND CAMERAMAN: JOHN WEILER (*UN-CREDITED*)
2ND CO. GRIP: TOMMY MATHEWS (*UN-CREDITED*)
ASSISTANT DIRECTOR: BERT GLAZER
ASST. PROP MAN: HARRY OTT (*UN-CREDITED*)
AUDIO SUPERVISOR: QUINN MARTIN
BOOM MAN: BILL FLANNERY (*UN-CREDITED*)

Construction Chief: Dee Bolhius (*un-credited*)
Director of Photography: Robert Hoffman
Electricians: Calman Bassin, Mike Hudson and Louis Kreiger (*all un-credited*)
Film Coordinator: Donald Tait
Film Editor: James Dyer
Gaffer: Calman Bassin (*un-credited*)
Key Grip: Mel Bledsoe
Make-up Artist: George Gray (*un-credited*)
Music Editor: Joe Inge
Production Coordinator: Joe Wonder
Production Supervisor: Barry Cohon
Property Master: Max Pittman
Recorder: Russ Schultz (*un-credited*)
Script Supervisor: Jeanne Lippman
Set Decorator: Clarence Steenson
Set Designer: Robert Kinoshita
Set Labor: Felix Felicia (*un-credited*)
Sound Editor: Monroe Martin
Sound Mixer: Jay Ashworth
Special Scientific Effects: Harry Redmond, Jr.
Still Man: Charles Rhodes (Sept. 28 only, *un-credited*)
Wardrobe: Alfred Berke (*un-credited*)

CAST: Jean Byron (Cathy Parker, $150); Ken Christy (Bill, $100); Donald Curtis (Dr. Roger Kiley, $150); Dick Foran (Jim Welles, $600); Charles Herbert (Tommy Parker, $100); and Riza Royce (Mrs. Tait, the nurse, $100)

PLOT: Broadway lighting director Jim Welles falls in love with costume designer Cathy Parker and discovers that her six-year old son, Tommy, is totally blind. Tommy's optic nerve was destroyed in a long-ago accident in which Cathy broke her back (which left her with a limp) and in which her husband met his death. Jim is unwilling to consider Tommy's case hopeless despite the verdict of specialists consulted by Cathy. Jim's friend, Dr. Roger Kiley, an up-and-coming eye specialist, examines the boy. Cathy, meanwhile, indignantly countermands the plan but is soon hospitalized for a series of

Donald Curtis as Dr. Roger Kiley in "The Miracle Hour."

operations. Learning she will be out of the picture for months, she implores Jim (because of his affection for the boy) to take care of Tommy in her absence. His "price" is permission to continue trying to help Tommy. Reluctantly, she gives permission. Because earthworms react to reflective light, Dr. Kiley conducts experiments on the boy; Tommy conceivably might be taught to "see" by proper training of the photosensitive cells in his skin. Three months later, Cathy is informed that she will soon be released from the hospital and the "experiments" with Tommy will have to stop. Kiley, however, succeeds in giving the boy the equivalent of rudimentary vision. This is demonstrated when Kiley and Jim bring the young boy to Cathy's hospital room and he is able to "see" the colored lights.

The Episode Guide: Season Two | 471

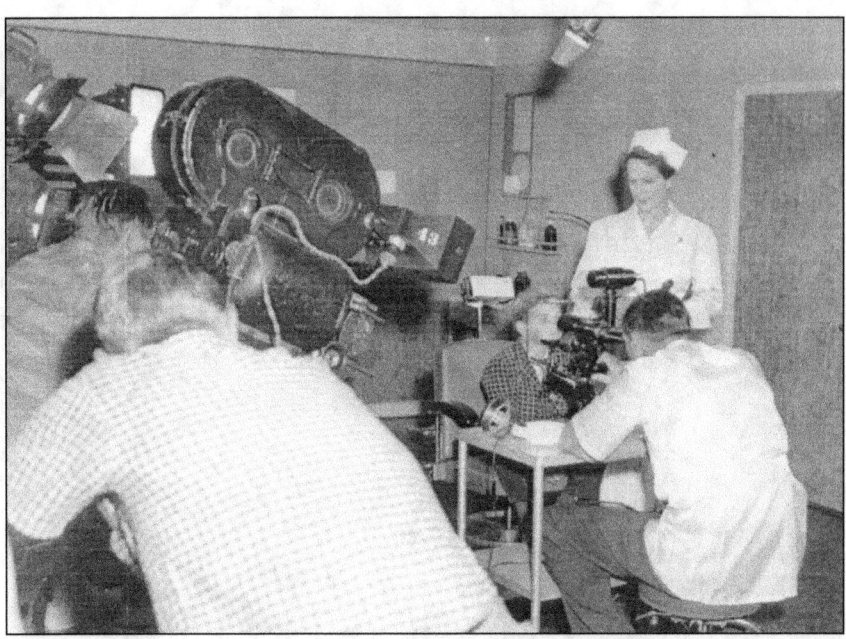

Camera Crew prepare to film the scene with Charles Herbert receiving a delicate eye test.

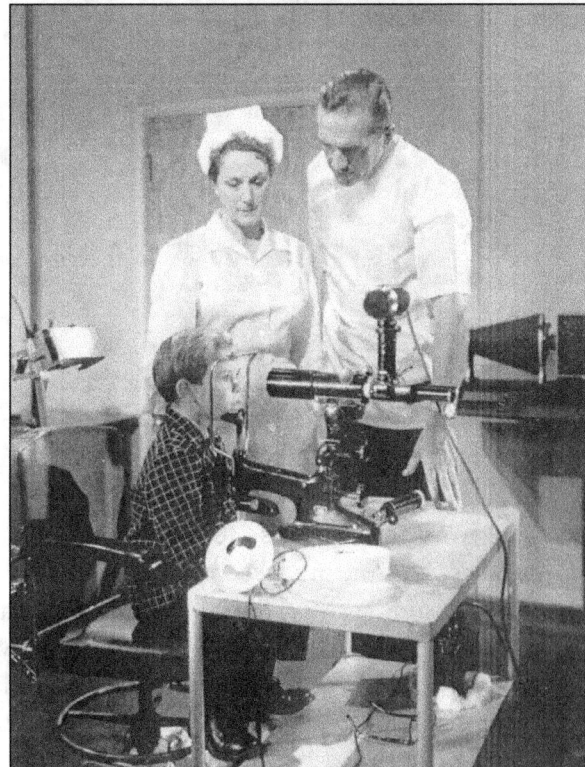

Tommy Parker (Charles Herbert) receives the eye test with Dr. Kiley (Donald Curtis) with nurse Tait (Riza Royce).

Dick Foran attempts to woo Jean Byron in the doctor's office in "The Miracle Hour."

NOTES

- The story for this episode was conceived a year previous for the first season, but never produced until the second season.
- This episode was produced under two separate titles. "None So Blind" and "Christmas." The teleplay was titled "None So Blind" but the reason why it was also produced under the title "Christmas" was because Ivan Tors was considering at the time to give the title a holiday flavor.

- The original script called for this episode to be a special holiday offering, with the concluding scene taking place in the hospital on Christmas day. Instead of the toy stage with lights, a Christmas tree was intended to be set up in the hospital room and it would have been the colored lights on the tree that young Tommy saw. For reasons unknown, the ending was changed and no Christmas celebration was referenced. Instead, it is commented that children were not permitted in the hospital rooms unless it was a special occasion, so Christmas Day was replaced with a reference that it was Tommy's seventh birthday.
- Among the electricians was an unnamed man from the Local 728.
- This is the only episode of the series to credit the key grip during the closing credits.
- The entire production was filmed on Stage 6.
- Production was held back 15 minutes on the second day of filming because Dick Foran was late to the set.
- Un-credited extras in the cast include F. Carter, M. Evans, John George, Frank Hunt and Duke Seba.
- Stock footage seen through Truman Bradley's microscope was lifted from a previous Ivan Tors production, *The Magnetic Monster* (1953).
- Truman Bradley holds a map of the solar system during his lab demonstration, happens to be the same hanging on the wall in the beginning of Bradley's demonstration in "Sun Gold." The same map appears on the wall during Bradley's closing remarks in "Stranger in the Desert."

Appendix A:
An Essay About Science Fiction
by Ivan Tors

Reprinted with permission from TV and Screen Writing *compiled and edited by Lola Goelet Yoakem. University of California Press, Berkeley & Los Angeles, 1958*

Since space satellites have become an accomplished reality, the whole realm of science fiction has taken on a new credibility in the eyes of the experts as well as of the general public.

A decade ago, Dick Tracy's wrist radio seemed altogether suitable to the somewhat juvenile vagaries of a comic strip. Today, tiny transistors make it an accomplished fact.

Fifty years ago, H.G. Wells wrote what were then termed "novels based on fanciful scientific speculation," such as *The Time Machine, The War of the Worlds, The Invisible Man, In the Days of the Comet,* and *War in the Air*. Almost a century ago, Jules Verne wrote "scientific romances with fantastic creations." Today, with so many of their "scientific speculations" having been turned into realities, their fictional "fantastic creations" do not meet with the same incredulity. In Jules Verne's time a radio receiver might have seemed as fantastic as today's nebulous Unidentified Flying Objects. Now we place a radio inside a space missile and shoot it out to orbit around the Earth. A few years ago, we may have wondered whether we should allow our children to watch TV shows about space cadets, rocket ships, disintegrator guns, and guided missile service stations that, so it is claimed, hung in space with nothing to anchor them. Today, scientists believe an Earth ship will make trips to the moon and to the planet Mars within the predictable future. In preparation for future space travel, the first lecture courses anywhere on Space Theory and Rocket Ship Technology have been given in San Francisco, Los Angeles, and San Diego. Among the learned faculty are such experts as Dr. Wernher von Braun, lecturing on "The Exploration of Mars"; Robert W. Buchheim, "Lunar Flight"; Krafft A. Ehricke, "Interplanetary Operations"; William H. Pickering, "Guidance Techniques"; Heinz Haber, "Space Medicine—Physical Factors of the Space Environment"; Dr. Hubertus Strughold, "Space Environmental Factors"; Samuel Herrick and Joseph W. Siry, "Earth Satellites"; John I. Shafer, "Propulsion—Solid Rocket Design"; Ernest E. Sechler, "Structural Materials, Configurations, and Analyses"; Alfred J. Eggers, Jr., "Recovery Dynamics—Possibility of Non-Destructive Testing"; L.M.K. Boelter and H. Guyford Stever, "Why Space Technology?"; and Herbert C. Corbin, "Time Dilation Effects in Space Travel."

The premise of science fiction as a new art form in movies, TV, radio, books, and magazines is simply that anything man is capable of imagining can happen. The imaginative word pictures conjured by authors can fire the creative talents of inventors, scientists, and engineers. Then, like wrist radio or a camera small enough to conceal in your hand, there it is—a reality and no longer fantastic.

Anything is possible in science fiction. This unique and fertile field is literally one market in which a producer or story editor may tell you that your story line is incredible or fantastic and mean that he likes it. Other kinds of fiction may find source material in past history or contemporary events; science fiction reaches into space and the future for its research.

Science fiction is here to stay; all indications are that this market will continue to expand in motion pictures and television. Writing in this field may become one of the most important forms of constructive literature within the next two decades.

Two basic qualities are requisite in the successful writer of science fiction: imagination and scientific curiosity. It goes without saying that he must have a solid basic understanding of science and familiarity with all its concepts. He must know, for example, the electrochemical nature of the brain and human nervous system, as well as the structure of the atom and the definition of the Einstein theory. Progress in medicine, aviation, ballistics, transportation, cybernetics, and automation must interest him. He must keep abreast of every development in the field of science, because he never knows when even an apparently insignificant item may spark a story for him.

There is a formula for science fiction literature, just as there is a pattern for all other types of writing. The writer can take any one of the basic plots and, by adding a fantastic new invention or an exciting but as yet unproved scientific theory, come up with a salable script. Science fiction is fantasy against a science background. The resolution of the plot explains the nature of the gimmick being used. It is almost as if the writer finds his gimmick, starts writing his story at the finish, and proceeds backward to the beginning.

Excellent examples of science fiction writing for television can be found in *Science Fiction Theatre*, a filmed series produced by ZIV. Poison gas is seeping along the roots of a "killer" tree in the desert. A scientist resolves the plot by determining that the gas is coming from the Earth's center; he injects a tube by means of which he is able to photograph the interior of the Earth.

A couple from outer space are controlled electronically by their native planet. They escape to Earth and take up residence near an electric power plant, which makes ineffective the other planet's electronic influence on the couple. Later, the master generator in the nearby power plant explodes, and the couple disappears from the Earth.

Because of extrasensory perception and an accidental short-wave transmission via a television microwave, an innocent woman is suspected of being a spy when she is able to receive secret information being recorded on a dictating machine several blocks away. A giant reflector is used to direct certain devastating sun rays into a secret laboratory, thereby causing a mysterious explosion.

Science fiction comprises more than robots, mechanical men, or ordinary automation, but if a story can be strengthened by such additions, so much the better.

An imaginative writer may place a human conflict against a background of outer space with the story conflict taking place inside a space ship or on a landing field poised strategically just beyond the Earth's magnetic field or on another planet. Again he may plot an interstellar conflict and give it a human earthbound resolution.

A fantastic premise is vital to science fiction. The writer may evolve a story so fantastic he may think an editor will reject it as being scientifically questionable. The editor may do so if the background material has not been thoroughly researched, but a rejection on the basis of incredible premise is not likely. For example, a plot might concern a man dying of an incurable malady and agreeing to an experiment in which he will be frozen in a block of ice for three weeks. At the end of this time the ice is removed and the man is still alive. Such a fantastic premise must be made believable, possibly by emphasizing the fact that a medical scientist has made a lifelong study of animal hibernation and discovered that in hibernation the body temperature drops twenty to thirty degrees and that animals never contract disease in hibernation because bacteria remain dormant at such temperatures. He may have observed that fish are often frozen within the ice of their habitat, but are still alive when the ice melts.

Well-researched science fiction has achieved added popularity since the advent of man-made satellites. Writers whose talents lie in this direction may sell not only to TV and movies but also to magazines. They can lease rights for TV and movies, later using the same plots for magazine stories or novels.

The trend is now definite toward more science fiction in motion pictures. These productions are often low budget, which means easier and more numerous sales. It is not impossible to sell such a subject for an hour or ninety-minute TV program.

The writer who can make a soundly constructed teleplay or a screen original in science fiction will have no trouble getting an agent. Agents are in business to earn 10 per cent on the sales they make for writers. If scripts are commercial in content and treatment, an agent can sell them quickly. I doubt if anything pleases an agent more than fast—and repeat—sales of a client's literary material.

The writer who knows his background data in science and who keeps his imagination working overtime can turn out science fiction scripts that will sell. Stories with a constructive premise command better prices, and also give the writer a greater satisfaction in his accomplishment. A prime example of high literary level in science fiction may be found in the prolific work of Ray Bradbury.

Yes, anything imaginable can happen in science fiction—even a writer who sells every script he writes, although the average professional writer might be inclined to think this kind of premise incredulous and altogether unbelievably fantastic.

Appendix B: Truman Bradley's Lab Demonstrations

The closing credits of each episode, in the episode guide, reflected only the dramatic part of the program, never the production crew responsible for Truman Bradley's opening and closing monologues. Television viewers today still suspect the closing credits reflected Bradley's lab demonstrations as well as the drama, which is not entirely true. The following information should help demonstrate Truman Bradley's infrequent appearances to the Ziv studios for both seasons of *Science Fiction Theatre*.

Episodes 3, 4 and 5

Date of Production: February 28, 1955
Director: Herbert L. Strock
1st Asst. Director: Marty Moss
2nd Asst. Director: Harry Jones
1st Cameraman: Robert Hoffman
2nd Cameraman: Bill Mautino
1st Asst. Cameraman: Jim Bell
Sound Mixer: Jay Ashworth
Recorder: Bill Denby
Boom Man: Jim Flannery
1st Co. Grip: Mel Bledsoe
2nd Co. Grip: Ted Mathew
Property Master: Max Pittman
Asst. Prop Man: Stan Walters
Set Dresser: Lou Hafley
Wardrobe Man: Alfred Berke
Script Supervisor: Helen Gailey

FILM EDITOR: JOHN B. WOELZ
GAFFER: J.C. BARTON
CONSTRUCTION CHIEF: ARCHIE HALL

Note: On this same date, February 28, Bradley recorded his off-screen narration for episode 3, and filmed the opening theme for the first season openers.

EPISODES 6 AND 7

DATE OF PRODUCTION: MARCH 14, 1955
DIRECTOR: HERBERT L. STROCK
1ST ASST. DIRECTOR: EDDIE BERNOUDY
2ND ASST. DIRECTOR: BOBBY RAY
1ST CAMERAMAN: MONROE "MONK" ASKINS
2ND CAMERAMAN: BUD MAUTINO
1ST ASST. CAMERAMAN: JIM BELL
SOUND MIXER: GARRY HARRIS
RECORDER: BOB POST
BOOM MAN: ELMER HAGLUND
1ST CO. GRIP: CARL MIKSCH
2ND CO. GRIP: COLEY KESSINGER
PROPERTY MASTER: MAX PITTMAN
ASST. PROP MAN: STAN WALTERS
SET DRESSER: LYLE REIFSNIDER
WARDROBE MAN: ALFRED BERKE
SCRIPT SUPERVISOR: LARRY LUND
FILM EDITOR: JOHN B. WOELZ
GAFFER: JOSEPH WHARTON
CONSTRUCTION CHIEF: ARCHIE HALL

EPISODES 13, 14 AND 15

DATE OF PRODUCTION: MAY 11, 1955
DIRECTOR: LEON BENSON
1ST ASST. DIRECTOR: BERT CHERVIN
2ND ASST. DIRECTOR: BOBBY RAY
1ST CAMERAMAN: CURT FETTERS

2ND CAMERAMAN: DICK RAWLINGS
1ST ASST. CAMERAMAN: ART BELL
SOUND MIXER: GARRY HARRIS
RECORDER: BOB POST
BOOM MAN: ELMER HAGLUND
1ST CO. GRIP: CARL MIKSCH
PROPERTY MASTER: MAX PITTMAN AND YGNACIO SEPULVEDA
SET DRESSER: BRUCE MACDONALD
MAKE-UP ARTIST: GEORGE GRAY
WARDROBE MAN: ALFRED BERKE
SCRIPT SUPERVISOR: LARRY LUND
FILM EDITOR: DUNCAN MANSFIELD, THOMAS SCOTT AND JOHN B. WOELZ
GAFFER: S.H. BARTON
CONSTRUCTION CHIEF: ARCHIE HALL

EPISODES 16, 17, 18 AND 19

DATE OF PRODUCTION: MAY 25, 1955
DIRECTOR: LEON BENSON
1ST ASST. DIRECTOR: DONALD VERK
2ND ASST. DIRECTOR: BOBBY RAY
1ST CAMERAMAN: CURT FETTERS
2ND CAMERAMAN: DICK RAWLINGS
1ST ASST. CAMERAMAN: JIM BELL
SOUND MIXER: GARRY HARRIS
RECORDER: BOB POST
BOOM MAN: ELMER HAGLUND
1ST CO. GRIP: CARL MIKSCH
PROPERTY MASTER: MAX PITTMAN
SET DRESSER: VINCENT TAYLOR
MAKE-UP ARTIST: GEORGE GRAY
WARDROBE MAN: FRANK TAUSS
SCRIPT SUPERVISOR: LARRY LUND
FILM EDITOR: ACE CLARK AND DUNCAN MANSFIELD
CONSTRUCTION CHIEF: ARCHIE HALL
ALSO FEATURES JOHN PHILLIPS AND GEORGE MATHERS WITH BRADLEY.

Note: For episode 17, Bradley only filmed the opening scenes. He had to return to the set on May 27 for additional pickups for episode 19.

EPISODES 17, 20 AND 21

DATE OF PRODUCTION: JUNE 13, 1955
DIRECTOR: HERBERT L. STROCK
1ST ASST. DIRECTOR: DONALD VERK
2ND ASST. DIRECTOR: BOBBY RAY
1ST CAMERAMAN: ROBERT HOFFMAN
2ND CAMERAMAN: BUD MAUTINO
1ST ASST. CAMERAMAN: JIM BELL
SOUND MIXER: GARRY HARRIS
RECORDER: BOB POST
BOOM MAN: ELMER HAGLUND
1ST CO. GRIP: MEL BLEDSOE
2ND CO. GRIP: TEX JACKSON
PROPERTY MASTER: MAX PITTMAN
SET DRESSER: VINCENT TAYLOR
MAKE-UP ARTIST: GEORGE GRAY
WARDROBE MAN: ALFRED BERKE
SCRIPT SUPERVISOR: LARRY LUND
FILM EDITOR: ACE CLARK (EPISODE 20) AND THOMAS SCOTT (EPISODE 21)
GAFFER: S.H. BARTON
CONSTRUCTION CHIEF: ARCHIE HALL

Note: For episode 17, Bradley was only filmed for the closing scenes.

EPISODES 25, 26 AND 27

DATE OF PRODUCTION: JULY 14, 1955
DIRECTOR: EDDIE DAVIS
1ST ASST. DIRECTOR: ED STEIN
2ND ASST. DIRECTOR: EDDIE MULL
1ST CAMERAMAN: ROBERT HOFFMAN
2ND CAMERAMAN: BUD MAUTINO

1st Asst. Cameraman: Spec Jones
Sound Mixer: Jay Ashworth
Recorder: Larry Golding
Boom Man: Jim Flannery
1st Co. Grip: Mel Bledsoe
Property Master: Max Pittman
Make-up Artist: George Gray
Wardrobe Man: Alfred Berke
Script Supervisor: Billy Vernon
Film Editor: Charles Craft (Episode 25), Thomas Scott (Episode 27) and John B. Woelz (Episode 26)
Construction Chief: Archie Hall

Note: On this same date, July 14, Bradley recorded his off-screen narrations for episodes 24, 25, 26 and 27.

EPISODES 28, 29 AND 30

Date of Production: July 26, 1955

Truman Bradley reported to Stage 7 for narration and lab demonstrations.

EPISODE 28

On July 30, 1955, Truman Bradley returned to the studio to re-record narration for episode 28, because the original narration had since underwent a re-write.

EPISODES 29, 31, 32 AND 33

On August 17, 1955, Bradley recorded narration for episodes 29, 31, 32 and 33 during the cast's hour-long lunch break of this episode, beginning 1:05.

On August 26, 1955, Eddie Davis directed Truman Bradley for additional pickup shots for episodes 31, 32 and 33.

EPISODES 34, 35, 36 AND 37

DATE OF PRODUCTION: SEPTEMBER 20, 1955
DIRECTOR: HERBERT L. STROCK
1ST ASST. DIRECTOR: ERICH VON STROHEIM, JR.
2ND ASST. DIRECTOR: BOBBY RAY
1ST CAMERAMAN: CURT FETTERS
2ND CAMERAMAN: DICK RAWLINGS
1ST ASST. CAMERAMAN: JIM BELL
SOUND MIXER: GARRY HARRIS
RECORDER: WILLIAM HANKS
BOOM MAN: ELMER HAGLUND
1ST CO. GRIP: CARL MIKSCH
2ND CO. GRIP: TEX JACKSON
PROPERTY MASTER: MAX PITTMAN
ASSISTANT PROP MAN: STAN WALTERS
SET DRESSER: BRUCE MACDONALD
MAKE-UP ARTIST: GEORGE GRAY
WARDROBE MAN: ALFRED BERKE
SCRIPT SUPERVISOR: RUTH BROWNSON
GAFFER: WADE HUFF
SET LABOR: ART SWEET
CONSTRUCTION CHIEF: DEE BOLHIUS
BEST BOY: MIKE HUDSON
ELECTRICIANS: CHARLES HANGER, FRED HOUNSHELL AND JOHN MILLMAN
3RD GRIP: CARL MIKSCH

THE FIRST SEASON CONCLUDES

On October 5, 1955, Truman Bradley recorded narration for episodes 34 through 39, while the cast was at lunch. He completed his job within 15 minutes. Bradley returned to the studio on October 6, for filming the opening and closing lab demonstrations for episodes 38 and 39 around 5 p.m., after the cast finished principal filming on Stage 3 and Stage 7.

THE SECOND SEASON

Documentation for the second season narrations and lab demonstrations have proven elusive. What little is known about Bradley's work follows:

EPISODES 40, 41 AND 42
DATE OF PRODUCTION: FEBRUARY 24, 1956

Truman Bradley filmed lab demonstrations and narration for all three episodes.

On this same date, the crew filmed the recurring opening and closing (also where the screen credits appear) for the second season.

EPISODES 43, 46, 48 AND 49
DATE OF PRODUCTION: MARCH 29, 1956

After filming was completed at 4:20 p.m., the cast went home while the crew remained behind with Truman Bradley to film the lab demonstrations.

EPISODES 43, 47, 49, 50 AND 52
DATE OF PRODUCTION: APRIL 4, 1956

After filming was completed at 3:45 p.m., Truman Bradley was filmed for additional pick-up shots for the lab demonstration for production 43. Bradley then recorded off-screen narration for productions 47, 49, 50 and 52.

EPISODES 47, 50 AND 51
DATE OF PRODUCTION: APRIL 13, 1956

After filming was completed on Stage 3 at 4:15 p.m., the cast went home while the crew remained behind with Truman Bradley to film lab demonstrations for episodes 47 and 50, and off-screen narration and lab demonstrations for episode 51. The entire task took almost four hours.

EPISODES 52, 53, 54 AND 55
DATE OF PRODUCTION: MAY 4, 1956

Truman Bradley was filmed all day for lab demonstrations. Tom Anthony was the extra used for two pictures. The entire direction was handled by Herbert L. Strock. Episodes 53, 54 and 55 took between 60 to 90 minutes to complete but episode 52 took three and a half hours to complete.

EPISODES 54, 56 AND 57
DATE OF PRODUCTION: MAY 23, 1956

While the cast and crew were away for lunch from 1 to 1:30 p.m, Truman Bradley recorded off-screen narration for episodes 54, 56, and 57.

EPISODES 60, 62, 63 AND 65
DATE OF PRODUCTION: JUNE 28, 1956

From 4:00 to 5:05 p.m., Truman Bradley was at the studio recording off-screen narrations.

EPISODES 61, 64 AND 66
DATE OF PRODUCTION: JULY 23, 1956

When the cast and crew left to film location shots at 12:40 p.m., Truman Bradley reported to Stage 5 to record off-screen narrations for productions starting at 1 p.m. He was also filmed for the opening and closing lab demonstrations for episodes 64 and 61.

EPISODES 65, 67 AND 72
DATE OF PRODUCTION: AUGUST 16, 1956

While the cast and crew went off to lunch, Truman Bradley recorded off-screen narrations within 30 minutes.

EPISODES 68, 70, 71, 73, 74 AND 75
DATE OF PRODUCTION: MAY 23, 1956

While the cast and crew departed for lunch from 1 to 1:30 p.m., Truman Bradley reported to Stage 5 for off-screen narrations, then reported to a different stage for the lab demonstrations. Property men Max Pittman and Stan Walters were on hand to assist filming and Herbert L. Strock directed.

EPISODES 73, 76, 77 AND 78
DATE OF PRODUCTION: OCTOBER 19, 1956

Truman Bradley recorded off-screen narration after the cast finished filming for the day.

Appendix C: "Y**O**R**O**"
Dated: November 1, 1954
A Teleplay Treatment
By Ivan Tors & George Van Marter

Fades in to an established shot of a large university campus.

Dissolves through to a plain, uncluttered room in which there is a wide table. Across the center of the table is a head-high partition which prevents those who are seated on opposite sides of the table from seeking each other. Dr. Curtis Lawton is on one side of the partition, Edna Miner is on the other. Lawton is an elderly man who radiates warmth and an intensity in an almost "Pickwickian" sense. On the table before him is a pad and pencil, a chart bearing cabalistic figures, and a small, bare light globe mounted in a base with a push button. Edna is young, lovely, and with lips that seem always ready to smile. She, too, has a chart, a light, a pad and pencil. Her chart is only partially filled with figures.

She presses the light button, sits with pencil poised. Lawton squints at his chart. There's a momentary pause, then Edna jots down a figure, once more presses the button. Lawton calls out to her that this is the end of the sequence . . . What was the last figure? She tells him. He shakes his head in amusement—and amazement and tells her the figures are correct—she was off only on the decimal point. He picks up a blackened pipe, comes 'round to her, sits on the edge of the table, tells her that she's the perfect assistant . . . One of these days he'll be able to stay home, work in his garden . . . she can carry on at the laboratory, read his mind at long distances. She chuckles, tells him that she has long suspected that they were "soul mates" . . . that's the reason for her ability to know "what he's thinking."

There is a timid, then a more persistent knock on the door. Lawton opens the door, confronts an apologetic secretary, and a medium youngish man in uniform of a full colonel. With quick amenities the colonel introduces himself. He's Peter Van Dyke, meteorologist . . . he's a man with a problem—a big problem—and he feels that only Dr. Lawton, the country's outstanding expert on parapsychology, can help solve it.

What is the problem?

Van Dyke has been in charge of the establishment of a weather station eighty miles from the North Pole. Recently, certain phenomena have occurred which are seemingly without plausible explanation. Seven men, three meteorologists, two radio and one radar expert, and two geophysicists, have suddenly shown hyper-sensitive and telepathic powers far beyond the normal range. These men are experts, scientists, men whose emotional equilibrium is well established. Recently they have been reading each others' minds, exhibiting psychic powers which are almost frightening. Each man shows an awareness of his companions' thoughts; some of them have called the run on events which have occurred thousands of miles away. Van Dyke cites several personal examples. The whole thing is amazing and disturbing.

Lawton is more than interested—he's excited. He tells Van Dyke that the cause of such phenomena are undoubtedly physical, and induced, perhaps by the locale and the isolation.

Van Dyke says that some of his men have decided that perhaps Houdini has at last determined to "get in touch." They find themselves doing things which they had not intended to do . . . they find themselves under momentary compulsions which are almost frightening.

Lawton's excitement mounts. Would it be possible for him to go to the weather camp and examine the men? Van Dyke chuckles and informs the professor that a plane is ready at the airport. They'll leave in three hours—with the blessings of the Defense Department.

Lawton tells Van Dyke that Edna Miner will accompany them—she's an able assistant, and she possesses telepathic powers far beyond the norm. Edna is equally excited and says she can be ready in twenty minutes. Then, while the professor launches into his preparations, she conducts the colonel through the laboratory. She tells about the "newness" of this field and says that Lawton claims that we use only five per cent of our brain potential. She exhibits an electroencephalograph and a toposcope . . . they'll take similar devices with them to the weather camp.

Van Dyke is fascinated and amazed by the hundreds of tubes in these machines. Edna tells him that Lawton likes to think of the brain as a "machine which contains not hundreds of tubes, but millions of them with connecting wires, scanning devices, controls, cut-offs, solenoids, and other machinery not yet imagined by man. The brain is a perfect machine not yet properly used . . . and compressed into a tiny mass of living tissue! This is God's greatest mechanical achievement!"

The flight to the weather camp is uneventful, yet exciting with all the vicious terrain that lies below.

Lawton and Edna find the situation even more absorbing than the colonel had described. Receptivity among the men has increased greatly. One of the men has kept a log of flight time of the plane which brought the three people from Washington. He is able to name the exact time of departure, the time over the check points, and has predicted the time of arrival. Everyone swears that this information was not received by radio.

Lawton conducts the classic experiments . . . the naming of cards, reproduction of geometric figures, sentence completion, etc. The incidence of accuracy is astounding. Lie detector tests are made. There is no chicanery!

Edna has been busy in her capacity as assistant. Suddenly she exhibits an almost mesmeric fatigue. Lawton says that this is what he has been waiting for . . . this girl is the most sensitive "reception instrument" he has ever encountered. Edna tells him that she seems to have more "awareness" than she has ever experienced, even in the most exhausting laboratory trials. The girl is placed on a cot. The electroencephalograph and toposcope are brought into use. Edna is "hooked up" . . . The needles on the graph machine begin their silent marking, and the lights of the toposcope play a dancing pattern.

The men in the room watch with complete fascination as Lawton controls the machine. The rising storm outside the hut makes the scene even more frightening.

Herb Dunne, one of the radar men, sits in a kind of half hypnosis. Lawton watches him and questions him. Dunne watches the flashing lights; his head nods in a rhythmic beat; it is almost difficult for him to speak. Slowly, he tells Lawton that there is a pattern to the way the lights are flashing.

How does he know? Has he ever seen a device like this? How can he distinguish a pattern?

Dunne insists he can see it . . . more than that, he can feel it!

Then he snaps out of it, comes back to full awareness. He says the "sensation" has stopped. Edna confirms this, says she is back to normalcy. The lights have changed pattern, lost regularity. Lawton released her from the machines. Van Dyke orders everyone to bed . . . everyone but Herb Dunne . . . It is his watch at the radar and radio.

The storm increases to a greater howling fury. The hands of the clock move into the night.

Herb Dunne sits before his observation and communication equipment. The lash of the Arctic wind screams against the hut. Suddenly Dunne becomes tense, his head begins to move in little rhythmic beats, his lips move without sound. His hand goes to the communication key. He begins to send a long series of dots and dashes . . . A pattern that is repeated over and over again! Then, with sweating determination, he pulls himself back to full consciousness, pushes the alarm button. The blast of the bell rings into the hut.

Everyone comes rushing into the room—everyone but Edna. Dunne tells the people of his experience, says he still feels the evidence of compulsion. Then Edna enters the room. Her movements are trance-like, compulsive, weird. She is almost fainting when Lawton places her on the cot, hooks up the electroencephalograph and toposcope. She goes into a complete trance as the lights begin to flash a regular pattern.

Then once more the lights lose their pattern. Edna recovers consciousness, says she feels actively ill. The radio key keeps hammering an insistent inquiry. The operator at Thule wants to know what this is all about. What is the meaning of these letters that have been transmitted to him? Y—O—R—D . . . over and over he has received Dunne's code. What does it mean?

Dunne remembers. That must have been the insistent thing coming into his brain. Y—O—R—D . . . These were the letters that he felt an uncontrollable compulsion to send.

Lawton examines the graph. Here, too, is a pattern . . . a long series . . . then a short one . . . repeated and repeated. This graph—this pattern—somehow found transmission from the electrical impulses emanating from Edna's brain!

He looks at the men, at the still pale Edna. Something . . . somehow . . . has found a way to intrude upon them. Topographically they must occupy an area of receptivity. They are intelligent people, yet each of them has felt mental compulsion in the same range of time. Apparently all the factors have been right for what seems to be a communication. Spirits? Somebody's dead grandmother? Subversive experimentation? Who knows? But here is certainly a pattern—even letters . . . a word! Y..O..R..D..! The significance of the pattern! This is the important thing! He must get back to Washington at once and start his analysis. When will the storm be over? When can he fly out?

Thule says the storm is abating. Van Dyke orders a plane for Lawton.

Lawton says he'll leave Edna at the camp. She's his most valuable telepathic contact—a valuable asset! Van Dyke agrees Edna is very valuable!

The Institute of Advanced Thinking . . . This is where Dr. Lawton meets his close friend and confidant, Dr. Arnold Samson.

Samson is a great bull of a man. He points a derisive finger at the pixie-like Curtis Lawton. With half laughter he tells the parapsychologist that he's been imagining things. Patterns! Messages! A strange word! Y..O..R..D..! It spells 'droy' backwards! Maybe an Eskimo was out in a droy and became lost? Maybe he's sending messages backward?

Lawton is insistent, tells Samson he's in constant communication with the weather base. The compulsive message patterns are still going on. Samson is one of our most advanced thinkers . . . Stop being a skeptic old bull and offer some help. Lawton shows the other man the electroencephalograph charts and the toposcope photos. Samson can see the regularity of pattern in certain portions.

Samson points out that if there is a coded message involved there is a way to "crack it" in a hurry. The Pentagon has a giant electronic computer which was developed for just one purpose—and that is to unscramble enemy codes in any language! If it is cryptography that is needed, then the Pentagon has the right machine. It can do in hours what the human brain can't do in months or years—or can't do at all!

Cryptographers examine Lawton's charts and photos . . . There is a definite pattern. Find the key word—that is the problem! Lawton tells them to try Y..O..R..D..

The giant computer goes into operation. Hour after hour it is fed the information that it needs. Then the key is found! One hundred and forty-nine words are the result of a translation from a completely unknown combination of letters. Hasty consultations are held with top officials.

Then Dr. Lawton finds himself in the great communications center in Washington. The chief operator is filled with amused skepticism. Is this what Lawton wants? Is he serious? Does he really want to blast a message into outer space?

The broadcast goes into operation . . . And no more has the message started on its way than Lawton receives a call from the weather camp . . . Only a few moments ago, at 2:44 A.M., in the midst of the greatest receptivity yet experienced, there was a sudden cessation of all extra-sensory or telepathic communication. There is sudden sagging disappointment in Lawton. He turns to a communication assistant, tells him to keep the message going into outer space until further notice.

Word keeps coming from the weather station. Hour after hour goes by . . . there is no further extra-sensory experience! Then Lawton receives a message from Meteorological Clearance. Wearily he reads it; he sends word to Communications . . . The message into outer space is no longer necessary.

All radio channels are cleared. All television channels are cleared. Dr. Curtis Lawton, parapsychologist, has a message to deliver. The whole world, from foreign deserts to Van Dyke's weather station, listens in.

In simple words Lawton explains that the people of this Earth had been in direct communication with the inhabitants of another planet. He tells how, by the wonders of extra-sensory perception, a message had been intercepted that a space ship from another world has found itself in trouble close to the Earth's atmosphere.

The passengers of the ship, by a form of telepathic communication, had been frantically asking for advice from the mother planet as to the best way to escape the Earth's gravitational pull. We, after decoding the spaceship's message, had sent word of encouragement and advice. However, our instructions had been transmitted too late. At 2:44 of the preceding night all telepathic receptivity had ceased . . . At that exact time the observatory at New Mexico had observed and photographed a fireball which entered and blazed brilliantly in the Earth's atmosphere. Spectrum analysis of the photographs has disclosed that the composition of the fireball was of alloyed materials . . . And alloys do not occur in nature!

Edna Miner, Colonel Van Dyke, and the other people of the weather station hear Lawton deliver his final words:

At least we are able to understand the language of the inhabitants of another planet. Certainly these space travelers were not on a war-like mission . . . and certainly their scientific advancement is far beyond ours! Perhaps these people have learned to live in peace and harmony . . . . Let it be God's will that they may teach us the secrets of longer life, freedom from disease, happy living! We have only to keep our eyes and ears—and our minds—open to the greater knowledge that flows about us and through us!

SELECTED BIBLIOGRAPHY

BOOKS

Brooks, Tim, and Earle Marsh. *The Complete Directory to Prime Time Network TV Shows, 1946–Present.* Fourth Edition. New York: Ballantine Books, 1988.

Broughton, Irv. *Producers on Producing.* Jefferson, NC: McFarland, 1986.

Cox, Jim. *Radio Crime Fighters.* Jefferson, NC: McFarland, 2002.

Duffin, Allan T., and Paul Matheis. *The 12 O'Clock High Logbook.* Duncan, OK: BearManor Media, 2005.

Dunning, John. *On the Air: The Encyclopedia of Old-Time Radio.* New York: Oxford University Press, 1998.

French, Jack. *Private Eyelashes: Radio's Lady Detectives.* Duncan, OK: BearManor Media, 2004.

Grabman, Sandra. *Plain Beautiful: The Life of Peggy Ann Garner.* Duncan, OK: BearManor Media, 2005.

Grams, Martin. *The Twilight Zone: Unlocking the Door to a Television Classic.* Churchville, MD: OTR Publishing, 2008.

Grams, Martin. *I Led 3 Lives: The True Story of Herbert A. Philbrick's Television Program.* Duncan, OK: BearManor Media, 2007.

Hayde, Michael. *Flights of Fantasy: The Unauthorized but True Story of Radio & TV's Adventures of Superman.* Duncan, OK: BearManor Media, 2008.

Hickerson, Jay. *The New, Revised Ultimate History of Network Radio Programming and Guide to All Circulating Shows.* Third Edition. Hamden, Conn.: Jay Hickerson, 2001.

Kindem, Gorham. *The Live Television Generation of Hollywood Film Directors: Interviews with Seven Directors.* Jefferson, NC: McFarland, 1994.

Kisseloff, Jeff. *The Box.* New York: Penguin Books, 1995.

Koper, Richard. *Fifties Blondes: Sexbombs, Sirens, Bad Girls and Teen Queens.* Duncan, OK: BearManor Media, 2010.

Lane, Girgenti. *Guy Williams: The Man Behind the Mask.* Duncan, OK: BearManor Media, 2005.

Phillips, Mark and Frank Garcia. *Science Fiction Television Series: Episode Guides, Histories, And Casts And Credits for 62 Primetime Shows, 1959 Through 1989.* Jefferson, NC: McFarland, 2006.

Pilato, Herbie. *The Bionic Book Reconstructed.* Duncan, OK: BearManor Media, 2007.

Rosin, James. *The Invaders: A Quinn Martin TV Series.* Philadelphia, PA: Autumn Road Company, 2010.

Rosin, James. *Naked City: The Television Series.* Philadelphia, PA: Autumn Road Company, 2007.

Rosin, James. *Route 66: The Television Series, 1960-64.* Philadelphia, PA: Autumn Road Company, 2010.

Weaver, Tom. *A Sci-Fi Swarm of Horror Horde: Interviews with 62 Filmmakers.* Jefferson, NC: McFarland, 2010.

Weaver, Tom. *I Talked With a Zombie: Interviews With 23 Veterans of Horror and Sci-Fi Films and Television.* Jefferson, NC: McFarland, 2008.

Weaver, Tom. *Mutants, Monsters and Heavenly Creatures: Confessions of 14 Classic Sci-Fi/Horrormeisters!* Baltimore, MD: Midnight Marquee, 2001.

Weaver, Tom. *Earth vs. the Sci-Fi Filmmakers: 20 Interviews.* Jefferson, NC: McFarland, 2005.

MAGAZINES

Filmfax #17, November 1989 issue, "SF Drama in Historical Perspective" by Gary Coville and Patrick Lucanio

Filmfax #17, November 1989 issue, "Science Fiction Theatre" by Charles Lee Jackson, II

Filmfax #55, March/April 1996 issue, "Strock Footage: An Interview with Herbert Strock" by Marc Zubatkin

SELECTED BIBLIOGRAPHY 497

Postcard promoting the series.

Index

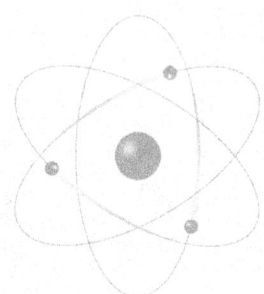

"100 Years Young" 167, 184-189, 290, 294, 421
"Are We Invaded?" 92, 113, 180, 184, 189, 287-291, 294, 299, 417
"Barrier of Silence" 207-210
"Beam of Fire" 367-371
"Before the Beginning" 224, 261, 274-278, 286
"Beyond Return" 90, 201, 270-274, 284, 286, 325, 331
"Beyond" 15, 62-65, 67, 71, 72, 113, 119-134, 165, 175, 179, 206, 284, 299, 337
"Bolt of Lightning" 459-463
"Brain of John Emerson, The" 83, 159-162
"Brain Unlimited" 76, 116, 399-405
"Bullet Proof" 110, 201, 273, 325, 327-332, 418
"Conversation With an Ape" 168-173
"Dead Reckoning" 217-220
"Dead Storage" 78, 210, 229-235, 383
"Death at 2 A.M." 152, 166-168, 188, 252, 284, 294, 421
"Death at My Fingertips" 406-408
"Doctor Robot" 85, 429-433, 467
"End of Tomorrow" 91, 309, 342-346
"Facsimile" 441-445
"Flicker, The" 49, 332-337

"Friend of a Raven" 55, 266-270
"Frozen Sound, The" 189-195
"Gravity Zero" 43, 451-455
"Green Bomb, The" 318-322, 391, 424, 436
"Hastings Secret, The" 252-257, 341, 418, 421
"Hour of Nightmare" 92, 132, 176-180, 206, 284
"Human Circuit, The" 117, 223, 424, 433-437
"Human Equation, The" 198, 235-239, 260
"Human Experiment, The" 88, 261, 357-362
"Jupitron" 210, 224, 232, 381-384
"Killer Tree" 95, 441, 446-450
"Last Barrier, The" 86, 88, 137, 320, 422-425, 436
"Legend of Crater Mountain, The" 371-375
"Living Lights" 376-381
"Long Day, The" 57, 215, 278-281
"Long Sleep, The" 97, 307-311
"Lost Heartbeat, The" 188, 199-203, 210, 273, 325, 331, 418
"Magic Suitcase, The" 455-459
"Man Who Didn't Know" 362-364, 366

"Marked Danger" 133, 173-176, 229
"Mind Machine" 60, 85, 346-351, 354
"Miracle Hour, The" 155, 441, 468-473
"Miracle of Doctor Dove" 59, 128, 320, 388-396, 441
"Missing Waveband, The" 56, 75, 229, 260, 351-356, 455
"Negative Man" 211-217
"No Food for Thought" 82, 83, 143-145
"One Thousand Eyes" 81, 101, 128, 396-399
"Operation Flypaper" 81, 99, 152, 184, 189, 206, 252, 284, 290-295
"Other Side of the Moon, The" 89, 288, 295-300
"Out of Nowhere" 76, 146-149
"Phantom Car, The" 364-367
"Postcard From Barcelona" 38, 57, 87, 132, 198, 223, 229, 239, 257-266, 277, 285, 289, 354, 360
"Project 44" 77, 93, 132, 152, 179, 206, 224, 245, 252, 261, 277, 282-286, 294
"Signals From the Heart" 106, 301-307
"Signals From The Moon" 426-429
"Sound That Kills" 256, 341, 409-411, 421
"Spider, Inc." 162-165
"Stones Began to Move, The" 195-199, 207, 239, 260
"Strange Doctor Lorenz, The" 172, 181-185, 189, 290, 294
"Strange Lodger, The" 455, 463-468
"Strange People at Pecos, The" 56, 134, 224-229, 260, 354
"Stranger in the Desert" 116, 153-156, 441, 473
"Sun Gold" 118, 155, 391, 437-441, 445, 450, 473
"Survival in Box Canyon" 55, 411-416, 458
"Target Hurricane" 240-246
"Three Minute Mile" 88, 167, 188, 252, 256, 418-421, 455
"Throwback, The" 214, 384-388
"Time is Just A Place" 77, 81, 82, 135-139, 148
"Unexplored, The" 58, 152, 167, 188, 249-252, 284, 294, 421
"Unguided Missile, The" 256, 337-342, 370, 418, 421
"Visit From Dr. Pliny, A" 152, 221-224, 252, 260, 277, 284, 285, 294, 383, 437
"Voice, The" 201, 256, 273, 325, 331, 341, 416-418, 421
"Water Maker, The" 247-249, 256, 341, 418, 421
"When A Camera Fails" 89, 201, 273, 322-327, 331, 345, 418
"Who Is This Man?" 112, 311-317, 378
"World Below, The" 203-207, 295
"Y**O**R**D**" 15, 32, 62, 65, 71-73, 113, 115, 149-152, 165, 252, 284, 294, 487-493

Abbott, John 187, 188
Ace, Goodman 11, 21, 22, 24
Ace, Jane 11, 21
Adams, Peter 236, 239
Adaptive Ultimate, The (1935 short story) 90, 91, 270, 273
Adventure Theatre (television program) 105
Adventures at Scott Island (television program) 17, 20
Adventures of Ellery Queen, The (radio program) 9

Adventures of Ozzie and Harriet, The (radio program) 29
Adventures of Superman, The (television program) 445
Adventures of Wild Bill Hickok, The (television program) 375
Agee, Maj. Gen. Walter R. 413
Alaskans, The (television program) 41
Albert, Darlene 378, 379
Albuquerque Journal (newspaper) 30
Allen, Gracie 27
Allen, John 166
Alper, Bud 240
Alpert, David 211, 312, 316, 407
Alpert, Tom 216
Alvin, John 174
Amazing Stories (television program) 138
Ameche, Don 27
Ames, Judith 150-152, 165, 225, 275-277, 333, 365, 456
Ames, Rachel 151
Anderson, Darwin 282
Andrews, Dana 16, 32
Andrews, Stanley 144
Andy Griffith Show, The (television program) 459
Ankrum, Morris 222, 253, 338, 342, 417
Anthony, Tom 206, 218, 340, 345, 364, 370, 434, 450
Aquanauts, The (television program) 41, 61, 65
Archer, John 186-188, 365
Arlen, Richard 147, 148
Arnold, Jack 82, 83, 135, 142, 143, 145, 157, 159, 162, 165
Arnold, Kenneth 44
Arnold, Phil 163, 434
Around the World in Eighty Days (movie) 172
Arthur, Art 62
Ashdown, Isa 267
Ashdown, Nadine 372, 374, 375
Ashworth, Jay 135, 146, 153, 157, 160, 163, 174, 177, 186, 190, 204, 208, 222, 230, 241, 267, 271, 279, 312, 323, 372, 397, 400, 407, 410, 412, 417, 423, 438, 447, 452, 456, 469, 478 and 482
Asimov, Isaac 44
Askins, Monroe "Monk" 129, 143, 150, 162, 173, 203, 207, 211, 224, 247, 253, 279, 307, 333, 357, 367, 376, 389, 406, 412, 419, 479
Asness, George 388, 391, 392, 418, 421
Astounding Science Fiction (magazine) 44, 90, 91, 273, 379
Attack of the Giant Leeches (1959 movie) 463
Auerbach, Lewis 324
August, Doris 271
Avery, Tol 204, 207
Ayers, Lew 98
Bacall, Lauren 15
Back to the Future (1985 movie) 70
Baer, Cynthia 410
Bailey, Raymond 279
Baker, Elsie 147
Bakken, Vicki 283, 286
Bankhead, Tallullah 22
Bari, Lynn 69, 177-180
Barker, Jess 147, 148
Barnes, Beverly 417
Barnes, Gordon 302
Barrett, Claudia 358
Barrett, Tony 179
Barrows, George 358, 423

INDEX

Barry Wood Show, The (radio program) 11, 19
Barry, Gene 40, 101, 163-165, 204, 205, 207
Barton, J.C. 135, 146, 153, 157, 160, 173, 479
Barton, S.H. 169, 200, 211, 217, 225, 235, 240, 247, 250, 257, 292, 296, 302, 307, 311, 322, 333, 480, 481
Bassin, Calman 426, 430, 434, 438, 446, 451, 456, 460, 464, 469
Bat Masterson (television program) 17, 20, 101
Batcheller, Dick 463
Battle Taxi (1955 movie) 62, 63
Baurmash, Leonard 48
Beast with 20,000 Fathoms (1953 movie) 71
Beaumont, Hugh 169-173
Beck, Jackson 10
Becwar, George 400
Behind the Mike (1947 film short) 30
Bell, Art 480
Bell, Jim 153, 157, 159, 166, 168, 173, 195, 199, 217, 224, 235, 247, 249, 253, 257, 274, 278, 287, 291, 296, 327, 332, 337, 342, 346, 351, 357, 362, 364, 376, 381, 384, 388, 419, 426, 429, 433, 437, 441, 451, 455, 478-481, 483
Below the Deadline (1946 movie) 39
Benay, Ben 271
Benedek, Lazlo 39
Bennett, Bruce 112, 130, 134, 312, 314, 316, 412, 413, 427, 428, 460, 461
Bennett, John 173
Bennett, Marjorie 236
Bennett, Ray 154

Benson, Leon 72, 99, 149, 152, 207, 287, 291
Bentham, Bill 323, 358, 368, 377, 382, 385, 389, 410, 419, 423, 427, 434, 438, 442, 447, 452, 456, 464
Bentley, Fred 181
Benton Sr., Bob 406, 411, 430
Benton Sr., Robert 229
Berg, Lee 135, 142
Berke, Alfred 135, 144, 146, 150, 154, 157, 160, 163, 166, 169, 174, 177, 181, 186, 190, 196, 200, 204, 208, 211, 218, 222, 225, 230, 236, 241, 248, 250, 253, 258, 267, 271, 275, 279, 283, 288, 292, 296, 302, 308, 312, 323, 328, 333, 338, 344, 347, 352, 358, 363, 365, 368, 372, 377, 382, 389, 397, 400, 407, 410, 417, 419, 423, 427, 430, 434, 452, 456, 460, 464, 469, 474,, 478-483
Berle, Milton 22
Bernard, Tom 283, 312, 385
Bernoudy, Eddie 157, 162, 479
Best in Hollywood (television program) 105
Beyond the Limits (television program) 126
Bice, Robert 419
Billboard (magazine) 15, 17, 82, 109
Bilson, Bruce 362, 364
Birch, Paul 169, 173, 225, 412
Bishop, William 177-180
Bissell, Whit 158, 159, 318, 319, 430-432
Blackman, Lonie 347, 349, 351, 407
Blanchard, Jackie 160, 161
Blanchard, Mari 91, 273

Bledsoe, Mel 129, 135, 146, 149, 153, 157, 159, 162, 168, 176, 181, 185, 189, 208, 217, 221, 229, 235, 240, 266, 270, 274, 292, 296, 301, 311, 318, 327, 337, 342, 347, 351, 367, 376, 382, 384, 388, 396, 399, 406, 411, 419, 422, 434, 441, 468, 469, 478, 481, 482
Bloch, Ray 100
Boelter, L.M.K. 475
Boesen, Vic 30
Bogart, Humphrey 15
Bold Venture (radio program) 15, 16
Bold Venture (television program) 17, 20
Bolhius, Dee 279, 282, 287, 292, 296, 301, 307, 311, 322, 328, 333, 338, 342, 352, 357, 367, 469, 483
Bolton, Irene 333
Bonestell, Chesley 124
Boston Blackie (radio program) 9
Boston Blackie (television program) 14, 17, 20, 106
Boswell Sisters, The 24
Boyd, Dallas 147
Boyle, Jack 9
Bradbury, Ray 44, 138, 477
Bradfoot, Walter 352
Bradley, Truman 3, 17, 21-35, 40, 55, 57, 64-68, 72, 73, 75, 77, 79, 83, 85, 93, 103, 113-117, 126, 132-134, 136, 139-141, 144, 147, 148, 161, 162, 164, 165, 167, 188, 194, 202, 206, 207, 210, 215, 216, 220, 223, 252, 256, 260, 269, 277, 281, 284, 286, 288, 304, 307, 309, 313, 320, 325, 334, 337, 339, 345, 346, 354, 364, 370, 373, 379, 380, 383, 386, 387, 390, 391, 408, 411, 414, 418, 421, 424, 425, 436, 437, 441, 445, 450, 455, 458, 459, 473, 478-486
Brady, Scott 69
Brasselle, Keefe 87, 258, 259, 261
Bratton, Myrla Ethel 34
Breese, Edmund 23
Brent, George 279, 281
Brian, David 16
Bridges, Lloyd 17, 20, 67, 118
Bright Star (radio program) 19
Brightmyer, Dick 221
Broadcasting (magazine) 111
Broadcasting-Telecasting (magazine) 7, 74, 103, 109, 126
Brodfoot, Walter 322
Brodie, Don 427
Brodie, Steve 218, 220, 279, 281
Bronco (television program) 41
Brooke, Peter R. 342, 346, 437
Broughton, Irv 9, 17, 94
Brown, J. 230, 267, 412
Brown, S. 455
Brownson, Ruth 287, 483
Bruce, Virginia 230, 233, 267, 270
Bryant, John 150, 243
Buccola, Guy 463
Buchanan, Bill 371
Buchheim, Robert W. 475
Buck, Connie 460
Buettner, Dr. Konrad 76
Burnet, Sir Macfarlane 145
Burns, George 27
Burton, Julian 417
Bury, John 302, 308, 318, 409, 422
Bushnell, John 441
Busick, Bud 279
Butler, Robert A. 172
Byron, Jean 81, 236, 238, 239, 279, 281, 397, 398, 469, 472

Cabin, Naomi 250
Caelecia, Felex 130
Cagney, James 96
Call Northside 777 (1948 movie) 29
Calling All Cars (radio program) 19
Calvin, Susan 441
Cane, Charles 258, 267
Cantor, Eddie 73
Cantrell, Norman 430
Capra, Frank 121
Captain Video (television program) 44, 60, 93, 286
Cardinali, Frank 406, 410, 412
Career of Alice Blair, The (radio program) 9, 19
Carey, MacDonald 236, 238
Carlson, Richard 40, 47, 50-53, 57, 58, 64, 121, 214
Carradine, John 69
Carroll, Irvin 222
Carroll, Toni 271, 283, 284, 286
Carson, Robert 130
Carter, F. 473
Carter, Helena 69
Carter, Janis 69
Cartwright, Lynn 442
Cary, Bill 385, 423
Casazza, Phil 146
Cassidy, Maureen 312
Castle, William 311, 315, 316
Cengia, John 318
Chaffee, Dick 163
Chambers, Jack 266, 270, 274, 292, 296, 311, 362, 364, 409, 416, 426, 429, 434, 437, 438, 442, 446, 451, 455, 460
Chambers, Wheaton 158, 159
Chandler, Ed 368
Chapman Jr., Harvey 139, 141
Chapman, Marguerite 69, 204, 207
Charlie Chan in Rio (1941 movie) 334

Cherry, Evelyn 325, 340, 345
Chervin, Bert 181, 185, 190, 208, 211, 217, 397, 411, 479
Cheshire, Pappy 9
Cheyenne (television program) 41, 403
Chicetti, Charles 267
Ching, William 267, 270, 423, 434, 435
Christine, Virginia 358, 385, 388
Christy, Ken 469
Cisco Kid, The (radio program) 11-13, 19
Cisco Kid, The (television program) 14, 17, 20, 80, 95, 106, 109
Clark, Ace 208, 230, 480, 481
Clark, Bonnie 413
Clark, Dane 69, 211, 213, 216, 275-277
Clark, Gloria 358
Clarke, Arthur C. 42
Clarke, Robert 163, 165
Clett, Tod 301
Cleveland, Madge 182
Clooney, Nick 13
Coates, Phyllis 208, 210
Coby, Fred 347, 442, 445
Coffin, Tris 69, 385, 388
Cohon, Barry 97, 302, 308, 309, 312, 318, 322, 328, 333, 338, 343, 347, 352, 357, 362, 365, 368, 372, 376, 382, 385, 389, 397, 400, 406, 409, 412, 417, 419, 422, 426, 430, 434, 438, 442, 446, 451, 456, 460, 464, 469
Colbert, Claudette 459
Colbert, Joe 365
Cole, Phyllis 174
Collier's (magazine) 137-139
Collins, Ray 29, 190, 191, 194, 243, 245, 410

Collis, Jack 174, 181, 190, 196, 200, 204, 208, 211, 218, 222, 225, 230, 236, 241, 247, 250, 253, 258, 267, 271, 275, 279, 283, 288, 292, 296, 302, 308, 312, 318, 323, 328, 333, 338, 343, 347, 352, 358, 368
Colman, Booth 230
Colt .45 (television program) 41
Commando Cody (film) 100
Como, Perry 22
Confidence Girl (1952 movie) 32
Conklin, Geoff 42, 43
Conklin, Heinie 197
Conquest (television program) 121
Conquest of Space (1955 movie) 93, 124, 286
Conrad, William 69, 70
Conried, Hans 69
Conwall, J. 230
Conway, Russ 158, 197
Corbin, Herbert C. 475
Corey, Wendell 69
Cornthwaite, Robert 69
Corrigan, Lloyd 69
Corson, Ken 460
Cortez, Stanley 52
Cory, Donald 451
Cosmopolitan (magazine) 5
Cowboy in Africa (television program) 36
Cox, Jim 3, 21
Cox, Jud 266
Coy, Walter 230, 233
Craft, Charles (Chuck) 129, 150, 221, 225, 230, 292, 372, 416, 419, 422, 482
Craig, James 218, 220
Crawford, Broderick 17, 18, 20
Crise, George 250
Cristo, Paul 158

Cropper, Roy 267, 271, 282, 312, 322
Culp, Walter 129, 249, 257, 371
Cummings, Susan 363, 412
Curland, David 371
Curtis, Donald 172, 182, 184, 417, 442-444, 445, 469-471
Cvetic, Matt 32
Dabke, Robert 322, 332, 347
Daktari (television program) 36, 41, 244
Daly, Tom 211, 216
Dangerous Assignment (television program) 65
Dark, Christopher 178-180, 328, 330, 332, 343, 344, 346
Daudette, Bob 307
Davidson, Lotus 129
Davis, Eddie 132, 224, 249, 252, 270, 274, 291, 295, 300, 418, 425, 429, 433, 437, 441, 446, 448-450, 459, 463, 466, 481, 482
Davis, Grant 147, 156, 320
Davis, Grant 172
Davis, Lee 129
Davis, Lisa 312
Davis, Nancy 69
Davis, Owen 460
Davis, Peter 211, 296
Davison, Robert 429
Daw, Kenneth 318, 357
Dawes, Maggie 468
Dawson, Hal K. 144
Day the Earth Stood Still, The (1951 movie) 45
Day, Kenneth 311, 338
De Angelo, Joe 367
de Corsia, Ted 166, 168, 275, 277
De Forest, Dr. Lee 42
de Graffenried, Tom 271
De Medici, Rod 158, 163

Dearest Mother (radio program) 8, 19
DeFore, Don 136, 137, 142
Dekker, Albert 91, 273
Delevanti, Cyril 258, 347, 351, 389, 392, 464, 466
Delmar, Armand 438, 446
Demon of the Himalayas (1936 movie) 39
Denby, Bill 135, 146, 157, 160, 162, 478
Dennis, John 368
Despite, Cesar 325
Destination Moon (1950 movie) 45
Dial 999 (television program) 17, 20
Diamond Lens, The (1858 short story) 90
Dillon, Tom 397
Dipetre, Cesar 302
Disney, Walt 36, 120, 142
Disneyland (television program) 142
Dixon, Granville 363
Dolenz, George 69
Dolinsky, Meyer 409, 459
Donahue, Pat 365
Donovan's Brain (1953 movie) 45, 65, 98, 161
Donovan's Brain (novel) 46
Dorothy and Dick (radio program) 19
Dorsey, Tommy 27
Douchette, John 208, 243, 245, 308
Douglas, Diana 343, 344, 346, 400-402
Douglas, George 456, 458
Douglas, Larry 11
Dowling, Constance 53, 71
Dowling, Doris 71, 225, 226, 283, 286
Dr. Christian (radio program) 95
Dr. Christian (television program) 17, 18, 20, 41
Drake, Kenneth 283

Drake, Tom 130, 134
Drew, Ellen 69, 70, 130, 131, 134, 160, 161
Dubov, Paul 204, 205, 207
Duff, Howard 67, 158, 159
Dugis, Frank 464
Dunbar, Dixie 307, 309, 328, 372
Duncan, Craig 147
Dunne, Peter 296
Dwight, David 410
Dyer, James 434, 438, 446, 451, 460, 464, 469
Earle, Edward 69, 158, 159
Earth vs. the Flying Saucers (1956 movie) 65, 133
Easy Aces (radio program) 11, 19, 21, 24
Eddie Cantor Comedy Theater, The (television program) 16, 20
Eddie Cantor Show, The (radio program) 19
Egan, Richard 53, 58
Eggers Jr., Alfred J. 475
Ehricke, Krafft A. 475
Eiseley, Loren C. 165
Eitner, Don 312
Eldredge, George 204, 205, 207, 250, 292, 295
Eldredge, John 292, 295, 328, 419
Elliot, Biff 283, 286
Elliot, Ross 438-440
Ellis, Juney 222
Emery, John 69
Enger, Charles Van 50
Engle, Jim 451, 455, 468
Epperson, William R. 455
Epstein, Jon 94, 202
Erdman, Richard 288, 289, 291
Erskine, Marilyn 118, 190-194, 372, 438-440
Erwin, William (Bill) 308, 363

Escape (radio program) 91, 273
Esenther, Evelyn Jane 34
Euard, Opal 324, 326
Eustrel, Antony 69, 288, 291, 417
Evans, Charles 179
Evans, David C. 413
Evans, Gene 69, 154, 156
Evans, Howard 441
Evans, M. 473
Everglades (television program) 18, 20
Eye Witness News (radio program) 19
Eyer, Richard 267, 268, 270
Famous Playhouse (television program) 105
Fans of the Stands (radio program) 8, 19
Fass, George 278
Fass, Gertrude 278
Favorite Story (television program) 17, 20, 41, 95
Fawcett, William 365
Faylen, Kay 271, 389, 392
Felicia, Felix 469
Ferrari, William 129
Fetters, Curt 143, 166, 195, 200, 235, 250, 257, 275, 282, 287, 292, 296, 322, 338, 347, 362, 365, 372, 376, 382, 409, 416, 434, 438, 442, 446, 451, 456, 460, 464, 479, 480, 483
Ficker, Jane 258, 267, 275
Field, Jimmy 333, 372, 385, 419
Field, Margaret 241, 243, 245
Fierro, Paul 438
Filmfax (magazine) 63, 424
Fine, Morton 15
Fink, Hyman 222, 230
Finney, Jack 135, 137-139, 142
Fitghard, Bers 271
Fitz-Gibbon, Frank 221, 230

Fitz-Richard, Arthur 185, 189
Five Against Venus (1952 novel) 93, 286
Flannery, Bill 135, 146, 157, 162, 176, 185, 282, 311, 322, 397, 400, 406, 409, 412, 416, 422, 438, 446, 451, 455, 468
Flannery, Jim 153, 160, 173, 190, 203, 208, 221, 229, 240, 267, 271, 478, 482
Flash Gordon (television program) 120
Flato, Richard 196, 197
Flight to Mars (1951 movie) 45
Flipper (television program) 41, 61
Flournoy, Elizabeth 430
Foran, Dick 75, 308, 352, 353, 355, 407, 469, 472, 473
Forbidden Diary (radio program) 8, 19
Ford Sunday Evening Hour, The (radio program) 24, 25
Forester, John 204
Forrest, Hal 147
Forte, Joe 212, 216
Foster, Sally 9
Fox and the Forest, The (short story) 138
Fox, Michael 49, 52, 65, 70, 130, 151, 160, 161, 190, 194, 333-337, 352, 353, 355, 382, 427, 428
Fox, Michael J. 70
Fox, Victoria 222
Franklin, Joe 302, 368
Franz, Arthur 92, 174, 176, 225-228, 363, 400-402, 442-445
Franz, Edward 69
Fred Waring Show, The (radio program) 19
Freedom USA (radio program) 19
Freiwald, Eric 240

Fresco, Robert M. 143, 145, 153, 156, 295
Freshest Thing in Town (radio program) 7, 19
Friedkin, David 15
Friend, Bud S. 225
Froner, Barry 225, 308
Frost, Terry 447, 450
Fullman, Robert L. 193
Fulton, Ian 456
Furst, Esther 430
Gailey, Helen 135, 146, 153, 157, 160, 478
Galaxy Science Fiction (magazine) 44
Gallagher, Eddie 308
Gallagher, Glen 332
Galvin, Gus 169, 174, 177, 181, 186, 190, 196, 200, 204, 208, 211, 218, 222, 225, 230, 236, 241, 248, 250, 253, 258, 267, 271, 368, 372, 382, 410
Ganzer, Alvin 257, 261, 274, 277
Garber, T. 412, 419
Gargoyle, The (magazine) 5
Garland, Beverly 89, 212, 216, 296, 297-300
Garth, Michael 279, 302, 344, 378
Gates, Nancy 174, 176
Gaunt, Bud 195, 307
Gaye, Leslie 288, 289, 291
Gaye, Lisa 452-454
Gediman, Walter 257, 271, 287, 338, 372, 426, 430
General Hospital (television program) 151, 152
Gengia, John 307
Gentle Ben (television program) 36
George, John 473
Geray, Steven 69
Gerry, Toni 382, 384

Gerstle, Frank 218, 220, 360, 368
Gertsman, Jack 208, 235
Gibbs, Jim 181
Gibson, Mary Whitlock 39, 64
Gilbert, Doris 95, 195, 198, 224, 270, 273, 291, 295, 357, 416
Gilbreath, George 464
Gilliam, Ann 434
Gilmore, Lowell 154, 156, 382, 384
Glass, Everett 69, 218, 220
Glazer, Bert 282, 311, 318, 468
Glick, Andrew 225
Gog (1954 movie) 39, 53-59, 71, 73, 118, 132, 134, 139, 152, 184, 193, 224, 229, 261, 277, 284, 285, 340
Gold (1934 movie) 46, 48, 59, 463
Golding, Larry 153, 173, 177, 186, 190, 204, 208, 221, 230, 240, 482
Goodrich, Jack 130
Goodwins, Leslie 159, 161
Granger, Michael 407
Grant, Doug 460
Granville, Bonita 447-449
Gray, Colleen 69
Gray, George 83, 108, 129, 135, 143, 150, 153, 155, 157, 160, 162, 166, 169, 173, 177, 181, 185, 190, 195, 200, 203, 208, 211, 217, 221, 225, 230, 235, 240, 247, 250, 253, 257, 267, 271, 275, 279, 280, 282, 287, 292, 296, 302, 307, 312, 322, 328, 333, 338, 343, 347, 352, 357, 362, 365, 368, 372, 376, 382, 389, 397, 400, 406, 409, 412, 417, 419, 422, 426, 430, 434, 442, 451, 456, 460, 464, 469, 480-483
Green, Al 266, 282
Greenleaf, Raymond 69

Greer, Dabbs 225, 292, 295, 343, 344, 346
Grey, Virginia 248
Gries, Tom 98, 100, 257, 263, 266, 268, 270, 282, 286, 318, 399, 406, 426
Griffin, Donald R. 148
Griffin, Robert 243, 318, 319
Griffith, Andy 459
Griffith, Billy 417
Guha, Bhupesh 427
Guilfoyle, Paul 39, 69, 96, 97, 278, 281, 296, 307, 327, 329, 331, 332, 341, 346, 351, 357, 359, 360, 371, 372, 381, 382, 384, 388, 396, 398, 416, 422, 425, 426, 451, 454, 455, 468
Gulliver's Travels (1726 book) 42
Gunsmoke (television program) 161
Guy Lombardo Show, The (radio program) 11, 19
Gwenn, Edmund 89, 182-184, 222
Haber, Fritz 77
Haber, Heinz 76, 475
Hafley, Lou 130, 135, 146, 150, 160, 163, 174, 372, 478
Haglund, Elmer 129, 143, 150, 162, 166, 168, 195, 199, 211, 217, 224, 235, 247, 249, 253, 257, 275, 279, 287, 292, 296, 328, 333, 342, 347, 352, 357, 362, 365, 376, 382, 385, 388, 419, 426, 430, 434, 442, 480, 481, 483
Haglund, Elmer 217
Hahn, Paul 243, 250, 288, 296, 410
Hale, Barbara 69, 70, 169-173, 253-255, 257
Hale, Jonathan 147, 148, 196, 197
Hale, Nancy 308
Hall, Archie 129, 135, 143, 146, 150, 153, 157, 160, 162, 166, 168, 173, 176, 181, 185, 190, 195, 199, 203, 208, 211, 217, 221, 225, 230, 235, 240, 247, 250, 253, 257, 267, 271, 275, 362, 365, 372, 376, 382, 385, 388, 397, 400, 406, 409, 412, 416, 419, 422, 426, 430, 434, 438, 442, 446, 451, 456, 460, 464, 479-482
Hall, Bing 287
Hall, Lue 371
Hamilton, Joe 363
Hanes, Lloyd 419
Hanes, William 275
Hanger, Charles 235, 240, 250, 271, 292, 311, 367, 376, 382, 389, 434, 438, 442, 446, 451, 456, 483
Hanks, Elmer 338
Hanks, Lloyd 328, 333, 338, 343, 347, 352, 358, 362, 365, 376, 382, 385, 389, 426, 430, 434, 442
Hanks, William 181, 258, 279, 287, 292, 296, 483
Hanley, Frank 163
Hanson, Peter 106, 271, 274, 302-305, 338, 341, 342, 385, 387, 388, 430, 432, 433, 464-466
Harber, Paul 368
Harbor Command (television program) 17, 20, 41, 101, 403
Harbor Master (television program) 17, 20
Harris, Garry 130, 143, 150, 163, 166, 169, 196, 200, 211, 218, 225, 236, 247, 250, 253, 258, 275, 283, 287, 292, 296, 328, 333, 338, 344, 347, 352, 358, 363, 365, 377, 382, 385, 389, 419, 427, 430, 434, 442, 479-481, 483
Harris, Glen 464

Harris, Joe 60
Harris, Patricia 129
Harris, Robert 230
Harvey, Jean G. 410
Hauser, Bob 162
Heiligman, Sam 129
Heinlein, Robert 81, 92
Helfer, Ralph 41
Helton, Percy 452-454
Henderson, Douglas 166, 230
Henley, Charles 129
Henry, Bill 296, 419
Henry, O. 11
Henry, Thomas B. 400, 442
Henry, Tom Browne 338
Herbert, Charles 469, 471
Herman, George 121
Hermit's Cave, The (radio program) 95
Herrick, Samuel 475
Herzberg, Jack 130, 229, 233, 252, 255, 351, 355
Hess, Norman 327, 332, 342, 352
Hess, Victor 437
Hewitt, Lee 203, 206, 252, 253, 256, 327, 331, 364
Hewitt, Richard 324
Heydt, Louis Jean 69, 150, 152
Heyes, Herbert 236, 239
Highway Patrol (television program) 17, 20, 41, 95, 331, 360
Hinds Honey and Almond Cream Program, The (radio program) 27
Hodiak, John 69
Hoffman, Bob 135, 146, 150, 153, 157, 160, 168, 176, 181, 185, 190, 208, 217, 221, 230, 240, 267, 271, 275, 301, 311, 318, 328, 343, 352, 385, 397, 400, 422, 426, 430, 469, 478, 481
Holden, Joyce 106, 160, 161, 302, 304, 305

Hollaway, Delmar 146
Hollmar, Richard 10
Holmes, Taylor 69
Holt, Jacqueline 328
Home of the Brave (stage play) 71
Homeier, Skip 166, 168, 297-300, 378, 379
Hoover, Hal 417
Hopalong Cassidy (radio program) 13
Hopper, Lou 230
Horn Blows at Midnight, The (1945 movie) 29
Hounshell, Fred 230, 235, 240, 250, 257, 292, 307, 322, 328, 338, 347, 357, 382, 397, 400, 406, 409, 412, 416, 419, 422, 430, 434, 483
Hour of Stars (radio program) 19
Houston, Art 416
Howard, Ann 158, 163, 194, 269
Howard, John 144, 145, 160, 161
Howard, Ron 459
Howat, Clark 69, 150
Hoyt, John 69
Hudson, Larry 188, 410
Hudson, Mike 221, 224, 229, 235, 271, 275, 279, 307, 311, 322, 333, 343, 352, 371, 376, 382, 385, 389, 419, 426, 451, 456, 460, 469, 483
Hudson, William 452, 453
Huerta, George 318
Huff, Wade 279
Hughes, David 397
Hugo, Mauritz 292
Huiper, Dr. Gerard 121
Hunger, Anna 199, 201, 203
Hunt, Frank 147, 232, 387, 473
Hunter, James 385, 397, 400, 422
Hunter, Ken 406
Hunter, Virginia 166, 168

Hussey, Ruth 69, 70, 187, 188, 338, 340-342
Huston, Lou 82, 95, 176, 207, 282, 286, 332, 351, 411, 446, 455
Hutchinson, Dale 412
Hyland, Gus 147
I Led Three Lives (television program) 15, 16, 20, 41, 58, 94, 95, 103, 106, 110, 111, 214, 467
I Love Lucy (television program) 16
I Was A Communist for the FBI (radio program) 16, 32
In the Days of the Comet (novel) 474
In the Good Old Summertime (1949 movie) 39
Inge, Joe 451, 456, 464, 469
Inverso, Sol (Sal) 143, 150, 153, 225, 292, 296, 312, 328, 333, 338, 343, 347, 352
Invisible Man, The (novel) 474
Ireland, John 69
It Happened One Night (1935 movie)
It's Showtime from Hollywood (radio program) 19
Jack Armstrong (radio program) 24
Jackman, Joe 301, 318
Jackson II, Charles Lee 424
Jackson, Bradford 279, 333, 372
Jackson, Jack 391
Jackson, Selmer 69
Jackson, Tex 247, 249, 253, 282, 483
James, Lois 383
Jameson, Joyce 434
Jason, Leigh 173, 176, 181, 184, 189, 240, 245
Jay, Helen 347, 351
Jerome, M.K. 94
Jerome, Stuart 94, 95, 157, 159, 173, 176, 199, 203, 229, 233, 247, 301, 367, 396, 441
Jessel, John 270, 273

Jetsons, The (television program) 78
Johannes, Bob 311, 322
Johnson, Dick 135, 146, 181, 282
Johnson, Jason 378, 423
Jolley, Norman 181, 184, 189, 235, 239, 287, 291, 322
Jones, Bert 221, 271, 275, 282, 287
Jones, Bill 464
Jones, Harry 135, 143, 146, 153, 157, 159, 168, 173, 176, 185, 189, 478
Jones, Spec 211, 221, 229, 240, 266, 282, 482
Joplin Globe (newspaper) 34
Jordan, Julie 158
Jory, Victor 40, 69, 333-337
Kalmus, Hans 184
Kane, Bill 455
Kane, Byron 324, 326
Kane, William 279, 282, 451, 456
Karns, Robert 52
Kaufman, Lawrence 271, 318, 389, 427
Kaye, Danny 22
Keane, Edward 70
Keane, Robert Emmett 69
Keener, Joe 406, 412, 417
Keep Your Distance (stage play) 37
Keily, William 230
Kelley, DeForest 150-152, 279, 412, 413
Kelly, Barry 69
Kelly, Jack 90, 273
Kemmer, Edward 385, 387, 388
Kennedy, Arthur 69
Kennedy, Douglas 130, 134
Kennedy, Madge 58, 250
Kenny, Jack 129
Kenyon, Curtis 153, 156
Kerns, H. 455
Kerr, Larry 302

Kesler, Henry S. 95, 96, 153, 156, 166, 168, 176, 177, 180, 199, 203, 211, 216, 221, 235, 237-239
Kessinger, Coley 143, 166, 173, 479
Kilsten, Ellen 391
King of Diamonds (television program) 18, 20
King, Andrea 69
King, Charles (Chuck) 250, 397, 464
King, Ralph 318
Kingsford, Walter 70, 150-152, 200, 201, 203, 258, 259, 261, 302, 303, 305, 344, 346, 452
Kinoshita, Robert 363, 365, 372, 377, 382, 385, 389, 397, 400, 406, 410, 412, 417, 419, 423, 426, 430, 434, 438, 442, 446, 452, 456, 460, 464, 469
Kirkham, Willard 287, 322, 327
Kisseloff, Jeff 102
Knight, Glen 376, 388, 422
Knight, Loraine 230, 233
Knudsen, Barbara 425
Korn Kobblers, The (radio program) 9, 19
Kraus, Harold 275, 287, 292, 296, 357, 409, 416, 426
Kreiger, Louis 250, 257, 307, 352, 357, 367, 426, 430, 442, 469
Kruger, Otto 144, 145, 174, 176
Krupnick, Jack 370
La Cava, Joe 147
Labbe, Ned 301
Lady Esther Screen Guild Theatre, The (radio program) 27, 35
Landers, Lew 195, 198
Lansbury, Angela 69
Lantz, Walter 14
Larson, Christine 87, 158, 159, 258, 259, 261
Latham, Jack 162, 380

Latham, Philip 286
Laughton, Charles 429
Lawman (television program) 379
Lawrence, Hugh 464
Lawson, Bob 156
Le Picard, George 270, 322
Leadbetter, Roy 221
Leave it to Beaver (television program) 58
Leben des Galilei (1947 movie) 429
Lee, Ruta 250
Lehmann, Theodore 456
Leiber, Fritz 81
Leigh, George 352
Leonetti, Frank 282
LeRoy, Harry 468
LeRoy, Judd 162, 296, 338, 343, 451, 456, 460
Leven, Betty 460
Levitt, Gene 217
Lewis, Art 218, 220
Lewis, Herman 358, 368
Life (magazine) 93
Lightning Jim (radio program) 19
Lights Out! (television program) 214
Lilliquist, Jo Ann 372, 374, 375
Linder, Alfred 427, 428
Lipney, Herman 221, 343, 385, 397, 400, 406, 409, 412, 416,
Lippman, Jeanne 308, 312, 323, 358, 372, 377, 382, 397, 400, 406, 409, 412, 417, 422, 451, 456, 469
Lisse, Bea 129
Living Book, The (television program) 14, 17, 20
Llewelyn, Ray 100
Lloyd, Gene 249
Lock Up (television program) 17, 20
Lockhart, Gene 40, 69, 70, 320, 323, 324, 326, 345, 389, 391, 392
Lockhart, June 407

Loder, John 69
Lone Ranger, The (radio program) 9
Lone Ranger, The (television program) 375
Look (magazine) 5
Loose, William 100
Loper, George 129
Lopez, Vincent 11
Los Angeles Times, The (newspaper) 34
Lost Planet, The (1953 film) 70, 71
Louise, Anita 69
Lovejoy, Frank 67, 69
Lowell, Mark 130
Lscher, Martin 256
Lucanio, Patrick 3, 5, 125, 126
Lukather, Paul 363
Lund, John 67, 69
Lund, Larry 150, 166, 169, 190, 196, 200, 204, 211, 218, 225, 236, 247, 250, 253, 292, 296, 328, 333, 338, 343, 347, 352, 358, 363, 365, 377, 385, 389, 419, 426, 430, 434, 438, 442, 446, 448, 479-481
Lundigan, William 51, 52, 62, 63, 69, 124, 130, 131, 133, 134
Lung, Clarence 144, 145
Lustig, Milton 100, 101
Lux Radio Theatre (radio program) 95
Lux Video Theatre (television program) 105
Lyden, Pierce 200
Lytton, Herbert C. 365, 366
MacArthur, Gen. Douglas 42
MacDonald, Bruce 200, 236, 241, 247, 250, 253, 258, 267, 271, 275, 279, 283, 312, 323, 328, 338, 343, 352, 377, 389, 409, 438, 442, 446, 451, 456, 464, 480, 483

MacKenzie's Raiders (television program) 17, 20
MacLeod, Kenneth 391
Magnetic Monster, The (1953 movie) 39, 46, 48-50, 59, 62, 70, 73, 239, 277, 433, 473
Man and the Challenge, The (television program) 17, 20, 36, 61, 65, 121-123
Man Called X, The (television program) 17, 20, 103, 158, 421, 441
Manhunt (radio program) 9, 19
Manriquez, Eddie 221, 229, 240, 275, 416, 430
Mansfield, Duncan 190, 195, 211, 235, 250, 302, 307, 311, 318, 322, 328, 333, 338, 352, 362, 367, 376, 397, 480
Mansfield, Sally 56, 139
Marcus, Ellis 166, 168, 346, 349, 376, 378, 380, 429
Mark, Del 267
Marks, Dane 181
Marley, J. Pervell 275
Marlowe, Hugh 133
Marquard, Brick 460
Marshall, Arthur 344, 382, 456
Marshall, Gary 241, 243, 245
Marshall, Gloria 419
Marshall, Herbert 53, 58
Martin, Monroe 275, 279, 283, 288, 296, 312, 328, 338, 358, 400, 430, 434, 438, 442, 447, 452, 456, 464, 469
Martin, Quinn 257, 267, 271, 275, 279, 282, 287, 292, 296, 301, 307, 311, 318, 322, 328, 333, 338, 342, 347, 352, 357, 362, 365, 367, 371, 376, 382, 385, 388, 397, 400, 406, 409, 411, 416, 419, 422, 426, 430, 434,

438, 442, 446, 451, 455, 460, 464, 468, 495
Martin, Tony 27
Marton, Andrew 39, 118
Mason, Sydney 347, 351, 423
Massen, Osa 58, 250-252
Mathers, George 204, 480
Mathew, Ted 153, 159, 168, 176, 181, 478
Mathews, Tommy 157, 185, 221, 229, 240, 362, 364, 371, 385, 396, 400, 406, 411, 422, 468
Mautino, Bill (Bud) 135, 146, 153, 157, 159, 162, 185, 189, 203, 208, 217, 240, 478, 479, 481
Maverick (television program) 41
Maxwell, Charles 158-160, 208, 318, 352, 354, 464, 465, 466
McCardle, Paul 130
McCaskey, Ted 247, 372, 397, 400, 406, 412, 417
McDonald, Francis 338, 342
McDonald, J.R. 129
McDonald, Maria 69
McGaskey, Ted 186
McGowan, Bill 459
McKee, Thomas 200
McKee, Tom 236, 352, 423
McNally, Steve 67
McVeagh, Eve 318
McVey, Tyler 365, 366
McWhorter, Richard 229, 249
Meader, George 236
Meadows, Roy 460, 464
Means, Claude 363, 365
Meeder, George 163
Meet Corliss Archer (television program) 16, 20, 41, 72, 94, 104
Meet the Menjous (radio program) 19
Meet the Press (television program) 105

Melton, Troy 365, 468
Men Into Space (television program) 41, 74, 101, 123, 124, 126, 445, 454
Men of Annapolis (television program) 17, 20, 41
Menjou, Adolphe 208, 210
Meredith, Charles 188
Merrill, Gary 67
Mestre, Goar 106
Michael, Dolores 410
Miksch, Carl 143, 166, 173, 195, 199, 203, 211, 224, 235, 247, 249, 257, 274, 279, 287, 291, 296, 322, 332, 337, 342, 346, 351, 357, 362, 364, 371, 376, 381, 388, 409, 416, 419, 426, 429, 433, 437, 441, 446, 451, 455, 456, 460, 479, 480, 483
Miles, Vera 144, 145
Millar, Lee 423
Miller, Glenn 38
Miller, Kristine 182, 184, 292, 295, 417, 460-462
Miller, Pat 212, 216
Miller, R. DeWitt 199, 201, 203
Millionaires in Prison (1940 movie) 30
Millman, John 185, 190, 195, 203, 224, 230, 287, 322, 347, 483
Milner, Martin 419
Mimi (stage play) 37
Missing Men of Saturn (1953 novel) 93, 286
Mitchell, Carlyle 147, 148
Mitchell, Irving 147, 148
Mitchell, Phil 181, 302, 308, 318
Mitchell, Steve 460
Mitchum, John 154, 174, 200, 248, 328
Moffett, Greg 302
Moore, Dennis 271

Moore, Mary Tyler 309
Morgan, Gloria 143
Morgan, Ralph 70
Morley, Hap 240
Morris, Chester 9, 10
Morris, Constance 130
Morris, Tommy 270
Morris, Wayne 69, 360, 368, 369
Morrison, Tom 464
Moss, Marty 160, 478
Movietown Radio Theatre (radio program) 19
Mowery, Helen 308
Mr. District Attorney (radio program) 9, 16, 19
Mr. District Attorney (television program) 16, 20, 72, 95, 102, 103, 106
Mudie, Leonard 368
Mull, Eddie 221, 224, 229, 240, 371, 481
Mullally, Donn 76, 146, 148, 149
Munday, Mary 283, 286
Mussey, Earl 307
Mustin, Burt 400
My Little Margie (television program) 62
Navarro, Anna 417
Naylor, Bill 460
Needham, Leo 148, 318, 434
Nelson Jr. Robert 283
Nelson, Bek 379
New Adventures of Martin Kane, The (television program) 17, 20
New York Times, The (newspaper) 42, 244
Newhart, Bob 22
Newmark, Stewart 429
Nibley, Sloan 76, 221, 257, 261, 399, 404
Night Before the Divorce (1942 movie) 30

North, Bill 468
Northwest Passage (1940 movie) 29
Nugent, Ed 176, 185, 189, 203, 396, 399, 406, 409, 411, 416, 422, 468
O'Brien, Edmund 69
O'Brien, James 90
O'Brien, Pat 288, 291
O'Connor, Peggy 136, 142
Ober, Philip 297, 300
Offord, Bert 438, 447
Og, Son of Fire (radio program) 24
Old Corral, The (radio program) 9
One for the Books (radio program) 8, 9, 19
Operation Air Rescue (1955 movie) 62
Othman, Frederick 32
Ott, Harry 247, 249, 253, 460, 468
Our Miss Brooks (television program) 105
Outer Limits, The (television program) 2, 65, 117, 126, 378, 379
Overhulser, Charles 407, 417, 419, 423
Pachet, Pierre 42
Pagel, Hayes 430
Paige, Alan 358
Pal, George 124
Paley, William S. 5
Palfy, Lou 363, 365, 442
Parents' Magazine of the Air (radio program) 19
Parsonnet, Marion 60
Parsons, Lynn 357, 367, 430
Parsons, Patricia 283
Pasco, Frances 464
Patryn, Renee 434
Patterson, Elizabeth 190
Patterson, Hank 144, 145, 225, 258, 447, 450
Payne, Bruce 368, 417, 460
Pembroke, George 368

Pendleton, Steve 174
Perkins, Voltaire 363
Perrett, Frank 129
Perrott, Ruth 158
Perry Mason (television program) 32
Peter Gunn (television program) 161
Peters, Paul 158
Peterson, Bob 147
Petrotta, Vic 292, 296, 333, 338, 347, 362, 365, 400, 422, 424, 442,
Peyton Place (television program) 379
Philbrick, Herbert 15, 16, 58
Phillips, Barney 267, 269
Phillips, John 204, 480
Phillips, Mark 4, 82, 86
Philo Vance (radio program) 10, 19
Phipps, Bill 417
Pickard, John 174
Pickering, William H. 475
Pierlot, Francis 70
Pine, Phillip 275, 277
Pitchard, Herb 267
Pittman, Max 135, 143, 146, 150, 153, 157, 160, 162, 166, 169, 173, 177, 181, 186, 190, 196, 200, 203, 208, 211, 217, 221, 225, 236, 240, 247, 250, 253, 258, 267, 271, 275, 279, 287, 292, 296, 302, 308, 312, 318, 322, 328, 333, 343, 347, 352, 358, 362, 365, 368, 372, 376, 382, 385, 397, 400, 406, 409, 412, 417, 419, 422, 424, 426, 430, 434, 438, 442, 446, 451, 455, 456, 460, 464, 469, 478-483, 486
Pittman, Tom 312
Pizanti, Victor 352, 367
Pleasure Parade (radio program) 11, 19
Plowman, Melinda 400
Pohlman, Virginia 389
Pollock, Ben 147, 148
Popular Mechanics (magazine) 142, 206
Post, Bob 130, 143, 150, 162, 169, 196, 200, 211, 217, 225, 236, 247, 253, 479-481
Postal, Charles 407
Powers, John 368
Preston, Robert 67
Price, Vincent 81, 99, 292-295, 397, 398
Princess and the Pirate, The (1944 movie) 65
Pritchard, Herb 308
Producers on Producing (book) 9, 94
Project Moon Base (1953 movie) 45
Public Defender (television program) 97
Pycha Jr. George 52
Qualen, John 69, 167, 168
Rabin, Jack 445
Rabinowitch, Eugene I. 384
Racket Squad (television program) 97
Radice, Conrad 416
Radio Guide (magazine) 9
Radio Showmanship (magazine) 12
Rain or Shine (television program) 105
Ramsey, Wanda 279, 282, 464
Ramstead, Jack 383
Ranaldi, Bill 307, 311
Randolph, Donald 69
Rapp, Joel Malcolm 406, 433
Rathbone, Basil 196-198
Rawlings, Dick 129, 143, 149, 166, 168, 173, 195, 199, 224, 235, 247, 250, 257, 275, 282, 287, 292, 296, 307, 328, 333, 338, 342, 347, 352, 357, 362, 365, 376, 382, 385, 388, 419, 422, 434, 442, 480, 483

Rawlings, Jack 357
Ray, Bobby 149, 162, 166, 195, 199, 203, 211, 217, 235, 247, 249, 253, 257, 270, 274, 279, 282, 292, 296, 307, 311, 318, 479-481, 483
Reason, Rhodes 389, 391
Record, Bill 217
Red Skelton Show, The (radio program) 19
Redbook (magazine) 6
Redmond Jr., Harry 39, 65, 74, 98, 130, 135, 143, 146, 150, 154, 157, 160, 163, 166, 169, 174, 177, 181, 186, 190, 196, 200, 204, 208, 211, 218, 222, 225, 230, 236, 241, 248, 250, 253, 258, 267, 271, 275, 279, 283, 288, 292, 294, 296, 302, 308, 312, 318, 323, 328, 333, 338, 344, 347, 352, 358, 363, 365, 368, 372, 377, 382, 385, 389, 397, 400, 407, 410, 412, 417, 419, 423, 427, 430, 434, 438, 442, 447, 452, 456, 460, 464, 469
Reed, Allen 416
Reid, George 129
Reifsnider, Lyle 129, 143, 153, 157, 160, 166, 479
Rennie, Guy 363
Repp, Stafford 352, 353, 355
Reynolds, Alan 271
Rhino! (1964 movie)
Rhodes, Charles 275, 296, 312, 323, 344, 347, 352, 358, 368, 377, 417, 469
Rice, Francis Owen 384
Richard Boone Show, The (television program) 403
Richards, Addison 279
Richards, Keith 447-449

Richardson, Dr. Robert S. 77, 93, 286
Richardson, Everett 311, 371, 388, 397
Riddle, Randy A. 10
Riders to the Stars (1954 movie) 39, 40, 51-53, 59, 62, 64, 71, 73, 76, 80, 116, 122
Ridgeway, Freddy 372, 374, 375, 412, 456
Rifkin, Bud 8, 112
Rifkin, M.J. 103
Ripcord (television program) 18, 20, 61
Ripley, Robert L. 8
Ritch, Steven 427
Rivero, Julian 438
Roach, Hal 57, 62
Roberts, Roy 69
Robinson, Gail 147
Rocketship X-M (1950 movie) 45
Rocky Jones, Space Ranger (television program) 113, 119, 120, 139
Roges, Budd 14
Ronso, Al 328, 338, 343, 347, 352, 357, 367, 376, 382, 385, 389, 397, 400, 406, 409, 412, 417, 419, 422, 434, 442
Rose, Charlie 241
Rose, David 100
Rossi, Bruno 224
Roth, Gene 302, 304, 305, 328, 352, 353, 355
Roud, Andrew 325, 413, 456
Rough Riders, The (television program) 17, 20
Royce, Riza 302, 469, 471
Rudley, Herbert 163
Ruick, Melville 318
Russell, Bing 412
Ruth, Phyllis 34, 35

Ruysdale, Basil 69, 70, 130, 133, 134
Ryan, Robert 69
Sackheim, Jerry 162, 165, 173, 176, 185, 247
Salvin, Gus 190
Sandrich, Jay 376, 381, 384, 416, 419, 422, 426, 430, 441
Sanford, Blaine 50
Saris, Marilyn 222
Sarnoff, David 5
Satterlee, Bruce 322, 391, 396, 400, 406, 409, 411, 416, 422, 433
Saturday Review of Literature (magazine) 6
Scar, Sam 312
Schaefer, Robert 240
Schallert, William 222
Schiff, Don 437, 446, 460, 464
Schnee, Thelma 211, 214, 384, 387
Schultz, Russ 438, 446, 451, 456, 469
Schwartz, Howard 221, 229, 396, 400
Scientific American (magazine) 51, 95, 145, 148, 165, 172, 184, 193, 224, 244, 256, 269, 383
Scott, Eugene 232
Scott, John 458
Scott, Martha 9
Scott, Thomas (Tommy) 157, 169, 217, 225, 240, 253, 267, 275, 282, 287, 343, 347, 357, 365, 382, 409, 419, 422, 426, 430, 464, 480-482
Scott, Zachary 200, 201, 203, 271, 274
Sea Hunt (television program) 17, 20, 36, 41, 61, 65, 117, 118
Seay, James 271, 456, 458
Seba, Duke 473
Sechler, Ernest E. 475
Secret Life of Walter Mitty, The (1947 movie) 65
Seely, John 100
Sehner, Virginia 214
Self, Clarence 301, 307, 318
Sepulveda, Ygnacio 282, 338, 342, 376, 389, 419, 434, 480
Shafer, John I. 475
She Devil (1957 movie) 90
Shearer, Norma 26
Sheldon, Jim 347, 423
Shepard, Jan 200, 385, 388, 464-466
Sherman, Robert 319, 412
Sherwood, Robert E. 15, 16
Shield, Robert (Bob) 427
Shore, Dinah 27
Short, Robin 197, 198, 389, 391, 392
Silverman, Stanley H. 468
Simon, Robert F. 160, 161, 212, 213, 216
Simpson, R.H. 244
Sinatra, Frank 27
Sincerely, Kenny Baker (radio program) 11, 19
Sinclair, Joan 377-379
Sinn, John 8, 11, 12
Siodmak, Curt 39, 45, 46, 49, 50, 52, 64
Siry, Joseph W. 475
Skelton, Red 27, 29
Slifer, Lizz 271, 338, 452
Slocum, Roy 275, 279, 296
Slosser, Ralph 168, 173, 176, 195
Smith, Alexis 69
Smith, Cecil 143, 146, 162, 279, 301
Smith, Charles (actor) 312, 314, 316
Smith, Charles (special effects) 230
Smith, Charles B. (writer) 311, 316
Smith, Don 240
Smith, E. 275
Smith, Kent 58, 250-252

Smith, Maxwell 48, 62, 73-75, 78, 80, 135, 143, 146, 150, 153, 157, 160, 163, 166, 169, 174, 177, 181, 186, 190, 196, 200, 203, 208, 211, 217, 221, 225, 230, 236, 240, 247, 250, 253, 258, 267, 271, 275, 277, 279, 282, 287, 292, 296, 302, 308, 312, 323, 328, 333, 335, 338, 343, 347, 352, 354, 358, 362, 365, 368, 372, 376, 382, 385, 389, 399

Smith, Richard (Dick) 301, 311, 333, 342, 367, 372, 400

Smith, Robert 52, 65

Smith, Robert E. 332, 446

Smith, Sydney 460

Smith, W.C. 357, 367

Song of Love (1947 movie) 39

Songs of Good Cheer (radio program) 19

Soule, Olan 158, 159

Space Patrol (radio program) 95

Space Patrol (television program) 113, 291

Sports Album (television program) 13, 14, 17, 20

St. Leo, Leonard 419, 421, 425, 456, 468

Stager, Dr. Kenneth E. 76

Stanton, Guy 172

Stanwyck, Barbara 95

Star Trek: Deep Space Nine (television program) 223

Star Trek: The Next Generation (television program) 223

Star Trek: Voyager (television program) 223

Steenson, Clarence 288, 292, 296, 302, 308, 318, 333, 347, 358, 363, 365, 368, 382, 385, 397, 400, 406, 412, 417, 419, 426, 430, 434, 460, 469

Stein, Ed 135, 149, 166, 221, 247, 292, 338, 352, 357, 362, 365, 367, 371, 382, 388, 426, 434, 439, 446, 451, 455, 460, 464, 481

Stelle, Martin 371

Stephens, Harvey 250

Stephenson, John 222, 407, 430

Stevens, Craig 248

Stevens, Warren 136, 142, 208, 209

Stever, H. Guyford 475

Stockwell, Charles 224, 240, 249, 271, 296

Stoddard, Ray 230, 250, 416

Stone, Gene 185, 221, 224, 230

Storm Over Tibet (1952 movie) 39

Story of Mary Marlin, The (radio program) 24

Story Theatre (television program) 14, 17, 20

Stossel, Ludwig 163, 165, 410

Stout, William 204

Strock, Herbert L. 32, 39-41, 63, 64, 86, 98, 108, 129, 134, 146, 149, 168, 172, 173, 185, 203, 207, 217, 220, 247, 301, 304, 305, 322, 326, 332, 336, 337, 340-342, 346, 360, 362, 364, 367, 369, 376, 380, 388, 391, 392, 409, 411, 413, 459, 478, 479, 481, 483, 485, 486, 496

Strudwick, Shepperd 69

Strughold, Dr. Hubertus 76, 475

Studio One (television program) 91, 273

Stuhlinger, Dr. Ernst 121

Sturgeon, Theodore 44

Such Interesting Neighbors (short story) 135, 137, 139

Sukman, Harry 52

Suspense (radio program) 29

Sutherland, Sidney 135, 143, 146, 150, 154, 157, 160, 163, 166, 267, 292, 302, 308, 323, 333, 343, 347, 352, 363, 365, 377, 385, 397, 412
Sweeney, John 426
Sweet, Art 253, 275, 279, 283, 287
Swift Revue, The (radio program) 24
Swift, Jonathan 42
Switzer, Carl "Alfalfa" 212, 216
Tait, Donald 129, 135, 143, 146, 150, 153, 157, 160, 162, 166, 169, 173, 176, 181, 185, 190, 195, 200, 203, 208, 211, 217, 221, 225, 230, 235, 240, 247, 250, 253, 257, 267, 271, 275, 279, 282, 287, 292, 296, 302, 307, 311, 318, 322, 328, 333, 338, 343, 347, 352, 357, 362, 365, 367, 372, 376, 382, 385, 389, 397, 400, 406, 409, 412, 416, 419, 422, 426, 430, 434, 438, 442, 446, 451, 456, 460, 464, 469
Talbot, Lyle 460
Tales of the Texas Rangers (television program) 379
Tales of Tomorrow (television program) 44, 60
Tallman, William 248
Tanner, Frankie 271
Target (television program) 17, 20
Tauss, Frank 186, 196, 200, 204, 222, 230, 480
Taylor, Vincent 169, 177, 181, 186, 190, 196, 204, 208, 211, 218, 222, 225, 230, 480, 481
Telephone Time (television program) 105
Television Magazine (magazine) 16
Telmie, Rob 371
Temple, Shirley 27
Templeton, Bob 327, 332, 337, 342, 347, 351, 357, 430
Templeton, Robert 147
That Forsythe Woman (1949 movie) 39
Thaxter, Phyllis 69
Then and Now (radio program) 24
Thielman, J. 279, 282
This Man Dawson (television program) 17, 20
Thomas, Bill 130
Thomas, Gretchen 389, 434
Thomas, Harry 129
Thompson, Marshall 110, 154, 156, 190, 192-194, 241-243, 245, 328-330, 358, 420, 434, 435
Thompson, Peggy 230
Thorpe, Ted 200
Thurston, Carol 197, 279
Time Machine, The (novel) 474
Time Square Playhouse (television program) 17, 20
Tobey, Kenneth 150, 152, 319
Tom Corbett, Space Cadet (television program) 44
Tombstone Territory (television program) 17, 20, 95
Toomey, Regis 69
Top Secret (television program) 60
Tors, Anthony 36
Tors, Erwin 36
Tors, Ivan 1, 3, 15, 32, 36-41, 43-47, 50, 52, 53, 57-62, 64, 65, 67, 69-73, 75, 76, 79-82, 88, 89, 92, 94-96, 98, 109, 115, 117, 118, 122, 123, 129, 131, 134, 139, 142, 149, 152-154, 156, 157, 159, 163, 166, 168, 173, 175, 180, 181, 184, 185, 189, 194, 195, 198, 201, 202, 206, 207, 211, 214,

216, 229, 233, 235, 240, 244, 245, 248, 251, 256-259, 261, 262, 274, 277, 287, 300, 301, 304, 305, 307, 310, 318, 320, 322, 326, 331, 348, 351, 355, 357, 360, 367, 369, 370, 373, 376, 378, 380, 381, 384, 388, 391, 394, 399, 403, 411, 414, 415, 425, 428, 433, 439, 472, 473, 473, 487
Tors, Margaret (Bohm) 36
Toss, Frank 190
Totter, Audrey 163, 165
Towne, Aline 442, 443
Travis, Merle 9
Treacy, Emerson 275
Treat 'em Rough (1942 movie) 28
True, L.L. 455
Truez, John 194
Trumbull, Brad 347, 351
Tuber, Richard Joseph 266, 295
Tucker, Forest 69
Tuttle, Helen 172
TV Guide (magazine) 59, 80, 119
Twilight Zone, The (television program) 2
Tyndall, Henry 172
Unchained Goddess, The (television special) 121
Underwater Warrior (1957 movie) 41
Unexpected, The (television program) 14, 17, 20, 95, 106
Unger, Maurice 61, 65, 67, 72, 73, 76, 113, 115
Vacation from Love (1938 movie) 27
Vaiana, Jim 143
Valentine, Don 372
Vallee, Rudy 27
Van Camp, Helen 197
Van Dine, S.S. 10
Van Enger, Charles 73

Van Marter, George 62, 65, 71, 72, 94, 149, 151, 487
Van Zandt, Julie 358, 359
Variety (periodical) 9, 11, 25, 27, 50, 52, 111, 122, 124, 134, 142, 145, 149, 152, 156, 159, 161, 162, 165, 168, 172, 175, 180, 184, 194, 198, 202, 206, 210, 215, 220, 233, 239, 245, 252, 256, 261, 269, 273, 277, 281, 286, 291, 295, 300, 304, 316, 326, 331, 341, 346, 351, 355, 379, 384, 387 and 391
Varno, Roland 417
Vaughan, William 292, 368, 407, 456
Verk, Donald 129, 199, 203, 224, 240, 253, 257, 287, 296, 332, 342, 347, 376, 419, 442, 480, 481
Verne, Jules 42
Vernon, Billy 169, 174, 177, 181, 186, 208, 221, 230, 240, 482
Victor, Charles 410
Vincent, Elmore 248
Vohs, Joan 271, 272, 274
Vollaerts, Rik 88, 159, 161, 162, 168, 172, 362, 422, 425
Von Braun, Dr. Wernher 121, 475
Von Stroheim Jr., Erich 271, 275, 279, 301, 391, 400, 406, 409, 483
Von Zell, Harry 24
Wade, Ed 357, 367
Wagenheim, Charles 145, 182, 389, 392
Wallaby, Jim 468
Walter, Stan 157, 160, 328, 357, 367, 382, 385, 409, 416, 424, 426, 438, 446, 451, 455, 464, 478, 479
Walters, James 422
Walters, Joe 328, 372, 389, 397, 400, 407, 412, 434, 438, 442, 447, 452, 456

Walters, Stan 157, 160, 235, 282, 287, 357, 382, 385, 409, 416, 424, 426, 438, 446, 451, 455, 464, 478, 479, 483, 486
War Correspondent (radio program) 19
War in the Air (novel) 474
War of the Worlds, The (1953 movie) 93, 286
War of the Worlds, The (novel) 474
Warde, Harlan 360, 368, 412
Washburn, Beverly 225, 227, 228
Watch the Birdie (1951 movie) 39
Waters, James 204, 434
Wayne King Show, The (radio program) 11, 19
Weaver, Tom 4, 39, 40, 49, 71, 82, 86, 161, 228, 495, 496
Webb, Amanda 283
Wehling, Bob 400, 403
Weiler, John (Bud) 409, 426, 430, 437, 468
Weinbaum, Stanley G. 90, 270, 273
Weiss, Arthur 249, 251, 274, 277, 307, 337, 381, 383, 384, 463
Wells, H.G. 42, 474
Welles, Orson 281
Welsh, Bill 385, 387
Wendell, Bruce 363, 397, 423
Wengraf, John 69
West Point (television program) 17, 20, 463
West, Robert 301, 378
Westerfield, James 92, 225, 227
Weston, Robert 378, 430
Wharton, Joseph 129, 150, 153, 154, 166, 181, 479
Wheeler, Charles 406, 411
Whelan, Arleen 69, 218
White Heat (1949 movie) 96
White, Daniel 464
White, Will J. 243

Whiting, Margaret 11
Whitney, Elizabeth 236
Wilcox, Harlow 312, 316
Wilcoxan, Henry 69
Wilder, Bud 416
Willes, Jean 197, 198
Williams, Adam 218, 220
Williams, Bill 60, 253, 254, 257, 283, 347, 349, 351, 382, 384, 447-449
Williams, Ken 253
Williams, Mack 283, 286, 297, 324, 326
Wilson, Doug 400, 430
Wilson, Harry 367
Wilson, Stanley 100
Wind Without Rain (stage play) 37
Windbeil, Morgan 190
Windsor, Marie 136, 142
Winkelman, Michael 236, 238, 239, 279
Winninger, Charles 70, 456, 457
Winters, Ralph 69
Winterset (1936 movie) 96
Woelz, John B. 135, 143, 146, 153, 157, 160, 162, 166, 169, 173, 176, 181, 185, 200, 203, 221, 235, 247, 250, 257, 271, 279, 296, 322, 328, 357, 385, 389, 400, 406, 409, 412, 438, 442, 456, 479, 480, 482
Wohlman, Howard 358
Wonder Who's Kissing Her Now?, I (1947 movie) 29
Wonder, Joe 129, 143, 146, 153, 186, 190, 195, 200, 203, 208, 211, 217, 221, 225, 230, 236, 240, 247, 250, 253, 258, 267, 271, 275, 279, 282, 287, 292, 296, 302, 308, 312, 318, 322, 328, 333, 338, 343, 347, 352, 357,

362, 365, 368, 372, 376, 382, 385, 389, 397, 400, 406, 409, 412, 417, 419, 422, 426, 430, 434, 438, 442, 446, 451, 456, 460, 464, 469
Woods, Donald 69
World of Giants, The (television program) 20
Worth, L.B. 129
Wright, Howard 222
Wright, Mac 307
Writer's Digest (magazine) 6
Wyenn, Than 324, 326, 442

Wynn, Gordon 200
Yeats, Murray 413
Yesterday's Newsreel (television program) 13, 14, 17, 20
You Are There (television program) 62
Yutronich, Larry 253
Zaremba, John 458, 464
Zeoran, Joe 320
Ziv, Frederic W. 1, 3, 5-18, 58, 60-62, 71, 73, 82, 95, 102, 103, 109, 118, 126
Zorro (television program) 403

About the Author

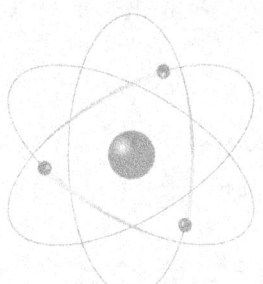

Martin Grams Jr. has authored or co-authored over a dozen books about radio and television. He wrote a number of magazine articles for *Blood n' Thunder, Filmfax, Scarlet Street,* and SPERDVAC's *Radiogram*. He contributed chapters, short stories and appendixes for various books including Ken Mogg's *The Alfred Hitchcock Story* (1999), BearManor Media's *It's That Time Again* (all three volumes, 2002–2005), Midnight Marquee's *Vincent Price* (1998), Arthur Anderson's *Let's Pretend* (2004) and Ben Ohmart's *Alan Reed Biography* (2009).

Martin is the recipient of the 1999 Ray Stanich Award, the 2005 Parley E. Baer Award and the 2005 Stone/Waterman Award. His name appears in the acknowledgements of more than 100 books about radio and television. His 2008 book *The Twilight Zone: Unlocking the Door to a Television Classic* won the Rondo Award for "best book of the year." He is presently finishing a book about *77 Sunset Strip* and *Duffy's Tavern*. Martin is presently a member of the convention staff for the Mid-Atlantic Nostalgia Convention, held annually in Maryland. He presently lives in Delta, Pennsylvania with his wife and three cats.

Other Books by Martin Grams Jr.

The History of the Cavalcade of America (1999, Morris Publishing)

The CBS Radio Mystery Theater: An Episode Guide and Handbook (1999, McFarland Publishing)

The Have Gun—Will Travel Companion (2000, OTR Publishing, LLC)

The Alfred Hitchcock Presents Companion (2001, OTR Publishing, LLC)

The Sound of Detection: Ellery Queen's Adventures in Radio (2002, OTR Publishing, LLC)

Information, Please (2003, BearManor Media, LLC)

Gang Busters: The Crime Fighters of American Broadcasting (2004, OTR Publishing, LLC)

The Railroad Hour (2006, BearManor Media, LLC)

The Radio Adventures of Sam Spade (2007, OTR Publishing, LLC)

I Led Three Lives: The True Story of Herbert A. Philbrick's Television Program (2007, BearManor Media, LLC)

The "Lost" Sam Spade Radio Scripts (2008, BearManor Media, LLC)

The Twilight Zone: Unlocking the Door to a Television Classic (2008, OTR Publishing, LLC)

Car 54: Where Are You? (2009, BearManor Media, LLC)

The Green Hornet: A History of Radio, Motion Pictures, Radio and Television (2009, OTR Publishing, LLC)

The Shadow: The History and Mystery of the Radio Program, 1930–1954 (2010, OTR Publishing, LLC)

BearManor Media

New books on Classic Stars.
The books, audio books, and DVDs of your genre-nation.

For the best in film, TV and radio books

coverout.com

www.ingramcontent.com/pod-product-compliance
Lightning Source LLC
Chambersburg PA
CBHW051332230426
43668CB00010B/1236